Despite All Adversities

SUNY series, Genders in the Global South
———————
Debra A. Castillo and Shelley Feldman, editors

Despite All Adversities
Spanish-American Queer Cinema

Edited by
Andrés Lema-Hincapié
and
Debra A. Castillo

Cover image (movie still) courtesy of Argentine filmmaker Marcelo Piñeyro, from *Plata quemada* (2000).

Published by State University of New York Press, Albany

© 2015 State University of New York

All rights reserved

Printed in the United States of America

No part of this book may be used or reproduced in any manner whatsoever without written permission. No part of this book may be stored in a retrieval system or transmitted in any form or by any means including electronic, electrostatic, magnetic tape, mechanical, photocopying, recording, or otherwise without the prior permission in writing of the publisher.

For information, contact State University of New York Press, Albany, NY www.sunypress.edu

Production, Diane Ganeles
Marketing, Anne M. Valentine

Library of Congress Cataloging-in-Publication Data

Despite all adversities : Spanish-American queer cinema / edited by
  Andrés Lema-Hincapié and Debra A. Castillo.
      pages cm. — (SUNY series, genders in the global South)
  Includes bibliographical references and index.
  ISBN 978-1-4384-5911-0 (hc : alk. paper)—978-1-4384-5910-3 (pb : alk. paper)
  ISBN 978-1-4384-5912-7 (e-book)
  1. Hispanic Americans in the motion picture industry. 2. Homosexuality in motion pictures. 3. Gays in motion pictures. I. Lema-Hincapié, Andrés, editor. II. Castillo, Debra A., editor.

PN1995.9.H47D47 2016
791.43'652968073—dc23   2015005100

10 9 8 7 6 5 4 3 2 1

To those who, at certain moments of my life, gave me various reasons to feel reality from different angles: James Mariucci, Andrés Felipe Calero (†), Andreas Dollinger, Rodolfo Puente, Ross Halvorsen, Facundo Echavarría, Mariano Zaleski, Lisandro Moisés Enrique, Walter Karam, Pablo Hernán Aguirre, Nicolás Matías Tabares, Diego Martín Grillo, and Ariel Li Gotti.

—Andrés Lema-Hincapié

Contents

Acknowledgments   xi

Introduction   1
    Andrés Lema-Hincapié and Debra A. Castillo

Part I
Queer Subjectivity, Desire, and Eroticism

1. Queer Couples in *Señora de Nadie* (María Luisa Bemberg, 1982)   19
   David William Foster

2. *Fresa y chocolate*: The Allure of Passions and Controversies
   (Tomás Gutiérrez Alea and Juan Carlos Tabío, 1993)   31
   Cristina Venegas

3. A Gaynster Quasi-Tragedy: Eroticism and Secrets in
   Plata quemada (Marcelo Piñeyro, 2000)   53
   Andrés Lema-Hincapié

4. Pathology, Poetry and Pleasure: HIV/AIDS, Confessional
   Writing and S/M in *Un año sin amor* (Anahí Berneri, 2005)   71
   Robert Deam Tobin

Part II
Gay Authorship—Queer Agency and Spectatorship

5. *La venganza del sexo*: The Curious Mutation from
   Horror Fantasy into Sexploitation Film (Emilio Vieyra, 1967)   99
   Esteve Riambau

6. Inside-Out: A Socio-Spatial Reading of *Mecánicas celestes*
   (Fina Torres, 1995) 111
   Cecelia Burke Lawless

7. *La Virgen de los Sicarios:* From Novel to Film
   (Barbet Schroeder, 2000) 125
   Óscar Osorio

8. A Case Study in Transnational Gay Auteurism:
   Mil nubes de paz cercan el cielo (Julián Hernández, 2004) 143
   Paul Julian Smith

9. Haunted: *XXY* (Lucía Puenzo, 2007) 155
   Debra A. Castillo

Part III
Bisexuality Experiences and Lesbian Identities

10. Excluded Middle? Bisexuality in *Doña Herlinda y su hijo*
    (Jaime Humberto Hermosillo, 1985) 173
    Daniel Balderston

11. The Construction of the Bisexual Subject in *No se lo digas a nadie* (Francisco Lombardi, 1998) 185
    Alfredo J. Sosa-Velasco

12. Lesbians Made in Mexico: Sexual Diversity and Transnational Fluxes 203
    María de la Cruz Castro Ricalde

Part IV
Queer Relations with Families, Government, and Nation

13. Clothes Make the Man: Closet, Cabaret, Cinema in
    El lugar sin límites (Arturo Ripstein, 1978) 221
    Claudia Schaefer

14. Families, Landowners, Servants, and Siblings in *La ciénaga*
    (Lucrecia Martel, 2001) 237
    David Oubiña

15. Mapping Guilt, Betrayal, and Redemption: *En la ciudad sin límites* (Antonio Hernández, 2002)   247
    Chris Perriam

16. *Ronda nocturna*: A Homage to Buenos Aires (Edgardo Cozarinsky, 2005)   263
    Dieter Ingenschay

Contributors   281

Index of Terms   287
Index of Names   293
Index of Concepts   301

Acknowledgments

If the patience of Job is mythic, so is that of each one of the colleagues who participated in the production of this book.

Andrés Lema-Hincapié conceived the idea of this book in 2007, while teaching an advanced course on Spanish-American queer cinema at Whitman College. Each collaborator approached on this project responded with enthusiasm, some more rapidly than others, and despite the delay in seeing the book into print, none of them showed the slightest amount of concern—confirming to us the value and importance of this task.

Publishing an academic book always relies on an indefinite number of variables, as any book editor will recognize. The unwavering confidence of the collaborators as well as that of Beth Bouloukos at the State University of New York Press, along with the hope in satisfying expectations of the readers who will consult this book, have given its editors the patience to see it into print despite roadblocks and unexpected challenges along the way.

All but one of the chapters in this book are original, previously unpublished works in English. We acknowledge New York University Press for granting rights to reproduce Daniel Balderston's essay. We are also grateful to Marcelo Piñeyro, the Argentine director of *Plata quemada*, for providing us with the still from his film and the permission to use it as a cover image.

Un cálido *gracias*—now in Spanish—para cinco excelentes traductores, exalumnos y amigos: Michael Clarkson, John Byron Lema, Bécquer Medak-Seguín, Alec Sugar, and Marsea Wynne. Y, claro, para otros dos amigos incondicionales que nos ayudaron en las largas etapas de edición: Michael J. Carr y John Didier Anaya.

Introduction

ANDRES LEMA-HINCAPIÉ AND DEBRA A. CASTILLO

Meeting the Macho

Inevitably, when we talk about LGBTQ issues in a comparative Americas context, references to histories of colonization ground the discussion: Latin America was colonized in the first wave of European expansionism, by Iberian powers from Portugal and the newly united principalities we now call Spain. In this respect as well, scholars are quick to point out that the histories and expressions of gender and sexual difference in Latin America do not align neatly with the histories of gender and sexuality from English-speaking parts of North America. Thus, while the rich panoply of cultures, languages, and traditions of the people inhabiting the many countries south of the Rio Grande argue for a diverse and incommensurable reality that makes comparison unwieldy, the common heritage of Spanish and Portuguese brings them together. One of the common touchstones for defining this difference is the concept of the "macho," used to talk about a specific, objectionable form of heteronormative masculinity.

This is a word that seemingly needs no definition. It is, in fact, a sign of our times that that "macho" and "machismo" have slipped into an international usage and daily expression in wildly divergent contexts around the globe. For instance, "macho" has in recent years become a common reference in Bollywood movies to define an attractive heteromasculinity. In the United States "machismo" has entered English as a stereotype or slur for an overbearing sense of entitlement, often used in what is—to ears accustomed to Spanish—a gratingly ungrammatical form. Yet, parallel to the overbearing macho, there is another, equally pervasive stereotype (this is the one Bollywood seems to have discovered): the instantly recognizable filmic image of the Latin lover, who is terrifyingly attractive, powerfully heterosexual, just a touch effeminate, and all the more sexually irresistible because of it. Italian-American actor Rudolph Valentino of silent movie fame was the archetype of this image, consolidated in his 1921 silent film *The Sheik*, but also refined in Spanish-tinged roles like his Argentine gaucho in the 1921 Hollywood version of Vicente Blasco Ibáñez's *The Four Horseman of the Apocalypse*, and his bullfighter in *Blood and Sand* (1922). In each of these cases, curiously, the idea of the macho trails a persistent sense of foreignness, of something imported, for good or ill, from other climates to describe a local reality that remains slightly out of alignment with local mainstream sexuality and gender histories. In a word, "macho" is already slightly queer.

It is not surprising that non-Latin traditions flatten out the term. Nonetheless, even considering Latin America's own variants on the stereotype for a certain style of heterosexual masculinity, something about the "hombre macho, pero muy macho" slips through the cracks. One needs to go no further than the classic 1946 Pedro Infante film, *Vuelven los García*, in which the macho is so strong, so powerful, that when he loses the woman most important to him in his life—his grandmother, naturally, played by the inimitable Sara García—he can bring a mariachi band to her tomb and weep inconsolably in a way that only enhances his masculinity. This portrayal of the macho strong enough to weep, like the macho strong enough to admit he is wrong, is a tradition in Golden Age Mexican cinema of the period. Contrasting with this image, the other familiar Latin American variation on the macho is, of course, the bully, familiar to us from so many evil drug kingpin roles. Here too, there is a touch of the feminine. This is a man who is so completely assured in his masculinity, so unbreachably *chingón*, that he can have sex with other men without impugning his heterosexuality. In fact, he is even more macho because of it.

The macho also has a feminine counterpart in Latin America, not the weepy *mujer abnegada*, but rather the *machorra*, the woman who is perceived to channel the power of the macho in a feminine body. The Latin spitfire, for example, is too hot, too independent, and too openly sexual for mainstream tastes, while the femme fatale too cold and calculating—but both channel strains of heteromasculinity in attractive women's bodies. The machorra takes too wide a stance, her gazes are too direct and piercing, she troubles gender arrangements by holding more power than is appropriate to a heterosexual woman. She is, naturally, a persistent source of fascination in literature and folklore, from Venezuela (Doña Bárbara) to

Chile (La Quintrala), and more recently as embodied by kick-ass heroines of narcodramas like *Rosario Tijeras* (2005) and *La Reina del Sur* (2011). The 1943 version of *Doña Bárbara,* starring the woman everyone had already been calling "La doña," Mexican superstar María Félix, is an iconic case in point. She is the absolute ruler of her little kingdom, all phallic weapons and blazing sexuality, but none of it under control or hetero-focused. She is such a strong woman that she conveys a bit of butch lesbianism, making her just that much more exotic and desirable.

With the always ambiguous (but denied) sexuality of the macho/machorra dominating commercial cinema,[1] Latin American film history was always a bit queer even before the release of the film that for many scholars marks the most notable beginning point for modern Queer Cinema in the continent: Arturo Ripstein's *El lugar sin límites* (*Hell Without Limits,* 1978) based on José Donoso's eponymous 1966 novel, and featuring the stunning performance of Roberto Cobo as La Manuela, a tormented transgender inhabitant of a run-down brothel.

LGBTQ in Latin America

It may surprise some readers to learn that the USA is not necessarily the leader in this respect, and indeed, one of the explicit charges of this book, written in English and published in a U.S. academic press, is to give scholars and students of film from Latin America, and of LGBTQ studies in general a ground for challenging U.S.-centric perspectives through productive comparisons with a history that has often been opaqued behind a dominant focus on Hollywood in popular culture, and U.S. understandings of LGBTQ lives and histories.

The academic institutionalization of the fields of women's studies, gender studies, and more recently queer and LGBTQ studies, has had important repercussions in the way we teach. Parallel social and academic movements in Latin America have had signal impacts on the film industry throughout the continent. Filmmakers who address queer topics with intelligence and sensitivity have become more prominent since the mid-1990s, paralleling these national trends toward legal recognition of sexual and gender diversity and greater levels of social acceptance.

As Deborah Shaw observed in 2007, "the strength of the most successful films from Latin America, in contrast to many (but not all) of their Hollywood counterparts, is that high-quality entertainment is produced without the loss of a socially committed agenda." Adding strength to the general and growing interest in Latin American film histories is the fact that Spanish and Spanish-American films have achieved international recognition and a considerable serious critical attention beyond their relative commercial success. Indeed, the éclat of Oscar Awards for Juan José Campanella (Argentina, 2010), Pedro Almodóvar (Spain, 2003), Luis Puenzo (Argentina, 1985) is only one index of a tradition of high quality filmmaking, with auteurs of the level of María Luisa Bemberg (Argentina), Arturo Ripstein (Mexico), Lucrecia Martel (Argentina), Tomás Gutiérrez Alea (Cuba), and Marcelo Piñeyro (Argetina), among many others. Equally importantly for our purposes, the best known of these films combine commercial success with a social edge. The films studied in our collective volume come from histories and cultures with a rich and complex relationship to issues of gender and sexuality that are not always straightforwardly aligned with U.S. dominant understandings. They also clearly fight for a queer agenda.

There is another history that needs to be briefly discussed as well, as the backgrounds out of which these films arose have been changing dramatically in the last decade and a half. This book comes into print at a time of tremendous transition in the legal status and social acceptance of LGBTQ peoples throughout the continent. One common indicator of cultural change is the growing acceptance of gay marriage; the United States is improving rapidly, and many commentators have focused on the effects of the rapid cultural shift that has followed in the wake of the first legalization efforts in Massachusetts in 2004. As of November 2014, slightly more than 60 percent of Americans now live in jurisdictions that recognize and perform same-sex marriages (35 states).

However, putting this evolution in a more continental context, in terms of gender activism, Argentina is still the only country in the world to allow people to change their gender identity on official documents without first passing through a legal or medical intervention, thanks to a progressive 2012 gender identity law: no hormone therapy, no psychiatric visits to diagnose gender dysphoria, no surgeries required. In May 2013, Brazil became the fourth country in the Americas to accept same-sex marriage nationally, following the lead of Uruguay, Ecuador (2008), and Argentina (2010). In addition, these changes were already in place in other forms in Colombia and Mexico as well, meaning that gay marriage or civil unions are nationally accepted in all of the most populous countries in the continent except the United States. In 2007 the Colombian Constitutional Court ruled that same-sex couples are entitled to the same inheritance rights as heterosexuals in common-law marriages, making Colombia the first South American nation to legally recognize them. Same-sex marriages were legalized in

Mexico City in 2009 (by law in Mexico only civil marriages are officially recognized), and legalization of marriage or civil unions quickly followed in other Mexican states. By August 2010, same-sex marriages performed within Mexico had been officially recognized by all 31 states without exception.

About this Book

Our anthology responds to the need for a work conceived for use by instructors and students of the college and university courses on Spanish-American cinema, as well as survey courses on Latin American literature and culture. This book, in other words, offers essays on a reasoned, representative selection of important films by Spanish America's most important directors since the 1950s, films that instructors are likely to include in their courses and for which they may wish to have useful materials on hand. Our goal is to offer a book with pedagogical applications that at the same time maintains intellectual sophistication. For that reason we have pooled the very best scholars, creating a cast of contributors known for their brilliance and solidity or for their expertise on the directors and films they discuss. Each of them chose or were assigned a specific, important film as the focus of their study. The analyses are rich and thoughtful, united by the thematic focus of the volume and the editorial decision to focus on a single film per chapter (rather than, for example, a filmmaker's body of work, or a topical point of entry).

The book is divided thematically into four parts. "Queer Subjectivity, Desire, and Eroticism," "Gay Authorship—Queer Agency and Spectatorship," "Bisexuality Experiences and Lesbian Identities," and "Constructing Queer Relations with Families, Government, and Nation." The first part includes reflections on some of the most iconic and commercially successful queer films, the ones that have crossed over into the general Latin American film canon. In the second part of the anthology, our authors explore a set of films that associated with auteur cinema, often somewhat more edgy or experimental in aesthetics or in style. Most of the fiction films indexed in Latin American LGBTQ studies focus primarily on the gay male; our third section gives space to two key groups often excluded in studies of queer cinema: lesbians and bisexuals. Finally, "Constructing Queer Relations with Families, Government, and Nation" groups together a set of analyses that go beyond individual expressions of identity to query the relation of the LGBTQ figure to questions of larger social and political structures.

Part I includes the following films: María Luisa Bemberg's *Señora de Nadie* (*Nobody's Wife*, 1982), Tomás Gutiérrez Alea and Juan Carlos Tabío's

Fresa y chocolate (*Strawberry and Chocolate*, 1993), Marcelo Piñeyro's *Plata quemada* (*Burnt Money*, 2000), and Anahí Berneri's *Un año sin amor* (*A Year Without Love*, 2005). María Luisa Bemberg's film is an important film for its representation of a woman strong enough to leave her husband and, eventually, to freely construct a queer subjectivity with the help of a gay man. In this queering of the Argentine matrimonial couple in late 1983, Bemberg explores the discourse of the heterosexist/homophobic patriarchy in Argentina. *Fresa y chocolate* builds a larger political context by indirectly talking about homophobia and desire as well, but this time the film studies the repression of homosexuals in Cuba at a critical historical juncture. *Plata quemada* represents the urban politics of gay bodies in Argentina at the end of the twentieth century. The film is an answer to a contemporary city audience that is ready to accept homosexual eroticism as long as male interaction does not go against certain petrified prejudices about homosexuality, and as long as its physical expressions are not publically visible. That is why Piñeyro skillfully connects the two gay main characters, Ángel (Eduardo Noriega) and El Nene (Leonardo Sbaraglia), very closely with the thoroughly macho heterosexual El Cuervo (Pablo Echarri), on the one hand; and, on the other, Piñeyro systematically avoids showing Ángel and El Nene engaging in effeminate gestures, sexual intercourse, and what could have been an authentic love freed of religious guilt. Finally, Anahí Berneri's *Un año sin amor* seems to echo the life and works of Pablo Neruda—a kind of paradigm for Spanish-American poetry, politics, and love. Her film can be understood as a cinematic love poem showing how love itself has changed from romanticized relationships—bundles of letters neatly tied up like a nineteenth-century talisman—to complex sadomasochistic relationships. But all of these changes happen after the appearance of HIV/AIDS, which has created a new world of human relations.

Part II, entitled "Gay Authorship—Queer Agency and Spectatorship," starts with the study of *La venganza del sexo* (*The Curious Dr. Humpp*, 1967). This Argentine low budget production by Emilio Vieyra mixes thriller and fantastic genres, dealing with classic topics such as the medieval myth of Doctor Faustus, the sexual connotations of vampirism, and a mad doctor following orders from a talking brain or a monster who rebels against his creator. Four years after the release in Argentina, an American distributor added seventeen minutes of a rich variety of edited soft porno scenes. The film includes a set of "traditional" sexual perversions: onanism, lesbianism, voyeurism, printed pornography, and couple exchanges. For English-speaking spectators *La venganza del sexo* received the name of *The Curious Dr. Humpp*, a bizarre sexploitation film released in the crossroads between eroticism and science fiction. If Vieyra expressed his authorship by creating a fantastic thriller, Venezuelan filmmaker Fina Torres's *Mecánicas celestes* (*Celestial Clockwork*, 1995) puts in place another literary genre to explore queer issues: the fairy tale. As an apparent *film d'auteur*, Fina Torres directs this film from her own nomadic positionality as a woman director from Venezuela who grew up in France. In *Mecánicas celestes* Fina Torres throws herself into the postmodern pastiche so common at the time, where not only gender roles but also social spaces are turned inside out, inverted, converted into a lightly subversive reworking of the traditional Cinderella story. As the film begins, the credits roll across a celestial star-studded sky until arriving at Earth, then Venezuela and a small colonial church where Ana, one of the protagonists, is on the verge of breaking away from her marriage ceremony. This opening scene's spatial play infuses the whole film as gravity pulls Ana in unexpected ways. From grand universal structures the film focuses on the struggles of an individual's sense of sexual space.

Space, as the concrete coordinates of queer agency, is also a central aspect of Barbet Schroeder's *La Virgen de los Sicarios* (*Our Lady of the Assassins*, 2000). This eponymous film adaptation of the 1994 Colombian novel by Fernando Vallejo dramatizes a gay love story in the violent, bloody, and deadly city of Medellín (Colombia). A comparative analysis of the screenplay and the novel induces the conclusion that the film represents a process of extension, suppression, and even embellishment of essential elements included in the novel. Readers and spectators differently assist to diverse cultural events: while violence dominates in the novel, passionate love dominates in the film; while the screenplay tells a story about duplicitous love, the novel is a dense story of violent action with occasional relief found in passionate love—always in the context of a ferocious city. In other words: spectatorship for the film and readership for the novel, both build around the queer interactions of the protagonists, are reciprocal filtered, enriched, or impoverished.

The critical analysis of *Mil nubes de paz cercan el cielo* (*A Thousand Clouds of Peace Encircle the Sky*, 2004) by Mexican filmmaker Julián Hernández shows that this film and his other works appear to be of restrictive or minority interest (homophilia, cinephilia). Hernández has constructed a transnational auteurism (*cinéma d'auteur*) that has achieved, however, wider distribution than more commercial Mexican cinema. Hernández's success in reaching faithful spectators and distributing his creation depends, on one hand, on a fine balance between artistic elements held to be local or indigenous, and those that stake a claim to an international cinematic tradition, on the other. In other words: in order to build strong bonds with his audience/spectatorship, Hernández appeals to a mediascape of fluid and irregular representations. Such representations are at once materially embedded in the authentic shooting locations of Mexico City and aesthetically abstracted from that very particular context in ways that render them accessible to international audiences. Whereas Hernández's *Mil nubes* situates its cinematic narrative in a megalopolis context, Lucía Puenzo's *XXY* (*XXY*, 2007) develops within domestic, even theatrical settings. This film, a clear example of queer/unstable agency, explores and questions a binary sex/gender system through the story of a young unmutilated intersex person, Alex. Moreover, Puenzo makes it an unusual contribution in the feature film subgenre of gender-questioning narratives. The ambiguous desires of the intersex adolescent remind the viewers of the artificial limits imposed by unquestioned styles of knowledge production—male, female, gay, straight—and the stricture "to be" one and only one of the above even in progressive circles. In Alex's case, the potential for fluidity underscores the performativity of gender roles in our species: more generally, the performativity of sex itself.

"Bisexuality Experiences and Lesbian Identities," Part III of this volume, begins with a study of a 1985 film from Mexico: Jaime Humberto Hermosillo's *Doña Herlinda y su hijo* (*Dona Herlinda and Her Son*). A central concept in queer studies is brought into play here: *bisexual*. This word would obviously seem to describe the sexual life and choices of Rodolfo, one of four protagonists. Nevertheless, as the study develops, "bisexual" becomes a difficult concept to grasp when put in connection others, such a homosexuality, gender roles, sexual identity, sexual politics and, particularly, the Mexican archetypes of the matriarchal mother and the macho male. Thought-provoking enough, at the end, the label "bisexual" loses its easy meaning to characterize an individual sexuality and rather points at Rodolfo's mother, Doña Herlinda. Doña Herlinda has successfully orchestrated a way to maintain, under her roof and subtle control, the heterosexual and homosexual relationships of his son. Her "construction" of Rodolfo's bisexuality will allow her to create an appearance of harmless, social normalcy, while she is still presiding as a matriarchal puppetmaster over every pusillanimous puppet in her little theater. *No se lo digas a nadie* (*Don't Tell Anyone*, 1998) presents more elements for the unstable concept of bisexuality. In the chapter devoted to this Peruvian film it is argued that filmmaker Francisco J. Lombardi heterosexualizes Jaime Bayly's eponymous novel: Joaquín, the main character, "comes out of the closet" in heteronormative Peruvian society, but at the same time his subjectivity is bisexually constructed—in comparison to the homosexual subjectivity constructed in the novel. In this way, the film adaptation of Bayly's novel criticizes more strongly such a society, reaffirming, then, its hypocrisy doubly. In other words: if Bayly's novel can be read as an exploration of the queer metaphor of "coming out of the closet," Lombardi's film can be seen at the same time as an answer to the literary text. In this vein, it is suggested that the impossibility of "coming out" brings with it the emergence of a bisexual subject, and by this emergence such a subject would attack more directly and efficiently Peruvian traditional discourses on sexuality and gender of normative heterosexuality.

"Bisexuality Experiences and Lesbian Identities" ends with a chapter analyzing, first, film representations of lesbians in Mexican cinema until the twenty-first century—or rather the meaningful lack of those kinds of representations. And then, the analysis moves forward to consider cinematic depictions of lesbianism at the beginning of Mexico's twenty-first century. Mexican films such as *Niñas mal* (*Charm School*, 2007) by Fernando Sariñana, Gustavo Moheno's *Hasta el viento tiene miedo* (Even the Wind is Afraid, 2007), *Así del precipicio* (Close to the Edge, 2006) by Teresa Suárez, and Rodrigo Ortúzar's *Todo incluido* (*All Inclusive*, 2009) show a common denominator, that is, sexual diversity in the global context of transnational fluxes. Including lesbian characters who are young, beautiful, upper-middle class, and inhabitants of urban enclaves, the characters of those films suddenly "discover" their "true" sexual preference in their attraction to another woman. This chapter focused on the transnational reconfiguration of lesbianism. It would perhaps make finally visible some lesbian exchanges in a Mexican environment. Nevertheless, the exchanges reveal blatant obstacles: lesbian encounters only originate in cosmopolitan settings; are reduced to members of a privileged social class; are posed either as a game or a "need" for experimentation; and, finally, are narratively explained by a foreign presence, alien to Mexico's idiosyncrasy.

The last part of the volume, entitled "Constructing Queer Relations with Families, Government, and Nation," opens up with an essay of another film version of a literary work from the Latin America "Boom." Directed by Mexican filmmaker Arturo Ripstein from a screenplay by José Donoso, the Chilean author of the homonymous novel on which it is based, and with uncredited assistance from Spanish writer Manuel Puig, *El lugar sin límites* (*Hell Without Limits*, 1978) elides the conventions of melodrama, the *fichera* film, and the road film. The film leaves no doubt about the human figure as the essential part of the *mise-en-scène*, while counterpointing between national cinema and the cinematic semiotics of clothing (the red dress, sewing, dance, bathing, Pancho's red shirt and tight jeans). Both aspects end up uniting visual representations of the clothed body to reveal the naked truth about gender in 1970s Mexican rural society. Ripstein's interior world in its death throes makes visible intersecting and tense anxieties written on two spaces: the dying "caserío" (hamlet) of El Olivo and La Manuela's own body—the tragic/martyr protagonist. La Manuela, performed by Mexican actor Roberto Cobo, reminds spectators of that greater social angst of national identity. Manuela is an icon of a nation at odds with itself, conjured up by Ripstein as that "uncanny" ghost within prevailing discourses of masculinity. Mexican President José López Portillo's *sexenio* (1976–1982) encompasses and gives root to these asphyxiating spaces of conventional melodrama as national backdrop for Ripstein's *Hell on Earth*.

Neither are national bonds a mere background for Lucrecia Martel's opera prima *La ciénaga* (*The Swamp*, 2001). *La ciénaga*, as a pitiless metaphor of Argentina, does not allow for a protagonist character or a central line of narration. Instead, the story unfolds according to a drift or flow. It progresses in a diffuse manner without knowing in which direction it is heading. It is based on an associative and cyclic model. There is no development, no continuity, and no alternation. The effect is of promiscuity and contamination. Martel makes no effort to distinguish the characters: at first sight it is difficult to identify them and to establish the links between them. Nevertheless, that confusion is not due to a sparse elaboration of their personal qualities since, although they intermingle, each one conserves his or her singularity. In any case, the film works with this light but abrupt disparity between similarity and difference. The characters belong to different classes, different generations, different families, and even different geographies of a "homogenous" nation; although that may not prevent them from permanently mixing, the juxtaposition of all the film characters does not suppose that there is anything to share either. Their relationships oscillate between small differences blown out of proportion to mark distance and a tight knit closeness that, by accentuating itself, does nothing but show incompatibility.

If by zooming-in a family can be understood as a sort of microcosm of a whole nation, *En la ciudad sin límites* (*The City of No Limits*, 2002) by Spanish director Antonio Hernández is interpreted according to the interconnectedness of issues of class- and family-based sexual politics and the reclamation of historical truths. The dying protagonist Max's falsified memories of a betrayal in Francoist Spain of his communist activist and militant homosexual lover are studied as a narrative device which highlights cinema's engagements with temporality—with the time-image—and its potential for witness. The way these memories are further falsified by the framework of bourgeois family politics and heterosexuality's privileged positioning as the arbiter of silence or declaration is studied in relation to both the subgenre of the family-dynasty movie and the melodrama of the unmentionable secret. The film thus becomes a dramatization and visualization of truth in the sense of a new—queer—version of both a family and a transnational history. Finally, the city spaces directly evoked and indirectly invoked by the film—Paris, Madrid, Buenos Aires, a fictional dystopian symbol referred as *En la ciudad sin límites*—will be shown to create patterns of emotion and haptic spaces. These patterns not only fill out and thicken the texture of the queering of histories which is one of the film's concerns, but also act as pointers to the way filmmaking, sexual, and political commitment are processes of mapping or plotting.

Edgardo Cozarinsky's *Ronda nocturna* (*Night Watch*, 2005) clearly echoes a deadly, nocturnal game of sex for sale, living dead, friendship, and laughter. For Cozarinky, the city of Buenos Aires becomes an imaginary chart where queer relations, a failing government, and a hopeless nation are at stake as well. *Ronda nocturna*, a night film including elements of social reality, fantasy, and desire, tells the story of Víctor (played by Gonzalo Heredia), a young hustler. From sunset to dawn spectators follow Víctor on his way through several corners of Buenos Aires. In an aesthetics of seemingly incoherent scenes, Cozarinsky gently develops his subject and his particular film language: the police officer who protects and exploits the young protagonist, the friend who shares his excess of sex and drugs, the visit to an expensive gym, the ambulant flower seller who donates Víctor a red carnation, Víctor's former, diaphanous girl wanting to drag him to death, the authentic comradery between Víctor and the other night and marginalized "creatures"—the waste recyclers and other hustlers—and finally, in the last scene of the film, the dribbling football tango with a couple of boys on their way to school. *Ronda nocturna* is full of memorable takes of typical Buenos Aires spirit and localities: the metropolitan avenue, the cheap hotel, the suburban cafe, and the rails of the train. Notwithstanding, this urban landscape appears less emblematic and less expected, since Buenos Aires is the genuine, loving setting for Víctor's precarious life, which he deeply experiences under the sign of condoms, cocaine, and a few dollars.

Readers of any anthology will always wonder about criteria for inclusion and exclusion of material. The films included in this book all participate in one way or another in an emergent canon of fiction films with LBGT emphases from Latin America. Certainly, the rapidly changing political and social climate as demonstrated in important legal victories in countries from Mexico to Argentina suggest that the future will open up rich new possibilities for queer production, distribution, and viewership. Besides their histories of production, distribution, and exhibition, there were other reasons why other now canonical films were not included in this book. *Kiss of the Spider Woman* (1985) by Héctor Babenco, for instance, inspired by the eponymous novel by Manuel Puig, was always well received, and included a star-studded international cast (William Hurt, Raul Julia and Sonia Braga). However, the film was made in English. In contrast, all the films chosen for *Despite All Adversities* were made in Spanish and, with very few exceptions—notably Eduardo Noriega (Spain), Ricardo Darín (Argentina), Fernando Fernán Gómez (Spain), Leonardo Sbaraglia (Spain), and Jorge Perugorría (Cuba)—the actors in these films were generally little known outside their countries of origin.[2]

Likewise, we did not include *Sin destino* (*Without Destination*, 2002) by Leopoldo Laborde or *Simón, el gran varón* (*Simon, the Great Male*, 2002) by Miguel Barreda. *Sin destino* is the last film of the great Roberto Cobo (1930–2002), but he was also the protagonist in *El lugar sin límites* (*Hell Without Limits*, 1978), and the latter film is sited in the great queer metropolis of Mexico City, an urban space beautifully portrayed by Julián Hernández in his film *Mil nubes de paz* (*A Thousand Clouds of Peace*, 2004). *Simón el gran varón*, for its part, deals with transvestism, a topic explored with greater aesthetic, political, and literary complexity in *El lugar sin límites*.

Another frequently cited queer film, *Mariposas en el andamio* (*Butterflies on a Scaffold*, 1996), by Luis Felipe Bernaza and Margaret Gilpin, offers a fascinating documentary peek into the lives of gays and trans people in Castro's Cuba, but *Mariposas en el andamio* is not a fiction film. Likewise, *Confesión a Laura* (*Confessing to Laura*, 1990) by Jaime Osorio Gómez—considered one of the greatest of all Colombian films—combines fictional and documentary materials referring to April 9–10, 1948 in Bogotá. Because fiction and documentary are so interwoven, we preferred to retain our emphasis on fully fictional films for this volume.

Argentina has the richest and most robust tradition of films engaging sexual diversity, including nearly half of the films studied in this book. Our anthology includes *La venganza del sexo* (*The Curious Dr. Humpp*, 1967), *Señora de Nadie* (*Nobody's Wife*, 1982), *Plata quemada* (*Burnt Money*, 2000), *La ciénaga* (*The Swamp*, 2001), *Ronda nocturna* (*Night Watch*, 2005), *Un año sin amor* (*A Year Without Love*, 2005); and *XXY* (2007). An anthology solely dedicated to Argentine film would certainly include films like *Otra historia de amor* (*Another Love Story*, 1986), by Américo Ortiz de Zárate, and *Adiós, Roberto . . .* (*Good Bye, Robert . . .* , 1985) by Enrique Dawi, or the tender *Besos en la frente* (*Kisses on Your Forehead*, 1996) by Carlos Galettini. However, for reasons of space and balance, we preferred a wider sampling from other filmic traditions.

We close with a final question: why the almost complete absence of lesbian film in *Despite All Adversities*? Up until now there has been, unfortunately, a very limited body of Spanish-American queer cinema with lesbian themes. In her film *Camila* (1984), Argentine filmmaker María Luisa Bemberg synthesized repudiation for single women in the words of her character Camila's father, Adolfo O'Gorman (Héctor Alterio), "A single woman is chaos, Camila. A disorder of nature . . . Marriage is order. Neither people nor a country can live without order."[3] Here and there, other some short and medium-length films have appeared, such as *Lesbianas de Buenos Aires* (*Lesbians of Buenos Aires*, 2000) by Santiago García. However, they have been hampered by weak distribution. Independent movie theaters and Internet sites have been unable to create a broad audience to access Spanish-American lesbian film. Fortunately, however, chapters by María de la Cruz Castro Ricalde and Cecilia Burke Lawless in this volume provide an introduction to a few lesbian films still little known outside specialized circles.

Lesbians continue to strive in an oppressive filmic silence, which turns into a muffled scream because there are only a few films of aesthetic value to serve as points of reference and inspiration.[4] They also struggle with the ubiquity of porn cinema of lesbian content. As Santiago García says, "for lesbians it meant the emergence of their sexuality stemming from a very patriarchal masculine gaze." Nonetheless, adds García, "lesbians have not yet been successful at creating heroines like those of other genres: terror, adventure or science fiction. There isn't a lesbian Indiana Jones or anything equivalent or remotely similar" (García "Lesbianas en el cine").

Why *Despite All Adversities* as the title of this book? In his famous *Death in Venice* (1912), Thomas Mann thinks through Gustave Aschenbach, his third-person, anonymous narrator about the word "despite." Aschenbach believes "that almost everything great that exists exists as a 'despite,' that is, comes into being despite grief and agony, poverty, abandonment, physical weakness, vice, passion, and a thousand hindrances."[5] This book aspires to continue fighting inveterate fears and to continue unleashing stifled truths within Spanish-American cultures. Within such cultures being as adversaries, in any case *and despite everything*, queer individuals endure and can hope to thrive.

Appendix: Further Readings

In the last twenty-five years, the study of film has increasingly become a curricular staple in literature and culture departments in United States and foreign colleges and universities. In our own field of Hispanic literatures and cultures, the analysis of visual media products is now a central aspect of the discipline, with film the privileged medium for these analyses. Works such as John King's *Magical Reels: A History of Cinema in Latin America* (2000), Alberto Elena and Marina Díaz López's *The Cinema of Latin America* (2003), Stephen M. Hart's *A Companion to Latin American Film* (2004), and Deborah Shaw's *Contemporary Latin American Cinema: Breaking into the Global Market* (2007) attest to a growing academic field.

English-language film students will be able to avail themselves of complementary texts with an LGBTQ focus such as Richard Dyer's *The Culture of Queers* (2002), Vito Russo's *The Celluloid Closet: Homosexuality in the Movies* (1987), Susana M. Villalba's *Grandes películas del cine gay* (1996), Jenni Olson's *The Ultimate Guide to Lesbian and Gay Film and Video* (1996), Boze Hadleigh's *The Lavender Screen: The Gay and Lesbian Films* (2001), Michele Aaron's *New Queer Cinema* (2004), Steven Paul Davis's *Out at the Movies: A History of Gay Cinema* (2008), and Darwin Porter and Danforth Prince's *Fifty Years of Queer Cinema: Five Hundred of the Best GLBTQ Films Ever Made* (2010). Unfortunately, these important studies pay only scant attention to queer film in Spanish, or made in Latin America—the few examples they address are generally limited to films from Spain.

Complementing these studies are two books that are especially important in marking Latin Americanist attention to LGBTQ issues in Latin American film in this contemporary moment: David William Foster's *Queer Issues in Contemporary Latin American Cinema* (Texas, 2003) and Gustavo Subero's *Queer Masculinities in Latin American Cinema* (Palgrave, 2014). We echo Subero's sentiments when he writes, "This book emerges, then, from a personal and academic desire to try and make sense of the way fiction cinema provides more than merely visual pleasure to audiences through its ability to portray snippets, or whole chunks of reality, and show audiences the felt experience of groups that would otherwise remain voiceless in their fight for equality" (xii). This book is in dialogue with these important studies.

Notes

1. Alongside the fascinating/repulsive macho and machorra, other manifestations of queerness in Latin American film and television, like those seen in the productions of other countries and cultures since the first days of moving pictures, tended to reduce openly gay characterizations to the vile stereotypes around pitiful *maricones*, who flutter limp-wristed through execrable plots and serve as comic relief in minor roles. These are the least interesting films of all for serious analysis, although historically they help us index the challenges for LGBTQ Latin Americans

in finding positive self-images in their local mediascapes. And there is some hope that these degrading images can soon be relegated to the past, as social mores evolve toward more equitable treatment of LGBTQ individuals.

2. Ricardo Darín became even more prominent outside his country with *El secreto de sus ojos* (*The Secret of Their Eyes*, 2009) by Juan José Campanella, the second Argentine film to win an Academy Award for Best Foreign Language Film (2010). With Fernando Fernán Gómez, his roles in *La lengua de las mariposas* (*Butterfly*, 1999) by José Luis Cuerda and in *Todo sobre mi madre* (*All About my Mother*, 1999) by Pedro Almódovar, gained him wide acclaim outside of Spain. *Todo sobre mi madre* won the 2000 Academy Award for best foreign film.

3. Nevertheless, those words from *Camila* seem over-stated. More gay men refuse (or are denied) paternity than lesbian women motherhood. María Luisa Bemberg also produced the aesthetically exquisite *Yo, la peor de todas* (*I, the Worst of All*, 1990), about the life of Sor Juana Inés de la Cruz (Mexico, 1651–1695). Because this anthology already includes another film by that director, *Señora de Nadie* (*Nobody's Wife*, 1982), the editors have chosen not to include two films by the same director. *Señora de Nadie* is important because Bemberg succeeds at intimately linking Hispanic women's assertions with those of Hispanic gay males.

4. "Películas." <http://www.pseudoghetto.com/>.

5. "dass beinahe alles Grosse, was dastehe, als ein Trotzdem dastehe, trotz Kummer und Qual, Armut, Verlassenheit, Koerperschwaeche, Laster, Leidenschaft und tausend Hemmnissen zustande gekommen sei." The Project Gutenberg EBook of *Der Tod in Venedig* by Thomas Mann. Robert Deam Tobin and Andrés Lema-Hincapié are the translators of the previous words by Thomas Mann.

Part I

Queer Subjectivity, Desire, and Eroticism

1

Queer Couples in *Señora de Nadie*[1]

(María Luisa Bemberg, 1982)

DAVID WILLIAM FOSTER

> Mirá si nos viera la tía Lola.
>
> —Pablo to Leonor

Señora de Nadie is undoubtedly one of María Luisa Bemberg's masterpieces, notwithstanding the enormous success of her last film, *De eso no se habla* (1993), with Marcello Mastroianni, and even the success (albeit more academic) of *Yo, la peor de todas* (1990), with Assumpta Serna. Although there is an important queer thread in all of Bemberg's films, *Señora de Nadie* is perhaps the queerest of her filmic texts.[2] Although *Yo, la peor de todas* is rightly recognized as a significant film for its transparent treatment of the lesbian dimensions in the life of the Mexican poet Sor Juana Inés de la Cruz (1648–1695), a balanced assessment of Bemberg's ideological commitments along a line that connects feminism with queer attitudes must give preeminence to *Señora de Nadie* for the way it engages in an unflinching and intransigent revision of heterosexist matrimony.[3]

Anyone who has seen the film treasures the moment, about two-thirds into the story, when Leonor, played by Luisina Brando, has, with all due deliberation, walked out on her chronically philandering husband in an assertion of prideful self-esteem, when someone who barely knows her unwittingly presents her to the man from whom she is estranged. The man making the introductions, because he barely knows her, pauses, at a loss for her name. When asked her proper married name (for surely any woman her age must be properly married), she looks her former husband in the eye and says, "Mrs. Nobody."[4] Of course, the trope works better in Spanish. Since the occasion is a formal party, a married Argentine woman, who is likely for everyday use to be known by her maiden name, becomes a "Señora de," the "wife of," a man. Here the possessive particle exercises not so much the much-vaunted function of signaling the way in which a woman must necessarily belong to a man. This is, of course, an operant point, though not the principal one. Rather, it marks the established imperative order of the hierarchy, in which men and women are paired off in what is very much the ground zero of the social order. Men and women may be flirting with each other with abandon, disappearing into bedrooms and bathrooms in the recesses of the house or exchanging phone numbers for subsequent assignations. But when the circumstance arises to evoke social formulas, such as in the moment of introducing guests to each other, there is a sudden, even if fleeting, reversion to accepted social order in which married affiliations, as signaled by the proper gender distribution of names, assume enormous significance.

As delightful as the moment is when Leonor goes on to introduce herself to her host and to the man from whom she is separated, by using her maiden name, the spectator must realize that Leonor is, after all, in no way a Mrs. Nobody. Fernando Morales (played by Rodolfo Ranni) is completely comfortable with attempting to woo Leonor all over again, both at the party and later, when he makes sure to show up at a remote and closed-up summer house in Punta del Este that she visits in preparation for trying to sell it in her job as a real estate agent. While they share a bottle of wine in front of the fire and make love on the plush carpet, Leonor realizes in the end that he will never be anything other than a conquering macho. And yet, Leonor's renunciation of her married identity at the party, and the unswerving conviction that she comes to hold that she can never return to Fernando, must inevitably come up against the hard social reality of Argentina in the early eighties.

It is important to remember that when Bemberg made her film, Argentina was still under military dictatorship: indeed, the film premiered the evening before the April 2, 1982, announcement of the invasion of the Islas Malvinas (the Falkland Islands) by Argentine forces. The country was still dominated by an effectively unchallenged masculinist supremacy that would attain a new peak as the majority at first supported the military takeover of the British-held islands. Although the initial enthusiasm for the operation, which was a desperate attempt to regain public support for the dictatorship, quickly waned as unquestioned defeat at the hands of the British became evident (the misadventure ended with an Argentine surrender on June 14, at a terrible cost in lives to the Argentines), divorce did not formally become legal in Argentina until June 3, 1987, fully three and a half years after the return to constitutional democracy in late 1983.[5] (It was approved by the Congress on May 7, 1987.)

In the film, Leonor uses the term "divorciada," but clearly she is not referring to what is understood as divorce in post-1987 Argentina. Nor is she referring to the legal process that existed in Argentina before 1987: the *separación de bienes,* in which the courts could recognize the separation of the married partners—what in popular terms has been called in the Spanish tradition *un divorcio de cama y mesa*—and the distribution of common property between them. Such an arrangement might call for alimony for the woman and also for child support, but neither partner would have the option of legally marrying again in Argentina, and the father would also, in all likelihood, retain the final word in decisions involving the children.[6] Leonor's total abandonment by the legal code, reinforced by social convention, is apparent when she appeals to her boss to let her rent one of the apartments they have on the market, without paying the customary signing expenses. She confesses—with great reluctance, since she is loath to discuss her personal affairs—that she receives no alimony from her husband, has no bank account, and has no one to turn to as a guarantor. Leonor is truly in a no-win situation: she cannot gain access to her husband's abundant assets, and she essentially has no financial standing of her own. Indeed, since she has announced to her sons that she has never worked a day in her life, it is remarkable, in the narrative universe of the film, that she can earn something of a living selling real estate. No information is given on how she lands such a competitive job.

Throughout the film, we see the interplay of two micronarratives of the heterosexist patriarchy.[7] One involves the way in which Leonor must be convinced that she has made a mistake in walking out on her husband. The principal agent of this micronarrative is her mother (played by China Zorrilla). When her mother tells her that she had better be careful or she will lose her husband, Leonor is quick to reply that he may lose her. In fact, she is determined to forget him and refuses her mother's advice to talk to him, for "hablando la gente se entiende." Later, when Leonor does in fact talk to her husband, after they have made love, she describes to him why she finds his way of being a husband wholly unacceptable, to which he replies that her case against him applies to all men—or, at least, to all Argentine men as he understands them to be (as they *must* be, in conformance with the role he is playing). It is abundantly clear that talking things through has hardly been a profitable undertaking. One trace of the unequal role is his insistence on calling her "chiquita" during this discussion. And she replies that he is never to use that diminutive with her again. At issue here, then, is a formula that allows them either to comply with their patriarchally defined roles or to fall short of them. In this formula, women's needs must be greater because of the dependent role women must play. Therefore, they have much to lose when the formula goes awry. Yet the stance that Leonor assumes is a blunt negation of dependency on him—a point that she makes forcefully by repudiating the affective address of "chiquita." Leonor speaks to him both directly and indirectly, through other agents of the social system (her mother, her boss, and even the maid, who efficiently administers "her" household after she has walked out). Fernando even gives the maid a raise. If we subscribe to the proposition that language is less a trace of social discourse than it is its very substantiation, the errant instances of actual discourse involved in the micronarrative being described here are resounding.

The other micronarrative at issue in *Señora de Nadie* concerns the dynamics of matrimonial relations. We have already seen how Leonor cannot accept Fernando's understanding of what it is to be a man and a husband—an understanding that appears rather conventional within the context of a masculinist, macho-dominated society such as Argentina under military tyranny.[8] What is notable is Leonor's rejection of this model. And even more remarkable is her apparent ignorance, in the beginning of the film, that such a model even exists. The separation between Leonor and Fernando is set in motion when, while out shopping for a birthday present for him, she spies his car with another woman in it. That woman kisses Fernando and gets out with affectionate gestures, including the hand gesture indicating that they will be in touch by phone later—one will later assume, for purposes of setting up a new tryst.

Leonor follows the woman, Gloria (played by Susú Pecoraro) into her place of business, an antique store. She gets Gloria's attention by knocking over a valuable crystal chandelier. Apologizing and offering to have her husband pay for any damage, she hands Gloria Fernando's business card. That Leonor would be carrying her husband's business cards is one of the many passing details of the patriarchal identity that she is about to rupture. Gloria looks at the card and realizes what is going on. What is interesting here is that Gloria does not apologize in any way but, rather, confronts Leonor to the effect that she could hardly not have known what was going on, that businessmen like Fernando are inevitably going to have lovers. Leonor thinks aloud of the trips abroad, of late-night board meetings and similar commitments, weekend symposia, and the like.

In the micronarrative of marital relations, such as the long list of Argentine films that constitute the viewer's horizon of knowledge in this regard, what is surprising is not the existence of Gloria (and many others, from A to Z), but Leonor's blindness to it. In short, she has been a deficient student of the system. Confrontation with Fernando at his office (which we see only as a flashback when they end up making love in the house in Punta del Este) may be a conventional chapter in the micronarrative, but Leonor's decision to abandon Fernando is very much a rupture in that narrative. Leonor will later tell her group therapy colleagues[9] about how her mother abided unquestioningly by the narrative, at the hands of a physically abusive husband who subsequently abandoned her, and there is the implicit message that Leonor will not.

There is an ironic twist here because Leonor's mother reads the cards to her and prophesies that she will meet a handsome bearded stranger. When the handsome Fernando shows up, he has acquired a beard, thereby not only fulfilling the mother's prophecy but also complying unknowingly with her admonition that the two of them meet, talk their differences out, and get on with their lives. There is no mention of the children here, and it is a master stroke of Bemberg that we see the two young male children (about seven and nine), to whom Leonor confesses—as though somehow asking permission from her sons—that she has never held a job before in her life. But *Señora de Nadie* steps immediately away from the typical Hollywood divorce film in which the fate of the children becomes a high-stakes stratagem in the story. After all, in the stereotypical Hollywood film, the children's very presence is confirmation that the work of the patriarchy is being satisfactorily pursued.

The two boys soon disappear from the film, and the fact that we do not hear Leonor refer to them again, except in passing (to the effect that she has nothing to offer them), or see her visit them again is a very hard-nosed decision on Bemberg's part. She is, in effect, dismissing the role that these children play in the matrimonial dynamic of which they are, in a very real way, the expected fruit—and, moreover, the privileged fruit, since both are boys. As the younger one says in the one conversation between the two of them in the film, things are better with just us men here in the house: seven years old and already well on his way to win honors in the training course for preparing fully functioning Argentine males. Just as Bemberg gives short shrift to the Argentine macho—one of the most pathetic segments of the film is when Leonor has a humiliating tryst with a client—she appears to be unmoved by the emotional clichés attached to children, as one can perceive in her filmmaking in general.

Señora de Nadie opens and closes with a man and woman in bed. In the opening scene, it is Leonor and her husband, making morning love before the alarm clock goes off and they start the routine of their bourgeois day (which, in Leonor's case, will include buying a birthday present for her husband, whom she subsequently sees with a lover, and so on). It appears to be a conventional sexual act, missionary style, with the man apparently in control in the top position. Now, this is a very remarkable scene, for it effectively establishes the patriarchal control of his wife's body by Fernando, and when he finishes with her, he simply rolls off and seemingly goes back to sleep. Leonor checks the clock: it is time to get on with her many responsibilities.

Moreover, this scene is notably invasive, as the camera makes the bedroom its set. After all, patriarchal sex is a matter of the public record, because it is what gets the business of control and reproduction done. Perhaps not quite an act of voyeurism, Bemberg's record of appropriate matrimonial commerce nevertheless satisfies the audience's demand—indeed, its right—to know that the matrimonial unit is working out, as well it should.[10]

Although censorship had not yet been lifted in Argentina (that would come in November 1983), the portrayal of such a scene, no matter how brief, and no matter how fleeting the view of Fernando's stockily masculine derriere, prefigures the transgressive nature that Bemberg's film will assume.[11] Not surprisingly, Leonor appears to be appropriately satisfied by her husband's manly attentions, as she faces her domestic responsibilities with exemplary verve.

Bemberg will later ironize this verve a bit because, before this latter-day Nora shuts the front door, she has taped instructions all over the place about the cleaning that needs to be picked up, the leaky faucet that needs fixing, the refrigerator that needs defrosting. One such note is the message she tapes to the gift she has bought for Fernando, wishing him a happy birthday. This nice touch of irony regarding top-level home economics can hardly be read as Leonor's clinging to her matrimonial base of operations. Rather, the implied message is that she will no longer be there to perform these functions, whether it be remaining at her husband's sexual disposal or checking (as she does at one point) the ring around the collar of one of his dress shirts.

The opening sexual scene of the film, complete with the sounds of good copulation, is complemented by the final scene of the film. In the course of her life away from Fernando, when Leonor joins a therapy group, she meets a young gay man (played by Julio Chávez, whose most notable parts will come in 2002 as the lead in Adrián Caetano's *Un oso rojo,* the story of a brutish ex-convict who is a case study of Argentine masculinity in crisis; and Rodrigo Moreno's *El custodio* (2006), where he plays a murderous bodyguard at the service of corrupt politicians). Pablo's part has much of the gay stereotype about it: after all, it is still 1982, the gay movement has not yet come to Argentina, and nothing approximating a queer discourse has yet become part of the national consciousness, as it is today.[12]

Thus, Pablo is called a pitiful *maricón* by Fernando and is persecuted by the aunt with whom he lives as *puto y depravado*. Pablo is engaged in a humiliating relationship with a married Brazilian, who pithily observes that he acts just like a woman in their relationship. Finally, as Leonor goes out one night to a party in which she allows herself to be set up by another conquering macho, only to come to her senses and bluff her way out of his arms (actually, she is not in his arms, because he quickly gets his hands up her dress, apparently closing in for the five-minute kill as he pins her against a tiled bathroom wall). Pablo has invited Leonor to move in with him after his aunt dies suddenly, promising her her own sector of the house. As Leonor returns to the house and turns on the lights, she sees a battered Pablo, barely conscious on the bottom steps of the staircase. He had gone out hoping to engage in his own sexual "killing" (he actually uses this sort of forceful Porteño vocabulary) but instead has almost been killed himself.

We do not learn the circumstances of this gay bashing, but the military regime explicitly encouraged this sort of social hygiene, engaging in it itself in the particular violence reserved for men in the armed forces suspected of being gay (not until several years after the return to democracy will this treatment be proscribed); practicing forms of entrapment of gay men in public spaces, particularly in the restrooms of bars and railway stations; and reserving especially brutal treatment for gays who fell into the clutches of the torture, imprisonment, and disappearance apparatus.[13]

Leonor helps Pablo up to his bed, treats his wounds as best she can, serves them both up a Valium, and turns to leave for him to rest as the drug takes effect. But Pablo begs her not only not to leave him but, moreover, to spend the night with him. She crawls dressed into his bed, and they snuggle like comfortable lovers, holding hands and kissing (albeit not on the mouth). It is at this point that Pablo asks Leonor what Tía Lola would think. Tía Lola is the stern, Spanish-accented administrator of a boarding house for older women. Although the sister of Leonor's mother, she has none of the other woman's sympathy, and it is apparent that her establishment is rule driven. Leonor at first lives in Lola's boardinghouse after she leaves Fernando. When Leonor invites Pablo to an intimate dinner in her room, Lola invades their space, puffed up with disapproval, invoking the decency of her home and the respectability of her boarders. It is not clear whether she disapproves of Pablo's presence because she sees him as a sexual predator (when she walks out of the room, Pablo pretends that he has impressed her with his studliness) or because she sees him as sexually abnormal. It is difficult to understand which condition, in Tía Lola's moral universe, is more reprehensible, but then, possibly in her asexual world of aging pensioners, all sex is reprehensible.

The closing scene of the film must be considered in tandem with the opening scene of lovemaking between husband and wife. The camera now zooms back, outside the bedroom, where Pablo and Leonor lie acting silly, as sincere lovers are wont to do. And as we hear their giggles and laughter, the final credits begin to roll over Pablo's warmly lighted bedroom window (pink curtains, of course). The lovemaking—regardless of how conventionally erotic or non-erotic it may be—is now a private affair, not open to public scrutiny, and part of the personal narrative between Leonor and Pablo that is no longer part of the prevailing heterosexist narrative. It is clear that not only does Leonor have no adverse feelings toward Pablo, but the level of intensity their relationship has reached underscores how, after a series of disastrous relationships with putatively "real" men, Leonor has found a measure of peace and happiness in the arms of a gay man.[14]

It is important that Bemberg's Pablo is what can be called a conventional *maricón*—that is, a man who is stereotypically gay because he is softly handsome, dressed in a nonstandard fashion, and with precisely the sort of hairdo that was cause for persecution in the early days of the 1976–1983 round of authoritarian/neofascist military tyrannies. He is softspoken, attentive, artistic, too good a dancer, and thin, as all Argentine women are supposed to be. He says that Leonor is jealous of his body. And most importantly, he is both attentive and responsive to Leonor. There is a closed-eyes touching scene conducted by the director of their therapy group that could be judged to be far more erotic than the scene of copulation that opens the film, even with Fernando's bare backside in view.

Pablo's acting here is emphatically gay, although never swishy or campy.[15] It certainly stands in sharp contrast to the fully embodied masculinity displayed by Oso in Caetano's film.[16] But what Pablo's character accomplishes is to stand in vivid contrast to the unsavory machismo of Fernando, which, he says and the others demonstrate, is the masculinity of all (Argentine—i.e., all "real" Argentine) men. Feminism always has lurking in the background the crucial question: *Don't these women ever learn?* After passing from her husband to the dentist, back to her husband, then to the quickie artist she meets at a party, Leonor does finally learn. And her decision to spend the night with Pablo in his bed is her definitive passage out of the jungle of the compulsory heterosexism, enforced in especially exaggerated terms by the military dictatorships of the period. The fact that those dictatorships may have been perceived by Bemberg to be taking their last gasp (she could not have known about the plan to invade the Malvinas—an invasion that was not just the last gasp but the final death rattle of the dictatorship) is what made it an especially propitious moment to launch a film such as *Señora de Nadie*.

It is immaterial what Leonor and Pablo may eventually do together in bed, although to laugh and talk together might be more important sexually, given the circumstances, than the gymnastics that open the film. Rather, the important thing is to consider carefully the point Leonor has reached in her education as a woman, and the determining role played in that education by, as her husband calls him, "*ese maricón lamentable.*" It is an education also abetted by a notably liberated female friend, as though there were a synergy to be sought in aligning herself with these two marginal social subjects. Does this mean that Bemberg might support the queer couple as a displacement and replacement of the institutionalized heterosexual one? Perhaps, although this is hardly an ideological pamphlet,[17] since it focuses on only two socially isolated individuals working out their own place in Argentine society. The patriarchy does a very good job of guarding its own interests, which exclude those of queer social subjects, whether a nonconforming man or a nonconforming woman, who must make their own way on their own.[18]

Because of its deconstruction of the naturalized category of marriage as propounded by the heteronormative social matrix, Bemberg's film is every bit as important ideologically for mid-1980s Argentine filmmaking as Luis Puenzo's *La historia oficial* (*The Official Story*, 1985) with its own deconstruction of stable matrimony. And it is singularly important in the context of the discourses over sexuality that will begin to emerge in Argentina after 1983, in terms of both female and homoerotic desire.[19]

Notes

1. An electronic version of this essay appeared in 2011 with the same title at http://argus-a-ensayos.blogspot.com/2011/09/queer-couples-in-maria-luis-bemberg.html. Here in its first printed form, it is reproduced with the author's permission.

2. I discuss *De eso no se habla* as a queer film text in David William Foster, *Queer Issues* (1–18), separating the concept of the queer from its often intended synonymity with gay sexuality. Rather, "queer" here is to be understood as that which transgresses the entire array of norms of the heterosexist patriarchy, not just the erotic ones. Thus, a heterosexual married couple who refuses to have children is, in this sense, queer.

3. Catherine Grant underscores how Bemberg's first two films deal with "female stasis" (95). The other film Grant discusses is *Momentos* (1980). See also Eduardo Rojas's characterization of the issues of women's lives in these two films.

4. There's a play on words here, since the English translation could well be "Nobody's Wife." We privilege "Mrs. Nobody" because it is symmetrical in English with such introductions in Spanish.

5. Of the four reviews extracted by Raúl Manrupe and María Alejandra Portela, three are very favorable, with one speaking of "la amistad sincera de un homosexual" (530). This is important, since one of the features that the discourse of homophobia at the time associates with the ideologeme "homosexual" is the incapacity for friendship and sincerity. But the fourth review speaks alarmingly of "todo lo que encierra como negativo y riesgoso [el ejemplo dado]" (530). One assumes that what is so dangerous is the audacious liaison of affection between a woman and a gay man, since Bemberg's film is hardly the first Argentine example of a woman walking out on an unfaithful husband. Miguel Ángel Rosado mentions Bemberg briefly but enthusiastically in his survey of the films of the period of dictatorship, 1968–1983 (156). Because of the clothes and the appearance of Buenos Aires in the film, it is clear that the action of the narrative is simultaneous with its filming.

6. One of the arguments in favor of divorce consisted of underscoring the considerable irregularities arising from subsequent non-legalized unions of the original spouses, including marriage in countries where divorce was legal. It should be noted that annulment of marriage for cause has also been a part of the Argentine legal system. Further restrictions may also arise from church weddings, although in Argentina marriage is always a civil matter and only occasionally a religious affair. Since churches in Argentina do not perform civil marriage, the concept of so-called gay marriage is not an issue on the level of civil law: all unions are civil unions. As for the father's default control of the children of any marriage, Argentina has long abided by the Roman concept of *patria potestas*.

7. Ana Forcinito's discussion of the feminist gaze of Bemberg's films is unquestionably the best analysis of her filmmaking. But the article places emphasis on Bemberg's last films; *Señora de Nadie* is not discussed.

8. Ana María Shua undertakes a fine parody of the Argentine husband in her *El marido argentino promedio* (1991).

9. Like a good Argentine, Leonor joins such a group. Psychoanalysis and other kinds of psychological therapy are the inevitable option for middle-class Argentines in times of crisis and conflict.

10. It is worth remembering here that in this patriarchal dynamic, a man can never rape his wife, for, with few exceptions (menstruation in some formulations), the wife must be always at her husband's beck and call.

11. Grant relates how the making of *Señora de Nadie* was blocked in the late 1970s by military censors, and includes the famous anecdote about how she was told that it would be better to have a son with cancer than one who is gay (92).

12. At this writing in mid-May 2009, Judith Butler has just been one of the featured authors at the Buenos Aires Feria del Libro; she also conducted a doctoral seminar at the Universidad de Buenos Aires. Coverage on her presence abounds in the local press, including the prestigious pages of the daily *La Nación*, which, in addition to a lengthy interview with Butler, published an equally long primer on Butler's contributions to queer theory. The presence of queer theory in Buenos Aires is yet one more demonstration of how its intellectuals must always be *toujours modernes, toujours à la page*. For an outstanding example of Argentine filmmaking in this respect, see Lucía Puenzo's *XXY* (2007), which won the 2007 Goya for the best film made in Spanish outside Spain. The film is a deft and persuasive queering of the important Argentine cultural narrative strain involving obstacle-fraught young lovers, as in David José Kohon's award-winning *Breve cielo* (1969).

13. For this history, see Flavio Rapisardi. Osvaldo Bazán devotes the ninth part of his history of homosexuality in Argentina to "La Dictadura."

14. It is worth mentioning that the film's theme song, "El tema de Leonor," was composed and is sung by María Elena Walsh, one of Argentina's legendary lesbian cultural figures.

15. Not that there is anything wrong with being swishy or campy. However, it is here a question of what the Argentine market would likely be able to bear in the closing years of the military dictatorship, when a swishy or campy character had little hope of engaging the sympathy of film audiences and could never be taken seriously as a human being of lasting interest.

16. Julio Chávez won the award at the Festival Internacional de Panamá in 1982, the Premio Mejor Actor de Reparto. And yet, interestingly, none of the three stills from *Señora de Nadie* in Clara Fontana's book includes Pablo, while two include Fernando (and one of these is reversed [15]). There is a nice still of Imanol Arias and Susú Pecoraro in bed together in the 1984 María Luisa Bemberg film *Camila* (21); it would have been nice to see it complemented by the scene of Chávez and Brando in bed together in the closing scene of *Señora de Nadie*.

17. Fontana, however, identifies a "soplo didáctico" in the film (26), although she does go on to recognize the importance of the film's closing scene. Of particular importance is her excellent metaphor regarding Argentine machismo: "Los varones tienen una concepción autista de la relación heterosexual" (29).

18. In a sense, *Señora de Nadie* prepares the way for the two major Argentine gay films to emerge from the return to democracy: Enrique Dawi's *Adiós, Roberto* (1985) and Américo Ortiz de Zarate's *Otra historia de amor* (1986). The two films are examined together in Foster, "El homoerotismo y la lucha." *Otra historia de amor* is also discussed in Foster, *Contemporary Argentine Cinema* (135–49).

19. John King recounts how Bemberg filmed two endings for *Señora de Nadie*. The one she did not use has Leonor returning to her children (21). The importance of the film as a queer document would certainly have been completely vitiated by

such an ending, and Pablo would have been only a way station in her return to heterosexual "responsibility."

Works Cited

Bazán, Osvaldo. *Historia de la homosexualidad en la Argentina: De la conquista de América al siglo XXI*. Buenos Aires: Marea, 2004. Print.
Bemberg, María Luisa, dir. *De eso no se habla*. s.d. 1993. DVD.
———. *Yo, la peor de todas*. GEA Cinematográfica. 1990. DVD.
———. *Camila*. Buenos Aires; Madrid: GEA Cinematográfica; Impala. 1984. DVD.
———. *Señora de Nadie*. GEA Cinematográfica. 1982. DVD.
———. *Momentos*. GEA Cinematográfica. 1980. DVD.
Fontana, Clara. *María Luisa Bemberg*. Buenos Aires: Centro Editor de América Latina, 1993. Print.
Forcinito, Ana. "Otra vez María Luisa Bemberg: Transgresiones, fragmentos y límites de la mirada cinemática." *Confluencia: Revista Hispánica de Cultura y Literatura* 21.2 (2006): 33–53. Print.
Foster, David William. *Queer Issues in Contemporary Latin American Cinema*. Austin, TX: U of Texas P, 2003. Print.
———. "El homoerotismo y la lucha por el espacio en Buenos Aires: dos muestras cinematográficas." *Tramas* 6 (1997): 13–42. Print.
———. *Contemporary Argentine Cinema*. Columbia, MO: U of Missouri P, 1992. Print.
Grant, Catherine. "*Intimista* Transformations: María Luisa Bemberg's First Feature Films." *An Argentine Passion: María Luisa Bemberg and Her Films*. Ed John King et al. London: Verso, 2000. 73–109. Print.
King, John. "María Luisa Bemberg and Argentine Culture." *An Argentine Passion: María Luisa Bemberg and Her Films*. Ed John King et al. London: Verso, 2000. 1–32. Print.
Manrupe, Raúl, and María Alejandra Portela. *Un diccionario de films argentinos*. Buenos Aires: Corregidor, 1995. Print.
Rapisardi, Flavio. *Fiestas, baños y exilios: Los gays porteños en la última dictadura*. Buenos Aires: Sudamericana, 2001. Print.
Rojas, Eduardo. "*Momentos y Señora de Nadie*: Señoras de nadie, nada, nunca." *Revista Canadiense de Estudios Hispánicos* 27.1 (2002): 59–73. Print.
Rosado, Miguel Ángel. "Entre la libertad y la censura." *Historia del cine argentino*. Nueva edición, corregida y aumentada. Ed. Jorge Miguel Consuelo. Buenos Aires: Centro Editor de América Latina, 1992. 139–65. Print.
Shua, Ana María. *El marido argentino promedio*. Buenos Aires: Sudamericana, 1991. Print.

2

Fresa y chocolate:
The Allure of Passions and Controversies

(Tomás Gutiérrez Alea and Juan Carlos Tabío, 1993)

CRISTINA VENEGAS

> Well, some say I'm a dissident because I criticize Cuban reality; others say I'm a propagandist for the government because with this criticism I try to show that in Cuba there exists freedom when in fact there is none. What a dilemma, eh?
>
> —Tomás Gutiérrez Alea (qtd. in Chanan)

The controversial and unprecedented subject matter of the Cuban film *Fresa y chocolate* (1993), co-directed by Cuba's most respected filmmaker Tomás Gutiérrez Alea and one of his protégés Juan Carlos Tabío, has largely defined the critical debates and reception of the film. *Fresa y chocolate* was the first Cuban film produced under the auspices of the state's Instituto Cubano de Arte e Industria Cinematográfica (ICAIC) to ever focus on homophobia. Based on the award-winning short story *El lobo, el bosque y el hombre nuevo* (*The Wolf, the Woods, and the New Man*) by Cuban novelist Senel Paz, which previously had also been adapted for the theatre, the film promised to reach a larger audience. Having come across Paz's short story even before publication in 1990, Gutiérrez Alea was shaken by the first reading and felt an urgency to bring it to the screen.

In *Fresa*, Gutiérrez Alea turned his attention to the way political culture constrained gay subjectivity by rendering sexual difference as a disease incompatible with the Revolution's ideals. The backdrop for the conflict is a rich national cultural history and Havana's deplorable physical decay. To get at the issue of sexuality, its repression and representation, Gutiérrez Alea adopts a classical narrative focus on the gay protagonist Diego (Jorge Perugorría), who tries to seduce a young, handsome, and straight revolutionary. Diego's character, defined by his staunch individuality, is aligned with a broader Cuban intellectual culture that is further nuanced in the emotional content of spaces and sounds. The critique of homophobia can hence be read through *Fresa y chocolate*'s multiple narrative layers and beyond a focus on an optical relationship to the film.

The film's classical structure and editing emphasizes vision—constantly cutting on the exchange of looks and thereby creating a connection between gay sexuality and the desiring gaze. This connection has led critics to focus almost exclusively on the film's visual register (Smith, 1996). According to this argument, the position of the spectator relies on a heterosexual construction of looking at the gay man when it is in fact a queering of that vision that would be crucial to articulating a radical critique. Such a view fails to look at the broader social, historical, and political interpretation of the film because we don't see gay sex onscreen. Due to the film's huge and deserved success with audiences at home and abroad, we have to consider the larger social and historical context that helps us understand the critical work the film is doing. *Fresa y chocolate*'s use of melodramatic language, the recourse of nostalgia, the looming specter of Gutiérrez Alea's death, and the social and physical space containing these emotions and interrogations, suggest that there are multiple sensory and allegorical strategies at work. While the visual register in the film does suggest and at times make powerfully visible that which has been previously obscured, the emotive use of the city's geography, architecture, and temporality allows us to talk effectively about the question of political intolerance and the failure of socialist democracy. It suggests that the larger political context can also be used indirectly to talk about the repression of homosexuals. The ruins of the urban landscape are metaphor and index of failed political and social projects enveloping and overtaking the narrative while the appeal to change, in the form of tolerance, resolves the story's conflict. Spaces and discourses produce weariness, claustrophobia, and joy suggesting that the terrain of melodrama can contain the contradictions of collapsed ideologies as well as appeal to a broad worldwide audience. The film attempts to restore the value of affective experiences, including the invisible terrain of gay sex that doesn't appear on screen. If the crumbling cityscapes of Italy had once ignited the imagination of Gutiérrez Alea to make the connection between Italian neorealism and an emerging Cuban cinema in the 1950s, the ruinous landscape of post-Cold War Cuba would provide a melodramatic vehicle for a renewed neorealism.

Despite the novelty of the subject matter in Cuban cinema, homosexuality and the homosexual had a strong presence in Cuban intellectual culture before the Revolution. In the film, however, Diego's main problem—that his sexual preference is denied and is controlled politically—is defined specifically within the confines of revolutionary culture. In *Tropics of Desire*, José Quiroga argues that this limited perspective prevents the film from properly establishing the life-world of the protagonist within the bounds of a fuller cultural history thus rendering the critique disingenuous (132). For Quiroga, the film's emphasis on the punitive response to homosexuality in the 1970s obscures the richer intellectual debate about homosexuality in the pages of cultural journals of the early 60s thus positioning homosexuality as uniquely problematic. Quiroga's insightful critique notwithstanding, the film's effectiveness with audiences (including his own emotional response to the film's end) is precisely the way it allowed a limited if at times facile identification with a subjective position marked as marginal. The desiring gaze structured through Diego is thus shared both by heterosexual and the homosexual alike.

By the 1970s, homosexuals in Cuba were harassed and ostracized in the name of social progress; revolutionary masculinity was linked to heterosexuality and both to the project of constructing *el hombre nuevo*, the new man. Physical and moral fortitude was aligned with the armed struggle, courage with defending and fighting for the nation, and virility with the ever-present icon of Che Guevara, the exemplary revolutionary. According to extremist policymakers, gay, lesbian and transsexual individuals—who were equally labeled *maricones*—needed reforming in order to be of service to the revolutionary project. Thus, they established punitive institutions like the UMAP work camps and sent hundreds to toil in disgrace.[1] Part of the reason that gay identity met with such repression in Cuba during the 1960s and through the 1970s, Quiroga contends, was that "the question of the homosexual was important to the debate around public loyalties and private space as these were understood in a revolutionary situation such as Cuba's" (127). Especially during the 1970s, the Cuban government did not "allow for personal choices as these were seen by the identity-gay movement in the United States," instead subsuming the personal into the political identification with the Cuban state (128). Throughout Cuba's history, homosexuals appear as a threat in the national discourse, as detritus, and worms (130). *Fresa y chocolate* redressed what had become institutionalized homophobia at a time when Cuban cinema had begun to move toward the exploration of post-revolutionary individual identity; a move most especially evident in the work of Fernando Pérez whose film *Madagascar* (1994), the quintessential film of the Special Period, articulated a self adrift in the tide of revolutionary masses and provided new models for identification for Cuban audiences. Gutiérrez Alea's and Tabío's film, made under the horrendous economic conditions of the 1990s, a historical moment the Cuban government labeled the Special Period, would be credited with, among other things, opening the space for public dialogue about homophobia.

Gutiérrez Alea had returned to melodrama four years earlier when he made *Cartas del parque* (*Letters from the Park*, 1989), a romance set in 1913 based on a short story by Gabriel García Marquez. Stylistically, *Fresa y chocolate* moves away from the formal sophistication of *Memorias del subdesarrollo* (*Memories of Underdevelopment*, 1968) or of *Muerte de un burócrata* (*Death of a Bureaucrat*, 1966). It forgoes the surreal extremes of *Los sobrevivientes* (*The Survivors*, 1979) or of *Una pelea cubana contra los demonios* (*A Cuban Fight with Demons*, 1972) while making room for Yoruba divination. It lacks the lacerating postcolonial perspective of *La última cena* (*The Last Supper*, 1976). Instead, his next to last film zeroes in on melodramatic elements and relies on a "realist" *mise-en-scène* that accentuates the emotionality of the story. Private spaces were filled with the disappointment generated by staid political discourse effectively embracing the potential of the melodramatic mode to intensify the "public function of the cinema in the way that it mobilizes and keeps alive major social contradictions in contemporary Cuban society" (Balaisis 5).

A social comedy, *Fresa y chocolate* emerges from the chaos of the Special Period to look back on a deeply troubling moment of the Revolution when gays were sent off to work camps to become reformed men worthy of the Revolution. Given the politically and materially depleted environment of this historical moment, Alea's challenge was to effectively critique the very nature of intolerant thinking in Cuba amid the tired calls for unity by a beleaguered political leadership. The temporal distance of the events narrated displaces mistakes by the revolutionary leadership and bureaucratic henchmen onto the past while highlighting the collective history of these events and the combined emotional response of anger and betrayal.

Other Cuban films had been raising taboo subjects, but the films and their creators became targets for virulent attacks by party apparatchiks and critics. Claiming that social criticism handed tools of sedition over to the enemy, the officials often made the open discussion of taboo subjects—repression, censorship, or freedom of expression—tantamount to treason.

Forging a culture of open criticism from within and outside the intellectual community would continue to be plagued by the overwhelming power of the state over life in Cuba. During the Special Period everyday life became chaotic and a film about homophobia, intolerance, and the limits of individual freedoms generated heated debates and euphoric spectacles. Quiroga recounts tales that became part of the melodramatic excess of the film about audiences of the time where gays cheered not the two protagonists but the stern Miguel (143–44) who appears bare-chested in the film. Emphasizing an emotional national topic, the film seemed to arrive too late and to present too sweet a response to the tragic discrimination against gays in the name of politics. Nonetheless, *Fresa y chocolate* became an important reference point for critics and historians, visitors and locals, as is evident in Lawrence La Fountain-Stokes's anecdote that an invitation to tea while visiting Havana or a book pulled out of a paper bag makes him wonder if his local guide is pointing to a common knowledge of the film (23).

The Special Period was in its third year when food, fuel, and electricity were in short supply. But in the bleak haze of this atmosphere, *Fresa y chocolate* appeared to be a seditious pleasure. By the summer of 1994, the grim situation and a growing political crisis with the U.S. government resulted in riots in Havana and a ruling by Fidel Castro that his government would no longer prevent the departure of those wanting to leave the island. This decision led to the exodus of more than thirty-five thousand Cubans on makeshift rafts. The U.S. government tightened its then thirty-two-year embargo in the hopes of overturning the power structure, thus contributing to greater material decline.[2] In the context of the era, injustice was linked not just to the oppressive policies of the Cuban state but also to the U.S. embargo, which after the disappearance of the former Soviet Union appeared even more politically senseless. Given the unstable social and political situation and the censorship scandal generated two years earlier by the controversial Daniel Díaz Torres film *Alicia en el pueblo de Maravillas* (*Alice in Wondertown*, 1991) *Fresa y chocolate*'s success with local and foreign audiences opened new doors for Cuban cinema at a time when the survival of the once thriving state's ICAIC seemed tenuous.

The melodramatic nature of the film becomes evident in the following plot summary. Set in 1979 Havana—a period of harsh repression of gays—the film centers on the evolving friendship among three characters: Diego, a homosexual artist-writer, David (Vladimir Cruz), a straight card-carrying university student, and Nancy (Mirta Ibarra), a black marketer and best friend to Diego. Diego openly tries to seduce David, and David predictably resists, but is curiously drawn to a potentially subversive Diego. A committed revolutionary and sexual ingénue, David's strict ideological training and countryside origins, make him uncultivated in most matters of life. Attending university during the 1970s, the experience has apparently marred and impoverished his cultural education and ability to think broadly. What repeatedly lures him to Diego's lair is the possibility of exposing Diego as a sexual and political deviant, thus fulfilling his revolutionary duty. Encouraged by a hardline university student named Miguel (Francisco Gattorno), David feigns friendship with Diego in order to gain access to his apartment to gather evidence for his conviction. There he meets Nancy, who initially passes herself off as an informant. When, instead of exposing Diego's homosexuality, David begins to befriend and defend him, the hyper-heterosexual Miguel threatens official retribution. Meanwhile, in a fit of depression, Nancy attempts suicide and saving her brings the trio closer together. Attracted to Diego's individual courage and cultural knowledge, David spirals into an ideological crisis. The freer, more cosmopolitan Diego exalts different aspects of Cuban history and arts, but increasingly puts himself at political risk by personally denouncing a censored art show. Focused on surviving and on finding love, Nancy is less interested in politics and pursues David. Finally, Diego is less interested in having sex with David than on broadening his intellectual perspective, pushing him instead to connect with Nancy. When a defeated Diego decides to leave Cuba to avoid further harassment by the authorities, a changed David questions his decision and prompts the emotional crescendo of the long-awaited friendship.

Fresa y chocolate became one way for audiences to ask new questions about the political process in Cuba and viewers like Venezuelan producer Delfina Catalá identified with how the film showed the relationship of two characters "through looks, gestures, touching, humor, smells, and sounds," remarking in a letter to Gutiérrez Alea in 1993 that the film had an almost "feminine sensibility" to it (Ibarra 292). Foreign audiences understood the film in terms of the language of gay rights, but also through its shortcomings. Did the lack of an explicit critique of heterosexuality as wedded to repression nullify the attempt? Was the theme of tolerance sufficient to critique and denounce the state's repressive tendencies? Clearly, it was not. Self-aware of defining the moral parameters of Cuban tolerance, the film carries a heavy burden that is not easily shaken. In *Fresa y chocolate*, Gutiérrez Alea and Tabío pursued a different purpose: diverse social groups presumably seeking a meeting point to make socialism better *through* socialism. The climatic hug that closes the film acts as an emotional release and activates regret, acknowledging that things have gone badly. This closing gesture hopes to inspire a new dialogue, signified through the simple tale of a gay-straight friendship. It's an empathic response hoping to anticipate a forthcoming change.

The film makes full use of the story's emotional power. For instance, the repeated deferral of the moving final embrace throughout the film heightens the potential rejection while José María Vitier's melancholic musical theme extends the intensified feeling in the melody. The moment underscores longing for the experience of Cuba defined throughout the film as an emotional geography of sadness and solace but also triumph. It charges the act of departure with the possibility of never returning, or of returning to a place changed by the intervening experience. Departure is the goodbye to sights, sites, sounds, and textures that promises to burden future experience that already encompasses a collective social trauma. The film also mourns lost ideals giving way to despair and frustration. Gays could point to the failed promise of transformation at the level of individual participation. Eradicating the fundamental problem of homophobia and racism cannot occur through the will and the policies of the state in the revolutionary project. Each of these problems required different responses that would address old social structural patterns of racial and sexual exclusion.

No Stranger to Critique

Cuban post-revolutionary films have helped to construct a critical engagement with social issues since the earliest moments of the Revolution. They documented social, political, and human conflicts encountered by the immensity of Cuban socialist goals: to transform society completely. Headed by Santiago Álvarez, the Latin American Newsreel documentaries and fiction films all pointed to inadequacies, errors, social confrontations, and what was deemed as entrenched behavior. In the most general terms these critical forays showed that while enormous efforts were made to improve conditions and solve problems, each solution almost always carried with it a negative result. For instance, one newsreel focused on the state's inability to find housing for people left idling for years in shelters after their homes had been declared unlivable. In some way, these critiques constituted a constant tenor of warning, decay, and uncertainty while they showed the revolutionary process at work. Beyond social introspection, cinematic critiques questioned Cuban historical accounts, and even the evolving revolutionary narrative.

Rarely, though, did the most sensitive topics—racism, homophobia, or censorship—emerge onto cinematic screens. Government leaders have often perceived these taboo themes as the dirty laundry one doesn't wash out in public. This logic not only narrows the space of productive criticism, it obscures important work done by some filmmakers, and focuses critical thinking within the ideological parameters of the state. Moreover, critical ideas were developed in concert with revolutionary practice.

Arguably, one of the most sophisticated authors of critiques of the revolutionary process was Tomás Gutiérrez Alea, who would fuse a sharp eye on the social conflicts around him with an aesthetics that was also committed to altering ways of seeing. Gutiérrez Alea was thus no stranger to controversy since his films frequently addressed—often with dark humor—what he believed were the most intensely problematic aspects of society: opportunism, sexism, corruption, homophobia, and bureaucracy.

Embedded in a revolutionary political and aesthetic complexity, Gutiérrez Alea's perspective frequently stretched the boundaries of both. He defended his position often arguing that he was no counterrevolutionary. His films articulated a pointed critique that he repeated in interviews, essays, and letters. He described his own process in terms of a Brechtian language that allowed him to create an energetic and critical engagement in order to prevent ideas from stagnating (Gutiérrez Alea 1988, 191–209).[3] Applied to his aesthetic practice, this in part amounted to deploying conventions rooted in drama, comedy, melodrama, and documentary, which when woven together and juxtaposed produced fresh relational ideas. His aesthetic approach is honed through the use of recurrent themes and aesthetic collisions that are appealing because they make possible a "free interpretation of events rather than by their historical reconstruction" (Ibarra 107). In a 1964 letter to his friend, the French film critic Paul-Louis Thiriard, Gutiérrez Alea reflected on the possibility that such an approach could reveal the deeper dimensions of social and moral predicaments through the rich layering of form, genre, and discourses. As they clash, the juxtaposition and contrast of elements incite new ways of seeing, and for him this was deeply revolutionary. Events themselves could generate tremendous dramatic strength but only by setting them free from the confines of historical linearity or explanation. His approach would question the hierarchy of discourses—colonial or revolutionary—and investigate the dilemmas facing Cuban society through a focus on the pressure points of social conflicts like those of the middle-class Sergio in *Memories of Underdevelopment*, or of Diego in *Fresa y chocolate*.

The Fragile Culture of Critical Engagement

Gutiérrez Alea's critical position, however, did not always serve him well. His take on Cuba's culture of homophobia was burdened by an earlier confrontation with long-time friend Néstor Almendros with whom he had strongly disagreed about the tenor of *Improper Conduct* (*Mauvaise Conduite*, 1984) a French documentary Almendros co-directed with Cuban filmmaker Orlando Jiménez Leal. *Improper* denounced in the harshest terms the homophobia that ruled the halls of power and the streets of Cuba; the camps, the persecutions, the censorship, and the lives lost to senseless witch-hunts. At the time, Gutiérrez Alea's response to Almendros's film was characteristically frank and it ended their friendship, a consequence he would later admit troubled him. Alea argued that *Improper* was an unfair critique and beneath Almendros's talent as an artist (Santí 413). While Gutiérrez Alea regretted the loss of this friendship, he never stopped feeling that *Improper* was in fact reprehensible (414). The conflict with Almendros is not covered in the posthumous letters published by his widow and long-time collaborator Mirta Ibarra in 2008. It is not covered in her documentary *Titón: de la Habana a Guantanamera* (2008) that recounts his artistic life. Nonetheless, because of its content, *Fresa y chocolate* contains the specter of all these battles: the personal one with Almendros, the official one with Cuban bureaucratic institutions, and an intimate one as he was diagnosed with cancer when he began filming. *Fresa y chocolate* is enveloped in a melancholia that informs its appeal to tolerance as much as it channels the lost ideals of unity and solidarity during the catastrophic moment of the 1990s.

In an interview he did with Michael Chanan, Gutiérrez Alea revealed that Almendros's death a year before was subconsciously present as he and Tabío worked on the film, acknowledging that *Fresa y chocolate* "could be seen as a response to *Improper Conduct*" (2002, 52). To its critics—especially those outside Cuba, *Fresa y chocolate* did not sufficiently indict the Cuban government for its repressive policies nor did it formulate a real critique of heterosexuality outside of its regime of vision. Worse, some criticized Gutiérrez Alea (Tabío was spared) as an apologist for the Cuban state. Nonetheless, while it would not get it entirely right, *Fresa y chocolate* connected the notion of social progress to that of democratic rights for all Cubans and by so doing it positioned the film successfully in the foreign art film market. Even so, in an interview several months before the film's release in 1993, Gutiérrez Alea acknowledged that the film's timing was off by about ten years "when discrimination of homosexuals was more acute" and when it would have had greater social and political impact (Campa 56). Had it been made a decade earlier, the film's release would have coincided in the mid-eighties with *Improper Conduct.*

Persuasions of Melodrama

By emphasizing the tragic oppression of gays, the moral conflict this implies, and the dialectic of innocence and experience, *Fresa y chocolate* deploys characteristic elements of the melodramatic mode. Moral solutions, excessive emotions, surprising narrative twists, and a sentimental identification of the cityscape, are all tempered from extremes by the use of actual locations in Havana. More than providing "truth" and "realism," the settings connect the narrative conflicts with the emotional topography of crumbling buildings, dingy rooms, faded grandeur, and the gorgeous sea. Unlike Humberto Solás's *Lucía* (1968) that matches an excess of emotionalism with epic sized aesthetics flourishes, melodrama in *Fresa y chocolate* is confined within the interiority of lives and emotionality of spaces while loading the visual gesture with emotional excess. Gutiérrez Alea claimed that the film was bound to appeal to contemporary audiences if it appealed to the heart. He said as much to José Antonio Évora in a letter dated June 1994 in response to the warm reception the film had received in the United States (Ibarra 292).

The opening scene establishes key conflicting elements of the plot as well as David's moral tenor, earnest character, and heterosexuality. A student in Havana, he is in a relationship with the much savvier Vivian (Marilyn Solaya). When he takes her to a dingy motel room, he appears oblivious to the falseness of her sexual shyness and sincerely offers to defer their lovemaking as proof of honorable intentions. We learn this from Vivian's shocked expression at David's confident announcement that he will wait for the wedding day and the five-star hotel. That day never comes and instead Vivian marries a foreigner and leaves the country. David's heartbroken response is underscored musically while he drinks rum at an outdoor bar. Off screen, the lyrics of an old *bolero* performed by a painfully out-of-tune street musician drone on: "I am sad without your love which stole my heart," creating a direct association between his sentimental state and the decrepit life of the street.

More than establishing the economy of looking that pervades the film—and is significantly coded heterosexual—the opening scene and shabby motel room *mise-en-scène* provide an initial glimpse of the film's emotional language of space. Peeling paint, holes in the walls, broken light switches, rickety furniture, and its location across the street from the local Committee for the Defense of the Revolution, make the place David selects for the his sexual initiation comically and pathetically unromantic. While training viewers to identify with David's heterosexual perspective, the film also identifies the city of Havana and the spaces of intimacy as key characters in the emotional movement of the plot.

The Havana setting is indispensable for the evolution of the friendship between Diego and David. While the institutionalized homophobia that the film confronts was generalized through national policy, cultural differences and degrees of acceptance vary between urban and rural spaces, making the film's politics decidedly urban. As Cuban film critic Frank Padrón contends, "Havana is much more significant [in *Fresa y chocolate*] than in other films, not only because it would be difficult to conceive of the evolution of David and Diego's friendship in other provinces, but because for the protagonist and his cultural mission, the capital provides an essential place and worldview" (43).[4]

The story really begins when Diego lures the naive David to his apartment with the pretext of giving him photographs taken of him in a play. The unauthorized photographs further suggest the film's voyeurism. They bring David to *La guarida*, Diego's apartment, which is the site for the sexual, cultural, and political transgressions that repeatedly reposition the viewer's subjectivity. At the level of plot, homosexuality is not treated as a secret; its repression from discourse, however, boils over in the performative excess of Diego's affected mannerisms. David resists on moral and political grounds, informed by the belief system he has acquired under the revolution. At first, David's curiosity is aroused by Diego's sexual agenda and by the hope that he might uncover counterrevolutionary activities, but in reality he is seduced by Diego's deep knowledge of Cuban culture. This epistemological courtship brings David back to Diego repeatedly in a game that to the chagrin of many critics culminates in friendship.

At the level of visual transgression one scene stands out in particular. Harassed by the staunchly communist and unyielding Miguel for hanging out with a *maricón*, David seeks comfort in Diego's apartment with the bottle of whiskey. Diego watches the passed out and bare-chested David silently from across the room while the music of Maria Callas is heard in the background. The melodramatic tone of the scene emphasizes Diego's desire through the safety of a tender and compassionate look. Nancy enters the room and together they gaze at David. As Diego longingly savors David's half-naked body with his eyes, the camera slowly pans the length of the torso, pausing on the partially unzipped fly of his jeans. The highly charged moment presents the threat of the homosexual to the political discourse of the era through a desiring gesture, which is replaced by Nancy's longing dialogue for David, "he reminds me of a man from the 40s." Together they share an erotic gaze at once painful and delightful. The comparison of David's erotic appeal to the ambiguous cultural imaginary of another era, leaves the audience open to interpret if she's referring to a film hero of the period, or a particular type of non-straight masculinity and national identity, and in doing so the film's narrative further points to its narrative layering.

Reality in Counterpoint

As a text, *Fresa y chocolate* utilizes narrative levels, discourses, and viewpoints that serve to challenge a monolithic view of Cuba. These multiple "voices" produce a layered effect that goes beyond the problem of representing homosexuality, positioning the discourse about homosexuality as part of a larger Cuban history and problem. As Mikhail Bakhtin demonstrated with regard to the novel, discourse has a social life that emerges from outside the artist's study where discourse is a social phenomenon (259). This concept is quite appropriate for understanding the complexity of *Fresa y chocolate* thus opening up the text to nonverbal or visual elements that act as narrative devices. The décor of Diego's apartment is the most obvious case in point as multiple cultural and political icons crowd the walls and are constantly part of the frame. It is a private museum and archive of select items presented as a topography of culture: photographs of well-known writers, a portrait of Cuban patriot José Martí, famous singers, artwork, a baroque iron fence railing, but significantly no portrait of Che.

But other objects also enunciate their significance to the central conflict like favorite books (some banned others not), opera records, teacups, furniture, "strange" religious sculptures and the ever-present *orisha* altars. When David inquires about an object in the apartment, the response spirals into a lecture on literary history, musical history, or social history. Everyday life gets integrated into the collection—listening to records, reading books, or drinking tea—conflating the past into the present in dialectical relationship between memory and history. Diego's apartment functions as a repository of Cuban, Latin American, and world history. And, like the Museum of the Revolution in Havana, this personal museum reveals an ideological construct that importantly, has Diego as curator of a personal national history. In the plot, Diego also tries to curate an art show with Germán (Joel Angelino), a young gay artist whose sculptures parody the figures of Christ and Marx and are temporarily hidden in his apartment. *La guarida* is literally an exhibition space, where a version of history is sanctioned and re-articulated unofficially, as well as where physical, visual, and musical pleasures occupy center stage, thus positing the ideological emptiness of the Revolution.

The apartment's different spaces—altars, spiritual corners, kitchen—further stratify the levels of signification. Occasional references to the saint Santa Bárbara, Rocco, the named refrigerator—a reference to the masterful 1960 melodrama by Luchino Visconti *Rocco and His Brothers*—Diego's made-up family members, and the Virgen de la Caridad del Cobre point to other forms of knowledge and ways of sensing. The altars in domestic spaces replace the ever-present patriotic public altars to Cuba's heroes of independence. The figure of Santa Bárbara is the syncretizing of the Roman Catholic saint with Changó, Afro-Cuban god of fire and storms, a lover of music, and a womanizer. The fusion of the male god with the female virgin, according to Natalia Bolívar, "is less surprising if we remember that this god had to disguise himself as a woman" (1990). These entities, however, do not operate in the filmic text only as cultural reminders of African roots or colonization. They take on a dramatic function within the seduction. After David storms out of the apartment in response to Diego's outrageous behavior, Diego begs Santa Bárbara for help in bringing back David, thus involving *her* in the melodramatic tension. When David eventually returns, the victory is registered as an aside to the audience with a coy smile and an offering for Santa Bárbara. Likewise Nancy, who is concurrently pursuing David, makes offerings to her patron saint to help her bring about the desired romance. When their lovemaking culminates the pursuit and the history lesson, she turns to Santa Bárbara and asks her not to gossip with the Vírgen del Cobre. Moreover, Nancy's "conversations" with *orishas* (gods) also function as other voices of resistance in Cuban culture. Coincidentally, they foster a narrative hook in a booming consumer market for Afro-Cuban religiosity in the mid-90s.

The austere interior of David's university dorm equally connects that space to the political rhetoric that the film questions, and Nancy's apartment is a storehouse of clandestine black market goods. Outdoors, the marvelous architecture and its deplorable decay, give rise to an atmosphere—used here as part of the ritual of conquest—where building ornamentation, porticos, columns, and stained-glass windows bring forth a history of art and culture. Mario García Joya's handheld camera produces intimacy through physical proximity to the actors. To solve the logistics of shooting in small spaces, García Joya moved camera operator and technicians around the actors creating a dynamic atmosphere.⁵ Tight interior spaces, balconies, stairwells and public spaces fuse with the life of the characters. A long zoom selects images of bystanders, "real" people caught unawares, and colloquial street sounds offer a counterpoint to David's communist jargon. Inside these spaces ideologies collide as David's blind political rhetoric, strict prohibitions, and moral taboos come up against Diego's more liberal and conciliatory position. Their battling discourse destabilizes the singular official line by valuing the multiplicity of cultural signifiers.

Colloquial expressions, appropriated as oppositional discourse, are also re-articulated through a homosexual context. The title of the film is a humorous and horrific reference to the significance of selecting ice-cream flavors at Coppelia, a popular ice-cream spot in Havana, serving ice cream to hundreds every day. It is a metaphor for accepted binaries. *Fresa* (strawberry) in street idiom suggests the pastel color used to refer to *locas* and *chocolate* to male virility. Chocolate also references the image of naked blacks supposedly conjured up during horrific torture sessions, which further references a colonial past and the hybrid nature of the culture. These coded expressions are thus deployed with pointed playfulness, calling attention to the deep cultural layers of homophobia implied in the binary opposition of the film's title. When they first meet, Diego exclaims in an exaggerated feminized gesture: "Look! It's my lucky day, I got a strawberry," announcing his preference for a queer position and initiating the seduction.

A key element of *Fresa y chocolate* is the "realism" evoked by the use of a hidden camera in the streets and neighborhoods that became the film's locations. The camera mobilizes looking and reveals the emotion of the cityscape and seascape. Gutiérrez Alea's and Tabio's Special Period neorealism reflects contemporary Havana and the harsh economic conditions of film production as both studios and processing labs had shut down two years earlier. The film's style thus ends up being inspired by historical circumstances. Dilapidated locations provided a savings and an emotional texture to the space. The dense cultural and political crosscurrents of the island are represented in Old Havana's narrow streets (where Diego's apartment is located) and in the multiplicity of architectural styles. The economic problems were recorded in the dark and dense interiors of decaying buildings that often housed multiple families and animals. City streets crowded with bicycle traffic instead of cars pointed to fuel shortages and collapsed buildings to the impermanence of things. The loaded emotional and humorous context of interior spaces is rendered in a telling scene where an enormous squealing pig is ushered up a dilapidated staircase as Diego enters his apartment unfazed. The film thus produces an emotional attachment to interior and exterior spaces, which is deployed dramatically throughout the narrative. Seduction has more potential in the airiness of Coppelia than in the ramshackle hotel room of the film's opening. Political discussion has greater allure in the enveloping baroque interior of Diego's apartment than inside the barrack-style dorms of the university. The glistening Havana harbor is a romantic backdrop for the exile subplot that gets deployed when Diego decides to leave the country. Out for the first time in public, the two men go to a favorite spot, which has a breathtaking view of the harbor. The visualization of exile is palpable in this shot, which like a tourist photograph centers the two men with the Havana cityscape and the sea in the background, evoking Gutiérrez Alea's earlier film *Memories of Underdevelopment* (1968) and Sergio's dialogue observing that "the city doesn't seem real, it's like a cardboard rendering."

Timothy Barnard has discussed the significance of the representation of historical retrieval in Cuban films, as it works to create a new history, a controlled history, whereby images of the past are carefully reconstructed, re-inscribed with one ideological dimension (230). The images seem to have a historical specificity. But on closer reading Barnard sees a conflation of imagery from the past and present that refers to an imaginary history, in this case how *Fresa y chocolate* imagines reconciliation with the past. The historical reconstruction also occurs aurally through the soundtrack and in the diegetic use of songs that also evoke the syncretic nature of the music. Diego uses music to begin the seduction and dramatically to conceal conversations in case the neighbors are listening. He treats David to an aria sung by Maria Callas, to the tropicalist music of Ernesto Lecuona, a Cuban pianist from the 1960s, and the classic *sones* of Ignacio Cervantes, who Diego points out "wrote *Adiós a Cuba* when the Spaniards threw him out during the war." They listen to *boleros* and *danzones* that embellish the inescapable nostalgia. With greater emphasis music captures the sonic hybridity and melancholia of the island. As the noted Cuban novelist and musicologist Alejo Carpentier once explained, the unique unraveling of an artistic process in Latin American music was "governed by the constant replay of confrontations between one's own and the foreign, the native and the imported" (1977).[6]

Watershed Film

Produced in the throes of a cataclysmic historical moment, *Fresa y chocolate* forms part of a new era of filmmaking that reflected the social acceptance of new forms of Cuban identity. New generations of filmmakers were training in film schools and on video, embracing alternative modes of production. As a Cuba-Mexico-Spain co-production, *Fresa y chocolate* contributed to the wave of co-productions that sustained ICAIC throughout the 1990s and beyond (Venegas). It was the first Cuban film to be commercially distributed in the United States—by Miramax—since the early 70s and to receive distribution in major territories throughout the world. A breakthrough in Cuba for tackling gay sexuality—which only a few other mainstream Latin American films had done in the 1980s—makes it twice a revelation.[7] While not as shocking as Pedro Almodóvar's early film *Laberinto de Pasiones* (*Labyrinth of Passion*, 1982), which Brad Epps suggests is the quintessential film of the *Movida*—the post Franco movement that seemed to "sweep Spain into postmodernity" (319)—*Fresa y chocolate* attempts a similar intervention by positioning the homosexual protagonist as a model Cuban and attractive lover in an attempt to shift the fixed heterosexuality of the regime's vision while the regime was still in place. As Marsha Kinder argues with respect to Almodóvar, his outrageous interventions in post Franco Spain used gay sexuality, indeed all marginality, centrally in the narrative as a way to disavow "the past and pretend the Francoist era had never existed." In this way, the film's gay label, accessible story line, and artistic pedigree made it an easy entry into international film festivals worldwide where it received multiple awards. At the 1993 Havana International Film Festival, the film walked away with all the major awards and its box-office success would follow during an eight-month run at the Yara Theatre in Havana's popular La Rampa neighborhood. At the Berlin Film Festival, the film won a Teddy for Best Feature and a Special Jury Prize. It received a Goya Award in Spain for the Best Spanish Foreign Film and a Special Mention from the Sundance Film Festival in Utah. It was also the first Cuban film ever to be nominated for an Academy Award in the United States.

The theme was thus considered internationally marketable for a Cuban film because of its controversial nature, and this aspect was successfully marketed to "art cinema" patrons. National audiences rushed to enjoy it and this double success squarely puts the film at the pressure point between national and transnational audiences. During the early 1990s, as the Cuban government navigated calamities and catastrophe, it also looked to the global sphere for its survival, which led to greater visibility for Cuban culture. As David William Foster argues, Cuban filmmaking "presents all sorts of issues of transnationalism . . . [as] . . . films not only bespeak concerns within Cuba but also take those issues to the Cuban American community, to the U.S. community at large, and to an international community" (117).

Fresa y chocolate re-opened international doors for Cuban cinema and it did so with a controversial subject matter. Given the film's content and the loaded emotional moment, Gutiérrez Alea's pragmatic approach to completing the film's production was again informed by events. As they shot the film, the team formulated a strategy of survival in concert with the sensitive political environment and the worsening economic crisis. Should the production of *Fresa y chocolate* meet with censorship a visual record was captured in the British "making of" documentary *Rear Window: Tales from Havana* (Anderson 1994), produced by Channel Four in Britain. Moreover, they sought advantage from the closing of the laboratories in Havana, which meant that daily footage was to be processed in Mexico, allowing filmmakers to safeguarded a copy of the negative in that country. Despite obstacles, the film's success marks a subversion of sorts.

In *History of Sexuality,* Michel Foucault re-orients the debate on power away from the repressive Law and instead onto the strategies of a field of mobile force relations (92). His proposal that "we must not imagine a world of discourse divided between accepted discourse and excluded discourse . . . but as a multiplicity of discursive elements that can come into play in various strategies" allows us to think of this film and its relationship to Cuban society as being "tactically productive" regarding the discourse of homosexuality and the mode of its production (102). Even though *Fresa y chocolate*'s treatment of the homosexual taboo was sanctioned by ICAIC, the behind-the-scenes account indicates that the completion of the project and its dissemination were far from guaranteed and had to rely on extra-state strategies of support both locally and outside Cuba to counterbalance the unpredictable economic and political situation. Despite the existing homophobic culture and material difficulties, the film is an example of how it becomes impossible to completely suppress a discourse, just as it is impossible for the filmmaker to ignore that the cultural tensions exist (*Rear Window: Tales From Havana*, 1994). Filmmaker and work have a direct political nexus to the process of production and to the contradictory discourse about sexuality, and the multiple tensions are incorporated into the final text. The film relies on the existence of a repressive discourse about homosexuality in Cuba, which it both dramatizes and contradicts using a double-voice approach analogous to its narrative and visual strategies.

The contradictory relations between text, bureaucracy, and state would also be in evidence in the context of exhibition as the film's Cuban television broadcast was endlessly postponed. The delay indicates the highly charged political terrain that television occupies in Cuban society. Incredibly, *Fresa y chocolate* would not be broadcast until May 5, 2007, fourteen years after its premiere at the Havana International Film Festival and then in response to a crisis about the repressive role of television personalities in the policies of the 1970s when intellectuals and cultural critics insisted that Cuban television officials needed to prove a greater openness. Cuban critic Jesús Laó writing on a blog about Cuban cinema lauded the broadcast presentation on the show "Espectador crítico" because it advocated very clearly a "perfectible Cuba," that is, a Cuba that aspired to participatory and inclusive democratic values. Laó observed that the network had the sense to feature Cuban film critic Frank Padrón, a specialist on gay-lesbian cinema, as the onscreen host and commentator for the film.[8]

The state itself has found novel strategies for incorporating the tenor of controversies while revamping its image of a more tolerant socialism. More than fifteen years after the film premiered, the state has aggressively and positively embraced an open policy on sexual diversity, promoting sexual diversity through television, education, health care, and cultural events. The Centro Nacional de Educación Sexual (CENESEX), an official policymaking institution founded in 1989 and headed by Mariela Castro—daughter of Raúl Castro—orchestrates a multi-prong approach from the highest level of leadership. The changes are publicly palpable, and Mariela Castro has brought the center to national and international attention. On a recent interview available through the CENESEX website, a writer suggests that small gains in representational strategies are afoot. Nelson Simón, noted Cuban author of homoerotic poetry contends that, "twenty years ago, if someone dealt with these topics [gay sexuality], gays would be portrayed as a strange species in danger of extinction. Now we can talk about recognition, co-existence and understanding."[9] CENESEX also sponsors a space for international gay cinema through the *Cineclub diferente* showing films that openly embrace gay sex. Newer and established Cuban filmmakers like Pavel Giroud and Gerardo Chijona contribute to this educational mandate by making public service announcements for Cuban television that promote respect for sexual diversity.[10] In 2006, *The Dark Side of the Moon*, a gay-themed Cuban soap opera produced by official Cuban television, sought to address sexual diversity and HIV education through the melodramatic mode once again. It aired on television even before *Fresa y chocolate* did (Rasverg 2006).

I am not suggesting that there is a deliberate connection between *Fresa y chocolate* and the institutionalization of sexual diversity through CENESEX, which in any case is not what the film advocates. What I am suggesting is that *Fresa y chocolate* made the debate and its contradictions broadly popular and public through a reliance on melodramatic conventions and audience appeal. Furthermore, both of these outcomes coincided with critical junctures that made state repression and its role in the intellectual life of Cubans much harder to ignore. Whatever its success at the level of redirecting the gaze, the film ultimately occupies an indelible place in Cuban cinema and culture that continues to generate new texts, evidence of which I offer in these two closing examples. First, an indirect reference, indeed a ghostly presence, in the film *Afinidades* (*Affinities*, 2010) in the form of a closing dedication to directors Gutiérrez Alea and Tabio by the film's co-directors and co-stars Jorge Perugorría and Vladimir Cruz acting together for the first time since *Fresa y chocolate*. The subtext of the film's existential treatise on sexuality and contemporary problems facing Cuban couples is precisely the reverberating effect of the co-stars and their self-conscious reference to their earlier onscreen pairing. Second, a direct intervention into the original text in the form of a short story by Cuban critic Rufo Caballero, which re-enlivens the postulated, but frustrated pleasures of the film. In "Silicona," Caballero—whose forceful dedication to Senel Paz has the tone of an unwanted intervention ("To Senel, even if he doesn't want it")—rewrites one scene of the 1993 film, queering the original text by positioning Nancy as first-person narrator (2010). Caballero's bold intervention into an existing text leads him to borrow and rewrite Paz's original story and in so doing he replenishes the original intention and confuses the line between one writer's words with another's. By turning Nancy into the protagonist, he changes the subjectivity of the conflict and its heterosexual bias. In confessional mode, Nancy reveals the disadvantage she feels in her courtship with David, as she competes for David's curiosity, attention, and his sex. Diego gets it all. In Caballero's version, Nancy doesn't share the attraction to David with Diego, she loses David to Diego altogether during the same afternoon that, in the earlier versions, Nancy and Diego had shared a silent longing for the passed-out David in Diego's apartment. Caballero leaves her out of the room entirely, but not out of the seduction, as her narration becomes the distant interlocutor of the men's sexual act. Listening intently through the walls of her apartment, Nancy overhears the ecstatic moaning in Diego's apartment as the two men delight in each other's sexual rhythms. Moreover, when Diego leaves Cuba, David disappears from her life completely until one day Germán—the gay author of the strange religious figures—reappears in her apartment and asks her not to worry about David because they have been together since Diego left. Caballero has performed an outrageous reversal of the tables positing homosexuality itself, even as the sex in the story is still unseen, albeit loudly heard, as the means to reinvent the revolutionary and re-direct the ideological crisis. It is as much in the inexorable force of the original to generate new narratives, as in the daring iterations of the same, that we can finally see the lasting power of the film's critique.

Notes

1. The Unidades Militares para la Ayuda de Producción (UMAP) existed between 1965 and 1967.
2. The Torricelli Act of 1992 further tightened trade with the island as the United States moved to complicate trade with any ally that attempted trade with Cuba. Its implementation concurred with the fall of the Soviet Union and marked the beginning of what the Cuban's refer to as the Special Period.
3. Gutiérrez Alea discusses his creative process in his essays "Dialectic with the Spectator," included in *New Latin American Cinema* and "Notes on *Memories of Underdevelopment*," in *Hojas de Cine*.
4. My translation.
5. Mario "Mayito" García Joya, who worked on many films with Tomás Gutiérrez Alea (*The Last Supper*, *Letters from the Park*, *The Survivors* among others), developed a unique method of shooting, which allows him to choreograph the handheld camera. With the help of assistants he moves freely about the set with the actors while obstacles are removed from his path and a wooden pole steadies the camera as hits a predetermined mark.
6. My translation.
7. Two films in particular boldly stand out in the 1980s: the Mexican production *Doña Herlinda y su hijo* by Jaime Humberto Hermosillo (*Doña Herlinda and Her Son*, 1985) and Argentine/Brazilian Héctor Babenco's *Kiss of the Spider Woman* (1985). While Babenco's film had international producers, Hermosillo's film was nationally produced and financed.
8. "*Fresa y chocolate* o la nación 'perfectible.'"
9. "CENESEX, interview with poet Nelson Simón."
10. "La diversidad es natural."

Works Cited

Acosta, Dalia. "Homosexualidad: Nelson Simón, la libertad de reconocerse gay." *Cenesex Portal*. Web. July 28, 2011.
Almendros, Néstor, and Orlando Jiménez Leal, dir. *Improper Conduct*. Antenne 2; Les Films du Losange, 1984. Film.
Anderson, Alexandra, dir. *Rear Window: Tales from Havana*. Channel Four, 1994. Film.
Babenco, Héctor, dir. *Kiss of the Spider Woman*. City Lights Pictures; Independent Cinema Restorative Archive, 2008. DVD.

Bakhtin, Mikhail Mikhailovich. "Discourse in the Novel." *The Dialogic Imagination*. Trans. Caryl Emerson and Michael Holquist. Austin, TX: U of Texas P, 1981: 259–422. Print.

Balaisis, Nicholas. "The Publicness of Melodrama in the Cuban Special Period." *Public* 37 (2008): 48–56. Print.

Barnard, Timothy. "Death is not True." *Mediating Two Worlds: Cinematic Encounters in the Americas*. Ed. John King et al. London: British Film Institute, 1993. 230–41. Print.

Bolívar Aróstegui, Natalia. *Los Orishas en Cuba*. La Habana: Unión, 1990. Print.

Caballero, Rufo. "Silicona." *Seduciendo a un extraño*. La Habana: ICAIC, 2010. Print.

Campa, Homero. "Expectación en Cuba por ver el film de Gutiérrez Alea coproducido con México: Homosexualidad, intolerancia, crítica social." *Proceso* 24 (1993): 56–57. Print.

Carpentier, Alejo. "América Latina en la confluencia de coordenadas históricas y su repercussion en la música." *America Latina en su música*. México, D.F.: Siglo XXI, 1977. 7–19. Print.

Chanan, Michael. "We Are Losing All Our Values: An Interview with Tomás Gutiérrez Alea." *Boundary* 2. 29.3 (2002): 47–53. Print.

Díaz Torres, Daniel, dir. *Alicia en el pueblo de Maravillas*. ICAIC, 1991. Film.

Epps, Brad. "Blind Shots and Backward Glances." *All About Almodóvar: A Passion for Cinema*. Ed. Brad Epps and Despina Kakoudaki. Minneapolis: U of Minnesota P, 2009. 319–20. Print.

Foster, David William. Rev. of *Cuba Transnational*, edited by Damián J. Fernandez, *Cuban Studies* 39 (2008): 113–17. Print.

Foucault, Michel. *The History of Sexuality*. Trans. Robert Hurley. Vol. 1. New York: Vintage, 1978. Print.

Hermosillo, Jaime Humberto, dir. *Doña Herlinda y su hijo*. IMCINE, 1984. Film.

Giroud, Pavel, and Gerardo Chijona. "La diversidad es natural." Web. Aug. 10, 2011. http://www.youtube.com/watch?v=b8ePMebWa4U.

Gutiérrez Alea, Tomás, dir. *La última cena*. Impulso; ICAIC, 2007. DVD.

———. "Dialectic with the Spectator." *New Latin American Cinema: Theory, Practices, and Transcontinental Articulations*. Ed. Michael T. Martin. Wayne State UP, 1997. 108–35. Print.

———, dir. *Cartas del parque*. ICAIC; TVE, 1989. Film.

———. "Memories of Underdevelopment." *Hojas de Cine: Testimonios y documentos del nuevo cine latinoamericano*. Vol. 3. México, D.F.: Dirección General de Publicaciones y Medios (SEP); Fundación Mexicana de Cineastas; Universidad Autónoma Metropolitana, 1988. 191–209. Print.

———, dir. *Los sobrevivientes*. ICAIC, 1979. Film.

———. *Una pelea cubana contra los demonios*. ICAIC, 1972. Film.

———. *Memorias del subdesarrollo*. ICAIC, 1968. Film.

———. *Muerte de un burócrata*. ICAIC, 1966. Film.

Gutiérrez Alea, Tomás, and Juan Carlos Tabío, dir. *Fresa y chocolate*. Libro sin Fronteras, 2005. DVD.

Ibarra, Mirtha, ed. *Titón: Volver sobre mis pasos*. La Habana: Unión, 2008. 107–108. Print.

———, dir. *Titón, de la Habana a Guantanamera*. Brothers and Sisters, 2008. Film.

Kinder, Marsha. "All about the Brothers: Retroseriality in Almodóvar's Cinema." *All About Almodóvar: A Passion for Cinema*. Ed. Brad Epps and Despina Kakoudaki. Minneapolis, MN: U of Minnesota P, 2009. 267–94. Print.

La Fountain-Stokes, Lawrence. "De un pájaro las dos alas: Travel Notes of a Queer Puerto Rican in Havana." *GLQ* 8.1–2 (2002): 7–33. Print.

Laó, Jesús. "*Fresa y chocolate* o la nación 'perfectible.'" *La pupila insomne blog*. Web. Dec. 9, 2009.

Padrón, Frank. *Sinfonía inconclusa para cine cubano*. Santiago de Cuba: Oriente, 2008. Print.

Paz, Senel. *El lobo, el bosque y el hombre nuevo*. México, D.F.: Era, 1991. Print.

Pérez, Fernando, dir. *Madagascar*. ICAIC, 1994. Film.

Perugorría, Jorge, and Vladimir Cruz, dir. *Afinidades*. Hispafilms, 2010. Film.

Quiroga, José. *Tropics of Desire: Interventions from Queer Latino America*. New York: New York UP, 2000: Print.

Rasverg, Fernando. "Amor de hombres en telenovela cubana." *BBC Mundo*. Web. September 7, 2011.

Santí, Enrico Mario. "*Fresa y chocolate*: The Rhetoric of Cuban Reconciliation." *Modern Language Notes* 113.2 (1998): 407–25. Print.

Smith, Paul Julian. *Vision Machines: Cinema, Literature and Sexuality in Spain and Cuba, 1983–1993*. London: Verso, 1996. Print.

Solás, Humberto, dir. *Lucía*. ICAIC, 1968. Film.

Venegas, Cristina. "Filmmaking with Foreigners." *Cuba in the Special Period: Culture and Ideology in the 1990s*. Ed. Ariana Hernandez-Reguant. New York: Palgrave MacMillan, 2009: 37–50. Print.

Vincent, Mauricio. "Aires de apertura en La Habana." *El País*. Web. July 5, 2007.

3

A Gaynster Quasi-Tragedy: Eroticism and Secrets in *Plata quemada*[1]

(Marcelo Piñeyro, 2000)

ANDRÉS LEMA-HINCAPIÉ

> Love is the burning of two souls compelled to grow and to manifest themselves independently.
>
> —Lawrence Durrell, *Justine*

In *Plata quemada* (*Burnt Money*), Marcelo Piñeyro (Buenos Aires, b. 1953) proposes as a central thesis the oscillation among expressions of erotic desire: Ángel and El Nene experience different intensities in the relationship of their reciprocal desire. That oscillation occurs on at least three levels: the archaeological, the diegetic, and the cinematic. Just as the protagonists' eroticism eludes any rigid or ultimate definition, the levels are likewise mutable, overlapping, and mutually enriching. Before continuing, we may assume that "erotic desire" transcends mere physical interest in the other person. Or, in the words of Patrick Anderson, "Eros is by no means generally 'erotic' and has intensities which may or may not involve sensuousness quite apart from carnality" (10).

Mythological traditions can aid our comprehension of the oscillating eroticism lived out between Ángel (Eduardo Noriega) and El Nene (Leonardo Sbaraglia). According to Orphic traditions, Eros "set the Universe in motion" (Graves 30). The same phenomenon occurs when Ángel and El Nene have their first casual sexual encounter in the public restroom of the

Constitución train station. Nevertheless, beyond just setting two lives in motion, the turbulent and socially devastating Eros—the archetypal "wild boy"—likewise causes "uncontrolled sexual passion." Graves goes on to say that Eros not only "showed no respect for age or station" (58), he also employs a specific element of nature—fire—to damage the hearts of his victims. The presence of physical fire and emotional passion in the myths of Eros immediately lead us to think of the fire that literally consumes the lives of Ángel and El Nene while, at the same time, causes their rebirth. Eros enjoys "wantonly setting hearts on fire with his dreadful torches" (58).[2]

At the *archaeological level,* this film, from 2000, is both preceded and succeeded by cultural filters that blur any definitive interpretation of the erotic desire between Ángel and El Nene. The critical viewer of Piñeyro's film quickly becomes aware of many filters linked to actual criminal events that took place in Argentina and Uruguay in 1965. These filters are the television broadcast of the event, the newspaper reports, the forensic accounts, the fictional reconstruction in Ricardo Piglia's eponymous novel published in 1997, the screenplay of *Burnt Money* (written by both Piñeyro and Marcelo Figueras and published in 2000), Piñeyro's film itself, the critical reviews generated by the film, and even this chapter. All these cultural filters oscillate to create a kaleidoscope, distancing us from the true-life crime and exposing us instead to a marvelous cultural creation. *Burnt Money* is, above all else, a cultural achievement. It is a human creation stitched together by historical opinions, words, and images in motion.

The oscillating tension at the *diegetic level* is displayed in three well-defined moments. The first is the fortuitous *cruising* encounter between El Nene and Ángel in the train station restroom of the Constitution Station and the following enigmatic rift between them. The second moment comprises the multiple actions taken in preparation for the robbery, the robbery itself, the escape to Uruguay, and the unsuccessful hiding out in that country. And the third moment is the final confrontation of El Cuervo (Pablo Echarri), El Nene, and Ángel against the forces of order. It is in this third moment that the erotic connection of physical desire and reciprocal caring that occurred earlier, quite unexpectedly, in the Constitución bathroom is reborn. Another enigma may be even more meaningful: while El Nene is dying in agony in Ángel's arms, what is it that he whispers into Ángel's ear? Here is the vexing kernel of *Burnt Money:* the secret becomes a conspicuous reality for the viewer, since its pervasive reality serves both to open and to close the plot. A secret, known only to the intimate couple, could explain the rupture of their initial relationship; and a secret, told in the intimate whisper of a dying man, is a sign sealing their rekindled love.

Burnt Money also involves the interweaving of diverse and complex elements at the level of *cinematography*: film camera work, still photography, staging, lighting, costume design, locations, soundtrack, and editing. The diversity, complexity, and interconnectivity of these elements respond fittingly to the erotic oscillation of desire that permeates the film.

Greek Tragedy and the Reviews

At least four types of cultural filters are in play. They are inevitable for all interpretations of *Burnt Money* and are equally responsible for the oscillating criticisms of it. These four categories of filter are Piglia's novel, the Piñeyro and Figueras screenplay, Piñeyro's other films, and critical commentaries about *Burnt Money*. This section focuses on only two categories of filter: the critical commentaries on *Burnt Money,* and Piñeyro's filmography.

The first critique of *Burnt Money* is the rating given to the film by the INCAA (National Institute of Cinema and Audiovisual Arts) of Argentina. The INCAA considered the film inappropriate for viewers under the age of eighteen, given that "the film depicts shady characters, drug addicts, and homosexuals in a positive light" (Piñeyro, personal interview). In this way, with a rating that, according to Piñeyro, "[negatively] affected the commercial success of the film" in Argentina—fewer viewers, decreased revenue—the reception of *Burnt Money* began with INCAA's deeming the film an apology for immorality. It is impossible, however, to make a detailed analysis of *Burnt Money*'s effect on filmgoers. David William Foster put it aptly: "There exists no published sociological or market studies about who goes to the movies in Argentina, and hence it is difficult to speak in anything other than impressionistic terms about audience values, expectations, interpretative horizon, and the like" (470). All that is left, therefore, are the critical reviews, which have appeared in publications in Argentina and outside the country.

Before considering the critical reviews, the lines which journalist Emilio Renzi—an *alter ego* of Ricardo Piglia—used to describe the criminal gang's actions at the end of the novel come to mind. The gang has a "tragic brilliance" (Piglia 188) and its bloody demise was a "tragic ceremony that no one who was there will ever forget" (188–89). The narrative voice of the novel's "Epilogue" speaks even more directly. The narrative voice reports experiencing *Greek tragic pathos* upon hearing the story "by chance" from the mouth of Blanca Galeano, a mistress of El Cuervo Mereles, and in doing so offers a brief definition of *tragedy*. Blanca Galeano, continues the epilogist, "spoke of the twins, of El Nene Brignone and of Gaucho Dorda and of Malito and of El Chueco Bazán, and I listened as if I found myself before an Argentine version of a Greek tragedy. The heroes decide to confront the impossible and resist it, choosing death as their destiny" (251).

French criticism tries to situate the film in a genealogy of genres: as *film noir* or as a gangster flick (Collin, Brisset, Leherpeur).[3] By contrast, criticisms written in English opt to classify the film in relation to other films: *Gun Crazy*, *Kiss or Kill*, *Bound*, *Butterfly Kiss*, *Pulp Fiction* (Harvey), *Bonnie and Clyde* (Thomas), *Reservoir Dogs*, *Ocean's Eleven*, and again *Bonnie and Clyde* (Scott). Meanwhile, reviews in Spanish prefer to focus on the acting of Noriega or Sbaraglia (Molina, García-Posada, Quiroga, *La Prensa*, Monteagudo), or on drawing connections to previous Piñeyro films (Otero, Quiroga). In any case, there is a common denominator in almost every review of *Burnt Money*: Piñeyro's work is *a tragedy*. For this reason, critics insist that Ángel and El Nene are "tragic heroes" (Molina); they identify the "certainty of a tragic ending" (Quiroga); they discover "two tragic heroes" (*La Prensa*) only implied in Piglia's novel; they speak of "a beautiful, tragic and original love story" (Baudin); they characterize the pair of lovers as the "living dead" (Schettini) "submerged over their heads in a battle they know they cannot win" (Otero); they admire "these doubly cursed lovers" (Khan); they describe the film in terms of a "grand romantic tragedy" (Thomas); or they think that the off-screen extradiegetic voice serves "à commenter l'action comme le chœur antique la gabegie de la fatalité" [to comment on the action in the way the ancient chorus comments on the chaos caused by fatality] (Péron).

Is it possible to justify connecting Piñeyro's *Burnt Money* with tragedy—that uniquely Greek invention? We can provide at least a partially affirmative answer to this question. It is not fair to say that the off-screen voice heard in the film is identical to the Greek chorus. Rather, it is more of a fading echo of the Greek chorus, or—more precisely still—an echo of the coryphaeus that momentarily takes on the role of the chorus. This off-screen narrative voice, beyond providing commentary, informs the viewer of elements seemingly undeveloped in the story itself, though it does not become as "intrusive" as the coryphaeus. In the words of Jacqueline de Romilly, in the tragedies of Aeschylus, Sophocles, and Euripides, "rien ne se passe jamais sur la scène sans que le chœur, ou le coryphée en son nom, n'intervienne pour donner, fût-ce brièvement, son avis sur la situation et ses derniers développements" (223) [Nothing takes place on stage without the intervention of the chorus, with the goal of expressing its opinion—even briefly—about the situation and its final developments]. Romilly also emphasizes that, on the one hand, Greek tragedies derive their "substance" from Greek myths or epics, and that their "form," on the other hand, consists of characters engaged in dialogue onstage, accompanied by a chorus that sings in the *orchestra* (186).[4] It could be said that Piñeyro obtains the *substance* of his film by aesthetically and erotically reworking elements of Piglia's novel as well as of the historic robbery. It is more by way of the protagonists—the way they live their lives and die their deaths—that the thread of epic-tragedy and other Greek elements come to light in *Burnt Money*. In order to identify possible echoes of ancient Greece in the love story of El Nene and Ángel, I want to begin with Plutarch. He mentions the existence of a very special group of soldiers, of a "sacred" nature, defeated only by Philip II of Macedonia in the Battle of Chaeronea (338 BCE). This group is made up of a "cohort of lovers" (84, 85). The intimate ties of love that united this group also gave it an unusual efficiency in military combat. "Because in risky situations," continues Plutarch, "members of the same curia or tribe pay little attention to one another, while the union established by loving relationships is indissoluble and indivisible; fearing dishonor, lovers will persevere in times of danger for sake of each other" (84).

    Lovers fight the enemy with greater fervor, because the life of a loved one is worth more than one's own life, because a lover should avoid allowing his or her beloved any suffering, and because fear of shaming a loved one eliminates all cowardice, encouraging acts of audacity and even temerity. In this way, the cohort perfectly embodied the idea of "brave men and warriors." To this day, no critic of *Burnt Money* has noted that the viewers' admiration of El Nene and Ángel contains a feeling similar to Philip II of Macedonia's admiration upon contemplating the cadavers of three hundred lovers.[5] Plutarch records Philip's admiration as follows: "And he found them piled on top of one another, which he found unusual, and when he knew it was the cohort of lovers, he began to weep, and he exclaimed: 'Cursed be anyone who could think that there was any reprehensibility among such men'" (85). With limitless courage, El Nene and Ángel entwine their bodies for the final siege, the pair of lovers earning at last the viewer's respect and admiration. The viewer in turn feels sadness for the fatal outcome of the cinematographic fiction: the certain death of El Nene and the very likely death of Ángel.[6]

    As in the Greek tragedies, and their antecedents in Homeric epics, the existence of Ángel, El Nene, and El Cuervo is determined by a two-faced destiny manifested through suffering and projected onto death—in accordance with the characters' physical beauty and the virtue of their courage (Romilly, 35). Even without the intervention of the gods, there is a theological dimension to Ángel and El Nene's march toward death. In Ángel, the strong presence of holiness is expressed in his very name, in the Virgen del Pilar medallion (*Guión* 146), in the way he thinks of himself as Nene's savior, in his visit to church, and in the religious gestures he uses while studying English. El Nene experiences the theological dimension through contact: he touches Ángel's medallion three times—moments before the robbery, while tenderly caressing Ángel's chest, and as he lays dying. Miguel Ángel's *La Pietà* comes to the critical viewer's mind on two occasions: when contemplating the elemental composition of the frame in 01:38:03–01:39:24 and in 01:57:55–02:01:05.[7] There is also tragedy, because the characters live in extremes. To this point, Romilly writes: "La tragédie voulait l'extrême—l'extrême du crime et l'extrême du sacrifice—afin d'offrir par là un spectacle plus saisissant" (191) [Tragedy attempts the extreme regarding crime and sacrifice, so that it will be able to present a more captivating spectacle]. The universe in *Burnt Money* is a secular one. That is, the gods have ceased to impose their wills over those humans. It is possible to draw a list of "caprices du destin" [caprices of fate] (Romilly 199). Fatal caprices pop up in different ways: for instance, an ongoing love relationship seems to have broken down, Ángel's behavior is uncontrollable—at the beach, and when he attacks a police officer by a park in Uruguay—and a series of betrayals, particularly those of El Cuervo, of Vivi, and finally of Giselle. In the end, the siege sequence draws the film to a tragic close. That sequence, which on the one hand rekindles the lovers' relationship and offers them their last hours of profound happiness, also brings them to a disastrous end. What better words than Romilly's to describe that final sequence: "À l'intérieur des tragédies [. . .] la joie est à son comble quand va à surgir la catastrophe" (200) [In Greek tragedies the height of joy occurs just before catastrophes].

Thus there is tragedy in *Burnt Money*, because the human will faces insurmountable obstacles that prevent it from realizing its most profound desires. Those obstacles come and go in oscillation. They come from numerous sources: sometimes, the obstacles come from the will of the characters; at other times, it is the unfavorable intervention of fortune.

Piñeyro's Cinematography

Beyond the traditional differences in styles of narrative, choice of settings, and differing content of the plots, in his body of cinematographic work Piñeyro tells stories in which his characters are extraordinary individuals, doomed to struggle. In their struggles—very specifically—they all try to survive the fatal attacks of anonymous forces guided by inhuman systems: systems of art, race, repression, and psychiatry in *Tango feroz, la leyenda de Tanguito* (*Wild Tango*, 1993); systems of media and finance in *Caballos salvajes* (*Wild Horses*, 1995); systems of justice and business in *Cenizas del paraíso* (*Ashes from Paradise*, 1997); the police system in *Plata quemada* (*Burnt Money*, 2000); the military system in *Kamchatka* (2002); the labor system in *El método* (*The Method*, 2005); classist capitalism in *Las viudas de los jueves* (*The Widows of Thursdays*, 2009); and race, childhood, fatherhood, and family in *Ismael* (*Ismael*, 2013).

In his decisive defense of humanity and rejection of institutions, Piñeyro advocates a certain illegality that is not immoral, and places a strong ethical value on the individual. This individual finds support, recognition, and hope in the unlimited love of a partner, in group friendship, in music and in non-biological fraternal bonds (*Tango feroz*); in companionship among strangers (*Caballos salvajes*); in the family nucleus of parents and siblings (*Cenizas del paraíso, Kamchatka*); in homosexual love and friendship (*Plata quemada*); in an old love story (*El método*); in the painful truth of a husband, a father, and two young people of the same generation (*Las viudas de los jueves*); and in an interracial family context (*Ismael*). In his defense of the individual who is always embodied in the protagonist characters—Piñeyro creates heroes. The heroism of these protagonists complements their tragic destiny.

In *The Human Condition*, Hannah Arendt recalls that for Homer a hero was simply a "name that was given to any free man who participated in the Trojan enterprise and about whom a story could be told" (210). In Piglia's novel, some of the narrative voices resort to a powerful adverb, characterizing the "terrible wrongdoers who had fought heroically for sixteen hours" (241). Piñeyro's heroes are not free in the Arendtian sense, since they are enslaved under consumerist forms of art and unjust laws (*Tango feroz*); under corrupt justice (*Cenizas del paraíso*); under unconscionable standards of labor productivity (*El método*); under State terror (*Kamchatka*); under the tedium of meaningless comfort and economic structures of capital (*Las viudas de los jueves*); under racial prejudices (*Ismael*); and under bloodthirsty police (*Plata quemada*). Nevertheless, Piñeyro's protagonists are heroes in a different sense. It is a more quotidian or even banal, but no less real, sense. They are heroes because, in accordance with the valor they show in their desire to exist fully, their smallest gestures equally confirm "[t]he will to act and to speak, to insert their own identities into the world and embark on a personal story" (Arendt 210).

In spite of the fact that the gods no longer exist as a cause of human hardship, it is possible to identify a human origin to that hardship: not a sin or shortcoming, but rather that "tragic flaw" that Plato (*Laws*, VIII, 838c8) and Aristotle (*Poetics*, XIII, 1453a10) called *hamartia*. Just like Oedipus and Antigone, Piñeyro's three semi-tragic heroes—El Cuervo, El Nene, and Ángel—respond to inevitable disaster in the only way they humanly can: with virtue (*arête*), "which is in essence strength in the face of adversity" (Festugière 23).

Oscillating Desire in the Plot

Hope is the *primum movens* of the action in *Burnt Money*—rather than the robbery itself, as is the case in the novel—and its absence from Piglia's novel is a main reason why the film and novel are such clearly separate works of art. In Piñeyro's film, El Nene and Ángel hope to use the heist and the ensuing drama to revitalize the erotic bond that united them. Understood as such, *Burnt Money*'s narrative begins with the lost bond, passes through several diegetic oscillations as the bond remains broken, and ends when the erotic bond is finally reestablished. In spite of the few flashbacks through cinematography, dialogues, monologues, and the off-screen voice, and although the viewer comes upon the love story of Ángel and El Nene *in media res*, Piñeyro's film maintains the classic narrative structure of *still*, *while*, and *already*.[8] It is during the narrative segment of *while*—the segment of longest duration (00:02:54–00:03:56 and 00:06:27–01:38:01, a total of 1 hour, 45 minutes and 18 seconds)—when the viewer witnesses the erotic oscillations of the two protagonists; and only during the brief segments of *still* (00:03:57–00:06:25, that is, 3 minutes and 28 seconds) and *already* (01:38:02–02:01:10, that is, 23 minutes and 12 seconds), that the viewer sees the erotic bond of El Nene and Ángel, which brings them happiness and stability.

At the same time, there are other aspects of the diegetic content of Piñeyro's work that set it apart from that of Piglia's. Two aspects are particularly notable: the secret and the unambiguous homosexual love between El Nene and Ángel. In Piglia's novel, there is no secret between Brignone, also nicknamed "el Nene" (Piglia 14), and Dorda, whose nickname was "the Gaucho Rubio." In Piñeyro's film, the secret constructs a full narrative circle for the viewer, since the relationship of the couple begins and ends with a secret. Out of respect, Piñeyro does not break the circle, and as a result the unrevealed secret—which is ultimately *two* secrets—becomes a true enigma.

The double secret, or the two secrets, can be expressed in the following two questions: Why did El Nene and Ángel's relationship fall apart? What words does El Nene whisper in Ángel's ear before dying?

This secret, which Piñeyro chooses not to violate and sincerely respects because it frustrates the insatiable voyeuristic curiosities of any viewer, is also one of the mechanisms by which the film avoids the pitfall of moralism. At least two critics have been sensitive to the importance of the secret. In that way, writes Monteagudo, "the film has the intelligence to not try to explain the difficult homosexual relationship between Ángel and El Nene." Óscar Kahn expressed the same sentiment with great perspicacity:

> It is fascinating how in Marcelo Piñeyro's hands, silence, tedium, and lack of communication can be so overwhelmingly expressive. The most important elements in *Burnt Money* are not visible. Nor are they audible. In this beautiful and brutal film, the most valuable gems are what these doubly cursed lovers never say to each other. They are damned by virtue of being both homosexuals and delinquents. For that reason, each glance and each gesture, each murmur and each display of attitude acquire an immeasurable value. ("El estruendoso silencio")

The secret can be integrated into the story through an architectural metaphor: Piñeyro's film consists of a story arc that begins when the two men lose their erotic connection and ends with the reestablishment of erotic intimacy: a joyful, playful, and deeply satisfying feeling between the two characters. The arc is constructed out of two materials. One is visible: the hope that under new conditions of conflict and criminality, they can regain the bond of erotic intimacy that was lost; the other is invisible: the two secrets that the viewer will never learn. The off-screen voice—or "off-screen narrator" as the script calls it—unambiguously identifies the hope and the secret: "But recently Ángel has been refusing contact without explaining why. Something is broken between them. [. . .] That is why they look forward to the raid. They know very well that when they are at work, they go back to being the twins" (*Guión* 111–12). Later in the script, there is a stage direction: "[Ángel] glues his ear to Nene's mouth, which finally speaks; we do not hear what he says" (*Guión* 250).

The film version of Ángel and El Nene's story leaves no ambiguity about the homosexual love shared by those two characters. Piñeyro and Marcelo Figueras, in the latter's words, noticed something in Piglia's novel: "Piñeyro and I discovered to what extent the writer's [Piglia's] imagination had intervened to transform a police matter into one of the most powerful love stories of Argentine literature" (*Guión* 18). Sequence 139 of the script, for example, goes even further than the film itself. Although in the film a short dialogue on the beach ends with Ángel's questions and an image of the two lovers who cannot look each other in the eyes—"My voices? What's going on? Am I the only one who hears them? What about you? Don't you hear voices that laugh at you, that point out everything you do wrong, all your mistakes? *That's wrong! Stop it or you'll fail! He's going to meet someone better. You'll see!*" (01:14:51–01:15:47)—the original script went on for two more lines, concluding with a definitive promise from the lover:

> NENE: Are you going to do something tonight, or are you going to keep wallowing in filth behind that closed door pretending to be deaf and dumb, getting drunk on paint thinner or whatever's lying around, or, or?
>
> ÁNGEL: You and I. Tonight. It's a promise. (202)

This is not the case in the homonymous novel by Piglia. The ambiguity of El Nene Brignone and El Gaucho Dorda's homosexual love is a product of the novel's own narrative characteristics. It is impossible to determine the truth about the relationship, because Piglia builds the story about the pair of criminals from multiple sources. Unlike the film, in which the viewer is provided with *ex visu* information by a single narrative and with some *ex auditu* testimony—the "narrator" or off-screen voice—the novel makes use of information provided by voice recording, direct or indirect witnesses, chronicler (cronista) Emilio Renzi, a nameless narrator, police reports, newspaper articles and psychiatric reports. Within this documentary web, the wary reader must limit him- or herself to conjecture, avoiding definitive conclusions. In other words, Piglia weaves *multiple threads* of information about Brignone and Dorda to form a piece of fiction; the film consists of *a single story*, without alternate versions.

Two critics have attempted to classify the basic relationship between the novel and the film. There is some truth to their statements, although I regard them as exaggerated. Molina wrote: "Piñeyro chose the same formula Orson Welles used to transpose Kafka into film: violate the book and use it to tell a different tale." In turn, a film critic from *La Prensa* noted rather forcefully: "Piñeyro accentuated the homosexuality that was implicit in Piglia's novel." There was neither "violation" nor "accentuation." What happened was simpler, less irreverent, and more obvious: the director of the film and his scriptwriter cunningly took advantage of the diegetic ambiguity inherent to the novel itself. The active homosexuality of the characters in the novel is not explicit, *but it is entirely plausible*. Piñeyro and Figueras use the plausible to create a possible narrative reality.

The fact that Ángel and El Nene's homosexual love is unambiguous in the film does not mean that it is free from oscillations and difficulties. As Julia Kristeva would say: "desire proves to be mercurial. It is intoxicated by novelty and is unstable by definition" (143). Displaying the details of those difficulties is an achievement of Piñeyro's film. The challenges for Ángel and El Nene to realize their love appear diegetically in several forms. They are symbolized, for example, by various objects.[9] The most important of these object-symbols for them is probably the little gold medallion that usually accompanies Ángel, whose Roman Catholic religiosity is expressed by more than just the name "Ángel" and his behavior. The medallion expresses the affectionate and tense intimacy between Ángel and El Nene: a medium shot shows Ángel handing it to El Nene as a protective talisman seconds before the robbery (00:13:59) and the latter clutching it in his hand (00:14:19). The medallion also obstructs access to physical pleasure: in a close-up, El Nene's hands reach out to Ángel's nude body and caress his nipple (00:39:30). In the end, Ángel gives the medallion back to El Nene as the latter lays dying. By the same token, it is not unreasonable to think that the image of the Virgen del Pilar on the medallion projects itself onto the two characters. Perhaps echoing the Virgen del Pilar, who cradles baby Jesus in her arms, parts of the final climactic sequence (01:58:40–02:01:09) are structured in accordance with elements of Catholic iconography. The first of these parts begins when Ángel recites the Ave Maria prayer while placing the Virgen del Pilar medallion on his lover. The musical *leitmotif* is now painful, almost lethargic; and in consonance with the physical and emotional pain of the moment, the camera slowly zooms out, leaving the two characters in their last lovers' embrace. They lose their heroic persistence in a setting that resembles an alcove for saints. There Ángel, torn apart by the loss, cradles his lover-son in his arms, a bereaved Virgin Mary like that of Miguel Ángel's *La Pietà* embracing her son: a flaccid and dead Jesus.

The Sexual Dynamic of the Male Bodies

In Piñeyro's film, it is impossible to study El Nene and Ángel's bodies without holding them in permanent contrast with El Cuervo's heterosexual body. This is undoubtedly a marvelous novelty of the film, since Piglia is very skeletal, or vague, in giving details about the physical appearance, mannerisms, gestures, and dress of the three criminals. The first narrative voice in the novel says the following of Dorda and Brignone: "They were striking and extravagant. They looked like a couple of boxers or a couple of funeral home employees. They were dressed elegantly, in dark double breasted suits, with short hair, and delicate hands" (12–13). El Cuervo Mereles was "slender with bulging eyes" (20), and also elegant (26). In the novel, El Nene is "morocho," meaning dark haired. He appeared to be an adolescent—maybe fifteen years old—with fair skin and definitely was not tall. The rather abstract vagueness on the reader's part is caused by the lack of concrete details from witnesses to the robbery: "Two guys jumped out and one of them had a woman's stocking over his head (say the witnesses)" (35). Even during the police investigation, when shown photos of suspects to help jog their memory, "the baffled witness could not recognize a single face (said the newspapers)" (36). Abraham Spector, a key witness in the criminal investigation because he worked for the Municipality of San Fernando (Province of Buenos Aires) and because he was inside the pay truck when the assault occurred, described precise features of the assailants—but still in a very general way. Referring to Brignone (El Nene) and Dorda (Ángel, in the film), respectively, Spector says: "One was dark haired and the other blonde. They were both young and had military style haircuts" (39).

Appearances are different in Piñeyro's work. The frame that opens the narration and sets the tone for the film focuses on Ángel's half-naked body. Ángel "flexes his arms while lying on the floor of a dark bedroom" (*Guión* 99). And, from that very moment, a unique sound takes on an unusual protagonism of the utmost significance: the Virgen del Pilar medallion jangles rhythmically against the floor as Ángel does his exercises. The script has also established that El Nene as well as Ángel is young and physically attractive. El Cuervo looks so similar to the two lovers that one might think of the three protagonists as triplets: they are of the same age, have the same haircut, and wear the same clothing, because "they all dress the same, with suits, nice shirts and ties purchased by Fontana" (*Guión* 113). The three men's mannerisms belong to an undeniably heterosexual cultural prototype of masculinity. This is despite the fact that Ángel walks deliberately, with sluggish and rigid movements; El Nene walks with subtle and coquettish movements, like a model on a fashion runway; and El Cuervo moves his hands and legs hyperactively, ostentatiously dancing and gesticulating.

Keen viewers may be aware of the strong homophobia toward effeminate gays in Argentina, even in the twenty-first century. Claiming that Piñeyro falls into anachronism is beside the point, because in the sexual climate of Argentina both in 1965—diegetic date—and in 2000—year of the film's release—the effeminate gay is a maligned and marginalized figure. This is why El Nene insults and even threatens the effeminate boy in the bathroom at the fair; it is also why Ángel furiously kicks the man with the megaphone. Bearing close resemblance to El Cuervo (Echarri), and in their capacity as heterosexual sex symbols of Ibero-American cinema and beyond, Noriega and Sbaraglia play Ángel and El Nene in a way that masculinizes gays. Argentina, especially Buenos Aires, is receptive to this type of masculine gay that Piñeyro constructs through the homogenizing metonymy of the gestures, physical appearance, age, and dress of the three men.

Do those three men embody the psychosexual metaphor of a three-faced Janus? By pursuing unhindered physical pleasure, El Cuervo, the heterosexual of the group, embodies the *id* of this Freudian trinity. Nene, who engages without guilt in bisexual behavior, may be the *ego*—a bridge between "pure" heterosexuality and "pure" homosexuality. The vehement religious devotion of Ángel causes his own body to be the martyr of repressed homosexual pleasures, whether real, dreamt, or fantasized. Thus, Ángel may symbolize the *superego*.

Second, living together and getting to know each other intimately let the three characters go from rejection and distrust to the life of a joyful sexual community. The three individuals glimpse the possibility of being a balanced trinity. In this sense, Piñeyro's tale is one of an emotional and undeniably erotic journey: a *Bildungsroman* of male sexuality. The three protagonists experience self-denial: Ángel with his "voices," fleeting bonds with no distinction of sex; El Nene's *cruisings* with men in restrooms and at the movies, and with a woman, Giselle; and the exclusive heterosexuality of El Cuervo, who looks down on El Nene and calls him a "fag" (*Guión* 131). They transition from the camaraderie of mutual insults to the point where the three criminals show true human respect for one another: El Cuervo is no longer a straight homophobe when he observes the homosexual couple's passionate kiss with calm and perhaps an embarrassed respect (01:52:10–01:52:13); Ángel protects El Cuervo's life with his own, the same Cuervo who had taunted him with cruel sarcasm days before—"Are you looking because you're retarded, queer, or both?" (*Guión* 151)—and El Cuervo wishes to die in the company of Ángel, *who he finally considers his friend*, rather than to die alone (01:52:15–01:53:35).

The sequence of the bullet removal deserves special consideration. Without any embellishment beyond several medium and long shots, many close-ups, and light that changes to darkness, one might think Piñeyro only wants to show the body truculence of removing a bullet. Nevertheless, the scene reveals much more. On one level, El Nene does not allow any third party, neither Vivi nor Fontana, to get near the couple. On another level, if one listens closely to the soundtrack without watching the images, it is easy to imagine that El Nene is sexually penetrating Ángel. Throughout the process of removing the bullet, which is accompanied by reciprocal caressing, three distinct types of sounds can be heard in the soundtrack: Ángel's grunting, El Nene's tender, brief, and profoundly sexual words, and some knocking sounds. This scene is not about sex; it is about love. The symbolic penetration is accompanied by three elements: first, *a desire to care for the other* in the visual content of the sequence; second, the familiarity with which the lovers come into *contact with one another's bodily fluids*—Ángel's blood, sweat, and saliva drench El Nene's skin and shirt; and third, the homosexual *physical excitement* made explicit in the soundtrack.

The sequences using bird's-eye view shots and the scene of the bullet removal also confirm a plainly evident contrast between heterosexual and homosexual intercourse. Piñeyro's comments about El Nene probably also apply to El Cuervo: "The sex El Nene has with Giselle," Piñeyro affirms, "lacks tenderness; it is more of an athletic activity" (Piñeyro, Personal interview). In the heterosexual sex scenes, the absence of erotic intimacy is echoed in the plain composition of the frames, which lack any special lighting. This is in contrast with the four moments of homosexual intimacy shared between Ángel and El Nene. Physical and verbal displays of affection are evidently more frequently made by El Nene toward Ángel. It is only during the final siege that Ángel can freely reciprocate his lover's tenderness.

Obstacles of an Oscillating *Eros*

While Ángel's sexual obstacles are grounded principally in religious belief, El Nene's repression of his own homosexuality comes from an understanding that his homosexual desires began randomly when he was in jail: "In jail I became a queer." Examples of El Nene's sexual repression are as often verbal as they are behavioral. The repression is verbal when El Nene will not admit to Giselle that he prefers sex with men, claiming that his homosexuality is only intermittent: "It happens in spurts," says El Nene, quoting *verbatim* words that Piñeyro and Figueras lifted from Roberto Artl's novel *El juguete rabioso* (*Mad Toy*) (102). El Nene also reveals a repressive self-loathing when he viciously insults the gay man in a restroom in Uruguay, one of the many "effeminate strangers" (Jones 9) he encounters in restrooms and movie theaters.

The paradoxical oscillation of El Nene and Ángel's erotic desires is described perfectly by a song that plays an important role in *Burnt Money*'s soundtrack. The song is the tango "Vida mía" ["My Life"] by E. Fresedo and O. Fresedo. The script mentions another tango: "La luz del fósforo" ["Match Light"] (103), but that song does not appear in the film. "Vida mía" provides a key to interpreting Ángel and El Nene's difficult relationship. The first lines of the tango proclaim: "Vida mía, más lejos te quiero" ["My life, I love you more from afar"]. Ángel loves El Nene, but systematically distances himself from him; El Nene loves Ángel, but continues to act on his desires far outside of the couple's relationship.

Fortunately, the oscillation of *eros* for the lovers that is driven by paradox eventually comes to an end. In the climactic moment of reciprocal eroticism, what Ángel and El Nene experience is best described by D. H. Lawrence in *The White Peacock*: "We looked at each other with eyes of still laughter, and our love was perfect for a moment, more perfect than any love I have known since, either for man or woman" (qtd. in Jeffrey Meyers 257). The final hours of calm before the storm of death bring to Piñeyro's two lovers a brief but profoundly intense gift: the gift of perfect love, including physical desire without orgasm, reciprocal affection, laughter, and no concern for money. And so, for a few moments, the tragic destiny of the two lovers remains suspended.

Notes

1. I want to express here my sincere thanks to Marcelo Piñeyro, Alejandra Piñeyro, and Arena Films for all the information they gave me while writing this essay. For the English translation of this essay, written originally in Spanish, my former student Alexander Sugar, my patient friend Michael J. Carr, and my Cornell mentor and colleague Debra A. Castillo deserve thousands of heartfelt thanks.

2. This alone could be a comprehensive and adequate summary of *Burnt Money*. It is perhaps due to the oscillating nature of erotic desire that "Eros was never considered a sufficiently responsible god to figure among the ruling Olympian family of Twelve" (Graves 59).

3. Marcelo Piñeyro also referred to his film as belonging to a hybrid genre, and even coined the term "urban gaynster" to describe it. The suffix -nster corresponds as much to gangsters as to Western "cowboy and Indian" movies. *Burnt Money* takes place in an urban context where criminals struggle against the omnipresent police of Buenos Aires and Montevideo. Thus, it belongs to the gangster genre. *Burnt Money* can also be considered a Western, because there is a faceless sheriff (Chancho Aguirre), four criminals live outside the law just like cowboys in

the movies, and two of them are *others*: different and strange. That is, they are "Indians" by virtue of being gay (see interview, July 7, 2008). During the final siege, El Cuervo's words to Ángel can be seen as documentary evidence as well as a key to interpreting the film: "You look like the Last of the Mohicans!"

4. The tightly limited space of the *mise-en-scène* in which Piñeyro's characters live forces one to think of the spatial limitations of an actual theater. Two critics were conscious of the limited atmosphere inhabited by the four protagonists: "a film of interior settings, with a claustrophobic atmosphere," writes Miguel García-Posada. For Xavier Leherpeur, "The *huis clos* of refugees where Piñeyro decides to place his heroes reflects the prison in which their passion has enclosed them, and it justifies his [Piñeyro's] choice of a primarily claustrophobic *mise-en-scène*."

5. Moreover, it should be recalled that armies are still referred to as a "band of brothers." Even though the word brothers do not want to openly imply any sexual bond, it could try to metaphorically express a linkage founded on affection and blood.

6. David Halperin's words about the death of Enkidu, in the context of his friendship with Gilgamesh, resonate here: "Death is the climax of the friendship, the occasion of the most extreme expressions of tenderness on the part of the two friends, and it weds them forever (in the memory of the survivor, at least). Indeed, it is not too much to say that death is to friendship what marriage is to romance" (79).

7. In the first case, one sees rays of light and shadows on the wall and in the bedroom. That light has the same texture and density of the light in a church, and it provides a mystic atmosphere in which El Nene holds Ángel in his arms, cradling him in his lap with his hands, and kissing him. In the second case, there is a nearly parallel frame in which El Nene lays dying in the arms of Ángel, with Ángel kissing him as well. Both bodies are marked within a sacred space—it is a temple—making one think of the niches for saints in Catholic churches. These frames can also lead one to see echoes of the Greek epics: In the *Illiad* (XXIII, 136–37), during Patrocles' funeral, the mourning Achilles cradles his companion's head in his arms.

8. By the words "still," "while," and "already" I am reinterpreting Aristotle's narratological concepts of beginning, middle, and end according to his *Poetics* (before 323 BCE).

9. There are two other objects, more closely linked to Ángel than to El Nene: a pocket dictionary and "a snow globe containing an image of New York" (*Guión* 99). In the fourth take, the beginning sequence of the film—after the credits—that object takes on an unusual protagonism. In the lower left-hand corner of the frame, the New York snow globe can be seen in an extreme close-up. The snow globe, along with the pocket dictionary, helps Ángel to construct a future utopia for the couple: far from Buenos Aires, in an idealized New York, El Nene can be saved. By the sympathetic magic of the two lovers—a sympathy composed cinematically by frequent parallel narrative segments—the utopia is revealed to be unattainable. Ángel destroys the New York snow globe in despair, fury, and sadness

(01:27:00), at the same time as El Nene resigns himself to heterosexual intercourse with Giselle in contempt, despair, and also sadness (01:27:02–01:27:07).

Works Cited

Anderson, Patrick, and Alistair Sutherland. *Eros: An Anthology of Male Friendship*. New York: The Citadel, 1963. Print.
Arendt, Hannah. *La condición humana*. Trad. Ramón Gil Novales. Barcelona: Paidós Ibérica, 1993. Print.
Baudin, Brigitte. "*Plata quemada*." *Figaro Scope*. Web. Feb. 14, 2000.
Collin, Philippe. "*Vie brûlées*." *Elle*. Web. Feb. 12, 2001.
Festugière, André-Jean. *De l'essence de la tragédie grècque*. Paris: Aubier-Montaigne, 1969. Print.
Figueras, Marcelo, and Marcelo Piñeyro. *Plata quemada: La película, Guión cinematográfico y Diario de rodaje*. Buenos Aires: Norma, 2000. Print.
García-Posada, Miguel. "Plata que quema." *El País*. Web. Sept. 21, 2000.
Graves, Robert. *The Greek Myths*. Vol. 1. London: Penguin, 1955. Print.
Halperin, David. *One Hundred Years of Homosexuality and Other Essays*. New York; London: Routledge, 1990. Print.
Harvey, Dennis. "Hot Shots: Two cruel desperadoes only have eyes for each other." *San Francisco Guardian*. Web. Dec. 14, 2011.
Homero. *Ilíada*. Trad. Emilio Crespo. Madrid: Gredos, 1991.
Jones, Teresa. "Desconstruyendo el odio." Denver: U of Colorado Denver. 2011. TS. 11. Print.
Kahn, Oscar. "El estruendoso silencio de dos amantes malditos." *Cinemanía*. Web. Sept. 27, 2000.
Kristeva, Julia. "Romeo y Julieta o el amor fuera de la ley." *La mirada de Orfeo: Los mitos literarios de Occidente*. Ed. Bernadette Bricout. Trans. Gemma Andújar Moreno. Barcelona: Paidós, 2002. 113–49.
Leherpeur, Xavier. "*Vie brûlées*." *Cine Live*. Web. Feb. 2001.
Meyers, Jeffrey. *Painting and the Novel*. Manchester, England: Manchester UP; Barnes and Noble, 1975. Print.
Molina, Daniel. "*Plata quemada*: el destino de un amor de varones." *Clarín*. Web. May 21, 2000.
Monteagudo, Luciano. "*Plata quemada*." *Página 12*. Web. May 11, 2000.
Otero, Marita. "*Plata quemada*." *Ahora*. Web. May 14, 2000.
Piglia, Ricardo. *Plata quemada*. Buenos Aires: Planeta, 2000. Print.
Piñeyro, Alejandra. Message to the author. Sept. 23, 2008. E-mail.
Piñeyro, Marcelo. Message to the author. Oct. 32, 2010. E-mail.
———, dir. *Las viudas de los jueves*. Buenos Aires: Haddock Films, 2009. DVD.
———. Personal Interview. July 7, 2008.
———. *El método*. New York: Palm Films et al., 2005. DVD.

———. *Kamchatka*. Buenos Aires: Patagonik et al., 2002. DVD.
———. *Plata quemada*. Buenos Aires: Oscar Kramer et al., 2000. DVD.
———. *Cenizas del paraíso*. Buenos Aires: Artear et al., 1997. DVD.
———. *Caballos salvajes*. Buenos Aires: Mandala Films et al., 1995. DVD.
———. *Tango feroz: La leyenda de Tanguito*. Buenos Aires: Mandala Films et al., 1993. DVD.
Plutarco. *Vidas paralelas*. Vol. 2. Tran. Antonio Ranz Romanillos. Barcelona: Iberia, 1979. Print.
La Prensa. "*Plata quemada*." Web. May 11, 2000.
Quiroga, Osvaldo. "La pasión por la muerte en un film de gran densidad dramática." *El Cronista*. Web. May 11, 2000.
Romilly, Jacqueline. *Pourquoi la Grèce?* Paris: Fallois, 1992. Print.
Schettini, Adriana. "*Plata quemada*." *La Nación*. Web. May 7, 2000.
Scott, A. O. "*Burnt Money*: After the Heist, It's Time to Worry." *New York Times*. Web. Oct. 19, 2001.
Thomas, Kevin. "Misfit Criminals Find Love in the Nuanced *Burnt Money*." *Los Angeles Times*. Web. Nov. 2, 2001.

4

Pathology, Poetry, and Pleasure: HIV/AIDS, Confessional Writing, and S/M in *Un año sin amor*

(Anahí Berneri, 2005)

Robert Deam Tobin

In Anahí Berneri's *Un año sin amor* (*A Year without Love,* 2005), based on the published diaries of the same title by Pablo Pérez (1998), the protagonist, an HIV-positive writer and tutor of French named Pablo Pérez living in Buenos Aires, undergoes three parallel journeys: (1) abandoning his faith in herbal remedies, he overcomes his skepticism of modern medicine and accepts a medical regimen based on a new drug cocktail that includes the possibly toxic AZT; (2) setting aside his hopes of publishing poetry, he compiles a novel or memoir based on his diaries as a gay man living with HIV; and (3) giving up the comforts of traditional bourgeois romance, he experiments in the world of leather and masochistic pleasures. In all cases, one can see a kind of acceptance of a submission to authority, be it medical, economic, or erotic. Berneri uses Pérez's depiction of these developments in his medical treatment, his writing, and his lifestyle to intervene in the global cinematic discourse on queerness in Argentina, on HIV/AIDS, on sadomasochism, and on the creative process itself.

Mise en abîme

Un año sin amor is a movie about a year in a man's life during which he writes a book. The HIV-positive protagonist, Pablo Pérez (Juan Minujín), spends a year detailing his life without love—a year in which he writes about his writing, his health, and his experiences in the leather scene of Buenos Aires. At the end of the movie, he has completed a book called *Un año sin amor*. Insofar as the book is self-referentially about its author's own writing process, it becomes a book about a book, making this a movie about a book about a book. This self-referentiality means that—even insofar as the movie is about other aspects of Pablo's life (his sexuality and his illness)—it is never transparently about Pablo's year without love: it is always already about that year as filtered through his autobiographical novel, *Un año sin amor: Diario del SIDA (A Year without Love: An AIDS Diary)*.

To complicate matters further, outside the framework of the movie, an actual person named Pablo Pérez in fact wrote a book, published in 1998, called *Un año sin amor: Diario del SIDA*, about his own experiences as an HIV-positive man in the S/M[1] and leather scenes of Argentina, which culminated in the publication of the book. *That* Pablo Pérez also contributed to the writing of Anahí Berneri's 2005 film script. From this perspective, then, the movie is about the writing of the book, *Un año sin amor*, which itself is about its own production. But while the book can at times be helpful in orienting the viewer of the film, to regard the film as simply a documentary of the novel would be to downgrade the creative influence of the director and the actors and even to diminish the importance of Pablo Pérez's own commentary, as the film's cowriter, on his work as a novelist. While we might be tempted to think that the film is a straightforward biographical, and even autobiographical, account of a person's life, it is crucial to think of Pablo Pérez as a fictional character, one whom the viewer sees through a series of lenses.

These lenses—the film, the book, the book described within the book—afford the film a chance to comment on the discourses that it uses. It is not just a film about Argentina, AIDS, or leather; it is a film about the languages, narratives, symbols, and metaphors surrounding Argentina, AIDS, and leather. The multiple perspectives of the artists (to name just a few examples: Berneri, the director; Pérez, the scriptwriter; Pérez, the novelist; Pérez, the character; Minujín, the actor) present a global audience (with its own varied perspectives) with an artwork ripe for analysis of the many ways of thinking about the questions posed by HIV/AIDS and sadomasochism in a queer Argentina.

Argentina at the Turn of the Millennium

The depiction of everyday life in Argentina in the 1990s provides a concrete and easily comprehensible example of the multiple lenses featured in *Un año sin amor*. One lens would be that of the characters, living in 1996 and described in the book that appeared in 1998; another would be that of the viewers after the film came out in 2005.

The 1996 lens presents a picture that is, on balance, positive: a forward-looking, prosperous Argentina shedding the burdens of its past. After horrific military repression in the 1970s, a humiliating loss to the UK in the war over the Malvinas, or Falkland Islands, and the devastating hyperinflation in the late 1980s, the 1990s saw a kind of neoliberal normality in Argentina. Carlos Menem had become president and pegged the peso to the dollar, which brought the inflation under control. In 1995, he had been reelected. Although there was some left-wing resistance to Menem's initiatives, in general the government was able to pursue business-friendly policies, promote free trade through MERCOSUR,[2] and encourage foreign investment. Relationships with the West, above all the United States and the UK, flourished. Menem even spoke before the joint houses of the U.S. Congress.

In the interests of "national reconciliation," Menem pardoned many of the leaders of the military dictatorship that terrorized Argentina from 1976 to 1983. This move swept obvious injustices under the carpet, but it also allowed Menem to sideline the military and keep it from meddling in politics. For the characters in *Un año sin amor*, the reign of state terror is relegated to the subtext of pointed questions about when and why someone returned to the country. Pablo says he came back from three years in France for "family matters"; his leather master, Baez, the "Sheriff," doesn't really answer why he came back from San Francisco. One can speculate that there is a connection between the fall of the military dictatorship and the return of at least some of these characters. Nonetheless, the film is a long way from *La historia oficial* (*The Official Story*), Luis Puenzo's Oscar-winning 1985 drama on what the Germans would call *Vergangenheitsbewältigung*—coming to terms with the crimes of the fascist past.

Domestically, the bourgeoisie hoped to catch its breath after the disastrous economic policies of the 1980s. Many accepted that some would have to suffer under neoliberal policies, as newly privatized companies shed previously subsidized positions and unemployment grew. The story in *Un año sin amor* subtly reflects this quiescence. There is neither direct political action nor involvement with political groups.

Economically, on the one hand, it seems that Pablo Pérez has drawn the short stick. He is suffering from the neoliberalism of the 1990s. He tells his father that his monthly salary from the gas company has fallen from 700 pesos to 220. On the other hand, the viewer never sees him actually *working* for the gas company, so perhaps the neoliberal economists are right and his position is indeed superfluous. Additionally, Pablo earns twenty pesos now and then teaching French to pupils such as Julia (Bárbara Lombardo), who stands in for the children of the bourgeoisie eager to turn their newly regained prosperity into cultural capital. With virtually no money, Pablo relies on his father (Ricardo Merkin) for support. His father's unkempt hair suggests bohemian leftist leanings, but he nonetheless seems able to provide that support for both his sister and his son. The film gives the viewer a sober, although nonmelodramatic view of the life of the downwardly mobile in Buenos Aires. Pablo gets medical care, but he shares an unattractive though functional room in the hospital. The apartment he and his aunt live in is tight and cramped. His plight becomes most vivid when he appears before a housing agency bureaucrat who, utterly without empathy, tries to fit the complexities and nuances of his life into the spaces on her forms.

Besides Pablo, however, most of the other characters in the film are doing fine—at least in 1996. Pablo's father and his pupil Julia both seem reasonably well off, for instance, as do most of Pablo's friends. His old friend Nicolás lives a more than comfortable bourgeois life, with book-lined shelves, Internet access, and nice wines. When not jetting off to Neuquén on business trips, Nicolás can afford to take Pablo out to dinner and treat him to a night at the dance club. Pablo's new friends in the leather scene have ample space to fulfill their desires. Baez, "the Sheriff" (Omar Núñez) lives in a luxury apartment high above the city. Somewhat more ironically, the hot young master Martín (Javier van de Couter) lives on a lavish estate featuring a beautiful swimming pool—with his parents. Nonetheless, money does not seem to be an issue in his life. The accoutrements of the leather scene themselves are not cheap, but everyone seems to have enough of them. Members of the leather community talk about their trips to San Francisco and Paris, which are presumably affordable in the 1990s because of the unrealistic one-to-one exchange rate between the peso and the dollar.

The 2005 lens is not as forgiving and generous. While the actions of the film take place at the height of the Carlos Menem boom in 1996, the film *Un año sin amor* was released in 2005, after the recovery had turned out to be chimerical. In 2001, five years after Pablo's "year without love," a national economic crisis was in full bloom. Restrictions were placed on withdrawals in order to prevent runs on the banks. In December, Argentina defaulted on 93 billion dollars in foreign debt—at that time the largest and most spectacular national default in history. A string of governments, one falling after the other, made Argentina seem ungovernable. Eventually, dollar accounts held in Argentina were converted to pesos, and then the pesos were devalued, ultimately to a quarter of their previous values. Middle-class assets were wiped out, while the wealthy, whose dollar accounts were deposited outside the country, continued to thrive. All this took place in the years preceding the distribution of the film. Thus, both the film and its audience know that the apparent success of the Menem era that *Un año sin amor* depicts would soon come crashing to a close.

Argentina's Queerness from a Global Perspective

In 2005, *Un año sin amor* won such awards as Best Foreign Narrative Film at the New York Lesbian and Gay Film Festival, the Grand Jury Award for Outstanding International Narrative Feature at the Los Angeles Outfest Film Festival, and the Teddy Award, which is for gay and lesbian films at the Berlin Film Festival. Outside the festival circuit, it was reviewed in French, English, Spanish, and German, in many newspapers and periodicals throughout the world, especially those with an interest in gay and lesbian culture. The film made an impression on the international gay and lesbian cultural scene, in part because it inserts itself into a preexistent discourse about queer Argentina. It makes an intervention into what had become an image of a sexually tolerant land characterized by Evita, the politics of *Kiss of the Spider Woman,* and a certain exoticism. *Un año sin amor* successfully counters all these tropes to create a more convincing image of the everyday life of gay Argentines around the turn of the millennium.

At least since Argentina, in 2010, became the tenth nation in the world to permit same-sex marriage (and the first in Latin America), the country has enjoyed a reputation as a progressive country, tolerant toward sexuality minorities. Indeed, private, consensual, noncommercial sex acts had been legal since the nineteenth century, because Argentina had followed the Napoleonic code in this matter. (Religious concerns still held sway over the institution of marriage, however—meaning that even heterosexual divorce and remarriage remained prohibited until 1987.) Nonetheless, despite this laissez-faire attitude toward private sexual behavior, homosexuals were periodically persecuted throughout the twentieth century. Politically activist homosexuals working as the "homosexual liberation front" joined with leftist opponents of the military dictatorship in the 1970s, which resulted in more persecution by the government. After the fall of the military dictatorship in 1983, however, a modern mainstream gay movement emerged. By the beginning of the twenty-first century, Argentina, particularly Buenos Aires, had come to stand out globally as one of the world's most attractive destinations for gays and lesbians.

Un año sin amor takes this progressive and tolerant culture more or less for granted. As Paul Julian Smith points out in his short but thought-provoking review of the film, Pablo seems sheltered from overt homophobia. The only explicit example takes place when his aunt hurls the epithet "*maricón*" at him and one has the sense that she doesn't mean it seriously. It's just an easily available insult. For Smith, the most significant achievement of the movie is its "depiction of the everyday life of an Argentine gay man" (84). This everyday life would be recognizable internationally by gays and lesbians from throughout the developed world. There is a vibrant infrastructure of gay magazines, personal ads, cafés, porn theaters, and dance clubs in which Pablo can act out his gay life. He has friends and plenty of sexual partners. Although there is certainly a story to be told about how Buenos Aires developed such a flourishing gay subculture in the last decades of the twentieth century, that is not the story that Berneri chooses to tell. Pablo does not seem to be part of any gay political organizations. He is simply trying to lead his life in a relatively well-developed gay culture that is basically a given.

Besides its recent record of progressive sexual politics, perhaps the primary connection that many outsiders make between Argentina and homosexuality is Eva Perón, "Evita," who—whatever else one can say about her—has become an international camp phenomenon, in part because of the Tony Award-winning 1979 musical *Evita*. There is some historical justification for this development: an impoverished, vulnerable, illegitimate child, Eva Perón mobilized her marginalized sexuality to become the most important woman in the country. Many gay people could use this model as an identificatory fantasy. Once she was in power, her stylish self-representation appealed to many gays worldwide. It did not hurt Eva Perón's gay audience that the pop star Madonna (no stranger to the strategies of mobilizing one's sexuality in order to control one's self-representation) played her in the Oscar-winning 1996 movie *Evita*. An Argentine film, *Eva Perón* (distributed in English as *Eva Perón: The True Story*) which also appeared in 1996, made an explicit claim that Eva Perón understood homosexuals to be among society's weak and vulnerable whom she could help. Given that particularly the selection of Madonna to play Eva Perón was controversial in Argentina at the time, it is noteworthy that in *Un año sin amor,* neither Pablo Pérez nor any of his friends wastes a single breath on Eva Perón. Neither he nor his friends are fans of Madonna or Evita; neither he nor his friends are outraged by Madonna or Evita. Outsiders might associate queer Argentina with Eva Perón, but not Pablo Pérez, not Anahí Berneri.

Besides Evita, perhaps the globally strongest cultural association between Argentina and homosexuality was forged by the movie *Kiss of the Spider Woman*, based on Manuel Puig's novel *El beso de la mujer araña*. Although Puig is Argentine, the film, directed by Héctor Babenco, is a Brazilian-American production, featuring such international stars as William Hurt, Raul Julia, and Sonia Braga. Hurt won the Oscar for best actor for his role as Luis Molina, the effeminate homosexual hairdresser who falls in love in prison with Valentin Arregui, the macho terrorist (Raul Julia). Published in Spain in 1976, the novel is actually not about the most notorious government-sponsored repression in Argentina—it was written just before the military coup ushered in the so-called National Reorganization Process. But by the time *Kiss of the Spider Woman* appeared as a film in 1985, it seemed shockingly prescient. (In this respect, 1985's *Kiss of the Spider Woman* comments on its 1976 novelistic source much as 2005's *Un año sin amor* comments on its 1998 textual origins.)

Despite their different historical positions, both the novelistic and cinematic versions of *Kiss of the Spider Woman* propose a Latin-American alliance between homosexual activism and leftist politics. Military governments repressed both sexual and political rights, meaning that gays and lesbians should turn out on the streets to fight for broad social change that would include (though not be limited to) sexual freedom. This was certainly Puig's hope, as well as that of many radical homosexual activists in North America and Europe. But it is not the vision promulgated by *Un año sin amor*. Pablo Pérez's openly gay culture is worlds apart from Luis Molina's furtive and persecuted group of drag queens. Nonetheless, Pérez, while openly and self-confidently gay, seems in many ways apolitical, even if he is a victim of neoliberal politics. In this respect, too, *Un año sin amor* disrupts the understanding of Argentine homosexuality previously dominant in global cinema.

Other representations in global cinema of homosexuality in Argentina include Kar Wai Wong's award-winning 1997 film *Happy Together*. *Happy Together* is a kind of anti-orientalization, whereby gay tourists from Hong Kong find in Buenos Aires a dysfunctional, incomprehensible, exotic place of fading beauty, where reality is altered, the rules are suspended, and the hopes and dreams of the men from Hong Kong are doomed to shatter. David Moreton's *Testosterone* (USA, 2003), one of those gay noir tango cartoon movies, wittily plays with a variety of clichés about Argentina: the virile masculinity of its men, the beauty of its women, and the seductive tangos that take place between and within the sexes. The gay American graphic novelist who stumbles into this world never really understands it. Wong's visual palette shares many similarities with Berneri's vision of Buenos Aires and may well have influenced her, but both *Happy Together* and *Testosterone* represent Argentina as an essentially unknowable foreign place, mysteriously incoherent. While Pablo Pérez may be confronted with complex and difficult situations in his life, the otherness of Argentina per se is obviously not his problem.

The Global Cinema of HIV/AIDS

From a global perspective, HIV/AIDS has been the subject of endless cinematic analyses. AIDS is a disease that thrives on globalization. Accounts of its spread focus heavily on stories of truckers moving up and down the highways of Africa, picking up and passing on the illness through a variety of sexual partners (see Patton). Similarly, the spread from country to country has been attributed to tourists who contract the disease, often through sexual intercourse or intravenous drug use, in one country and fly to the next. The ability of certain "disease vectors" to move from one sexual or drug-using community to another further underscores the mobility associated with this disease.

To a certain extent, *Un año sin amor* plays along with these tropes, as Pablo Pérez presumably acquired the disease from, or with, his partner in France, who also had AIDS. But just as the movie intervenes in the global cinematic arena to correct simplistic attitudes about queer Argentina, it also makes a specific contribution to global HIV/AIDS cinema. Paul Julian Smith provides a good starting point for analysis:

> Pablo's position is hardly grim and contrasts with more pessimistic AIDS narratives in earlier films. Berneri provides him with a loyal best friend (whom he should not have hooked up with if he knew what was good for him) and a caring doctor, who gently insists on Pablo taking the treatment that will save his life. Pablo is also supported financially by his long-suffering father. (84)

While there is room for discussion of some of Smith's claims, it is true overall that this film represents a step forward in the depiction of AIDS, away from films depicting it melodramatically or tragically as a death sentence for the individual and an apocalypse for society.

In the context of HIV/AIDS films, *Un año sin amor* runs a distinctive course between what Douglas Crimp has identified as the twin imperatives of mourning and militancy in response to the epidemic ("Mourning" 3–18). On the side of mourning are a range of films that move from a bittersweet and thoughtful look back at the passing of gay men and their world (*Parting Glances*, 1986) to more sentimental movies designed to provoke empathy for the victims of AIDS (such as *An Early Frost*, 1985 or *Philadelphia*, 1993). The "militant" films designed to provoke outrage at the policies that helped the epidemic make a similarly wide variety of political interventions. Nearly all attack the inefficiencies of the government, the insensitivities of the medical research community, and the small-minded fear-mongering of many religious institutions—Rosa von Praunheim's bitterly sarcastic *Ein Virus kennt keine Moral* (*A Virus Knows No Morals*, 1986) is one of the best. Some include a critique of a self-indulgent gay culture that won't give up its sexual pleasures in the face of incontrovertible evidence of the plague (*And the Band Played On*, 1993). Responding to precisely that charge—and, specifically, its incarnation in the so-called patient zero, a flight attendant who allegedly contributed to the spread of the epidemic in its early days by flitting from bathhouse to bathhouse in one major city—the 1993 Canadian film *Zero Patience* argues that this approach is nothing but self-righteous, nonscientific bunk. It instead insists that societal attitudes about the disease and sexuality are at fault for the spread of the disease (Hansen 324–40). There are films that promote the heroism of AIDS activists in films such as Praunheim's AIDS Trilogy (especially *Silence = Death*, 1990 and *Positive*, 1990).[3] Others, such as Gregg Araki's 1992 *The Living End*, promote a kind of *Thelma and Louise* aesthetics, poised between nihilism and life-affirmation, of living life to the fullest after one's diagnosis.

Two Pulitzer Prize-winning literary works, Michael Cunningham's 1998 novel *The Hours* and Tony Kushner's 1993 play cycle *Angels in America*, were adapted for the screen, with star-studded casts. If Cunningham's novel was dedicated more to mourning than to militancy, its beautiful writing gave a kind of serene afterlife to the victims of disease. Tellingly, the 2002 film of *The Hours* was unable to duplicate this gorgeous style and, thus, seem trapped in an interminable melancholy rather than released in an uplifting mourning. Kushner's play, which became an HBO miniseries in 2003, tried, as successfully as any artwork, to meld empathetic mourning for the victims of the disease with political activism on a truly grand scale.[4] While *Un año sin amor* does not have the grandiose political and philosophical ambitions of Kushner's work, it does follow in the tradition of Kushner and Cunningham by charting a delicate course between mourning the fate of the young protagonist, Pablo Pérez, and taking a more militant line revealing how AIDS exposes society's political, economic, and cultural fault lines.

Medicine and Literature

Striving to make an intervention in the established cinematic contexts of HIV/AIDS films, *Un año sin amor* does not focus on assigning blame for the epidemic. Nor does it investigate the trauma of the individual's discovery of his diagnosis or his (mis)treatment by society. It is neither a paean to the heroic battles of HIV-positive rebels nor a call to action politically. It is not particularly interested in propagating safe sex (despite the odd—and unsubstantiated—insistence in Laura Kern's *New York Times* review that Pablo's sex is "protected" [E13]). Since Pablo is still alive at the end, the film is not primarily about honoring the lost dead. Instead, just as a relatively progressive society and well-developed gay culture are a given, so is Pablo's HIV status. In terms of HIV, the action of the plot lies in Pablo's gradual acceptance of the innovative medical treatments that emerged in the 1990s—the so-called "cocktail" of drugs that allowed many gay men to continue living with HIV. As this story unfolds, it becomes increasingly clear that HIV/AIDS also sheds light on the relationship between language, literature, and medicine.

As the twenty-first century progresses, the controversies of the 1980s and 1990s surrounding AIDS treatments in general and AZT in particular become more remote. *Un año sin amor* preserves and retells aspects of this story that might otherwise be forgotten. After a decade in which the diagnosis of AIDS was practically a death sentence, for which there were no cures with demonstrable success rates, the early 1990s saw the emergence of drugs that could treat HIV. The most famous and notorious of these was azidothymidine, or AZT, which was effective in prolonging the lives of people with AIDS but was also exorbitantly expensive and had seriously toxic side effects. For many people with AIDS, AZT was simply not good enough: it was evidence that the medical community was not trying hard and not taking people with AIDS seriously. Accusations of genocide accompanied charges of profiteering. With time, there would emerge a concern that policymakers worldwide were focusing more on drug therapy rather than prevention, both because the drug companies wanted to make money and because governments were afraid to embrace the sex-positive messages that would have to be part of prevention campaigns within the gay community. Many HIV-positive gay men resisted AZT and the drug cocktails, out of concern for the toxic side effects of the new drug regimen and because of broader concerns about a drug-based approach to the disease. Pablo Pérez begins with this mindset, sharing the general skepticism of AZT, but gradually comes to accept the advice of the medical authorities he consults.

Herbal teas figure prominently in many of the opening shots of the film, suggesting Pablo's initial desire to use mild, natural means to cure his ailment, which consists primarily of a stubborn cough. Considering homeopathy's long and vibrant history in Argentina, it is not surprising that Pablo takes that form of alternative medicine as well. He demonstrates his suspicion of establishment medicine early in the film, when he walks out of the hospital after getting some oxygen. He had come to the hospital in the middle of the night after a particularly severe coughing fit. The nurse suggests that his condition is serious, but once he has gotten some relief, he gets up and walks out of the dark and gloomy building. This could be simple denial of the reality of his disease, but the film itself seems to share Pablo's view of medicine. The long shot of the hospital hallway doused in an eerie green light, with Pablo in the background attached to an oxygen tank, gives the view a sense of Pablo's own suspicions of the medical establishment. Intercut with this scene are close-ups of Pablo's face with an attached mask delivering the oxygen—a mask that makes him look alien and scarcely human. The camera presents a worldview that closely reflects Pablo's own suspicion of the medical establishment.

Moreover, other aspects of the film suggest that Pablo's rejection of establishment medicine is principled, not merely the product of denial or fear. When his physician recommends AZT, Pablo makes clear that he knows of the drug's dangerous side effects. He resists the authority of his physician in a way that suggests that he has learned from the activism of organizations such as ACT UP, which, throughout the 1980s and 1990s, encouraged patients to take charge of institutions of medicine and fight back against authority figures such as physicians, medical researchers, and medical policymakers. HIV/AIDS activists, often heavily influenced by theoreticians such as Michel Foucault, had turned the tables on medical authorities, insisting that patients, too, could master medical discourses.

But moving away from the heroic model of the HIV-positive fighter for justice, this film shows Pablo eventually acquiescing to medical power, accepting his physician's advice, and taking the new drug cocktails, which include AZT. The drug cocktails would quickly become the new normal, at least in the developed world. By the movie's release in 2005, Pablo's difficult decision to accept the medical establishment's cure would—especially for viewers in the first world—already have the feeling of a documentary about how life was a decade earlier.

In 1996, Pablo Pérez is at the dawning of a new era in which HIV becomes a manageable disease. In 2005, viewers were ready to see someone like Pablo as the new face of AIDS. The film *Un año sin amor* is notable in that it gives no emphasis to the physical toll that AIDS could take on patients, as documented, say, by the photographer Nicholas Nixon.[5] The audience sees no disfiguring Kaposi's sarcoma (KS), which was a common result of HIV infection in the 1980s and shows up repeatedly in films from the first decade of the epidemic. (Tom Hanks's Andrew Beckett in *Philadelphia* and Steve Buscemi's Nick in *Parting Glances* both suffer from it, for instance.) Just as Pablo's life in a city relatively tolerant of gays and lesbians is taken for granted, his health is represented in a more realistic, less melodramatic way than had been the case with many earlier films. Yes, he is sick, coughs a lot, and has to go to the hospital. But he is not obviously physically marked with disfiguring characteristics that mean HIV/AIDS.

Berneri goes further than avoiding depicting the HIV-positive Pablo as a tragic victim of HIV, marked with some obvious symptoms that mean AIDS and only AIDS. She actually endows Pablo's body with a kind of eroticism that is empowering even as it is objectifying. There is a certain cinematic pleasure taken in Pablo's sickly body. When he coughs at night, tossing and turning in his bed, the extreme high-angle shot makes him seem vulnerable but also provides a flattering view of his lissome, trim body. When he undergoes a CAT scan, his body is similarly eroticized. Although *Variety* refers to actor Juan Minujín's Pablo Pérez as "gaunt" (43), *The Advocate* calls him "attractive" (64), and Smith describes him as "cutely brooding" (84). This eroticization perhaps feeds into a potential fetishization of Minujín's almost delicate brown-skinned male body among certain segments of the largely white gay audiences of the film festivals in Berlin, New York, and Los Angeles. But at the same time, it reconfigures the status of a gay HIV-positive Argentine man. He is no longer the victim with KS, identifiable by all and shunned by most. Instead, the film celebrates him as beautiful. Pablo is an object of desire within certain circles of Buenos Aires, and the actor who plays him is an object of desire for film viewers throughout the world.

Nor is Pablo's body the only place where beauty can be found in HIV and AIDS. Surprisingly, given his resistance to AZT, Pablo finds the AZT tablet symbolically attractive. Developed by the pharmaceutical company Burroughs-Wellcome, it seems to "welcome" him to a new world with its emblematic unicorn.⁶ The film reinforces Pablo's sense of self-worth by focusing visually, through extreme close-ups, on new moments of beauty: the dissolution of the tablets in water, the flow of blood into the syringe, and the patient's body as he submits to medical examinations. Certainly, the film does not indulge in a Romantic glorification of sickness, or any foolish comparison between AIDS and a Wagnerian *Liebestod*. It effectively documents the seriousness of Pablo's illness. But neither does it dramatize the disease as a tragic end without hope. Pablo and the film are able to find a path toward appreciating moments of beauty and poetry in accepting and submitting to the realities of the discourses of HIV and AIDS.

Medicine is one of the master scripts of this movie. The power of this establishment medical discourse is reemphasized throughout. Overwhelming shots of the names of hospitals, close-ups of medical reports on T-cell counts, names of drugs such as AZT moving across the computer screen, handwritten doctors' prescriptions, and labels of pills showcase cinematically the prose of HIV and AIDS. This new language is full of acronyms and scientific terminology that seem to wring the humanity out of the individual. The semiotics of medicine—the reading of the signs of the body, the arcane results of medical tests, legible most clearly to the physician—is the language that dominates Pablo's life now. Visually, this language is represented by the architecture of the hospitals, shabby and severe—places where one has to fight to keep one's dignity. Narratively, the film's contribution to the cinema of HIV/AIDS is its dramatization of the decision to submit to medical authority and accept a drug cocktail based on AZT, a *pharmakon* that is both a poison and a cure.⁷

Poetry: Pablo Neruda/Pablo Pérez

In a conversation with his sweet but bourgeois gay friend Nicolás (Carlos Echevarría), Pablo reveals his early love for Pablo Neruda, the Chilean poet of great love and passionate politics. An idol of leftist artists and intellectuals throughout Latin America and beyond, Pablo Neruda has been cinematically immortalized in the Italian film *Il postino* (*The Postman*, 1994) as the exiled poet who teaches the poor fisherman to express his love in words.⁸ Just as *Un año sin amor* rejects the radical leftist sexual politics of *Kiss of the Spider Woman*, it also implicitly leaves behind Neruda as a model of romantic sexual and political revolution. Instead, it reframes Pablo as a point of bonding with his friends from his earlier pre-HIV life—he shares a love of Neruda not only with his gay friend Nicolás but also with his aunt. The depiction of overcoming the Neruda model of literary activity sets up Pablo's eventual move into the memoir and the confessional.

Pablo shares his love of Neruda with Nicolás. They recite the lines "Joy, I was a taciturn young man, I found your head of hair . . . wild." The two young gay men are able to appropriate Neruda's famous heterosexuality for their own homosexual desire, which is a testament to the power of literature in general to build community, and Neruda's power to cement erotic communities. However, while the cinematic world of *Il postino* associates Neruda with deep desire and radical politics, *Un año sin amor* places the iconic poet on the bookshelves of conventional liberal bourgeois society. Well-established Nicolás has all the comforts of a successful *Bildungsbürger*. Only his homosexuality puts him on the fringe of conventionality, a quasi-exile that doesn't seem to create much trouble for him. He apparently participates actively and without resentment in the gay scene of Buenos Aires. A modern gay man in the modern world, all he needs is a spouse—and that spouse could well be Pablo, for whom he cares deeply and with whom he may even be in love.

The limits of Nicolás's bourgeois liberality emerge, however, in his inability to understand Pablo's forays into pornographic theaters and dark rooms. His facial expression suggests that he is hurt when Pablo picks up tricks when the two of them are on a date. Nicolás's disappointment is understandable, but Pablo Pérez's desires are different from either what Nicolás wants or what Neruda describes. Pérez is interested in a different kind of erotic intimacy. He wants something more anonymous, more promiscuous, and ultimately more masochistic than anything that Nicolás or Neruda can offer. As Paul Julian Smith points out, Berneri's film makes no effort to explain or justify Pablo's desires—it takes them as a given and on their own terms. Pablo's rejection of a homonormative relationship with Nicolás, in a home where Neruda is cherished, goes hand in hand with his interest in a different kind of writing from Neruda's. (While the movie seems to spell out a rejection of the worldview that Nicolás represents, it is probably worth noting that Pérez's book, *Un año sin amor*, is dedicated to a certain Nicolás Gelormini.)[9]

In rejecting the model of a companionate relationship with Nicolás based in part on a shared appreciation of Neruda, Pablo is also rejecting the models that his family and childhood gave him. Pablo tells Nicolás that he learned about Neruda from his aunt, with whom he now lives in a cramped apartment owned by his father. When he was younger, he used to pretend he was Neruda on the Ouija board—stubbornly, his aunt believed that it really was Neruda in the afterlife, even after Pablo told her that he was moving the board. Under the influence of his family, he tried to bring Neruda back to life.

Pérez's aunt, with whom he shared his Neruda bond as a youth, presents a less domesticated version of Neruda among the bourgeoisie. Called Nefertiti (and Mimí Ardú), she is devoted to love and sex, but unfortunately, she's not the fun-loving Auntie Mame whom many twentieth-century gay boys have wanted. Impoverished and mentally unstable, she falls asleep on the bench in the hallway. While Nicolás can "like" Neruda yet lead a functional bourgeoisie life, Auntie has taken Neruda's passion for love to the point of mental instability and dysfunctionality. Simply to survive, Pérez must reject Auntie despite how much she loves and cares for him. Life in the small apartment, already cramped, is all the more difficult because of her. Concretely, she stands in the way of sexual and erotic freedom, observing him constantly and tying up the phone lines with her own assignations.

For Pablo Pérez, then, Pablo Neruda is caught up in a world with no future—as sweet as his relationships with his friend Nicolás and Nefertiti are, they will not satisfy him anymore. Nor is he alone. For despite the deep affection that Nicolás and his aunt have for Neruda, traditional poetry does not sell anymore. When Pérez finally meets with the editor (Carlos Portaluppi), he hears that his poetry, while good, is not marketable—because Argentina doesn't read poetry anymore. The Nefertitis and Nicolases of the world are receding in importance demographically. Perhaps the vicissitudes of dictatorship and economic crisis in Argentina have decimated the liberal bourgeoisie that they represent. Perhaps they would have lost importance even if a half century of trouble and turmoil had not taken its toll on them. But they—and the canonical Neruda whom they admire—have no future in this film.

Pablo's Writings: Poetry and Personals

The movie opens with a text that is both poem and personal ad. To the clackety-clack of an old-fashioned keyboard, the following words appear:

> Poet professor in autumn years
> seeks helpmate companion protector friend
> young lover w/empty compassionate soul
> exuberant spirit, straightforward handsome
> . . .
> to share bed meditation apartment . . .

help inspire mankind conquer world anger & guilt
. . . slave or master, mortally tender passing swift time
Find me here . . . alone with the Alone.[10]

As a voice-over reads the poem, the film prepares its viewers for Pablo's story with a montage of close-ups of Pablo's fingers typing on a keyboard, close-ups of Pablo's face as he considers his words, shots of occasional words such as "apartamento," "mortalmente," and "solo" in classic IBM script on the computer screen, and tight pans of Pablo's desk, featuring his tea and homeopathic medicines. Only after this segment does the title of the movie appear, suggesting that this kind of confessional thinking is already in place at the beginning of the year without love.

The author of this personal ad as poem is not Pablo Neruda, but another great poet of politics and love: Allen Ginsberg. While the novel explicitly cites Ginsberg,[11] the movie makes the point obliquely, simply providing a shot of a collection of Ginsberg's poetry at one point. For those in the know, the Ginsberg citation points once again to Pérez's location in global discourses of sexuality and poetics. But more importantly, the opening sequences of the film suggest that Pérez takes his personal ads seriously as a kind of existential poetry. For him, they are a chance to ask the deepest kinds of questions: "¿Qué soy? ¿Qué busco?" [Who am I? What am I looking for?] (Pérez, 55).

The first answer to those questions that Pablo publishes is the following: "30, 5'7" [1.73 m], 154 lbs [70 kg], cropped head, good body, seeks lover or masculine buddy, active, protector, well hung, for long-term relationship, safe sex." The romance of Ginsberg's poetry is gone, but the text still reveals a man expressing vulnerability and desire through words. The viewer sees him writing this ad, sees the words coming across the computer screen, and, ultimately, sees the printed ad as well. Visually, the film documents the process of conceiving, forming, and printing a verbal self-expression. Like any form of communication, a personal ad—be it a message in a bottle or an arcane poem—requires a receiver as well as a sender. Pablo's ad elicits only one response: a man who, he says, looks like an alien. Nonetheless, Pablo claims he would have followed him anywhere, until he stammers, "Soy petiso" (rendered in the subtitles as "I'm stubby").[12] Pablo had asked for someone who was "bien dotado"—well endowed.

More subtly, Pablo had hoped that readers would understand his reference to safe sex as indicating his HIV status. After much deliberation (suggested visually by images of him writing and crossing out the letters "HIV"), he decides to come out more forcefully as an HIV-positive man: "Sincere spirit, idealist, seeking to share pleasures, sex, friendship with a masculine man no older than 40. Me: 30, 5'7" [1.73 m], 140 lbs [64 kg], cropped hair, HIV+." Between the ads, Pablo has lost weight—probably because of his illness. Perhaps because of his encounter with the stubby man, he no longer specifies penis length, instead simply calling for a "masculine man." The language of sincerity and idealism underscores the earlier romantic roots of his writing.

Explicit about HIV, this ad likewise only produces one response—from a hairdresser, apparently not masculine enough. Just as with his poetry, Pablo's personal ads simply do not elicit enough good readers. Pablo therefore shifts his position and becomes a reader, responding to the advertisements of others. He has long been the reader of the erotic writings of others—poetry, of course, has been in his life since childhood. But he has also carefully preserved the letters and diaries of his deceased French lover. The ribbons and wrappings around the letters make them look positively Victorian. However, when he looks into these documents, he doesn't find the confirmation of Romantic love that he seeks. Instead, he finds only one reference to his name, next to someone else's telephone number. Based on his experience, it makes some kind of sense that he would be looking for a new kind of erotic intimacy—the intimacy that he finds in the sadomasochistic leather scene. The kind of romantic love that he had in France is now in the past for him, just as exhausted as the possibility of settling down with Nicolás or continuing to live with Aunt Nefertiti.

Pablo's Writing: Poetry and the Diary

When his editor sorrowfully confirms that Pablo's poems are not even minimally commercially viable, Pablo volunteers that he's writing a novel, really a diary, of a "writer with AIDS." The editor repeats the description as a diary of a "gay with AIDS," suggesting (perhaps) some sort of equivalency between writers and gays, but also (more likely) the power of AIDS to turn any noun into a signifier of homosexuality. Nonetheless, the editor is enthusiastic about the idea of this text, which, in fact, becomes the book *Un año sin amor: Diario del SIDA*. Structured as a diary, with daily entries from February 17 to December 31, the text does not fit easily into a genre. Interestingly, the Library of Congress catalogs it under the rubric of internal medicine, neither as a novel nor as a memoir. In the book, Pedro insists that "writing this diary is now a kind of autopilot of poetry."[13] Along with the personal ads, it replaces traditional poetry.

The film *Un año sin amor* covers the publication and initial responses to the book *Un año sin amor*, making structurally clear that the film is not simply a cinematic version of the book, or even a depiction of the writing of the book. It goes beyond the book to include reactions, both critical and laudatory. The responses include Pablo's own concern that the picture on the cover of the book makes him look effeminate. (And in fact, the illustration on the cover really does look like a woman.) He doesn't like that the marketing of the book focuses sensationally on his homosexuality. Nicolás tries to reassure him that such marketing is just the way of the commercial world, and takes him out to celebrate. His friends in the leather community are also supportive, although, toward the end of the film, Pablo actually uses the book as a means of avoiding them. It is telling that the gay friends, both vanilla and leather, are supportive of the book, even though it probably reveals private details about them. In contrast, however, Pablo's biological family is distraught. When his aunt reads how she appears in the memoir, she complains to his father. His father evicts him from the apartment, in what is clearly a draconian and cruel overreaction.

While the publication of the book marks the end of his old relationships with his biological family, the film suggests that it does not necessarily cement his relationship with his new families of choice in the gay and leather communities. Interestingly, he chooses not to ask Nicolás or the Sheriff for help when he is faced with homelessness, although both would clearly have offered assistance. Instead, the final scenes of the movie show Pablo returning to the pornographic film theater, where he will presumably spend the night. Is this refusal to reach out for help a masochistic, self-lacerating move? Or does it suggest a firm commitment to a new kind of interpersonal relationship, one that goes beyond both the bourgeois constraints that come with Nicolás and the ritualized conventions that come with the Sheriff? It is difficult to say. A neutral tracking shot follows Pablo as he walks from his apartment to the movie theater. An objective high-angle shot shows him walking down one set of stairs to buy a ticket for the pornographic film. Another objective high-angle shot shows him descending another flight of stairs into the theater proper. On the one hand, Pablo is going down, not once but twice. But on the other hand, the camera remains steadfastly objective, giving the viewer as much latitude to interpret the end of the movie as possible. Shortly before these final scenes, Pablo's intonation puts a question mark on the phrase "A Year without Love." In many respects, the movie's ending is open, perhaps nowhere more than in the question of where and how Pablo's love life will develop.

Leather and Masochism

For many viewers, the sadomasochistic scenes of the movie remain in the mind most vividly. Laura Kern of the *New York Times* sniffs that the scenes "aren't particularly hard core, or impassioned, even, like those, say, of Bob Flanagan, whose similar quest for finding pleasure in physical pain while fighting a debilitating disease was documented in the 1997 film *Sick*" (E13). Paul Julian Smith, however, in *Sight and Sound,* finds them "relatively graphic" (64). Visually, they are a striking and prominent feature of the film. The first sequence in which Pablo takes part in a sadomasochistic scene occurs after a meeting with the Sheriff. A shot of a glass tray of metallic paraphernalia looks almost medical, except that instead of medical implements, the tray holds clips, handcuffs, collars, and even knives. Then, in a medium shot, the camera shows the Sheriff and his friend whipping Pablo, followed by a close-up of Pablo's back as a leather strap caresses it. A sudden cut to a picture of Pablo as a child has shock value as a contrast, after which the viewer sees a montage of scenes from a leather club, including shots of men pushing Pablo to his knees, and many close-ups of unidentified hands on skin and leather. In the documentary footage that accompanies the Strand DVD of *Un año sin amor*, Berneri describes being inspired by the dramatic lighting of the leather clubs in Buenos Aires, and indeed, these scenes are typically lit with bright spotlights on certain bodies or body parts, while the rest of the scene is dark. The effect is memorable. Moreover, the leather scenes are an important part of the story. In this register, the narrative force of the story is Pablo's gradual entry into the sadomasochistic scene in Buenos Aires, and his experimentation with the limits of that scene.

Pablo's immersion in the world of sadomasochism emphasizes the importance of language in the construction of sexuality. The film *Un año sin amor* reinforces this issue when Pablo teaches his French pupil Julia to modify "je t'aime": "un peu," "à la folie," "pas du tout." Pablo gives Julia a language in which to say that she loves someone "a little," "madly," or "not at all." He himself needs such a language to navigate the world of sadomasochism and leather. In the book *Un año sin amor*, this language comes primarily from English. Not only are very specific practices, such as "fist-fucking," given in English, but so are "leather," "master," and "slave," for which there are easily available Spanish equivalents.[14] The italicized English words point to a new sexual vocabulary describing a new sexuality. In the documentary footage about *Un año sin amor* on the Strand DVD released in the United States, the director and the actors all use the term "leather" in English, although they are speaking in Spanish. Interestingly, the reviews of the film show that the English terminology is not particularly solidified, either. *Variety* refers to "S&M clubs" and "bondage" (Cockrell 43); the *New York Times* talks about "the S-and-M group" and "S-and-M activities" (Kern E13); *The Advocate* discusses "an intimate S/M-leather group" (Shannon 84). This unstable punctuation points to theoretical complexities in approaching the entire world to which Pablo gains access in his year without love.

In *Psychopathia Sexualis* (first edition 1886), Richard von Krafft-Ebing coins for the first time the terms "sadism" and "masochism" after, respectively, the sexual cruelty of the Marquis de Sade, and the submissive joy in pain of Leopold von Sacher-Masoch. Sacher-Masoch wrote numerous novels depicting sexual submission and the eroticization of pain, the most famous of which is *Venus im Pelz* (*Venus in Furs*, 1870).[15] Sade was, of course, long dead by the time Krafft-Ebing wrote, but Sacher-Masoch lived to see his name turned into a pathology, which he bitterly resented. This set up a long-standing conflict between the pathological and nonpathological understandings of sadism and masochism, comparable to the debates between those who would medicalize homosexuality and those who would not. *Un año sin amor* clearly does not consider any aspect of bondage/domination/sadism/masochism pathological.

More recently, a subsequent debate has put into question the worldview that sees people as "sadists" (who typically desire an unwilling victim) and "masochists" (who often have to instruct their tormentors.) The old joke about the sadist who cruelly refuses the masochist's plea to hurt him relies on this worldview, according to which sadists and masochists are actually not well-suited for each other at all (Deleuze, 193). More recent trends have emphasized a nonpathologizing vision of a more fluid community of people who enjoy playing with sexual power, often moving between various roles. This community is often called "sadomasochistic" and goes by acronyms such as "SM," "S-M," "S/M" or "S and M," which can carry subtle nuances of their own. (Some argue that the slash in "S/M," for instance, emphasizes a stronger distinction between the "sadist" and the "masochist," whereas the lack of punctuation markers in "SM" suggests a more fluid dynamic.) Some prefer the terminology of bondage and discipline, abbreviated as "B and D"; frequently the two sets of acronyms are joined as the term "BDSM." At times, "leather" and "fetish" are used to describe the SM community. The terminological free-for-all shows that sexuality is a linguistic matter as well as a physical one.

In *Un año sin amor,* Pablo seems to be much more masochistic than sadomasochistic. In the book, his desire to be a "slave" is quite explicit. In the movie, the viewer does not see him in a domineering position, inflicting pain or discipline on others. Instead, he is frequently the bound and tied-up victim of sadomasochistic bondage and discipline scenarios. In the documentary footage on the Strand DVD, Berneri reiterates that Pablo takes on the role of a slave. The world in which he finds his new friends is sadomasochistic, but he himself is on the masochistic side of the sexual equation. Leather seems to be a major feature of the sexual scenes, and bondage and discipline seem to be an important part of the action.

Pablo's interest in the world of leather and S/M predates the film's beginning. As he tells the Sheriff, he visited establishments such as Mec Zone when he lived in Paris, but it takes him a while to remember the name of the bar, suggesting that it was not a major part of his life. In Buenos Aires, he does not seem to know this world well at all at the outset of the movie. In the film, he sees a leather pair in the distance at a coffee shop and eyes them enviously, embarrassed by his cough, which indicates that he might be damaged goods in this new world that he wants to enter. His initial introduction to the Sheriff reveals him to be shy and a little slow on the uptake—he has to be reminded periodically to say "sir."

After his induction into the scene, Pablo violates the rules by starting a little affair on the side with Martín, a hot young sadist with a shaved head, whose Internet moniker is "masterinboots." (Once again, the language of leather is English.) The affair is transgressive because Martín is a favorite of the Sheriff. When the Sheriff finds out, he insists that Pablo come by his place, where the Sheriff and Martín submit the young masochist to a particularly severely choreographed session. Bound and gagged, Pablo cannot defend himself against knives that touch and nearly penetrate his skin and nipples, nor can he protect his neck from the heavy boots of Martín. The scene seems to move from sadomasochistic play to something more dangerous and serious. At the conclusion of the scene, Pablo is cured of his love for Martín and seems to understand the limits of what he can expect from his sadomasochistic friends.

For Paul Julian Smith, this second torture scene is "clearly non-consensual." While that may be true, it is also the culmination of several trajectories in the classical masochistic narrative. On the one hand, the climax of Leopold von Sacher-Masoch's *Venus in Furs* is Wanda's ultimate act of cruelty to Severin, when she hands him over to her new lover, "the Greek," and lets the Greek whip him. Even though he had previously declared that there were no limits, this goes beyond the limits of what Severin thinks he can endure, "curing" him of his masochistic desires. Although Martín does not need to learn to become a master in the way Wanda does, it does seem that Pablo entices him to enter into this new relationship outside the Sheriff's controlling sphere. In that respect, Martín is comparable to Wanda. Similarly, it is not certain that Martín reports the relationship to the Sheriff as an example of his extreme cruelty, in the way that Wanda hands Severin over to the Greek. Because the Sheriff finds out somehow, however, it seems most likely that Martín tells him. Martín's casual attitude about the matter, both before and after Pablo is tortured, has that same icily indifferent cruelty that characterizes Wanda. Just as Pérez and Berneri intervene in depictions of Argentina's queerness and global HIV/AIDS, they also work within a tradition of depicting masochism, while also altering it.

On the other hand, as the psychoanalyst Theodor Reik argues, the masochistic position fundamentally requires a witness: "The onlooker or listener is here also a *conditio sine qua non*" (339). What Reik calls "the demonstrative feature" of masochism mandates that "the imagined witness has to look on at the exposure and beating and share the pleasure. He cannot be left out for he is the carrier of the pleasure-bringing action" (341). The one-on-one with Martín is not as full an expression of masochistic desire as being whipped in front of the Sheriff by Martín—someone has to enjoy Martín's whipping of Pablo. Within Pablo's world, the Sheriff becomes the necessary witness to his pain. Perhaps more importantly, though, the film's viewer is a witness to Pablo's masochism, even of the scenes *à deux*. There is something of an overlap between the films that Pablo views in the pornographic theater and the somewhat less explicit but still quite titillating film that the audience of *Un año sin amor* sees. Occasional use of handheld cameras in the leather scenes contributes to a subjective feeling, as though the viewer were present in the room.

Conclusion

Anahí Berneri's *Un año sin amor* reflects on the discourses surrounding a broad range of cultural issues and cinematic tropes, including late-twentieth-century Argentine history, Argentina's queerness, representations of HIV/AIDS in a global context, medicine and literature, the radical love poetry of Neruda and Ginsberg, personal advertisements and diaries as literature, and leather and S and M. Often, the first and most important move that the film makes is to reposition twenty-first-century Argentina with respect to early cinematic images that misrepresent the current situation. Queerness in Argentina is not a matter of overt oppression as it was in *Kiss of the Spider Woman,* nor is it the campy extravaganza filled with drag queens who look like Madonna playing Evita. HIV/AIDS is neither a story of victims of society nor heroic resistance to capitalistic drug companies. Poetry doesn't sell, but people are still reading personal ads and confessional novels. The leather scene is not an arena where people playfully switch roles, but it does provide some measure of friendship and community and even the potential for something that could be love. Instead of melodramatic and sweeping gestures, the film details small, sober, realistic steps: accepting a regimen of AZT treatments, publishing a piece of confessional writing, learning the limits of masochistic play. Together, these small steps constitute a huge departure from previous discourses.

There is something ultimately submissive about Pablo Pérez's development—he acquiesces to the establishment in medicine, in writing, and in sexuality. Pablo comes to accept his subservience to modern medical discourses just as he agrees to publish his diaries rather than his poetry, just as he embraces the masochistic position in his sexuality. This submission can be read as abject—his father literally evicts from his apartment, severing all familial ties. Alone, he descends into what some might see as the netherworld of anonymous sex in a pornographic world. On the other hand, *Un año sin amor* has consistently emphasized the beauty of leather, poetic personal ads, and even aspects of Pablo's medical treatments. Cinematically, the film ends on a starkly neutral and objective note. It is up to the viewer to consider the directions that Pablo's fate might take him. But the viewer can make a more informed assessment of Pablo's situation because *Un año sin amor* has performed a thorough deconstruction of the myths surrounding homosexuality, HIV, and leather in Argentina.

Notes

1. "S/M" stands for "sadism and masochism," but see the discussion, in this chapter, of the language of S/M.

2. MERCOSUR stands for MERcado Común del SUR, created in 1991, and refers to a trading block of countries, primarily including the following members: Argentina, Brazil, Paraguay, Uruguay, and Venezuela. Bolivia, Chile, Colombia, Ecuador, and Peru are only associate members.

3. The third film, on AIDS in Germany, was never released.

4. For further thoughts on the relationship between mourning, melancholy, and militarism in television treatments of the disease, see Robert Deam Tobin, "Politics, Tragedy and *Six Feet Under*: Camp Aesthetics and Strategies of Gay Mourning in Post-AIDS America."

5. For a critique of this work, see Douglas Crimp's "Portraits of People with AIDS."

6. Burroughs-Wellcome became GlaxoWellcome in 1995, then merged with another company to become GlaxoSmithKline in 2000. The name "Wellcome" obviously fits Pérez's poetic needs best, though.

7. For a more thorough discussion of HIV and AIDS as signifiers, see Robert Deam Tobin, "Prescriptions: Medicine and Literature."

8. *Il postino* was released in Argentina in 1995 as *El cartero*. The movie is actually a remake of Antonio Skármenta's *Ardiente oscuridad* (1983), which itself is based on Skármenta's 1983 book *El cartero de Neruda*. There is, therefore, a previous cinematic tradition of Neruda as the leftist love of Latin film.

9. "a Nicolás Gelormini, / por nuestra bella amistad" (Pérez 15).

10. The poem is "Personals Ad," by Allen Ginsberg. The subtitles are slightly different, but I have quoted the original.

The movie draws on the translation in Pérez's diary novel (56):

> "Poeta mundialmente famoso profesor en sus años
> otoñales
> busca compañero pareja protector y amigo
> amante joven alma delicada vacía compasiva
> espíritu exuberante, franco y bello
> . . .
> para compartir cama meditación apartamento . . .
> ayudar a vencer la furia y la culpa del mundo,
> inspirar humanidad
> . . .
> . . . como esclavo o amo,
> mortalmente tierno al paso veloz del tiempo
> . . .
> solo con lo Solo
> . . . ."

11. Pérez, 55.

12. Pérez, 99.

13. "Escribir este diario, ahora es una especie de piloto automático de la poesía" (Pérez 93).

14. See, for example, Pérez, 64–65, 142.

15. For more thorough analysis of masochism and its history, see Finke and Niekerk.

Works Cited

Berneri, Anahí, dir. *Un año sin amor*. 2005. DVD.
Cockrell, Eddie. "A Year without Love." *Variety*, March 28, 2005: 43. Print.
Crimp, Douglas. "Portraits of People with AIDS." *Discourses of Sexuality: From Aristotle to AIDS*. Ed. Donna C. Stanton. Ann Arbor, MI: U of Michigan P, 1992. 362–88. Print.
——. "Mourning and Militancy." *October* 51 (1989): 3–18. Print.
Deleuze, Gilles. "Sacher-Masoch und der Masochismus." Trans. Gertrud Müller. *Venus im Pelz*. Leopold von Sacher-Masoch. Frankfurt am Main: Insel, 1980. 165–281. Print.
Finke, Michael C., and Carl Niekerk, ed. *One Hundred Years of Masochism: Literary Texts, Social and Cultural Contexts*. Atlanta, GA: Rodopi, 2000. Print.
Ginsberg, Allen. "Personals Ad." *Collected Poems: 1947–1997*. New York: Harper Collins, 2006. 970. Print.
Hansen, Ellis. "Undead." *inside/out: Lesbian Theories, Gay Theories*. Ed. Diana Fuss. New York: Routledge, 1991. 324–40. Print.
Kern, Laura. "A Year without Love." *New York Times*, Feb. 10, 2006: E13. Print.
Patton, Cindy. *Inventing AIDS*. New York: Routledge, 1990. Print.
Pérez, Pablo. *Un año sin Amor: Diario del SIDA*. Buenos Aires: Perfil Libros, 1998. Print.
Reik, Theodor. "The Characteristics of Masochism (An Excerpt)." Trans. G. Wilbur. *Essential Papers on Masochism*. Ed. Margaret Ann Fitzpatrick Hanly. New York: New York UP, 1995. Print.
Shannon, Kelley. "A Year without Love." *The Advocate*, Feb. 14, 2006: 64. Print.
Smith, Paul Julian. "A Year without Love." *Sight & Sound* 16.5 (2006): 84. Print.
Tobin, Robert Deam. "Politics, Tragedy and *Six Feet Under*: Camp Aesthetics and Strategies of Gay Mourning in post-AIDS America." *Reading Six Feet Under: TV to Die for*. Ed. Kim Akass and Janet McCabe. New York: Tauris. 2005. 85–93. Print.
——. "Prescriptions: Medicine and Literature." *Mosaic* 33.4 (2000): 179–92. Print.

Part II

Gay Authorship—Queer Agency and Spectatorship

5

La venganza del sexo: The Curious Mutation from Horror Fantasy to Sexploitation Film

(Emilio Vieyra, 1967)

Esteve Riambau[1]

La venganza del sexo (*The Curious Dr. Humpp*, 1967) does not have an assigned place in the annals of cinema history. At best, the film may enjoy offhand references in texts on fantasy cinema that are suitable only for the genre's most devoted followers.[2] Although there are those who describe it, generously, as "one of the most original and imaginative Argentine films of all time" (Curubeto, 172), its stylistic and industrial parameters are closer to the marginal cinema of Ed Wood or Russ Meyer, consigned to the grindhouse theaters of the 1970s, than to Universal's classic terror films of the 1930s or to those produced by Val Lewton for RKO a decade later.

It is not easy to obtain an original copy of this black-and-white Argentine production, directed by Emilio Vieyra in 1967. Easier to find is the DVD version, distributed in the United States beginning in October 2000. Frank Henenlotter discovered a copy left behind from an Argentine premier in the 1970s and released it as a part of the series Sexy Shockers from the Vault, under the Something Weird Video label.[3] Rechristened *The Curious Dr. Humpp*, the copy released in the United States is seventeen minutes longer than the original Argentine production of barely seventy minutes. The additions consist of interludes that nourish an already far-fetched plot emerging from an original story by Raúl Zorilla, a pseudonym for Vieyra himself. Halfway between a detective story and disparate subcategories of fantasy, the film unfurls topics of genre that include the myth of Faustus, the typology of the mad doctor, the sexual connotations of vampirism, a brain that talks, and the good-hearted monster that rebels against its creator.

The Argentine Emilio Vieyra, inventor of such a strange creature, began his artistic career as a theater, film, and television actor. He immigrated to the United States in the 1950s and, at the end of that decade, returned from New York with $500 he had invested in the creation of a film production company headquartered in Buenos Aires. *Detrás de la mentira* (*Behind the Lie*, 1961), one of his first films, is an anticommunist pamphlet built on the pretext of a detective plot. *Testigo para un crimen* (*Violated Love*, 1963), his next film, was the first Argentine film that included the presence of a transvestite, specifically hired for its release in the United States. This displacement of genre from film noir to eroticism—a field that Vieyra cultivated with the collaboration of actress Libertad Leblanc (*María M*, 1964; *Testigo para un crimen*), and within which his films competed with those of Armando Bó, whose star was the exuberant Isabel Sarli—soon directed Vieyra toward fantasy.

Five films released nearly consecutively, including *La venganza del sexo*, crowned Vieyra as a specialist in a genre whose tradition in Argentine cinema was as scarce as its popularity was vast. *Extraña invasión* (1965), the first of this series, arose from the initiative of a U.S. producer and was released in the United States under the title *Stay Tuned for Terror*. To reduce costs, it was filmed in the vicinity of El Palomar, near Buenos Aires, simulating a small town in the United States. The roles included the North American actors Richard Conte and Ann Strasberg, in addition to Mónica Mihanovich, a local star and, later, the unflagging news anchor for Canal 13. The plot revolves around a phenomenon that affects local televisions invaded by foreign cathodic cables that capture the attention of children and elders via hypnosis. After watching the infected televisions, the children and elders turn into dangerous zombies. Resolution of the problem unleashes a syndrome of abstinence and requires military intervention. *Placer sangriento* (*Feast of Flesh*, or *The Deadly Organ*, 1965), Vieyra's next film, combines detective and erotic elements in a low-budget psycho-thriller filmed over a ten-day span in Punta Ballena, Uruguay. The protagonist is a serial killer who wanders around psychedelic discotheques by night, assassinating his victims with a lethal dose of drugs. The police do not hesitate to use LSD to interrogate one of the heroin overdose survivors.

Vieyra also developed a North American version oriented toward a Hispanic audience, distributed under the title *The Deadly Organ*. Both metaphoric elements, the quashing of others' consciences for totalitarian ends, and the use of drugs as the murder weapon against those whose conduct is morally licentious, converge, as we will see, in *La venganza del sexo*.

Vieyra's subsequent fantasy films use a good part of the cast led by Ricardo Bauleo, Aldo Barbero, Susana Beltrán, and Gloria Prat and also develop the same elements that we find in *La venganza del sexo*—for example, the masked assassin who preys on the chorus girls of a vaudeville house in *La bestia desnuda* (*The Naked Beast*, 1967). This film includes an erotic happening with scenes of homosexuality, transvestism, and the effects of drugs and alcohol, at the pace of a bolero with sadomasochistic lyrics, titled "Castígame" ["Punish Me"], and vampirism—first approached in Argentine film by *Sangre de vírgenes* (1967). This delirious revisiting of classical mythology contradicts its own title with the inclusion of diverse sex scenes and makes up for its lack of funding by using seagulls filmed with a red filter as a substitute for the inevitable bats. It was shot in the Andes near Bariloche—a local emulation of the original Carpathians of Bram Stoker's novel, and released in the United States as *Blood of the Virgins* or *Red Horror*. In 1999, Vieyra contemplated doing *El Dr. Zoide contra la bestia desnuda* (literally, *Dr. Zoide versus the Naked Beast*), a film that would resuscitate the protagonist of *La venganza del sexo*, confronting him with a murder similar to the one in *La bestia desnuda*, but the project was never realized.

Vieyra's prolific career, including more than thirty feature-length films, would deviate in its latter years toward other popular genres: musicals with singers Sandro (*Quiero llenarme de ti* [*I want to Fill Myself with You*, 1968]), *La vida continua* (*Life Goes On*, 1969), and *Gitano* (*Male Gypsy*, 1969) and Leonardo Favio (*Simplemente una rosa* [*Just a Rose*, 1971]); the comedies *Villa Cariño está que arde* (*Villa Cariño is Almost Burning*, 1968) and *Yo gané al prode . . . ¿y Ud . . . ?* (*I Beat the Geek, and You?* 1973); the Argentine version of superagents inspired by Ian Fleming's James Bond (*La gran Aventura* [*The Great Adventure*, 1974]); the Western parody *Los irrompibles* (*The Unbreakable Ones*, 1975); an erotic film titled *Sucedió en el internado* (*It Happened in a Boarding School*, 1985); a prison melodrama called *Correccional de mujeres* (*Women's Reformatory*, 1986); and the exaltation of paramilitary groups in *Comandos azules* (*Blue Commandos*, 1980) and its sequel *Comandos azules en acción* (*Blue Commandos in Action*, 1980), filmed when the military dictatorship of General Videla prohibited Vieyra's release of erotic films and favored more traumatic kidnappings than those perpetrated by the mad scientist of *The Curious Dr. Humpp*. Still active in 2005, Vieyra directed *Cargo de conciencia*, a thriller about the decriminalization of drugs in the most moralizing tone of his filmic trajectory.

Crime Thriller and Horror Fantasy

The Curious Dr. Humpp vacillates between three of the great canonical genres: the *thriller* centered on the investigation, led by a *detective*-journalist and paralleled by the police investigation, seeking to uncover the mystery behind a series of disappearances; horror or strange tales, and fantasy, represented by the scientist who obtains, through sex, an elixir that guarantees his eternal youth—at the cost of converting the couples he kidnaps for his experiments into emotionless robots. Vieyra's film is heir to a tradition whose development dates back to the nineteenth century in certain novels by Gaston Leroux (e.g., *Le mystère de la chambre jaune* and *Le parfum de la dame en noir*), Sir Arthur Conan Doyle (the Sherlock Holmes mysteries), Jean Ray (Detective Harry Dickson mysteries), Mary Shelley (*Frankenstein; or, The Modern Prometheus*), and the short stories of Edgar Allan Poe. It poses an enigma that has less to do with discovering the guilty party—because the identity of the perpetrator is revealed at an early stage—than with finding the trigger to interrupt the chain of crimes triggered by the perpetrator's chimerical aspirations. Out of a diverse set of possible solutions, in the end only one turns out to be truly effective, and, according to Tzvetan Todorov, "It is already difficult enough, in the detective story, to find the point that 'defies reason' such that we are willing to accept the existence of the supernatural before the absence of any explanation" (54).

The Curious Dr. Humpp fits exactly with the definition that the Russian philosopher and mystic Vladimir Soloviov established in the nineteenth century when he affirmed, "[i]n true fantasy, the exterior and formal possibility of a simple explanation of the phenomena is always conserved, but, at the same time, this explanation is completely deprived of any internal possibility" (Tomachevski 288). In Vieyra's film, a scientist maintains his youthfulness for 200 years at the expense of the couples he has kidnapped, whose blood, enriched by libidinal fluids secreted after an orgasm, he needs for nutrition. This explanation, though logical, turns out to be unlikely. It becomes even more unlikely when the protagonist converses with the speaking brain of one of his first victims, who later turns into his oracle.

From the point of view of the journalist who investigates the kidnappings, *The Curious Dr. Humpp* responds to Gérard Lenne's definition of fantasy as "a fruit of the invasion, more or less irresistible, by the Imaginary into the Real" (16)—or, in Todorov's words, as "the doubt experienced by an entity that only follows the laws of nature, posed with an event that appears supernatural" (29). According to Todorov, the film that concerns us approaches the strange more than the marvelous, from the moment that "the story recounts events that can be perfectly described by the laws of reason, but are, in some way or another, incredible, extraordinary, shocking, singular, unnerving, unusual, and, because of this, provoke a similar reaction from the character as from the reader, to which stories of fantasy have had us grown accustomed" (51–52). Confronted by the two major directions (according to Lenne) by which fantasy cinema travels, *The Curious Dr. Humpp* distances itself from external threats generally deriving from other planets to stick closely to a threat that "finds its origin in human will, man acts with a tendency toward domination; he deliberately perturbs the universe's order, and his creation becomes a threat to itself" (64).

The Mad Doctor and His Henchmen

Lenne defines this typology as the "sorcerer's apprentice." The protagonist of *The Curious Dr. Humpp* adjusts himself to it but also echoes multiple other archetypes linked to fantasy. Dr. Zoide—the name given to the character in the Argentine version of the film and, as such, imbued with specific sexual connotations since his surname is an apocope of "spermatozoid"—is, above all, a mad doctor. Thus, he is an heir to the literary tradition occupied by Mary Shelley's characters or those of H. G. Wells in *Island of Lost Souls,* later introduced to cinema via their adaptations, or even by the model founded by *The Cabinet of Dr. Caligari* (Robert Wiene, 1919) and derived from the literary legacy of German romanticism.

Far from the myth of the double, identified by the journey of no return undertaken by Robert Louis Stevenson's Dr. Jekyll, originating in his laboratory and ending in the dark side of his subconscious, or of scientists who provoke catastrophes when they were only trying to save humanity by altering nature—*The Quatermass Experiment* (Val Guest, 1955), *Them!* (Gordon Douglas, 1954), *The Fly* (Kurt Neumann, 1958)—the doctor with megalomaniacal tendencies is a psychological monster. He is perfectly willing to create other physiological monsters in his desire to accomplish ancillary objectives: to "restore the beauty of the disfigured daughter—or lover—find the elixir of eternal youthfulness, resuscitate the dead, create a race of superbeings, or test Darwin's theories on live subjects" (Costa 65). The second of these aspirations, to find the elixir of eternal youth, is what connects *The Curious Dr. Humpp* with the myth of Faustus and that of Dorian Gray, one of its successors. Differing from Goethe's recreated literary character, who sells his soul to the devil for a life replete with pleasures and knowledge, Vieyra's protagonist does not resort to criminal means to retrieve the prized antidote, though he is faced with the inevitable aging of his cells, periodically manifest in the cutaneous lesions on his hands. His objective is, therefore, immortality, and to reach it he restores the superiority of his scientific work over the biological limitations of the human species. When failing to reach his objective, however, the doctor suffers the same fate as Oscar Wilde's protagonist, aging precipitously and thus reestablishing nature's order.

Far from totalitarian connotations that Nazism retrospectively imposed on Goethe's work and its filmic adaptation carried out by Friedrich W. Murnau (*Faust*, 1926), the scientist in *The Curious Dr. Humpp* does not evoke the typology of a demiurge that, through a disturbing form of seduction like that of the vampire, exercises a certain influence on the soul and conscience of his victims, kidnapped with the help of hit men. Borrowing from the extensive taxonomic classification of the fantasy genre proposed by Roger Caillois for literary models, Vieyra's film tackles the pact with the devil but, in one way or another, also "the specter condemned to a disorganized and eternal existence," "the vampires, the dead who are assured perpetual youthfulness if they suck the blood of the living," "the statue, the mannequin, the armor, the automaton, that soon become animated and acquire certain independence," "the woman ghost, who comes from the afterlife, seducer and mortal," and "the room, the apartment, the floor, the house, or the street erased from space" (Caillois 36–39).

The removal of revitalizing liquids to which the scientist submits his victims refers to vampirism. The vampiric resonances increase with the extractions of blood—a liquid that appears in fantasy "when the real surpasses the frontier of the symbolic" (Leutrat 60)—and especially because these bloodlettings go unpunished and produce a mental deterioration in the unfortunate donors. After several extractions, the donors turn into zombies, automatons lacking any sort of free will that does not conform to servicing the criminal activities of the tyrannical Dr. Zoide. Comparable to his kindred spirit Caligari, who uses a hypnotized automaton as an executioner, the protagonist of Vieyra's film has many servants at his disposal and, in particular, a monstrous creature fitted with heavy metallic boots and covered with a grotesque mask, which kidnaps its victims upon projecting its shadow against the nearest wall—as in *Nosferatu* (F. W. Murnau, 1922). But the monstrous creature also goes shopping at the local pharmacy to obtain the aphrodisiac drugs, until her robotic profile appears in the newspapers and raises suspicions. As a filmic clone of those "new Prometheuses" in the tradition of Frankenstein's hideous creature, the monster of *The Curious Dr. Humpp* is not a creature built from spare parts. Quite the contrary: its master subjects it to brain surgery to rid it of any human vestiges. (As

Henenlotter points out in his DVD production notes, Vieyra's monster echoes Frankenstein's in that he, too, is sick: "looking like he's contracted over 4,000 sexual diseases.") Even with this operation, the monster falls in love with one of the scientist's victims, offers her flowers, kidnaps her, and, in the tradition of *The Beauty and the Beast,* dies for her when it is gunned down by the police and drowns in a pond, perhaps in homage to *The Creature from the Black Lagoon* (Jack Arnold, 1954). Before succumbing to that tragic fate, however, the creature has already provided evidence of his kindhearted nature when, in one of the most deliriously fanciful shots of the film, he entertains the doctor's automatons by strumming languid chords on his guitar while they wander about the mansion's garden.

Dr. Zoide enjoys the help of another useful servant, a nurse and lover who, after being doped up with ether, surrenders herself sexually to a captive journalist when she confuses him with the scientist—and, from that point on, becomes determined to save him. But her surrender entails her dehumanization and, by extension, her death. An identical destiny corresponds to the brain preserved in formaldehyde, which is connected to some electrodes that give it the power of speech and allow the doctor to use it as an adviser. Her dramatic function within the film is much clearer in the American dubbing, which links her to an Italian scientist who would have initiated the very experiments Dr. Zoide is carrying out, than in the original, much more cryptic Argentine version. Whatever may be the intended case, the doctor's typology evokes other anatomical organs that have been a mainstay in the history of fantasy cinema, from the amputated hands of *Mad Love* (1935) to the hand that enjoys a life of its own in *The Addams Family* (1964), to the headless horseman depicted in filmed versions of Washington Irving's *The Legend of Sleepy Hollow,* and the hypnotizing head in *The Thing that Couldn't Die* (Will Cowan, 1959), not to mention its direct precedent, *Donovan's Brain* (Felix E. Feist, 1953), or the 1942 Curt Siodmak novel adapted into film on several occasions.

The Journalist as Voyeur

If the mad scientist occupies the territory of the prohibited and the supernatural, the journalist investigating the disappearances of his victims contributes a perspective mediated by the real and the rational. The journalist is more astute than the police and anticipates their every move. Having the benefit of studying a similar case that took place in Europe, he has no qualms about invading enemy territory when given the investigative opportunity. Captured by the mad doctor, the journalist soon falls in love with the stripper with whom he shares a room, he in ridiculous pajama shorts while she sports a transparent nightgown. Despite their love at first sight, he is quite happy to make love to his captor's nurse. She will be precisely the person who prevents him from having his free will taken from him via a ritual that resonates with those seen in exotic adventure cinema, from *The Mask of Fu Manchu* (Charles Brabin, 1932) to *Indiana Jones and the Temple of Doom* (Steven Spielberg, 1984).

In the end, the journalist succeeds in drawing the attention of the police so that they can find the uncharted mansion and ruin the plans of his adversary, whom the stripper stabs, thereby rapidly weakening a body that is biologically two hundred years old—a reference to the Mummy, another classic horror myth. The doctor's life is prolonged by sex—"Sex has dominated the world; now, I dominate sex," he pompously affirms—but, curiously, his conduct gives away his apparent impotence. His sexual activity is limited by the liquid he extracts and drinks from his victims and by his eager voyeuristic contemplation of them through a screen set up in his laboratory and connected to all the rooms of his aroused patients. He kidnaps his victims to extract the libidinal fluids present in their blood after sexual activity. At the same time, however, he is telling the journalist something altogether different: "You will possess that girl without even touching her body and you'll be aroused by that possession." Betrayed by his sick lover—whose frustrated desires to have sex with him make her able to confuse the journalist for him, whereupon she falls in love with the journalist—the scientist reprimands her when he finds out about her infidelity: "I warned you. Sex betrayed you."

The foregrounding of a saxophonist, whose music accompanies a striptease, reveals that Vieyra's sexual humor is of a dense caliber and unequivocally sexist: when the waiter at the gentleman's club is asked whether the kidnapped woman is his wife, he replies, "I wish!" In a later scene, the same character laments that the new stripper is fatter than the kidnapped stripper. An ideological reading of the film subverts the fantasy constant that makes the majority of its parables "obligatorily reactionary" (Lenne 1974, 46). The evil scientist's outlook on sex is merely subsidiary to his desire for immortality; he avoids physical contact and destroys bodies that engage in sex to his advantage. The journalist, however, is identified with "normality." He is very sexually active; he sleeps successively with the stripper and the nurse, at the same time performing the voyeuristic function for the audience, whose rejection of the scientist derives more from his impotence than from his transgression of the biological order. The reestablishment of order, therefore, implies a less repressive and castrating sexuality.

Double Versions

The version of *The Curious Dr. Humpp* released in the United States, both the one released in theaters at the beginning of the 1960s and the edited DVD version, is much more sexually explicit than the original. With merely partially uncovered breasts in the Argentine version, the North American distributor Jerald Intrator, director of such sexploitation films as *Satan in High Heels* (1962), *Orgy at Lil's Place* (1963), and *The Sexperts* (1965), added new scenes, much as he did with *La horripilante bestia humana* (*The Horrifying Human Beast*, René Cardona, 1969), a Mexican production released three years later in the United States under the title *Night of the Bloody Apes,* including the addition of several erotic scenes. In *The Curious Dr. Humpp*, Intrator filmed the added scenes in New York with North American actors, resulting in seventeen minutes of footage that included a lesbian couple making love, a drunk mariner who—only in the trailer, not in the film—identified himself as a homosexual; a nymphomaniac who masturbates to photographs of naked men that surround her, before having sex with one of the men; and an orgy involving two marijuana-smoking, hippie couples. Scenes capturing each of these situations were inserted into the original plot as if to suggest the kidnapping of hypothetical victims by the scientist's masked monster. The hypothetical victims later appear inside a mansion, framed by a screen through which the monster can observe them, superimposed like an erotic dream that includes the stripper and the journalist or like the patients he watches in different rooms. These images include nude backsides of individuals of both sexes, breasts, and female pubic hair, adhering to soft-porn standards.[4]

The film's North American title, *The Curious Dr. Humpp*, evokes that of *Jar ar nyfiken—en film i gult* (*I Am Curious [Yellow]*, Vilgot Sjöman, 1967): a Swedish film replete with erotic resonances that provoked a notorious international repercussion and whose exhibition in the United States was authorized only because of a Supreme Court sentence that underscored the film's merits as material for sexual education. Given these antecedents, the North American version of Vieyra's film not only included the word "curious" in the title and in the trailer—calling the film "the most curious of them all"—but also associated itself with the protagonist's scientific profession, re-christening him "Dr. Humpp." In an effort to avoid censorial problems, numerous sexploitation films released around the same time began with a supposed doctor dressed in a white coat, offering an educational introduction that justified the ensuing sexual scenes.

La venganza del sexo/The Curious Dr. Humpp thus benefits from the development of a second iteration—a precedent established by other films—to adapt its content to particular markets. This was a habitual practice in silent film. *Foolish Wives* (Erich von Stroheim, 1922), for example, had versions that contained much more suggestive shots in the copies for release in the permissive Italian market than those destined for the American market, which recently had established the Motion Picture Association of America. With the advent of "talkies," the big North American studios started exporting several of their films—*Dracula* (Tod Browning, 1931) was one of these—and creating new versions of the same screenplays, this time interpreted by Hispanic, Italian, French, or German actors. The European co-productions of the 1950s and 60s also gave rise to differing versions, especially those that included Spanish participation, whose strict censorship, a consequence of Francoism, demanded a conservative approach to erotic or violent scenes. Recent releases of director's cuts, commercialized in successive DVD editions that include deleted scenes or modified editing, also employ this practice.

Something similar occurred to the North American version of *The Curious Dr. Humpp*. Argentine cinema has had clear censorial limitations since the 1963 inception of the Consejo Nacional Honorario de Calificación Cinematográfica (National Honorary Council of Film Ratings). The film's North American distributor was quick to take advantage of the newfound tolerance gained from the elimination of the Hays Code, and it was these circumstances that allowed *The Curious Dr. Humpp* to be turned into a product akin to the sexploitation films produced in the United States since the early 1960s and destined for a targeted limited release. Vieyra steered clear of such manipulations and, as a result, reaped none of the benefits. But he paid attention to the new possibilities, and his next film, *Sangre de vírgenes* (*Virgin Blood*), was much more sexually explicit than the Argentine version of *The Curious Dr. Humpp*. Consequently, *Sangre de vírgenes* was banned until 1974. Then, after a few brief months in theaters, the military dictatorship removed the film from cinemas until deep into the next decade.

It is thanks only to the added sex scenes between two women in the U.S. version that one can categorize *The Curious Dr. Humpp* as a "queer" film. The borders between fantasy and sex have often been diffuse, and *The Curious Dr. Humpp* does not hesitate to include a generous repertoire of erotic situations that "illustrate various transformations of desire. Most of which really belong to the supernatural, if not to the social 'weird'" (Todorov 138). Besides incest, these correspond to homosexuality—a recurring subject in fantasy literature and cinema—or group sex, which Todorov calls "the love of more than two." Forty years after its release, Vieyra's film and its North American "double" continue to distill inevitably kitsch aromas. Both works create communicating vessels linking the two genres of fantasy and erotic cinema, through a catalogue of "curious" adventures that are unintentionally hilarious. And who knows? Perhaps such adventures will eventually find their way into an anthology of both genres.

Notes

1. Professor Esteve Riambau and the book's editors express their most sincere thanks to Cornell graduate student Bécquer Medak-Seguín for the English translation of this essay, written originally in Spanish.

2. See James L. Limbacher, R. G. Young, John Flowers, Paul Frizler, and Douglas Pratt.

3. The new edition includes a trailer to the North American version of the film, several production notes from the specialist Frank Henenlotter—whose passion for fantasy B movies led him to direct such cult films as *Basket Case* (1982), *Brain Damage* (1988), and *Frankenhooker* (1990)—and three erotic short films that have nothing to do with Vieyra: *Rasputin and the Princess*, *The Girl and the Skeleton*, and the Scopitone *My Teenage Fallout Queen*.

4. Omar Khan indicates that in the United States, "the film had been made available in a 'hot' version containing all the smut and a 'cold' version that was sans the dirty bits."

Works Cited

Caillois, Roger. *Images, images: Essais sur le rôle et le pouvoir de l'imagination*. Paris: Corti, 1965. Print.

Costa, Jordi. "¿Qué le pasa, doctor? Algunas notas sobre *mad doctors* y demás visionarios con carrera." *Nosferatu* 27 (1998): 64–69. Print.

Curubeto, Diego. "Argentina: ¡Carne sobre carne!" *Mondo macabre*. Ed. Pete Tombs. Londres: Titan Books, 1997. Revised and extended edition: *Mondo macabre: El cine más alucinante y extraño del planeta*. Barcelona: Círculo Latino, 2003. Print.

Flowers, John, and Paul Frizler. *Psychotherapists on Film, 1899–1999: A Worldwide Guide to Over 5000 Films*. Jefferson, NC: McFarland, 2004. Print.

Khan, Omar. Review of *The Curious Dr. Humpp*. Web. Oct. 15, 2009.
Lenne, Gérard. *El cine "fantástico" y sus mitologías*. Trans. Gustavo Hernández. Barcelona: Anagrama, 1974. Print.
Leutrat, Jean-Louis. *Vida de fantasmas: Lo fantástico en el cine*. Trans. María José Ferris Carrillo y Pau Rovira PérezValencia, Sp.: De la Mirada, 1999. Print.
Limbacher, James L. *Sexuality in World Cinema*. Lanham, MD: Scarecrow, 1983. Print.
Pratt, Douglas. *Doug Pratt's DVD: Movies, Television, Music, Art, Adult, and More!* Vol. 1.New York: UNET 2 Corporation, 2004. Print.
Todorov, Tzvetan. *Introduction à la littérature fantastique*. Paris: Du Seuil, 1970. Print.
Tomachevski, Boris. "Thématique." *Théorie de la littérature*. Paris: Du Seuil, 1965. Print.
Vieyra, Emilio, dir. *The Curious Dr. Hummp*. Ed. Frank Henenlotter. Something Weird Video, 2000. DVD.
Young, R. G. *The Encyclopedia of Fantastic Film: Ali Baba to Zombies*. New York: Applause, 2000. Print.

6

Inside-Out:
A Socio-Spatial Reading of *Mecánicas celestes*

(Fina Torres, 1995)

CECELIA BURKE LAWLESS

The screen fills with stars and sparks of planets, and so spectators find themselves in outer space pulled into a downward spiral toward the planet earth. Quickly, we realize that the continent laid out below us is South America, and the camera then descends on the top country, Venezuela, and into a colonial church. A baroque altar dominates the screen as the camera continues to pan down from the heavens to present us, from behind, a bride and groom standing in a marriage ceremony. Thus begin the first thirty-five seconds of the Venezuelan French co-production film *Mécaniques célestes* or *Mecánicas celestes* or *Celestial Clockwork* (1995) by director Fina Torres.[1] This introductory scene from outer space invites me to base this paper in a critique of gendered space turned inside out, an appropriate place for a film that begins from the outside of the world as we know it.

The plot of *Mecánicas celestes* as I will henceforth call it, is a simple one, made complicated through a series of bizarre twists and turns almost magical in their outcome, certainly guided by the "celestial" machinations referred to obviously in the title, and then later in the salsa song played at one of the various parties that occur during the next hour and a half.[2] The premise for the film's plot is the Cinderella fairy tale, a familiar narrative for both children and adults, a space where reality and fantasy meet. This well-worn story acts as a foundational myth of coming-of-age for young girls; or as many would say, a story based on eschewed expectations. A poor young girl lives with two stepsisters and their typically evil stepmother. She is made to do drudgery work for them until a fairy godmother appears and makes Cinderella beautiful in a gorgeous gown so that she can go to a ball, meet a prince, and fall in love. The midnight hour strikes, the spell is broken, and Cinderella must wait for her Prince Charming to find her with only a lost glass slipper to guide him. Of course, he does find her, and they marry and live happily ever after. Or so the story goes.

Mecánicas celestes takes this Grimm fairy tale and turns it inside out. Ana Mendoza is the Cinderella figure who flees her marriage in the Venezuelan church, flies to Paris in her disheveled gown, and lives with three adopted "sisters," also from Latin America, who stand by and advise her throughout the film as equally illegal immigrants in France. The fairy godmother appears in triplicate form as a Lacanian psychoanalyst, Ana's eventual lover, Alcanie; a Parisian gay waiter, soon to be Ana's husband, Armand; and Toutou, a bantu doctor of supposed white magic. The evil stepmother takes the form of the brashly postmodern Celeste, who also shares the apartment with the other Latin American young women. She is dressed in tacky clothes and almost always appears with a camera which she uses to film Ana. Celeste's magical qualities manifest themselves through special effects that emphasize her supernatural attributes, such as flames that come out of her eyes or a black cloud that rises from her dyed hair, and through the film's animated sequences that often accompany her appearance.

Within this array of characters, Ana searches for her own voice—literally—since she is a professional singer with initial doubts as to whether she still can sing—"Je veux savoir si je peux toujours chanter." For her, the idea of "happily-ever-after" consists in playing the role of a Cinderella in the movie adaptation of Rossini's opera *Cenerentola*. Ana must overcome many obstacles to achieve this goal, but unlike Grimm's Cinderella, she actively participates in forging her own fate with the help from the many members of her newfound community. In the end, after various struggles and setbacks and musical interludes, Ana does achieve her goal and the camera then zooms out from the initial sacred space—a church, now located in Paris, and falls back into the celestial heavens and outer space. Everyone thus has found their place, but along the way there have occurred many twists and turns of postmodern space that lead to a re-shaping of this classic story and the identity formation that it encompasses.

Inside the Box

Mecánicas celestes could be called a superficial film, as it presents a "melting pot" of soundtracks from opera, pop, and Latin salsa, as well as cultural hybridity in the intertwining languages of French, Spanish, and English people from the periphery interacting with those of the metropolis (Martí-Olivella 89). I would like to take this critique away from the domain of judgment and toward that of spatial studies. In fact, the camera rarely lingers in one location; rather it glides across a series of superficies that include a quick view of a colonial Venezuelan church and then a postcard collection perspective of relatively cliché images of Paris such as Notre Dame church, the Seine River, the Eiffel Tower, and the Bastille. These surface images of Paris—the apartment of the illegal Latin American women, the opera stage, the music studio in the graffiti laden building, the café, the "dangerous" police-filled streets, the white apartment of the psychoanalyst—all rub up against one another to create an almost absurd sensual zone of eroticism, or perhaps a parody of such a space. And this light eroticism plays into the emotions that evolve between Ana and Alcanie with a strong emphasis on the word "play." This reading then feeds into the theory of Elizabeth Grosz about lesbian bodies.

Grosz describes the concept of desire from Plato through Freud in "Refiguring Lesbian Desire," where she cogently lays out how desire has been framed over the centuries as a lack, from an accepted masculine position. According to Grosz's reading of Hegel, for example, the desire for what or whom is not present can only be fulfilled by the object or person that will, in effect, overwhelm this very desire; that is, paradoxically, once the desire is fulfilled it no longer exists: "The only object desire can desire is one that will not fill the lack or provide complete satisfaction. To provide desire with its object is to annihilate it. Desire desires to be desired" (176). Thus construed, lesbian desire would be difficult to understand in a traditional heterosexual society since it has been hard to imagine the desire for oneself, the Same, as opposed to desire for the Other—that which one is not, especially according to Freudian theories. But, if one begins to think of desire as a mode of production rather than as a passive receivership, then the idea of lesbian desire becomes much more viable: "to shift fixed positions and transform our everyday expectations and habitual conceptions schema" (175). Traditionally, women have been construed as the repositories of the lack constitutive of desire, caught between the opposition of presence and absence, reality, and fantasy; thus, women occupy man's Other. As Grosz claims, "For Spinoza, unlike Freud, reality does not prohibit desire but is produced by it. Desire is the face of positive production, the action that produces things, makes alliances, and forges interactions" (175). Such a conceptualization of desire creates multilayered possibilities for gendered space.

In *Mecánicas celestes* Ana goes beyond such oppositional positionalities as she appears present and yet is simultaneously threatened by disappearance from the immigration police, as well as the machinations of Celeste who seeks her obliteration. In effect, located in the fairy tale world of Cinderella, and the story within a story, Ana's life is a depiction of real-life struggles of an illegal immigrant and a woman in search of self, framed by fantasy both through the action and the form of the film. The film then plays with these binaries of absence/presence, heterosexual/homosexual, place/displacement through Ana and her predicament so as to ask, along the lines of Grosz, "Can desire be refigured in terms of surfaces and surface effects?" (175). *Mecánicas celestes* is, as already stated, all about the collision of surfaces. Let us examine such surfaces in close-up.

With its emphasis on stylistics, the wardrobes of *Mecánicas celestes*'s characters provide shorthand indicators of their personalities. Even though Ana during much of the film displays her androgynous self through masculine clothing, she begins and ends the film clothed in the bridal white gown of purity and innocence. As well as signaling the circularity of the film (and her life) "mi vida es un circulo vicioso" [my life is a vicious circle], her very name is a palindrome. The color white marks the virginity of Ana, which throughout the film remains unblemished. She is pure. She is untouchable, representing not a lack, but an absence of a reality that consists only of Manichean good and bad. Instead, Ana remains in an untouched, in-between space. This is not to say that she represents a static space. If we look closely at her white dress we do note a stylistic shift from that of the beginning and the end of the film.

In the colonial church of Venezuela, with its baroque altar, and formal groom, Ana's dress is the traditional lacey full gown crowned with a trailing white veil that is actually reminiscent of the Disney version of the gown in the film version of *Cinderella* (Soliño 77). She wears this as she escapes from the church, hops in a taxi, sits in a plane, and goes through French immigration, becoming progressively more disheveled. The trappings of a traditional wedding gown are fraying, losing their role as an indicator of ceremony and sacred space. This culminates when Lucila, later in the apartment, remarks in passing: "Muy original tu vestido" [very original dress]. The wedding dress, icon of submission and giving-over of oneself, has been converted into just one more outlandish outfit—an everyday dress, as if inverted, turned inside out from its usual significance.

At the end of the film, Ana once more is getting married, but this time the guests are casually dressed, and Armand, the gay groom, typically appears in crumpled clothes. Ana peers from behind the church door in a slim, modest white dress capped by a white turban and veil reminiscent of a nun or a Joan of Arc figure. She already has had a civil wedding where she wore pants and a grey top—not at all festive or indicative of a wedding moment. Now, regal in white, untouchable as a nun, she once more inverses the occasion as she presents herself as virginally alone, even while engaged in the "I do" moment of surrendering herself to her nontraditional husband who represents a means to an end. Through this marriage she can become legal and stay in France, and she also realizes a gesture of friendship to please Armand and his parents.

In both ceremonies Ana is simultaneously present and absent. The look on her face indicates that she does not in any way wish to participate in her own wedding. In the first instance, she does absent herself—literally—by running away and thus not completing the marriage. In the latter instance, she is tormented by the absence of her supposed real love, Alcanie—who surprisingly appears—and her unfulfilled goal of embodying Cenerentola in the opera/movie, which also surprisingly—or not—will come to pass, as the director Italo Medici also appears at the ceremony. The "marriage" here is the bringing together of Medici, as her professional if not personal "prince charming," and Mendoza; the last image reveals a star-struck Ana singing in what we assume is the film-to-be. Marriage here is not the joining together of man and woman, the woman to fulfill the man and his desires; rather, the woman here, through marriage, finds fulfillment of her dreams to be the singer she has longed to be, the fulfillment of a desire that the man concerned only mediates through his power as director. The presence of Alcanie indicates that "true love" will be consummated, but not through the traditional union of man and woman. Simultaneously, the positioning of the smiling Italo and Alcanie side by side fulfills the roles of Ana's patrons/ guides, prince/princess charming and parents. Identity roles become multiple, not one-dimensional as in a fairy-tale world of dichotomies. Surfaces collide and so proliferate.

In this reenactment of the Cinderella story, Ana does represent a lack for the prince charming, Italo, who holds the key to professional happiness/fulfillment. But, in fact, they need one another mutually: he needs her voice—not only her body—for his film, and she needs him as a tool for her voice, not his body or everlasting security. There is a lack on both sides, but the perfect shoe fit does not represent a fragmented body part, but rather a voice of identity that has already been described by Ana's Russian music teacher, and Italo himself, as a voice that speaks of a "stalwart soul and deep emotion." We are a long way away from the Grimm fairy tale of identity-less heroine, though still on the level of surface because of both the light stylistic form through which the story presents itself, and the formulaic story of Cinderella itself. Ironically, or interestingly, Ana exists as a full being, not a mythic voice, for Alcanie, her lover, and Celeste her enemy. As Grosz states: "The sites most intensely invested in desire always occur at a conjunction, an interruption, a point of machinic connection, always surface effects between one thing and another" (182). The interrupted marriages at the beginning and end of *Mecánicas celestes* represent an excellent example of an interrupted desire that produces an alternative unexpected desire—a trip to France; a role in a film. To understand this notion we must lose hold of our understanding of totalities and focus on surfaces, fragments, parts that exist outside of their integration and organization.

Throughout Ana's journey, *Mecánicas celestes* takes place in constant tension, wanting to present a coherent narrative and yet showing that reality inside-out, in terms of its presentation of characters and their sexuality, the urban space of Paris, the mixture of salsa and opera, animation and conventional comedy scenes. In fact, although the film has been called a "pastiche" or a "hybrid," I think, rather, that it is at play with this inversion of depth and surface and therein lies its strength and what makes it compelling.[3] As Grosz suggests, "As production, desire does not provide blueprints, models, ideals, or goals. Rather, it experiments, it makes: it is fundamentally aleatory, inventive" (180). *Mecánicas celestes* playfully presents a movement of resistance to a traditional socio-sexual structure, well-organized or chaotic, collective or fragmentary that implicitly combats this very structure and reveals space as transparent, while place appears as endlessly multiple.[4]

Outside the Box

By returning to the opening scene of *Mecánicas celestes* we can continue our study of gendered space through a "spectatorial topoanalysis" as Guiliana Bruno calls her spatial analysis of film (16). The classic diegetic panorama establishing shot of *Mecánicas celestes* is hyperbolic in that, rather than presenting a cityscape or an all-encompassing overview of a building or room to "set the stage" (as in Torres' other films), we are in fact presented with the celestial, deep dark-filled space flecked with planets and shooting stars. This establishing point-of-view shot, which also ends the film, presents the gods or destiny as a "celestial clockwork," as the point of view, the implicit narrator of the film—a *deus ex machina* in the old sense. Thus configured, the ensuing various absurd or magical occurrences would lead us to believe that we are witnessing not only the workings of the "witch" Celeste, but also the overall events managed by the heavens themselves. With such a view in mind then, the spatial similarities of beginning and end take on new resonance as in fact the difference in the superficial spaces here are of little concern, rather the voyage from one church to the next, the psychological journey of movement or e-motion takes front stage.

Let us replay once more the opening scene: from the heavenly diegetic view the camera zooms down to earth, then the continent of South America, then to Venezuela, to ultimately open up our gaze to a church and a wedding taking place there. What are the connotations here? From space we have arrived at place; that is, within the definitions of humanist geographers, such as Gillian Rose or Yi-Fu Tuan, place is considered imbued with a sense of history, of ontological attachment: "How a mere space becomes an intensely human place is a task for the humanist geographer; it appeals to such distinctly humanist interests as the nature of experience, the quality of the emotional bond to physical objects, and the role of concepts and symbols in the creation of place identity" (Tuan 269).

Or, as Berdoulay explains: "The idea of place implies a meaningful portion of geographical space. Place involves meaning for the people who build it, or live in it, or visit it or study it" (125). Having left the abstract astronaut view, the church excites the eye to place this spot within its cultural, religious, sociohistorical context. The intricately carved statues speak of Europe and its legacy to Latin America. The resounding notes of the Schubert's *Ave Maria* sound forth from a European context as well. Historically, the church speaks of Catholicism, a religion brought by the Old World colonizers to the New World, a place where, in particular, women, as well as the indigenous, traditionally have been marginalized, if not outright made invisible. This is a place where priests are men, and the ultimate authorities in the religious community, since women have little or no voice. In this sense, the music dominates and overshadows the actual words of the ceremony although we can see the characters mouth the words. But the words of Ana—the "I do"—do not come forth from the petrified face of the bride. Instead, with a violent pushing to the side of her veil and an athletic impetus unusual for a bride, Ana runs away from the altar, the men, and the ritual of the Church. A 1950s-style taxi takes her through the streets of a provincial-style colonial town typical of those left constructed by the Spanish. She enters her bedroom where walls are plastered with images of Paris and posters of Maria Callas. Obviously, from such images we can see that her gaze has been focused outside of Ángel Rama's *lettered city* and beyond the confines of the small town.[5] Ana carries little to no luggage except for the opera-singer poster. The flight seems spontaneous, although the room's decoration implies already that her desires to conquer other spaces have been in place for a while. We never find out how she learned French, which on her arrival in Paris we hear to be perfect. The usual ties of family, friends, discarded husband-to-be never enter into the dialogue or plot of the film. Ana is a woman who has cut all ties with her former home site. Because of her voyage by plane, to a new place, in search of identity, yet through scene after scene of almost a parodically superficial musical nature *Mecánicas celestes* can easily fall into the site-seeing theories of Guiliana Bruno: "Film is a modern cartography; its haptic way of site seeing turns pictures into an architecture, transforming them into a geography of lived, and living space" (9). Thus, in many ways, the viewing of *Mecánicas celestes* traces the cartography of superficial tensions between space and place, foreground and background, surface and depth. Let me give some examples.

The taxi ride provides comic relief at an expensive price, 700 francs or 100 dollars. The madcap ride contrasts with a former airport scene. In the taxi, Ana, glued to the window, watches the picture-postcard-perfect Paris unfold itself in small window-sized vignettes. The taxi driver has decorated the interior of his vehicle with French flags as if in no way to let us forget that the audience/Ana is now in France. But the taxi itself, the views of Paris, the Rossini opera that comes on the radio, the yapping/singing dog altogether serve to make light of this arrival scene so that we might focus on something else. All these are surface spaces that belie the background issue of the emancipation of Ana that is emphasized by the previous scene in the airport where, very quickly, as Ana walks to the immigration booth, there appears a dark-skinned man shouting to be let go as he is led away by immigration police. Not everyone has the freedom to choose their space, nor place. And it is this background scene of racial, politicized reality that serves as a contrast to the comic surface foreground of an escaping bride.

A similar scene of potential immigration disturbance occurs shortly thereafter when Ana arrives at the Parisian apartment, and there appears near the door a glimpse of an African woman looking very uncomfortable and on the verge of flight. Her appearance asks us to question why she looks fearful, where is her home, what does she do there, how does she fit in? This leitmotif of exile or spatial dislocation occurs throughout the film as the gendered space of Ana is questioned, develops, and turns itself inside out bringing with it questions of public/private, travel/home, and spaces in between as well. As the film unfolds, this immigration issue increasingly focuses on Ana's individual status as an illegal immigrant and the background predicament of others further recedes into an invisible space. For example, the police enter the café in search of Ana, the outsider, and when they ask the barman if he has seen any foreigners, he replies no and says sardonically "Je les reconnais toujours, tout de suite" [I always recognize them right away]. Of course, as they are discussing foreigners and their evident visual characteristics, Ana and her three Latin American illegal friends are sitting at a table in the background, once more emphasizing the tensions between foreground/background and what one should or should not see. Cities, in their multiple, intricate spaces can easily and simultaneously reveal and hide foreign elements. As Watts clearly states in his work:

> Thus bodies can be said to both produce and be produced by the city. And while cities obviously contain bodies, bodies also contain cities. . . . In other words, the various component parts of a city—its built environment, cultures, peoples networks and communication and so on—operate interdependently, producing—but importantly also restricting or suppressing—possibilities of expression, identification and, in a more acute sense, survival via any number of visible and invisible interactions and overlaps. (3)

The intermittent tropes of immigration make visible the power of the city in hiding and revealing the problems of being "different" that consume this film. Difference in *Mecánicas celestes* signals both the sexual and the ethnic. As Bruno suggests:

> to look with geographical eyes at feminist film theory, for example, could expose how travel in (film) space may map sexual difference and vice versa. . . . [This] could help us understand sexual difference in terms of space—as a geography of negotiated terrains. Thinking geographically could enable us to think of sexual difference in ways that integrate or even overcome symbolic notions as we venture into the terrain of an architectonics of gender. (85)

By delving into the background motifs of *Mecánicas celestes*, and turning inside out the various superficies of the film to find the in between spaces, this analysis corrodes the polarization of immobility/mobility, inside/outside, private/public, dwelling/travel so as to unloose the gender and ethnic boxing these oppositions entail.

Ana moves from one country to another, one culture to another, one language, Spanish, to another, French, and even one prescribed heterosexual position to lesbian status. All of this involves movement, so key to our spatial analysis here and antithetical to a traditional (Latin American) woman's position. Ana is not looking for a new home in her travel to Paris, and all that that site connotes.[6] To the contrary, Ana lives with four other women, then one woman, then a gay man; all casual living situations with little stability. Ana is truly depicted as a nomad, her anchors or points of stability being her poster of Callas, who magically sings at specific key moments during the film. In this sense, it does not seem that Ana necessarily has a destination for her travel as much as an existential goal or place—her "home" is her voice, and hence she can be at ease in any place if she has the freedom to exercise that voice. Ana desires what she has not had and thus looks for it where she has not been: "the desire does not take shape as a 'return' but rather as a 'voyage.' Nostalgia is substituted by dislocation" (Bruno 82). In this way Ana remaps dwelling to dwell within herself. Her travel is not that of territorial conquest. She dwells not to dominate; in fact, she is dominated and manipulated throughout the film. As a sign of her continued innocence, Ana is represented as completely malleable.

Reinventing the Box

Both Ana and *Mecánicas celestes*'s filmic texture are manipulated by Celeste. Besides issues of foreground/background, liberty, immigration and gender, we should also examine the animation scenes usually associated with Celeste. These scenes, in and of themselves, speak to surface and echo, parodically, the Disney conventions of "Cinderella." As well, the constant use of a camera that films within the film adds to *Mecánicas celestes*'s multiple layers. Both techniques emphasize the performativity of *Mecánicas celestes* and Ana's process of evolution.

The character of Celeste is most constantly accompanied by special effects and, of course, it is also she who wields a camera throughout the film. Her relationship to Ana from the very beginning is one of antagonism, once more following the inversion of tropes typical of the film. Although she is the "evil" character, she is blond, traditionally associated with the "good girls" of Hollywood, and in particular, Disney. And while Ana appears androgynous—it is Celeste who cuts Ana's hair to make her look more beautiful, but also more like a boy—it is Celeste, who with her hyper-sexy clothes and makeup, is truly androgynous or bisexual, at one point kissing Italo and later seducing Alcanie with whom she leaves to go to New York.

Celeste first appears on a rooftop with black clouds sprouting from her head. This designates her as from the heavens, but the dark heavens. Immediately, we realize that she will be personifying the role of the bad girl, "la mala." Another black moment occurs when she spray paints the screen of an art piece, which represents the actual camera lens for the audience, thus causing a "black-out," a clear indicator that she manipulates and trespasses the boundaries of filmic and outside space. In this way she less subtly inhabits an in-between space. But then, Celeste is not a subtle character. She is all bad and completely two dimensional, almost cartoonish. The cartoon aspect of Celeste comes forth most apparently in two scenes: her cabaret version of what it means to be a "modern woman," and in her video at the gala party where Ana first meets Italo.

In the first instance, Celeste appears through the eyes of Lucila as a 1950s female figure of what she interprets as a modern woman who will take New York by storm through her singing. She dominates the screen in a long gown with backup singers, in fact reminiscent of the real-life actress's (Arielle Dombasle) video clips and burlesque songs that she has performed throughout her career. So, the echo of real-life space intrudes through this mental-picture space in the larger filmic space of *Mecánicas celestes* itself. Celeste, however, immediately replaces this clip with her own mental picture of herself; much more postmodern in her clothing style, lyrics—"I eat spiders"—and multiple montage effect. Later, we witness the screening of her music video that is psychedelic and kitschy in its presentation, a very far cry from the lyrical sequences of opera that punctuate the film issuing from the voice of Ana—her character in opposition—the good girl. The weakness of Celeste is that she literally disappears in the film when she leaves with Alcanie for New York, never to return or be mentioned again.

Of course other characters also participate in musical numbers, always parodic in an Almodóvar-type style. The first appearance of Armand the waiter, and future groom of Ana, occurs as he issues forth from a trap door in the café singing. This instance represents pure comic relief. At another point, Alcanie does a cabaret musical number when she is in consultation with Toutou the Bantu witch doctor. Her theme is that of "hambre" [hunger] and again is a pure parody of the 1950s femme fatale, who in this case is attracted to someone of the same sex, not the traditional male figure. Both of these musical numbers throw into relief a certain frivolity or superficiality in contrast to the immigration troubles of Ana, and then her sexual conversion. They are "flat" sequences, stressing the superfice and the parody of the situation so as to add lightness. They also stress that, as Alcanie says, "space is laden with illusions."

Throughout *Mecánicas celestes* Celeste films Ana: at her arrival to the apartment in Paris, while cutting her hair, at the various parties and so on. In fact, she exerts from Ana a promise that she be allowed to film her as a condition for staying in the apartment. Celeste thus documents, manipulates, and edits Ana's life through film at the same time that she tries to negatively direct Ana's life. This adds a further layer of surface to the film as we acknowledge, or are forced to acknowledge through Celeste's filming, that we are actually watching a film. The sequences of the filmed Ana also serve to change the texture of *Mecánicas celestes* and add to the accumulated genre layers: fairy tale, opera, movie, comedy, romance, documentary, music video. This emphatically forces us to realize that *Mecánicas celestes* cannot be categorized, it resists closure, a characteristic that makes it, in part, difficult to attain commercial success.

Mecánicas celestes plays with various issues, not least with that of the surface, but also with the liminal spaces found between binary structures such as male/female, public/private, foreground/background. It is appropriate here to cite Samuel Delany:

> [T]he bulk of the extraordinarily rich, fragmentary and complex sexual landscape has been—and remains—outside of language. Most of it will remain there quite some time . . . But what is not articulated in certain orders of language—written language, say, and of a certain formality—does not mean that it doesn't exist. . . . The sexual experience is still largely outside language at least as it (language) is constituted at any number of levels. (107)

What appears to be a "light" film, taken in the context of Latin American film production, in fact questions such binaries and finds a power in the spaces of marginality if we scratch the surface, inside out.

Notes

1. I deliberately use here all versions of the film's title that emphasize the influence of globalization here. The title itself is linguistically unstable as, for example, researching the film involves using these multiple titles in order not to miss any reviews.

2. The songs "Mécaniques célestes" and "Mecánicas celestes (Final)" are in fact written by the actress who plays Lucila, Alma Rosa Castellanos.

3. See reviews of the film, such as those by Stephen Holden for the *New York Times*, Peter Stack of the *San Francisco Chronicle*, and James Berardinelli of *Reel Views*.

4. I rely heavily here on the work of humanist geography that clearly delineates between space as geometrical, a mathematical construct, and place as anthropological and imbued with vertical human relations.

5. Ángel Rama's *La ciudad letrada* (*The Lettered City*), published in 1984, clearly explains the hierarchy of architectonic power embodied in the construction of colonial Latin American urban sites, where the Church and the Government, housed in buildings along the plaza, or main square, hold full power that is gradually reduced as the buildings retreat further away from this central point.

6. Much has been written about the power of the "home" site in humanist geography studies. Let it suffice to say here that Gillian Rose in her work, along with many others, has made a critical impact in her analysis of the problems associated with the idealization of a home place in studies dominated by a "masculinist" perspective (53–56).

Works Cited

Agnew, John, and James Duncan, eds. *The Power of Place: Bringing Together Geographical and Sociological Imaginations*. Boston: Unwin Hyman, 1989. Print.

Bell, David, Jon Binnie, Ruth Holliday, and Robyn Longhurst, eds. *Pleasure Zones: Bodies, Cities, Spaces*. Syracuse, NY: Syracuse UP, 2001. Print.

Berardinelli, James. "*Celestial Clockwork*." Web. Jan. 15, 2012.

Bruno, Giuliana. *Atlas of Emotion: Journeys in Art, Architecture, and Film*. New York: Verso, 2002. Print.

Delany, Samuel R. *Longer Views: Extended Essays*. Hanover, NH: Wesleyan UP, 1996.

Grosz, Elizabeth. *Space, Time, and Perversion: Essays on the Politics of Bodies*. London: Routledge, 1995. Print.

Holden, Sephen. "*Celestial Clockwork*." Web. Jan. 15, 2012.

Keith, Michael, Steve Pile, eds. *Place and the Politics of Identity*. London: Routledge, 1993. Print.

Martí-Olivella, Jaume. "Textual Screens and City Landscapes: Barcelona and the Touristic Gaze." *Chasqui* 34.2 (2005): 78–94. Print.

Mitchell, Don. *Cultural Geography: A Critical Introduction*. Oxford: Blackwell, 2000. Print.

Rama, Ángel. *La ciudad letrada*. Hanover, NJ: Ediciones del Norte, 1984. Print.

Rose, Gillian. *Feminism and Geography: The Limits of Geographical Knowledge*. Minneapolis, MN: U of Minnesota P, 1993. Print.

Ross, Karen, and Deniz Derman, eds. *Mapping the Margins: Identity Politics and the Media*. Cresskill, NJ: Hampton, 2003. Print.

Soliño, María Elena. "From Perrault through Disney to Fina Torres: Cinderella Learns Spanish and Talks Back in *Celestial Clockwork*." *Letras femeninas* 23.2 (2001): 68–85. Print.
Stack, Peter, "Farce Runs Almost Like Clockwork." Web. Jan. 15, 2012.
Tuan, Yi-Fu. "Humanistic Geography." *Annals of the Association of American Geographers* 66 (1976): 266–76. Print.
Verstraete, Ginette, and Tim Cresswell, eds. *Mobilizing Place, Placing Mobility: The Politics of Representation in a Globalized World.* Amsterdam: Rodopi, 2002. Print.
Whybrow, Nicolas, ed. *Performance and the Contemporary City: An Interdisciplinary Reader.* London: Palgrave Macmillan, 2010. Print.

7

La Virgen de los Sicarios: From Novel to Film

(Barbet Schroeder, 2000)[1]

Óscar Osorio

La Virgen de los Sicarios, directed by Barbet Schroeder in 2000, is an eponymous film adaptation of the 1994 Colombian novel by Fernando Vallejo in 1994. According to most critics, the screenplay, written under the direction of Vallejo himself, is faithful to the literary text. Upon initial viewing, the audience is left with the impression that the film is "una adaptación bastante fidedigna de la novela de Vallejo" [a sufficiently faithful adaptation of the novel] (Jácome 153), and that it represents a successful translation of the literary text into the film medium. This impression is due to a series of direct links between novel and film in dialogues and a positioning of actors on location in the city. Additionally, the film is faithful to the original text as it follows Fernando's encounters with his lovers, crimes committed by the young assassins, circumstances surrounding their deaths, along with certain judgmental statements made by the narrator-protagonist. In the words of Edwin Carvajal, "La obra cinematográfica va captando paulatinamente las partes centrales de la obra, como una especie de sumario que va a plasmar con minuciosidad los acontecimientos o partes constitutivas del hecho literario" [The cinematography gradually captures the central parts of the novel, as if it were a form of summary meant to describe events or key parts of the literary work in a straightforward manner] (57).

In spite of these suggestions, a comparative reading of the screenplay and novel evokes the conclusion that the film represents a process of extension, suppression, and even embellishment of essential elements within the novel. These digressions bring about a transformation that fundamentally destroys the aesthetic purpose and ideological scope of the literary text. The film adaptation operates as an ethical-aesthetic sieve to produce a text that is not only different, but that in certain aspects contradicts the original.[2] The film's diegesis essentially follows the two texts, preserving the circular framework of the central stories: Fernando and Wílmar's story mirrors that of Fernando and Alexis. Vallejo's novel lucidly generates text-based processes to deepen this diegetic repetition through a series of events. Fernando finds Wílmar the day that Fernando leaves the apartment and enters the church of La América to plead "al Todopoderoso que puesto que no me mandaba la muerte me devolviera a Alexis" [to the All-Powerful who has not yet sent me death, I beg you to return Alexis to me] (90). This exchange suggests that God fulfilled Fernando's wish by returning Alexis to him in the form of Wílmar. A similar parallel is established that same day when Fernando and Alexis go to the church of San Antonio; at the church exit, Fernando reads a sentence written in Latin "bajo el reloj detenido" [under the stopped clock] (93). Earlier, the protagonist had entered the "templo de las mariposas" [temple of the butterflies] with Alexis and the clocks had stopped; with Wílmar he enters the temple of San Antonio where the clock has also stopped. In other words, Fernando sinks into eternity with both lovers. On numerous occasions Fernando refers to Wílmar as if he were Alexis (92, 95). When Wílmar undresses for Fernando for the first time, he sets aside his weapon in the same manner that Alexis had done earlier in the story (94, 15). In both scenes Fernando's character perceives the revolver as a symbol of his own death, and he further emphasizes its meaning, calling his lover "ángel de la guarda" [guardian angel] (12, 94). Other examples of Vallejo's circular intention follow: during the trip to Sabaneta with Wílmar, Fernando is engulfed by nostalgia, flashing back to playtimes with his brothers, "felices, inconscientes, despilfarrando el chorro de nuestras vidas pasábamos frente a Bombay persiguiendo un globo" [happy, unaware, frittering away our lives, we passed in front of the Bombay in pursuit of a paper balloon] (97). This mirrors precisely the scene from the old man's first trip to Sabaneta with Alexis when they also passed the Bombay, and it is the scene that opens and closes the initial sequence of the novel. When Fernando takes Wílmar to his apartment, the absence of music is disturbing to the boy, the same way that it had surprised Alexis when he arrived (17,93). Subsequently, when they go out into the streets and Wílmar unleashes his violence, the narrator tells us: "volvimos a lo de Alexis" [we are returning to the ways of Alexis] (98). Fernando venerates both Alexis and Wílmar with the same descriptive comment: ". . . mi niño, Alexis, el único" [my child, Alexis, the only one] (113), ". . . Wílmar, mi niño, el único" [Wílmar, my child, the only one] (118). Love songs inspire Wílmar's killings, earning Fernando's applause and delight, clearly recalling both motive and the protagonist-narrator's reactions to Alexis's crimes.

Delving more deeply into the story of Fernando and his lovers, there are additional textual elements supporting a cycle that completes three sequences within each of two segments in both narratives. During Fernando's journey with Wílmar, *El Difunto* tells the couple that *Ñato* had been killed. The narrator dedicates three pages to this story (106–109), which seems to have no verifiable connection to the main narrative. Fernando cannot believe that *El Difunto* is telling him that someone had killed *Ñato*, "el tira de Junín que detestaba a los maricas" [the shooter of Junín who hated gays], so he blends the present with the past, attesting that "al Ñato sí lo mataron, y ahí, en ese mismo punto del espacio, pero hace treinta años, cuando ni siquiera habían abierto la Avenida Oriental, que era una calle estrecha" [sure, they killed *Ñato*, and it was here, in the exact same place, but thirty years ago, when they hadn't opened up Oriental Avenue either, and it was a narrow street] (106–107). Fernando and Wílmar go up to Manrique to *Ñato's* house, to verify that it was the same *Ñato* that had been murdered thirty years earlier. When they open the coffin and see the body, he tells us that "en efecto era El Ñato, el mismo hijueputa. Las bolsas bajo los ojos, la nariz ñata, el bigotito a lo Hitler . . . Igualito. Era porque era. Pero si habían pasado treinta años, ¿cómo podía seguir igual? Ahí les dejo para que lo piensen el problemita" [it was indeed "El Ñato," the same fucker. The bags under the eyes, the pug-nose, the little Hitler mustache . . . the same little guy. That was just the way it was. But if thirty years had passed, how could he be the same? Here I leave you to think about this little problem] (109).

This pattern of repetition is contained in the Fernando-Wílmar saga, which replicates the story of Fernando-Alexis. Additionally, the narrator emphasizes this repetition, insisting that the reader not fail to notice it. I underscore his words here: "¿No sería que la realidad en Medellín se enloqueció y se estaba repitiendo?" [Wasn't it that reality in Medellín went crazy and kept repeating?] This question reveals the purpose and meaning of the *Ñato* episode, which is not just another story to support the idea of suspended time, but a story that repeats itself in a deadly, never-ending cycle. Throughout the text the narrator-protagonist continues to interject phrases to reinforce this circular vision: "Bombay era la misma como yo siempre he sido yo: niño, joven, hombre, viejo, el mimo rencor cansado que olvida todos los agravios por pereza de recordar" (13); "Que mi vida acabe como empezó, con la felicidad del que no lo sabe" (16); "La trama de mi vida es la de un libro absurdo en el que lo que debía ir primero va luego" (17); "Ese río es como yo: siempre el mismo en su permanencia yéndose" (31) [the Bombay was the same as I myself have always been: a child, young, a man, an old man, a resentful tired mime that forgets all insults because he is too lazy to remember; in fact my life ends as it began, with the happiness of not knowing; the storyline of my life is that of an absurd book in which what should come first comes later; this river is like me: always the same in its permanent state of going somewhere].

This repetition specifically refers to the reality of violence. *El Ñato* murdered homosexuals who were murdered twice, whose story is told in that of Wílmar (who will quickly be killed) who murders the murderer Alexis. It is the endless duplication of a violent story that repeats another violent story. By doing this, the narrative revolves around an especially incisive and explicit repetition of violence within the text: "Es que Colombia cambia, pero sigue igual, son nuevas caras de un mismo desastre" (12); "En el momento en que escribo el conflicto aún no se resuelve: siguen matando y naciendo" (28); "Una venganza trae otra y una muerte otra muerte" (29) [It's a fact that Colombia changes, but stays the same, with new faces of the same disaster; As I write, the conflict is still unresolved: they continue killing and being born; One vengeful act brings another and one death another death].

In all, this carefully choreographed repetition serves to convey a key precept of the text: that violence in Colombia is a recurring phenomenon. As the narrator states in the first paragraph of the novel, "es la sangre que derramará Colombia ahora y siempre por los siglos de los siglos, amen" [it is the blood that Colombia will spill now and always for centuries and centuries, amen] (8). This idea of never-ending violence has become commonplace in Colombia since the last century, as Daniel Pécaut concluded: "Un buen número de colombianos resultan persuadidos de que la violencia constituye la trama subyacente de su historia política y social. Una violencia que, más allá de su materialidad, comanda así un imaginario en el que adquiere la figura de un destino que estaría condenado a repetirse sin fin" [A substantial number of Colombians have been persuaded that violence constitutes the underlying storyline of their political and social history. This is a violence that, beyond its actuality, elicits the image of a national destiny condemned to be repeated without end] ("Reflexiones" 26–27).

In *Guerra contra la sociedad*, the French scholar insists on the idea of an image in which violence repeats itself without end: "No hay entonces nada de asombroso en que numerosos colombianos estén persuadidos de que la violencia no puede tener fin, ni en que, hacia 1978, cuando efectivamente resurgió, no hayan visto en ello sino el reinicio de la antigua violencia" [There is nothing surprising then about the fact that many Colombians are persuaded that violence couldn't end, nor that towards 1978 when violence effectively came back, they hadn't seen but the reemergence of the old violence] (111).

The cyclical structure of the text, defined by all of these repetitive elements is dramatized by an archaic and commonplace perception of violence in Colombia, which in turn is transformed into a hostile reality proposed by the novel. Vallejo's work supports a thesis of never-ending violence as defined in the apocalyptic spirit of the text, which concludes that it is impossible to escape its disastrous consequences. There is nothing more paralyzing in the search to understand Colombian violence than the idea that we Colombians are condemned to it, but in truth, violence can be controlled, except by those who believe that they cannot escape it. This explanation clarifies nothing and is undoubtedly confusing, still, as pointed out by Pécaut, "such mythical representation is completely contrary to anything that can be called history." (Pécaut, "Reflexiones" 65)Schroeder's screenplay for *La Virgen de los Sicarios* maintains the diegetic mirroring of the Fernando-Alexis and Fernando-Wílmar stories with the exception of various contrastive elements within the text. Certain supports for the afore-noted cyclical structure disappear: the identification between the assassin-lovers, duplicitous situations, Ñato's story, insistent statements by the narrator-protagonist about the idea of cycle, and the construction of the text itself. With the dissolution of this structural repetition, widely held interpretations are dismantled, bringing to light a clear discrepancy between the two texts.

This distinction is made clear in a comparative analysis of the beginnings and endings of the screenplay and the novel. The latter begins with a diegetic sequence that focuses on a yearning for the past and its dismantling by present corruption. From this temporal juxtaposition, a conceptual dichotomy is derived that deliberately drives the idea of the narrator's displacement. The initial movie sequence focuses viewer attention on the love relationship between Fernando and Alexis, and the introduction of Medellín as a city wracked by violence. Although an element of nostalgia appears in the layout of the Bombay cantina, the contrast is not as strong in the screenplay. Because of that, while the primary focus of the novel in the initial sequence is on the loss of the paper balloon at the end of the world (as in Fernando's childhood and happiness), the focus in the movie is on Alexis's nakedness with the gun placed on his penis, displaying it as a violent extension of the assassin's sexuality. The paper balloon image draws on the aesthetic structure of the literary text, pointing to the idea that yearning for an idyllic past reinforces the bitterness of a wasted present. It is precisely the perspective created by desperation for the present and the conviction of being condemned to its incessant repetition that causes the narrator-protagonist to advocate genocide as a solution. From the time it is introduced, the phallus-gun image also announces a central interest of the screenplay: interplays between love and death, sex and violence—these are integral relationships that are presented as a romantic relationship set in a city corroded by violence. It is evident that the aesthetic-ethical beginnings of both screenplay and novel successfully carry out their discrete intentions.

The endings are also different. In the novel, the narrator says goodbye, announcing that he is getting on a bus, creating an open framework which implies possibility for the cycle to continue. In the movie, the final picture is an ordinary scene of Fernando closing the curtains in his apartment as the screen fades into black while the song "Senderito de amor" ("Little Path of Love") is the background music. The whole scene emphasizes the concept of love and pain, and reinforces the impossibility of a continuation. It is clearly a narrative closure that leaves no room for any open-ended future possibilities, nor does it harbor the idea of a continuing cycle. In the novel's cyclical structure, violence in Colombia is ancillary to the idea of an inescapable tragic destiny, which is eliminated in the movie.

The screenplay does not incorporate a cyclical structure; instead it highlights the dialogue between love and death, exploring the experience of passionate love in the midst of violence. Because of this, the film emphasizes the erotic passion between the protagonists, which terminates with Wílmar's death. The suppression of cyclical formatting suggests a radical difference between the aesthetic-ethical statement of the screenplay and the movie.

There is also an enormous difference in the literary text and screenplay in the number and nature of crimes, characterizations of victims, and in portrayals of Fernando's reactions. One can compare the initial sequence of the novel—so poetic and effective in its launch, and so suggestive in its development of the characters—with the rest of the novel, which is filled with spasms of zealous homicidal entertainment. Not everyone has the book to hand. Everything is reduced to an exhaustive accumulation of repulsive comments and senseless crimes, animated by a few romantic references and language ploys.[3] The narrator seems to delight in it: "Y sigamos con los muertos que a eso es a lo que vinimos" [And we continue with the dead because this is what we came for] (62). Fernando seems to delude himself by delighting in the complicity and ferocious language to the point that the double character of Alexis-Wílmar is simply playing the role of an armed and murderous extension of the old lover, caught up in insane acts and verbal furor. Medellín is reduced to being a "fucking bitch in heat" filled with homicides, indigents, and the poor.

In the film, Alexis kills eight men, not a single woman, and no children. This is a much smaller number than the thirty-five homicides described in the novel. Beyond that, the screenplay mollifies the viewer by providing justification for each crime: four of Alexis's victims are assassins that had intended to murder the two protagonists; the two men in the metro and the taxi driver attempt to bully Fernando before Alexis reacts. In Wílmar's case, he kills one man (five fewer than in the novel): the whistler—who had attempted to pull his gun on them, and who turned out to be the murderous thief from the beginning of the movie. Because of this digression, partial justification for the murders can be found in a plea of self-defense. Additionally, when José Antonio Vásquez discusses the movie version of Alexis, he quips that the young killer "tiene tres o cuatro muertos" [has three or four deaths on his conscience] (00:06:55), but the novel states that Alexis committed ten murders before he met Fernando. Clearly, the reduction in the number of crimes, their justification, and the dispensing of the murders of women, of pregnant women, and of children (not counting the list that Fernando made of innumerable crimes by Wílmar), reveals a complex adaptation that intends, in principle, to avoid tiring the viewer, and to diminish moral sanctions against Fernando and his murderous lovers. Carvajal highlights this process, "También se debe decir que esta idea de mermar la carga emocional de las muertes se ve reflejada claramente en la película cuando se 'evitan' todas las muertes de niños que se producen en la novela" [One can also say that this idea of minimizing the emotional burden of the dead is clearly reflected in the movie when they 'avoid' all the deaths of children that occur in the novel] (66, nota 13). In the words of Osorio this generates "Un cambio importante en la postura del *ethos* que va de la novela a la película con respecto a este tipo de muertes" [An important change in the posturing of ethos that goes from novel to movie with respect to these kinds of deaths].[4] On the other hand, it destroys a fundamental poetic process from the written text: a mounting anticipation. The reiterated entertainment in the crimes is one of the most effective textual processes in the novel's plan to make violence visible, and to strike the reader, confronting him with violence to the point of saturation. The mitigation of intensity conveyed by the screenplay indicates an important transformation with respect to the ethical-aesthetic intent of the novel, deliberately modifying reader-viewer perception.

Along the same lines, Fernando's attitude toward these murders is completely different in the two versions. The taxi driver's death provokes a disapproving look in the screenplay, while in the novel, Fernando is impressed by the "espléndida explosión" [splendid explosion] of the car. In the movie, the murder of two men who try to bully Fernando in the metro[5] seems to inspire second thoughts in Fernando as he counsels Alexis "antes de disparar recapacita, cuenta hasta diez" [before shooting, reconsider and count to ten] (00:42:44) and he calls the assassin's attention to the fifth commandment: "No matarás!" [Thou shalt not kill!]. In the novel, the death of the female cafeteria employee is portrayed as senseless; the narrator comments that one should return to the scene of the crime because one can have an excellent lunch there, but in the screenplay Fernando stops Alexis when the youth pulls out his gun, and thus prevents the crime. In the film, before the murder of the "punkero," Fernando reacts with alarm: "¡Ay, niño, qué hiciste!" [Oh child, what did you do!], "¡Matar este pobre muchacho por nada! ¡Cómo pudiste!" [To kill this poor boy for nothing! How could you!] (00:33:06), "me siento culpable, niño" [I feel guilty, child] (00:34:52), "ya van siete noches" [it's been seven nights]. In the novel, Fernando watches the people approaching to look at the corpse and affirms, "Estaban ellos más contentos que yo" [They were happier than I] (27). Fernando happily counts off the 250 murders by his lover in the novel, but in the movie he reproaches Alexis: "¿Niño, qué está pasando? ¿Adónde hemos llegado? Todos estos muertos absurdos. Me remuerde la conciencia. ¿Cuántos llevamos?" [Child, what is happening? Where have we gotten to? All these senseless murders. My conscience is killing me. How many are we up to?] (00:55:41). The persistence of guilt in Fernando, to the point that it won't let him sleep, displays a film character that is diametrically opposed to the novel's narrator who jubilantly celebrates the crimes. It is essential to expose the absence of guilt in the character development of the novel's protagonist because it frames his criminal thought processes. Insisting on guilt in Fernando's film character distances him from the possibility of being completely criminal.

The film reinforces this distance with the notable absence of murders of children and pregnant women, resulting in the suppression of Fernando's celebrations of those deaths along with his humorous comments. However, this interpretation not only eliminates the protagonist's sense of humor with respect to the victims, but also his attitude toward nearly all the crimes that his lovers commit. It is important to note that Fernando does indeed react indolently and gleefully in the screenplay when confronted by some of his lovers' crimes, but only in the cases of assassins who try to murder the two of them. Upset by blood splashed all over his childhood home, Fernando insults the bleeding victim, and later laughs at Alexis's imitation of a pregnant woman, which the youth performs after shooting Fernando's would-be killer. Nevertheless, not even in these instances does the film allow Fernando to applaud or celebrate the crimes.

As noted in the above examples, the film justifies murder in various ways, and Fernando's reactions are presented as moral sanctions; in truth, as he himself declares, he is "contra toda violencia" [against all violence] (00:18:35) and because of this, "simplemente no hay que andar armados" [there is simply no reason to carry weapons] (00:35:26). This contradiction, combined with Fernando's repeated expressions of guilt for the crimes committed by his lovers, his efforts to admonish the boys, and the failure of the narrator-protagonist to glorify the crimes, suggest that the two Fernando characters—in the novel, and in the film—have opposing beliefs about human life. The screenplay's effort to moderate and soften the Fernando character results in lightening his burden of hate, giving the movie character a less repulsive personality with a distinctly moral dimension.

Furthermore, in the realm of universal values and in Fernando's discourse in the two texts, we find radically different presentations. In the novel, Fernando states that the community of his own adolescence embodied a deplorable ethnic and cultural condition: "No hay plaga mayor sobre el planeta que el campesino colombiano, ho hay alimaña más dañina, más mala. Pedir y pedir, matar y morir, tal su miserable sino" [There is no worse plague on the planet than a Colombian peasant, no vermin more noxious. Beg and beg, kill and die, such is his miserable fate] (83–84). This diatribe offers an explanation of the ethnic-historical character of the novel, according to which the perverted ethnic condition is a product of racial comingling during the Spanish conquest and colonization: "De mala sangre, de mala raza, de mala índole, de mala ley, no hay mezcla más mala que la del español con el indio y el negro: producen saltapatrases o sea changos, simios, monos, micos con cola para que con ella se vuelvan a subir al árbol" [Of bad blood, bad race, bad natured, of bad laws, there is no worse mixture than that of Spaniard, Indian, and Black: it produces a mixed race or should I say idiots, apes, monkeys, monkeys with long tails so they can get back up in the trees] (90). For Fernando, this upbringing instilled in him a profound rejection: "Me avergüenzo de esta raza limosnera" [I'm ashamed of this beggarly race] (15) and he offers a genocidal solution to the problem: "Esta es una raza ventajosa, envidiosa, rencorosa embustera, traicionera, ladrona: la peste humana en su más extrema ruindad. ¿La solución para acabar con la juventud delincuente? Esterminen la niñez" [This is an opportunistic race, jealous, deceitfully resentful, treacherous, thieving: human pestilence at its lowest extreme. The solution to end juvenile delinquency? Exterminate childhood] (27–28). Additionally, since one of the expressions of this ethnic and cultural perversion is poverty, he insists on a genocidal remedy directed at the poor: "Mi fórmula para acabar con ella [la pobreza] no es hacerles caso a los que la padecen y se empeñan en no ser ricos: es cianurarles de una vez por todas el agua y listo" [My prescription for ending it (poverty) is to pay no attention to people who suffer from it and who insist on not being rich: it is simply to poison them all at the same time with cyanide in the water, and there you go] (68), "Mi fórmula para acabar con la lucha de clases es fumigar a esta roña (los pobres)" [My formula for ending class warfare is to fumigate this filth] (96); "Por razones genéticas el pobre no tiene derecho a reproducirse" [For genetic reasons, the poor don't have the right to reproduce] (104). As central elements to reproduction, according to Fernando, women and children are responsible for the continuation of the race and poverty; he starts up against children: "La niñez es como la pobreza, dañina, mala" [Childhood is like poverty, infectious, evil] (106), and against women whom he categorizes as "putas perras paridoras" [fucking bitches in labor] (64) or "perra humana embarazada" [pregnant human bitch] (101). A genocidal thought is brought to light in the narrator's sentences, along with a radical misogyny, a deep disdain for others and for human life in general. Using ethnicity as an explanation for the idea that the Colombian disposition has no choice but to be inclined toward violence and disorder, he in turn argues about regulatory institutions and their influence in creating a malformed society. In the descriptive revealing of the violent and disorganized development of the Medellín gangs and their language, the narrator-protagonist builds a diagnosis for the problem of Colombian violence.[6] This diagnosis is consistent with the idea that defines the framework of the novel: that Colombian violence is cyclical and Colombians are condemned to suffer from it endlessly. Fernando believes that if a violent disposition in part defines our identity, in our ontological essence and in our genes (from races that are inferior and weaker due to their mixing), and additionally, that the institutions don't work properly, then we Colombians have no exit from violence nor from social decay. This verification permits the narrator-protagonist to repeatedly insist on what seems to him to be the only possible solution: annihilate the poor.

The aforementioned diagnosis and its proposed treatment are consistent with the argumentative development of the text, which revolves around crime and is key to the realization of the narrator's genocidal ideas. Claudia

Ospina notes: "Se propone en esta novela una fórmula genocida como solución al conflicto y caos reinantes que sólo llevan al exterminio total de su región y, por extensión, de su país" [In this novel a genocidal remedy is presented as the solution for conflict and reigning chaos which can only be alleviated by the total extermination of the region, and by extension, of the country] (164). Felipe Oliver comes to a similar interpretation: "Después de que todos los relatos políticos, religiosos, económicos, etcétera, han ido cayendo uno detrás de otro, ¿no es acaso un acto de necedad creer en algo que no sea la extinción de la especie? Se trata de una postura desde luego radical, pero en esta exageración reside el encanto de Vallejo" [After all the stories about politics, religion, money, etcetera, which have fallen one after another, isn't it perhaps a necessary act to believe in something beyond the extinction of the species? He describes a truly radical position, but in such exaggeration resides the appeal of Vallejo] (50). Nonetheless the critic's final accolade is disquieting. Oliver derives ethical and aesthetic pleasure from the novel in Fernando's proposition for a genocidal solution, which at the same time he perceives as a radical exaggeration. Ethically and aesthetically, I find this unacceptable.

In the screenplay, in contrast, most of these statements are suppressed and those that survive are not as ferocious; even some of these are completely stripped of their original aggression or diminished due to a less aggressive framing lent by the actor's interpretation of character and context. The interpretation of Fernando by Germán Jaramillo softens the negative baggage that his actions could provoke: warm voice, measured mood, harmonious manner, a permanent smile, modest and informal dress. Another important element in this process of mitigation is the laughter and festivity with which the assassin-lover celebrates Fernando's notions. In fact, it is recorded in a code of humor and the character returns to being a more pleasant individual.

For example, when asked if he likes women, Fernando answers that "depende de los hermanitos que tenga" [it depends on her little brothers]. This popular joke is the same in both texts, but the narrator-protagonist of the novel moves immediately into a "en serio" [serious] sentence: "Para mí las mujeres es como si no tuvieran alma. Un coco vacío. Y que por eso con ellas es imposible el amor" [For me, women are like they don't have a soul. An empty coconut. And because of this love is impossible with them] (18). The movie eliminates these words, which are so important in the written text to set up the narrator-protagonist's misogynistic characteristics. The suppression of this misogynistic content in the film relegates Fernando's offensive action to a mere popular joke, helping to mold the film character as a player in the film, and to elicit empathy from the viewer. The actor reinforces this character in the scene, so that the sentence is spoken clearly, with a naughty smile, thus depriving the novel's character of his poisonous traits. This process of elimination and recontextualization positively transforms a deeply condemning feature of the original text.

In tandem with the transformation of Fernando's character and the mitigation of his criminal thinking, the story of his amorous passion is enhanced in the movie. Although the narrator of the novel clearly and repeatedly avoids describing his passionate nights with the assassins, the screenplay delights in them. Already in the first sequence, the film offers up a set complete with a mirror in which the lovers are amusing themselves in multiple positions during an explicitly sexual act. Later on, camera shots also develop the sexual encounter between Fernando and Wílmar. Additionally, passionate kisses with Fernando and his lovers appear in the first scenes.[7] The same thing happens in the exchange of amorous expressions between the characters. In the novel these phrases arise in situations that carry a defiant message relative to Fernando's affectionate intentions: in front of the Virgin, or in a church (15, 94), in phrases laden with misogyny (19) or deprecating family or community (24–15, 30, 40, 45), or at the crime scene (25–26, 28, 71). In the movie, on the other hand, they take on an emphatic relevance; amorous exchanges are placed after the scene in which the assassins are murdered in front of a pregnant woman. The lovers appear in an apartment and Alexis, with a pillow under his shirt, mockingly imitates the desperate screams of the woman in front of the bodies. The scene ends as the camera zooms in on the lovers as they look into each other's eyes. Fernando says with heavy emotion, "Alexis, niño, eres lo más hermoso que me ha dado la vida" [Alexis, child, you are the most beautiful thing that life has given me] (00:59:40). The feeling of his voice is enhanced with soft piano music and full sunlight that highlights the lovers' gestures and the camera moves around, making the scene intensely compelling while the lovers kiss passionately. In the novel, the context of Fernando's statement is brought to light at the crime scene, but in the movie it is quickly separated in order to create a more intimate connection, one that reinforces the intensity of the words and the serious nature of the old lover's declaration. In the novel, the narrator-protagonist's amorous comments are obviously not intended for his lovers; they are for his readers, and they are a confrontation.

Another mechanism by which the love story is enhanced in the movie is the idea of sacrifice. In Alexis's death scene, they are walking along the avenue when Alexis sees the assassins approaching. Since he had lost his weapon in the gutter, the boy cannot defend himself and can only call out to warn Fernando, calling him by his first name for the first time, and move in front of him to stop the bullets from reaching the body of the old lover. Alexis also prevents Fernando's death in the novel, but he neither intervenes nor establishes the idea of sacrifice, which is so effective in bringing the love story to the forefront and elevating it to become the primary focus of the screenplay.

The grief for Alexis is also fundamental in signaling the dominance of amorous passion in the screenplay. In the literary text less than four weeks pass from the time of Alexis's death to the point at which Fernando finds a new love. Fernando met Alexis on a Monday in December, a little after the death of Pablo Escobar, which occurred on December 2, 1993 (61). It must have been very days after that because, before the year ended, he gave us detailed descriptions of twenty-four murders by Alexis (64–65). By the time Alexis was murdered, the lovers had been together for seven months (82). When Fernando met Wílmar, the same president, César Gaviria, was still in office; he would be replaced on August 7, 1994. During these few days of grief, Fernando visits Alexis's mother to give her some money and to confirm the name of Alexis's assassin. The few paragraphs that are focused on the experience of grief are cut by pages dedicated to an in-depth analysis of Medellín and its hate-filled neighborhoods. Only in the end of the passage does Fernando narrate a dream in which he sees himself in a church, surrounded by beggars and addicts, and he talks about his pain. What happens in the film is completely different. When Fernando emerges from his grief, there had been a change in government and president Ernesto Samper Pizano had taken over. That is to say that months passed before Fernando achieved some normalcy and would meet Wílmar. This allows the viewer to realize the intensity of feeling resulting from the loss of Alexis. The grief scene takes up several camera shots and lasts 10 minutes (1:40:00–1:50:00), which indicates its importance in the film. Additionally, the intensity of Fernando's pain is emphasized using fast-forwarded photography to convey the duration of inclement weather that closes the scene. The entire sequence serves to express Fernando's sense of loss over the death of his lover. Furthermore, when he visits Alexis's family, sorrow is brought to the forefront with scenes of bloody rivers of rain and in the image of a blue lagoon in which Fernando's happiness would die. Afterward, during a dream in which he sees himself on the Patio del Tango, Fernando appears bearded, bloated and wracked with pain, inconsolable on the church floor. The dream scene fades into a shot of Fernando crying on the dining room table in his apartment. In a subsequent sequence, Fernando and Wílmar enter the apartment for the first time to consummate their relationship and the camera focuses on trash: papers and bottles strewn in all directions. This disorder creates a violent dialogue within the character's personality and exposes his pain. Osorio highlights the way in which the screenplay emphasizes the character's pain: "Este lapso mayor de tiempo concentra en la mirada del espectador una mayor sensación del dolor que ha significado en Fernando la muerte de Alexis; lo hace más humano en este sentido, menos cínico frente al dolor" [This major time lapse focuses the viewer on the intensity in which Fernando experiences the death of Alexis, which makes him more human and less cynical when confronted by such pain].

In contrast with sections of the novel dedicated to the deterioration of Medellín, the movie only references this decay in the poor masses and criminal elements that build up around the church in Fernando's dream and during the visit with Alexis's mother describing the miserable state of her home filmed through Fernando's eyes. In the novel, this hate-laden point of view is aligned with the painful and pathetic images of the slums, and is replaced by a single statement from Alexis's little brother, about six years old, who swears to avenge his brother's death.

The preeminence of the love story over that of the violence is illustrated in the nude scene of Alexis in the "butterfly room," during the first sequence of the film. Alexis undresses at Fernando's command. In a full shot of the room, Fernando's partial figure is sharply outlined while Alexis's entire body is lit softly in the background. Alexis has his revolver in his right hand and the weapon is placed over his penis. Behind and to the left side of Alexis, there is a sculpture of the Archangel Saint Michael, and a wall full of clocks. Alexis moves toward the nightstand to deposit the weapon so he can cavort with the man who will become his lover. These camera shots are especially powerful because they highlight the key elements of the screenplay: the youthfulness of the assassin, and the old age of the lover (clear references to concepts of life and death, the bargain for murderous violence: the old live on, the young will die); the religious figure of the Archangel alludes to the Apocalypse, symbolizing the violence of Medellín and the solution of extermination; extreme close-ups focus on the details of the talismans and the revolver, pointing to definite traits of the assassin: religious fetishism and violence; the clocks reference time—suspended in the novel, dynamic in the movie; the penis-revolver merges sex and violence. Referring to this image of the weapon on top of the assassin's genitals, Gastón Alzate proposes that "la construcción social de la masculinidad para muchos jóvenes colombianos, sea esta heterosexual u homosexual y aunque muchos se nieguen a reconocerlo está mediatizada por las armas. Alexis se cubre el sexo con 'el fierro' como símbolo de esta construcción simbólica masculina" [the social structure of masculinity for many young Colombians, whether heterosexual or homosexual and even though many refuse to recognize it, is influenced by weapons. Alexis covers his penis with 'the steel' as a metaphor for this symbolic interpretation of masculinity] (9). It does not seem to me that one can generalize the relationship between weapons and masculinity among Colombian youth, certainly much more in the fringe sectors of the city. Nevertheless, it seems clear that this powerful image is not exhausted by its ironic connection to masculinity, but is actually served by the complex merger of violence and sex, or death and love, or *Eros* and *Thanatos*, which is the symbolic construct at the heart of the screenplay. The sequence combines violence and death, incarnate in the figure of the lover: the assassin services the fulfillment of Fernando's sexual desires at the same time that he materializes the old man's criminal inclinations. But the scene culminates when Alexis leaves the revolver on the stand and lies in bed waiting for his lover, which indicates that in this melding of violence and sex, passionate love overcomes all else: the take closes with a final scene of the two lovers engaged in bodily pleasures framed in the reflection of a mirror.

The same occurs in the final shots of the movie. Fernando appears, pulling the curtains of the apartment and fading into black while "Senderito de amor" is playing: a song that expresses intense nostalgia over lost love. In this way, it emphasizes Fernando's profound sense of desolation aroused by the loss of his lover. This song has already been heard at the beginning of the movie. When Fernando and Alexis visit Sabaneta, they hear it while they drink aguardiente in the Bombay bar and it causes such a strong emotional response in Fernando that he collapses sobbing on the table. The song symbolizes the definitive loss of family, of the past, and of happiness. In repeating it at the end of the film, the song, which comes with all this heavy baggage, creates a merger of lost loves and happiness of the past with the loss of recent love, conveying a final sense of absolute despair.

Other elements of the literary text that disappear in the adaptation to screenplay are the story of the slums, the ethnic explanation for the violence and its cyclical characteristic, and the story of the degradation of language as it mutates into the "slang" of the slums. All of this supports the idea of the film's failure to consider explanations based on historical and cultural origins, as well as its bypass of social mechanisms that encouraged violence in Medellín. The movie's inattention to these aspects, which are fundamental to the novel and which explain the hate of the narrator-protagonist and the violence of his assassins, once again points out the discrepancies between the ethical-aesthetic presentation of the film and the novel.

Passionate love, as much in the novel as in the movie, is the only thing that satisfies Fernando, and that offers some meaning to his existence.

It seems that in this Medellín full of the poor, of assassins, and of noise; all other aspects of life are disposable to Fernando. In conclusion, while violence dominates in the novel, passionate love dominates in the film: the screenplay tells a story about duplicitous love. The novel is a dense story of violent action with occasional relief found in passionate love, still in the context of a violent city. This reversal defines profound differences in the two texts. The powerful argumentative core of the novel, ideologically and structurally subject to the systematic whims of criminal thought, practically disappears in the screenplay. Through techniques of attenuation (minimization, suppression, or highlighting) of important elements within the literary text, the film distances itself from the mental intrigue and builds a vision of Medellín which, filtered by amorous interaction, results in a less devastating presentation.

Notes

1. With sincere gratitude to Marsea Wynne (advised by Professor Andrés Lema-Hincapié and M.A. Student Michael Clarkson) for her interpretive English translation of my essay. Marsea Wynne also translated into English all the excerpts from *La Virgen de los Sicarios* by Fernando Vallejo.

2. I am not unaware of the fact that the media of novel and film are different modes of expression and that, because of this, many of the transfigurations that arise in the adaptation are due to constraints of the film medium. [I give credit to professor and friend Alejandro López for this point.] However, the majority of digressions that I single out in this work fall under an authorial intent that can be traced back to an aesthetic-ethical production of the screenplay which substantially distances itself from that of the novel. In this case, these transfigurations, whether they are intentional, or whether they are limitations of the film media, are substantial, and radically alter the original text. Because of this, I do not share the judgment of Carvajal (2004), according to whom these variations "se presentan en detalles mínimos que por el estilo y la estética, seguramente del director, y del lenguaje propiamente cinematográfico, se hicieron pero que no afectaron la esencia misma de la historia, es decir, su argumento" [present themselves in minute stylistic and aesthetic details, surely due to the nature of cinematography. They were implemented without impacting the essential argument of the story] (57).

3. This overwhelming play of crimes is so exhaustive that critics cannot agree on the number of incidents: In the instance of the murders by Alexis, Erna von der Walde, in "La sicaresca colombiana," adds up 15; Carvajal counts 35; José Osorio approximates "more than 100." I agree with Carvajal: there are 35.

4. This essay does not have page numbers.

5. As Carvajal explains, this scene is a transformation of the passage from the novel in which a woman and children are murdered on the bus.

6. Fernando disparages other efforts to explain the phenomenon coming from disciplines such as sociology (100).

7. These scenes are tremendously provocative in the context of a society like Colombia's, so conservative in its views on sexuality and with almost no experience with "queer" cinema. Regarding the purpose of these scenes, Fernández L'Hoeste comments, "Explicit representations on the large screen, however, were still a remote event. Thus the personification of the world of *sicarios*—which in and by itself was an uncomfortable topic for many Colombians—contributes to an expansion in the construction of national identity in more than one way" (550). These were decisive for a certain sector of Colombian intellectuals who expressed furious judgment of *La Virgen de los Sicarios*, which was in fact embarrassing for the rest of them, given the quality of the discussion and the precariousness of the argument. I won't delve into the details of this discussion, but it was evident that the film circulation, as well as the novel, benefitted from the scandal.

Works Cited

Alzate, Gastón. "El extremismo de la lucidez: San Fernando Vallejo." *Revista Iberoamericana* 79.222 (2008): 1–17. Web. Oct. 10, 2011.

Carvajal Córdoba, Edwin. "*La Virgen de los Sicarios*: Entre el encanto literario y la frustración fílmica." *Estudios de Literatura Colombiana* 15 (2004): 51–78. Print.

Fernández L'Hoeste, Héctor. "From Rodrigo to Rosario: Birth and Rise of the Sicaresca." *Revista de Estudios Hispánicos* 42 (2008): 543–57. Web. Sept. 18, 2011.

Jácome Liévano, Margarita Rosa. *La novela sicaresca: Exploraciones ficcionales de la criminalidad juvenil del narcotráfico*. Diss. The University of Iowa, 2006. Web. Nov. 20, 2010.

Oliver, Felipe. "Después de García Márquez: Tres aproximaciones a la novela urbana colombiana." *Revista de Humanidades* 23 (2007): 41–46. Web. July 19, 2011.

Osorio, José. "*La Virgen de los Sicarios* y la adaptación cinematográfica." *Letralia* 219 (2009): Web. Sept. 20, 2010.

Ospina, Claudia. *Representación de la violencia en la novela del narcotráfico y el cine colombiano contemporáneo*. Diss. University of Kentucky, 2010. Web. Nov. 12, 2011.

Pécaut, Daniel. "Reflexiones sobre la violencia en Colombia." *Violencia, guerra y paz: Una mirada desde las ciencias sociales*. Trad. Anthony Sampson. Cali, Col.: Universidad del Valle, 2001. Print.

———. *Guerra contra la sociedad*. Colombia: Planeta, 2001. Print.

Rama, Ángel. *La ciudad letrada*. Hanover, NJ: Ediciones del Norte, 1984. Print.

Schroeder, Barbet, dir. *La Virgen de los Sicarios*. Colombia; Francia: Les Films du Losange. 2000. DVD.
Vallejo, Fernando. *La Virgen de los Sicarios*. Bogotá: Alfaguara, 1998. Print.
Walde Uribe, Erna von der. "La sicaresca colombiana: Narrar la violencia en América Latina." *Nueva Sociedad* 170 (2000): 222–27. Web. May 17, 2011.

8

A Case Study in Transnational Gay Auteurism: *Mil nubes de paz cercan el cielo, amor, jamás acabarás de ser amor*

(Julián Hernández, 2004)[1]

Paul Julian Smith

Much research on globalizing cinemas focuses on commercial genres. In the case of Mexican cinema, particular attention has been paid to the three directors held, outside Mexico at least, to have kick-started a "New Wave" of feature films that aspire to artistic quality while still achieving box office popularity around the world: Alfonso Cuarón (Mexico City, 1961), Guillermo del Toro (Guadalajara, 1964), and Alejandro González Iñárritu (Mexico City, 1963). As is well known, these three filmmakers have successfully combined feature-length films made in Mexico with international projects, shot in the United States or Europe. Some of those most recent projects of their Cha Cha Cha Company have been: *Biutiful* (2010), *Mother and Child* (2009), and *Rudo y Cursi* (2008).

It is somewhat paradoxical or even ironic that this perceived renaissance took place (as several commentators have noted) after changes in the state funding regime that many predicted would destroy, not revitalize, Mexican cinema. Industry sources such as Rosa Bosch (of Tequila Gang production company founded in 1998)[2] claim that is precisely because the new big three directors already mentioned, profiting from global distribution and promotion, were free from financial and artistic dependence on state-controlled Instituto Mexicano de Cinematografía (IMCINE) and that therefore they could stage a "take-over" of the industry from an older generation identified with the once canonized and now neglected Mexican filmmakers Artuno Ripstein and Paul Leduc (Wood 168).

This essay treats rather the phenomenon of a transnational auteurist film, in which the achievement of distribution depends on a fine balance between artistic elements held to be local or indigenous and those that stake a claim to an international cinematic tradition. As in the better known case of Carlos Reygadas (*Japón* [*Japan*, 2002], *Batalla en el cielo* [*Battle in Heaven*, 2005], *Luz silenciosa* [*Silent Light*, 2007]), Julián Hernández is a transnationally distributed young filmmaker from Mexico whose four features to date—*Yo soy la felicidad de este mundo* (*I am Happiness on Earth*, 2013), *Rabioso sol, rabioso cielo* (*Raging Sun, Raging Sky*, 2009), *El cielo dividido* (*Broken Sky*, 2006), and *Mil nubes de paz* (*A Thousand Clouds of Peace*, 2004)—are unapologetically art-house in narrative structure and film form. Unlike Reygadas, who has appealed to graphic, but notably unerotic, scenes of heterosexual activity, Hernández seeks to inscribe himself within a gay or homoerotic tradition that includes both European old masters like Reiner Werner Fassbinder (1945–1982) and Pier Paolo Pasolini (1922–1975) and gestures perhaps toward contemporary Asian auteurs, most especially Wong Kar Wai (1958) and Tsai Ming Liang (1957).

As we shall see, the theme of homosexuality is central, but contested and contradictory, here. The filmmaker and his critics both defend the specificity of a homoeroticism that is held to be hitherto absent from Mexican cinema—thus inadvertently obscuring the contribution of the prolific and durable gay auteur Jaime Humberto Hermosillo (Aguascalientes 1942)—and insist that Hernández's films are universal in both thematics and audience address: they are said to treat an erotic and psychic experience that is relevant, if not accessible, to all. Although the director insists, auteur-like, that "all of my films are about me," one of *Mil nubes*'s cast, more diplomatic or cautious, claims that the film "goes beyond homosexuality: it's a love story and love has no limits" (Cómo hacer cine).

I will suggest that, in spite of such disavowals, homosexuality is inextricable from auteurism here. Only when an overtly gay thematics—the common preoccupation of Hernández's oeuvre—is couched within the rarified aesthetics of the art movie is it acceptable to Mexican critics and audience alike, even as they decry the "homophobia" of their own cinematic tradition.[3] The conspicuous and very specific pleasures of young male bodies are thus bought at the cost of a transnational art-house technique, much of which is, ironically, shared by the very heterosexual Carlos Reygadas: an overtly aestheticized cinematography, an editing strategy that is (over-)reliant on the punishingly long take, and a style of narrative and characterization whose premises remain willfully obscure. Even the impassivity and affectlessness of the central performance in *Mil nubes* (attributed by unsympathetic critics to its young protagonist's inexperience) is reminiscent of grand European auteurs such as French director Robert Bresson (1901–1999). The cultural distinction that such cinema seeks, potentially threatened by the all-too-obvious pleasures of the naked ephebe, is thus assured by a self-conscious distancing from commercial aesthetics.

The unfeasibly long titles that are Hernández's trademark ("a thousand clouds . . ." claims to be taken from a poem by Pasolini)[4] are perhaps the most self-evident of these strategies. Indeed, in *The Rules of Art*, his study of the perilous balances and trade-offs between culture and commerce, Pierre Bourdieu cites "the obscure and disconcerting title" (137) as one of the essential characteristics of the artwork that aspires to distinction by offering consecrated critics the chance to display the ingenuity of their interpretative skills.

It is perhaps no accident that Mexico's most acerbic critic, Jorge Ayala Blanco, the scourge of both the official state cinema of Ripstein and the new transnational independent films of González Iñárritu, has been unusually supportive of Hernández, even naming *Mil nubes de paz* (*One Thousand Clouds of Peace*) as one of the top twenty films in the history of Mexican cinema (*La Jornada*). And if authoritative Mexican critics are eager to display their critical ingenuity when confronted by disconcerting obscurity, then those on the Left at least (in *La Jornada*, again) are equally anxious to show that, unlike their fellow Mexicans, they are unafraid of the rather different challenge of relatively graphic gay content that includes male frontal nudity.[5]

It is worth looking a little closer at the discourse used in support of Hernández by the licensed heretic, Jorge Ayala Blanco. Writing even before the first feature has been released in his collection *La fugacidad del cine mexicano*, Ayala Blanco has no qualms in calling Hernández's informally distributed short *Hubo un tiempo en que las noches dieron paso a largas noches de insomnia . . .* (*Long Sleepless Nights*, 2000) a "rare cult film of the precarious national [i.e., Mexican] gay cinema" (444). But he takes care to distance it from global gay film, which, Ayala Blanco claims, tends to aim for the "shocking" gesture—the word is given in English—or a "flamboyantly camp avant-gardism [that is] post-[Derek] Jarman." Praising Hernández for the subtlety of his "textures" and tones (white, grey, and black), Ayala also celebrates the narrative "reticence" ("pudor") whereby he carefully erases his own "footsteps" or "traces" ("huellas") from the script he has himself written (446). These "slippages of pleasure," we are told, go beyond a simple statement of the social exclusion of homosexuals in contemporary Mexico to address the "enigmatic splendour" of young men (or "young people" [jóvenes]) in general (447). According to Ayala Blanco, Hernández thus re-stages Pasolini's *Una vita violenta* (*Violent Life*, 1962), transferring the exotic Roman ragazzi to prosaic Mexico City.

Like Hernández himself, then, Ayala Blanco attempts to balance local reference with global resonance and to trump social testimony with an aesthetic ambivalence as fleeting and formless as the slippages of desire. The Mexican critic eases the way for the budding auteur to adopt a perilous and provisional—but potentially prestigious—position in the contested Mexican cultural field. It is no surprise that, in a book subsidized by the government institutions devoted to culture and cinema—the Consejo Nacional para la Cultura y las Artes (CONACULTA) and the IMCINE— *Mil nubes* was chosen as the first of just four Mexican films representing 2004, the year of its release (González Vargas 242–45). To propose institutional motives for Hernández's unlikely and qualified success is, however, not to diminish the sheer difficulty of his achievement, which may not have been helped by his brave and open self-identification with Mexico's gay community. Although he was a graduate of the official film school, the CUEC at Universidad Nacional Autónoma de México (UNAM), several sources (including Ayala Blanco, who has taught a course on film aesthetics at that same school) claim that Hernández was unpopular and unappreciated there. After numerous shorts, his first feature, *Mil nubes*, was shot on a micro-budget and temporarily abandoned midway through because of lack of resources. Hernández has thus been forced to embrace flexible accumulation in the low budget production of features with high-end production values—seen especially in his business partner Diego Arizmendi's luminous black and white cinematography—making highly uncommercial features against all the odds.[6]

Nevertheless, Hernández has attempted to offset production difficulties at home with distribution possibilities abroad. Like other independent Mexican directors—including, ironically, González Iñárritu—Hernández has managed to exploit a potent reverse cultural flow. Hernández's debut feature was consecrated at numerous foreign festivals before it received, a full year after screenings abroad, a limited theatrical release in Mexico that led to nominations for eight Ariel awards.[7] Once more, gay interest (far from harming prospects of distribution) may have actively helped: *Mil nubes* won the Teddy award at Berlin, a dedicated LBGT prize. In Madrid the film's only screenings have been at the dedicated Lesbian and Gay Festival and, subsequently, at an officially sponsored round up of Mexican cinema, a nice pairing of queer and nationalist showcases that points to a confluence of two brands of identity politics.[8] Likewise Hernández balances respectful nods to Pasolini—that immoderately long title again—with admiring references to that most Mexican of Golden Age directors, Emilio "El Indio" Fernández.

While Hernández has insisted in an interview that his first picture achieved its foreign success because it refused to recycle clichés of both homosexuality and *mexicanidad*, in fact his films appeal to a mediascape of fluid and irregular representations that are difficult to place. His features are at once materially embedded in the authentic shooting locations of Mexico City (*Mil nubes* offers—like *Amores perros* [*Love's a Bitch*, 2000]—an early brief glimpse of the central Torre Latinoamericana; *El cielo dividido* [*Broken Sky*] was filmed on the UNAM campus and in the gay-friendly Zona Rosa in Mexico City) and aesthetically abstracted from that very particular context in ways that render the films accessible to international audiences. Tellingly, Hernández, in spite of his preference for his native Distrito Federal and unlike other current directors, does not rely on that quintessentially national location of the Zócalo—Mexico City's central plaza—juxtaposed with a blowjob in Reygadas's *Batalla en el cielo* and, ten years earlier, the scene of a gay assignation in Jorge Fons's *El callejón de los milagros* (*Midaq Alley*, 1994). Rather than exploiting, and subverting, such symbolically charged locations, Hernández's national production processes are rooted in the Morelos Film Cooperative that he set up as part of a triumvirate with cinematographer Diego Arizmendi and producer Roberto Fiesco. Yet his first feature, which asserts its artistic and commercial independence, was still subsidized by the national film body IMCINE, while receiving development funding from the Rockefeller and MacArthur Foundations. The prestigious Sundance Festival in the United States, a crucial international source of both finance and legitimation, has also supported his work.

I would argue that Hernández's transnational reception is based on a hybridized revision of the homoerotic motifs that no doubt contributed to this sympathetic funding from abroad. On its limited release in the United States, critics in New York, Los Angeles, and San Francisco (where it was screened at the symbolic Castro Theater) were variably resistant to *Mil nubes*'s exacting tempo and opaque narrative (Holden, Dargis, Johnson). But they had no trouble placing it within a dissident auteurist tradition that was at much literary as it was cinematic (French author Jean Genet is the emblematic name that recurs here). Hernández thus emerged in his first feature with that prerequisite of auteurism—a signature style and subject—already fully fledged.

Let us look now in more detail at the textual composition of Hernández's film, which stakes its claim to distinction through the self-conscious asceticism of minimalist technique. After near-silent monochrome credits the film opens with a sex scene in an unestablished nocturnal exterior. Teenage Gerardo (Juan Carlos Ortuño) is performing fellatio, just out of shot, on an anonymous client in the latter's car. The camera focuses, as in Andy Warhol's *Blow Job* (but much more briefly), on the client's face.[9] Wiping cum or vomit from his lips with the banknotes that are his paltry reward, Gerardo next submits to a lengthy two shots in which he (and we) are driven through the shadowy city. The couple remain resolutely blank faced and depressingly silent, an impression ironically reinforced by the romantic ballad on the car radio ("Oh gente" by José José, the "Prince" of seventies Mexican pop). The impression on the viewer is particularly ironic, to the degree in which there is a strong and contradictory contrast between sex without love—and for money—that has just concluded, on the one hand, and the realization of idealized love in the song, on the other hand:

> Cada día, cada instante
> Con amor se van uriendo
> De tristezas y alegrías
> Pasan juntos muchos días,
> Van subiendo y buscando,
> Esperando su destino.
> ¡Oh, gente! ¡Cuánto amas, cuánto sientes!
> Das la vida y nunca mientes
> Y tu luz es la verdad.
> ¡Oh, gente! ¡Cómo entregas primaveras!
> Con amor la vida llenas.
> Tu esperanza es realidad.

[Each day, each instant / A love unting them / Of sadness and joy / Spending many days together/ They rise and seek / Waiting for their destiny / Oh people! How much you love, How much you feel! / You give your life and never lie / And your light is the truth. / Oh people! How you hand over springtimes! / Filling life with love. / Your hope is reality.]

Here minimalist technique (albeit leavened by luscious, grainy night shooting) is combined with existential thematics: Gerardo's alienation, apparently effected by a homosexuality that is presented through the opening sequence as a purely financial transaction, could hardly be more self-evident.

Blurring the boundaries between past and present, however, Hernández goes on to reveal that Gerardo's marginalization is due to more than a generalized and precocious *Weltschmerz*. As we see in flashbacks, intermittently inserted into the apparently aimless flaneurism of the present, Gerardo has been dumped by an older boyfriend who has left him a poetically enigmatic break-up note. A second scene is crucial here. As Gerardo lies frustrated on the bed in his grungy rented room, Hernández pans left over his still clothed body. Gerardo rises to examine his morose reflection in the cracked mirror, pulls down his pants, and caresses his crotch, before retiring once more to the bed. Masturbation is, however, interrupted by remembered or fantasized scenes of lovemaking with the lost boyfriend. And, crucially, in spite of the typical lack of dialogue, the whole sequence is played to music sourced to the youth's old-fashioned gramophone. The use of masturbation, as one of the few more or less effective paths that the lover has to recuperate the missing loved one, is a theme that will later reappear with more thematic force and daring in Hernández's *El cielo dividido* (*Broken Sky*, 2006). In Gerardo's case (Juan Carlos Ortuño), his masturbatory practice will be registered during more or less forty-nine seconds; whereas the character in *El cielo dividido*, another Gerardo (Miguel Ángel Hoppe), appears to be a more oblique, thematic device. In *El cielo dividido* the masturbation scene reflects realism without moral judgment as well, because there is no music either over or off-screen to accompany the short takes. Still, these short takes of the actual masturbation take place extra-dietically. In *El cielo dividido*, Gerardo (Miguel Ángel Hoppe) also masturbates as a way to recover and revive the fleeing presence of his beloved Jonás (Fernando Arroyo).

The song in *Mil nubes* is "Nena" by Sara Montiel, the grande dame of Spanish musicals, who also enjoyed a successful film career in Mexico. The chorus runs as follows:

> Nena . . .
> Me decía loco de pasión.
> Nena . . .
> Que mi vida llenas de ilusión.
> Deja que ponga
> Con embeleso
> Junto a tus labios
> La llama divina
> De un beso.

[Girl, he would call me, mad with passion; girl, who fills my life with hope. Let me in my enchantment place on your lips the divine flame of a kiss.]

The novelistic lyrics go on to tell of a man who swore eternal love to the singer, only to be separated from her by death: if his dark eyes shine even brighter now than the first time they pierced the singer's soul, it is because they now burn with mortal fever. The relatively graphic frontal nudity of this sequence is thus juxtaposed with the stylized and tortured romance of an earlier era—the song is taken from the soundtrack of *El último cuplé* (*The Last Torch Song*, 1957), a Spanish variant on *A Star is Born* (1954), directed by Francoist stalwart Juan de Orduña (Madrid, 1900).

What is striking in this sequence (00:28:42–00:31:35) is not so much the willed incongruity between image and sound tracks as the appeal to perhaps the most transnationally accessible figure of Spanish-language camp icons. Gerardo may be confined to his little room in Mexico City, but his obsession with singer Sarita Montiel (who would also feature as a gay youth's ego ideal in Almodóvar's *La mala educación* [*Bad Education*], just one year later) places him in the familiar mainstream of gay fandom. Homosexuality, squalidly commercial in the opening sequence, is now presented as narcissistic, but mediated by fantastic identifications that are experienced as collective by the target audience, if not by the character himself. Gerardo talks with characteristic vagueness of "No sé cómo se llama. Es la música de una película española. Se trata de una muchacha pobre, pero que canta muy bonito" [I don't know what the name is. But it is the music to a Spanish movie. It is about a poor girl who sings beautifully] (00:19:00–00:19:05). He is shown to be unaware of the song's source, even as he submits in time-worn style to the seduction of its extravagant masochism.

A third and final sequence offers yet another contradictory image of homosexuality (00:49:21–00:52:47). When Gerardo cruises a stereotypically masculine man on the city outskirts, Hernández exploits the squalid urban locations that are so successfully aestheticized by his cinematographer: soulless highways, deserted train tracks, and walls intricately scarred by graffiti. Here lengthy, silent takes are combined with frequent camera movement (tracks and pans) and directive editing strategies (point-of-view [POV] and crosscutting) to create a compelling, if slow-moving, chase sequence. The erotic pursuit leads, however, not to the expected embrace but rather to a punch in the face that will leave our impassive hero attractively bruised for the remainder of the film.

The sexual exploitation of the first sequence and the narcissistic camp of the second are here joined by a violence that is clearly eroticized, but not, however, presented as pleasurable to its victim. And once more, and for a third time, the source music tends to distance us from the social implications of the scene. For this queer bashing is set, with transparently ironic intent, to a liturgical, choral soundtrack. Now, there are hints elsewhere in the film that Gerardo's erotic and romantic odyssey is in some way spiritual—or even mystical. An older, deserted (drag?) queen tells him he should look to the sky or heaven: "Tú sigue mirando hacia el cielo. El secreto está en no abandonarse al odio. Nosotros no somos nada, pero Él . . . ¡Él es el Rey de Reyes!" [Keep looking toward the sky. The secret to it is to keep away from hate. We are nothing. But He . . . He is the King of Kings!] (00:39:34–00:39:58). It is not clear whether the older man is invoking the deity or the great dark-eyed man whose role is, as ever, to seduce and abandon the beloved.

I have already argued that Hernández attempts to walk a tightrope, striking a balance between the national and transnational, the homosexual and the universal. Here also he tries to distance himself from the sociopolitical arena to which much Latin American cinema has found itself confined, especially by foreign critics, even as he invokes those cinematic memories of underdevelopment in his favored locations. One further technique exemplifies this disavowal, which (barely) preserves what it seeks to deny. Diego Arizmendi often favors an extreme shallowness of field which tends to isolate the protagonist, shot in loving, sculptural close-up, from his fleeting, blurry background, a visual effect that perhaps echoes the "thousand clouds" of the title or, indeed, Ayala Blanco's "fugacidad" ("fleetingness") of Mexican cinema.

It is true that Hernández bears some witness in his narrative and locations to social deprivation and exploitation (from poverty to homophobia), an emphasis likely to be expected in a Mexican movie by European or American audiences, who have tended to value such films in socioeconomic rather than aesthetic terms. But Hernández clearly signals through his film techniques that this localist reading of his film may be to some extent necessary but is by no means sufficient for its interpretation. Familiar elements of social realism—authentic locations, amateur actors, vernacular dialogue—are preserved under erasure, fleetingly glimpsed only to be masked by the equally familiar, but often incompatible, aesthetics of the transnational art movie (monochrome photography, off-center framing, extended takes with little camera movement, human silhouettes that echo sculptures, bas reliefs with the density of forms).

I would suggest finally, then, that it is precisely through those elements of his oeuvre that appear to be of restricted or minority interest (homophilia, cinephilia) that Hernández constructs a transnational gay auteurism that has achieved wider distribution than has more commercial Mexican cinema. While it remains to be seen whether Fernández will be able to build a more substantial body of work that would fully justify the auteurist status to which his films to date clearly aspire, there is no doubt that he is already a unique and distinctive artist in a rapidly globalizing Mexican film industry.

Notes

1. This is the most recent version of Paul Julian Smith's essay. See Smith, Paul Julian. *Mexican Screen Fiction: Between Cinema and Television*. Cambridge, UK; Malden, MA: Polity, 2014.

2. This group includes figures like Guillermo del Toro, Alfonso Cuarón, and Alejandro González Iñárritu.

3. As a paradigmatic example of homophobia in Mexican cinema, it is sufficient to mention *Modisto de señoras* (*Tailor for Ladies*, 1969) by Eduardo Jiménez Pons.

4. The title of Hernández's film makes reference to lines from Pier Paolo Pasolini's book, *Poesia in forma di rosa* (1964): "Ah vergogna e splendore, vergogna e splendore! / Mille nubi di pace accerchiano il cielo, amore, / Mai non finirai di essere amore."

5. Male frontal nudity has largely been systematically avoided in Mexican cinema. Beyond pointing to this avoidance on the big screen, it also reveals the tremendous erotic panic buried in that culture, which has yet to propose a more open and comprehensive political-erotic understanding of the human body. The significant absence of male nudity in general, nonetheless, has been defied not only by Hernández, but also other directors like Carlos Reygadas (e.g., *Japón* 2002, *Batalla en el cielo* 2005).

6. See "Hernández y la prisión del deseo," by Luis Bernardo Jaime Vázquez.

7. Inspired by the work of Uruguayan author José Enrique Rodó (1871–1917), the Ariel Awards are the equivalent of the Oscars in the USA and the Prix César in France. The Ariels were first awarded in 1947 with the goal of recognizing high quality Mexican cinema.

8. According to the *Stanford Encyclopedia of Philosophy*, *identity politics* "has come to signify a wide range of political activity and theorizing founded in the shared experiences of injustice of members of certain social groups. Rather than organizing solely around belief systems, programmatic manifestos, or party affiliation, identity political formations typically aim to secure the political freedom of a specific constituency marginalized within its larger context. Members of that constituency assert or reclaim ways of understanding their distinctiveness that challenge dominant oppressive characterizations, with the goal of greater self-determination."

9. Andy Warhol's camera shoots a close-up of a client's face, with a fixed camera, that lasts more or less twenty-five minutes. Hernández would have paid

homage to this thematic daring of his predecesor by repeating the same framing with a focus on the client's face for an eleven-second take. However, this is not an isolated incident and includes editing. Like Warhol, the *fellatio* is off-screen, offering more opportunities for imagination.

Works Cited

Ayala Blanco, Jorge. *La fugacidad del cine mexicano*. México, D. F.: Océano, 2001. Print.
Bourdieu, Pierre. *The Rules of Art: Genesis and Structure of the Literary Field*. Trans. Susan Emanuel. Cambridge, UK: Polity, 1996. Print.
Cómo hacer cine. "*Mil nubes de paz* . . . de Julián Hernández." Feb. 26, 2004. Web. Oct. 19, 2008.
Dargis, Manohla. Review of *Mil nubes*. Web. Oct. 19, 2008.
González Vargas, Carla. *Rutas del cine mexicano 1990–2006*. México, D.F.: CONACULTA IMCINE; Landucci, 2006. Print.
Hernández, Julián, dir. *El cielo dividido*. México, D.F.: Mil Nubes Cine, 2006. DVD.
———. *Mil nubes de paz*. México, D. F.: Mil Nubes Cine, 2004. DVD.
Holden, Stephen. Review of *Mil nubes*. Web. Oct. 19, 2008.
"Identity Politics." *Stanford Encyclopedia of Philosophy*. Web. April 25, 2012.
Johnson, G. Allen. Review of *Mil nubes*. Web. Oct. 19, 2008.
La Jornada [Staff]. "En México se teme reconocer la homosexualidad: Julián Hernández." Web. Oct. 19, 2008.
Noble, Andrea. *Mexican National Cinema*. London; New York: Routledge, 2005. Print.
Pasolini, Pier Paolo. *Poesia in forma di rosa*. Web. June 26, 2010.
Vázquez, Luis Bernardo Jaime. "Hernández y la prisión del deseo." Web. Oct. 19, 2008.
Wood, Jason. *The Faber Book of Mexican Cinema*. London: Faber and Faber, 2006. Print.

9

Haunted: *XXY*

(Lucía Puenzo, 2007)

Debra A. Castillo

Diana Sanchez begins her review of the 2007 Argentine film *XXY* by saying, "[t]he case of Manitoba-born David Reimer has always haunted me." Reimer is, of course, the name of the patient pseudonymously called John/Joan in the famous and now discredited 1970s studies conducted by Johns Hopkins University researcher John Money on the efficacy of socialization (and, in Reimer's case, surgery) in determining a child's gender. As Judith Butler notes in her article analyzing this case, the John/Joan story has, over the years, come to be seen as an allegory, "or has the force of allegory" (Butler 627), as the seemingly inevitable point of reference for debates on intersexuality and current surgical practices for "normalizing" children of ambiguous gender. Despite the uproar, since the late 1990s, on the particulars of Money's methods and analysis, in much of current medical practice the case continues to be read as if it were incontrovertibly true that infants are born gender-neutral and can be surgically morphed, as if Money's questionable postulates should hold for intersexed individuals and as if there were exactly two sexes and exactly one way to be: either male or female (see Dreger *et passim*) Yet despite Money's allegorical status, his haunting of stories about gender and surgical "normalization," David Reimer was neither intersexual nor transsexual—he was the victim of a botched operation on his penis when he was a baby, and an even more botched and traumatizing series of scientific interventions after that point. This blurring of very different lives and gender expressions in the popular press and in scientific studies is at the heart of recent reflections such as Butler's, where justice and allegory come together, along with Alice Domurat Dreger's (and others') work on medical ethics.

It seems symptomatic that David Reimer's story is evoked in the Toronto film festival review as a rubric for framing analysis of the Argentine film *XXY,* and this paper will explore this haunting and this allegory in Lucía Puenzo's opera prima: *XXY.* Daughter of the highly regarded director Luis Puenzo, Lucía has a PhD in literary studies and an established career as a novelist and scriptwriter in her native Argentina. The film, set in provincial beachside Uruguay, tells the story of first love, between a sixteen-year-old boy, Álvaro, and a fifteen-year-old intersex person, Alex. While the plot's outline comes from "Cinismo," a short story from the collection *Chicos,* written by Puenzo's partner, fellow scriptwriter Sergio Bizzio, Puenzo is emphatic in interviews that much of the inspiration for *XXY*'s unusual plot derives from her consultations with medical personnel as well as trans and intersex individuals, especially the Austrian intersex person Alex Jürgen, whom she met in Paris and whose story, along with the documentary film about his life, *Tintenfischalarm (Octopusalarm,* 2006), she found particularly powerful.

XXY's questioning of a binary sex/gender system through the story of a young unmutilated intersex person makes it an unusual contribution in the feature film subgenre of gender-questioning narratives—a story that film reviewers almost gravitationally assign to a growing set of films tracing the complicated lives of characters with gender dysphoria, especially transsexuality, for dramatic or comic effect. The film carries with it the force of allegory in a banal sense—as soon as mainstream filmmakers realized that audiences were not running screaming from theaters or burning them down, transsexuals became an increasingly popular linchpin to anchor feature films about identity and family and love.[1] Again, the function of the allegory allows for this category shift, by which intersex is assimilated to the very different condition of the trans individual. At the same time, we should not discount the shift in social perceptions partly created by the increasingly ubiquitous filmic transsexual body that made it possible for a film on the topic of intersex to become Argentina's official entry for the 2007 Best Foreign Film Oscar as well as for Spain's Goya awards. And yet, it is important to remember that while film transsexuals, in their yearning for socially legible bodies that will "pass" as unnoticed representatives of the gender expressed by that individual, tend to comfortably support mainstream society's understanding of gender dimorphism, this is a position that real-world intersexed people increasingly reject in favor of retaining their rights to gender ambiguity. As Alex Jürgen comments in a note on *Tintenfischalarm*, "I realized that I needed to start accepting myself as I was: as a NON-MAN and a NON-WOMAN" (Pressbook).

One of the haunting aspects of Reimer's case was Money's use of male-to-female transsexuals—presumably because of the parallels in surgical procedures—to talk to the young child about the advantages of being a girl (Butler 624). That Sanchez finds in Puenzo's film, on the awakening sexuality of a young intersex person named Alex,[2] another manifestation of this allegorical tale reflects familiar aspects of this wholly comprehensible drive for context and meaning. This is born of Diana Sanchez's desire to anchor Puenzo's story in a more comfortable and intelligible one. The transsexual haunts Reimer's story as Reimer haunts this reading of Puenzo's film, if only as an allegorical ur-narrative of scientific hubris and unethical behavior.[3] Puenzo more explicitly traces out that ur-narrative in her characters' musing on the implications of pressuring Alex to agree to surgery now that s/he has reached adolescence. It is this pedagogical aspect of the film that most surely links it to the testimonial substratum that was an important aspect of its inspiration. It is also this aspect that opens the possibility of slippage between the fictional and the documentary—such that the movie has reportedly enabled discussion in Argentina concerning the intersex body that has not been subjected to surgery.

Puenzo's film accesses allegory in another sense, as well. While it tackles head-on the clinical question of surgical intervention (the Reimer allegory), Puenzo has commented that in her novels *El niño pez* and *Nueve minutos* "aparecen también los temas del intersexo de diferentes maneras" (Suárez), albeit in ways that are more subtle and metaphorical than in the film. Intersex and queerness, in this respect, serve as limit points to help explore the broad question of how to think about one's existential position as a sexual being in this world. Here Puenzo asks the viewer of her film, like the reader of her novels, to ponder the relation of personal identity to sexual identity, to meditate on the variable quotient of essence and social construction (and even speciation) in thinking beings' understanding of our place in the vast ecological and cultural web.

There is also a generic allusiveness, or haunting, to this film. One important and recognized style of Latin American filmmaking includes citing and responding interstitially to international cinema—for instance, by taking up familiar Hollywood plots and remaking them. In some sense, then, *XXY* offers a Latin American response to the current run of well-received international films on the transgender theme, such as *Transamerica* and *Boys Don't Cry*. In another sense, it is a radical Argentine reinterpretation of the familiar B-movie genre of the angst-ridden teeny-bopper romance, where identity and sexuality are transmuted in the crucible of youthful hormones. Whereas the Hollywood staple tends to be written as (tragi)comedy, Puenzo rethinks the core question of how to understand oneself as a desiring, sexual being, which serves as the heart and engine of these narratives, through the confused, tentative, burgeoning attraction between a boy discovering his homosexuality and an intersex person who is not yet certain about the form his/her erotic inclinations are taking. Here, the two characters, each outsiders in their own way and, hence, rejected or seen as freaks by their peers, respond to gay Argentine poet Néstor Perlongher's statement, cited by Puenzo: "We do not want respect, we want to be desired" (Tehrani). Inevitably, however, because this is a film (and, moreover, a film about teen sexuality), the imperative of desire occurs in the fishbowl of the visual, what is seen and what is not seen of the actors' bodies, and by whom: the adolescent couple, the other adolescents who form Alex's peer group, Alex's parents (especially the father), and, above all, the film's audience.

What is this desire? Whose desire is interpellated here, and where is it directed? These are important questions to ask regarding this film, where the exploration of desire and sexuality intertwines with a profound rethinking of individual identity. To return to our index case, David Reimer was, over many years, subjected to invasive scrutiny of a part of his body that most people consider intensely private, hence creating a specific hyperaware shame about his "wrongness," his difference from other girls or boys. Furthermore, despite the mutilation of his genitalia and the years of pressure to conform to stereotypical female social behavior, he never accepted the gender assigned him. His desires were always those of a heterosexual male. Even in writing this sentence, however, the intellectual stakes underwriting it loom large, in debates between those who espouse a concept of social construction of gender and those who respond with biological or psychological explanations for an essential core identity. Puenzo addresses the aesthetic analog of this question from an unexpected vantage point, asking us how to engage a film narrative about gender when performance doesn't fall into the expected binary, when meaning is contradictory and excessive (that is, too many sexualities are in play). At the same time, she underscores our investment in the gaze as a surrogate for knowledge. Like Reimer's therapists, we want to see. Bizzio's story and Puenzo's film continually bring us back to the concrete place of desire, the location of sexual pleasure. Crudely, constantly, everyone wants to know what Alex's ("Rocío's" in Bizzio's short story) genitalia look like, whether out of prurient curiosity or a desire to change them.

For Alex, ambivalent feelings about his/her ambiguous genitalia figure in the relationships between desire, pleasure, and identity in the most basic sense: how to become and express physically what one really is. Alex "tiene todo," and, having unilaterally made the decision to stop taking the prescribed hormones that have feminized his/her appearance, is beginning to explore whether the penis or the vagina (or both) is the site of his/her sexual pleasure. Traditional understandings of human sexuality are insufficient to account for Alex's situation, since Alex is outside the binaries of male/female, gay/straight, and Alex's conundrum exposes the limits of our imagination in defining the human. The ambiguous desires of the intersex adolescent remind the viewers of the artificial limits imposed by unquestioned styles of knowledge production—male, female, gay, straight—and the stricture "to be" one and only one of the above even in progressive circles. In Alex's case, the potential for fluidity underscores the performativity of gender roles in our species: more generally, the performativity of sex itself.

Alex's counterpart, Álvaro, more conventionally, through his/her tentative and fumbling sexual relations with Alex, learns that he is a gay male who finds pleasure in being anally penetrated.[4] In this respect, the film highlights the ironic quality of his father's relief that his somewhat "odd" (*raro*) son finally seems to be attracted to a girl—this despite the fact that the father is a plastic surgeon who has been called in specifically to consult with the family on the advantages of castration to turn Alex into an unambiguous woman. For Álvaro's father, Alex's visible body is legible to him only as female, and he clearly imagines Alex's unseen penis only as dysfunctional excess—"lo que le sobra."

This is, as Amber Wilkinson notes in a review, a film where the potential "to go very wrong was great." For my taste, Bizzio's story falls into the register of exploitative voyeurism, where things go very wrong, while Puenzo's film more successfully steps back from the edge of the adolescent freak show it could have been. In general, the stories in Bizzio's collection, including "Cinismo," offer a strange, capricious, often brutal primer for liminal worlds. For example, one story tells of the variously narrated encounters between a tribe of pygmies and a group of Westerners, ending with a scene of voyeurism on adolescent lovers; another, of the conversation between two tiny aliens and a Japanese writer on a beach; and yet another, of the meditations of a duck plotting revenge on rapist cats. "Cinismo," the first story, focusing on the tipping point into aggressively sexualized adolescence of a twelve-year-old intersex child and the child's fifteen-year-old gay Arab-Argentine lover, sets the stage for the progressively more extravagant stories, in a collection suggestively described by the press as "algo así como un costumbrismo border" ("De cerca nadie es normal"). In context, it scarcely causes us to blink.

In Bizzio's story, the homophobic father is played to stereotype as the film musician Muhabid Jasan. (In Puenzo's movie, at least one form of offensiveness—that of ethnic/racial stereotyping—is ameliorated by casting him instead as a white Argentine plastic surgeon named Ramiro.) Muhabid and his wife, an economist named Érika—with an un-Spanish "k" and a personality also defined in quotation marks (he is "interesante," she is "una mujer 'con inquietudes'" [17])—take their markedly effeminate son with them on a vacation to Punta del Este, to visit their friends Suli and Néstor Kraken, also "interesantes." Álvaro, as befits his genetics and class status, is smart but defined as somewhat repugnant; Rocío, the Krakens's intersex child, is the cynic of the story's title, and her (Bizzio consistently refers to Rocío with feminine adjectives) ambiguous sexuality pretentiously fits her genetics as the child of the all-too-obviously symbolic sea monster father. The opening conversational gambit between Rocío and Álvaro involves Rocío asking Álvaro if he just came from jerking off (10), a conversation that naturally leads to asking if he's ever had sex (12), followed by a series of conversations that range between seductive and hectoring on Rocío's part about getting together to lose their virginity. The parents have minor roles in this drama: Érika catches her son masturbating with his finger in his anus (15); Kraken interrupts the couple as they are initiating sex (20). The two young people never complete the sexual act to orgasm but have various tearful scenes indicating that they are now officially in love. On parting, Álvaro begs for—and begrudgingly gets—a final revelation scene of Rocío's genitals: "—Por favor . . . mostrame . . .—le dijo—. Antes de irme . . . dejame ver . . . Rocío se sonrió. La idea pareció divertirla, aunque en verdad la demolía" (34). ["Please, show me," he said. "Before I go, let me see . . ." Rocío smiled. The idea seemed to entertain her, although, in fact, it tore her apart.] Thus, the twelve-year-old's first exploratory experience of love is overdetermined by the insistent focus, so akin to that of the medical profession and the prurient public in general, on her genitalia. It is, finally, the only thing that makes this prickly, abrupt child "interesting," and Álvaro's insistence further confirms the perception once again that what people in general want from Rocío is visible difference, the freak show. By the very fact of her existence, the cynical child offers them an opportunity to sublimate or repress their own anxieties about their various grave dysfunctionalities in the assurance that the intersex person is even more "raro."

The contrast between Bizzio's exchange in the short story and the parallel parting conversation in Puenzo's film offers a telling contrast (notes in brackets added):

ALEX. Nunca pensé que me iba a enamorar de alguien como vos. Pero me pasó.

ÁLVARO. A mí también.

ALEX. No. [pause] A vos te pasó otra cosa.

ÁLVARO. [tearfully] No.

ALEX. ¿Qué te da más lástima? ¿No verme más o no haberlo visto? [pause, Álvaro continuing to look Alex in the eye without changing expression] ¿Quieres ver?

ALEX. I never thought I could fall in love with someone like you. But it happened.

ÁLVARO. Me, too.

ALEX. No. [pause] Something else happened to you.

ÁLVARO. [tearfully] No.

ALEX. What bothers you more: not seeing me again or never having seen it? [pause, Álvaro continuing to look Alex in the eye without changing expression.] Do you want to see?

When Alex pulls down his/her sweatpants and shows Álvaro, but not us, his/her penis, we film viewers know that we will not have our own prurient curiosity satisfied. Where Bizzio's story depends for its effort on the shock value of narrative flatness combined with sensationalist themes, Puenzo, if at times overly schematic, provides a more discrete and nuanced image of the fumbling young lovers and complicates the picture by developing an additional level of insecurity in both teenagers regarding their sexuality.

The first minute of Puenzo's film establishes the ambient color scheme and the rather obvious symbolism reinforced throughout the film, establishing an allegorical parallel to half-unseen, vaguely threatening sea creatures—a nod both to her own "niño pez" and to Alex Jürgen's "octopus alarm." The movie's opening credits run over a scene of murky green water and indistinct swimming shapes (they might as well be krakens), intercut with shots of two children (Alex and, briefly, a girl friend) running through the woods, also in the muted colors of the director's predominant green/blue/gray palette. With this title sequence, we already learn that this will be a border space, impeding clear vision, where one thing shades into another and where good intentions can sometimes lead people to trip and fall—as Alex does, at the end of the sequence. This liminality, where borders like those between land and sea are both absolute and crossable, is allegorically established in the repeated images of sea turtles, which haunt the film and serve as Alex's objective correlative: Alex wears a necklace made from a turtle's identification tag. The turtles, while amphibious, are endangered by fishermen's nets; they are frequently dragged out of their comfortable environment and mutilated or killed, or rescued, or dissected by Alex's father. This message of absolute and blurred horizons is reinforced throughout the film and brought home at the end in its final, more optimistic shot, where Alex's future, no longer that of the undersea monster about to be captured and dissected, is projected into an imagined amphibiousness with the vista of a clear blue-gray sky that meets an equally uninterrupted, slightly different shade of blue-green sea, just before the final credits run.

The title sequence gives way to a series of establishing shots. Alex smokes and broods. Kraken, the marine biologist, dissects an enormous (and somewhat amorphous-looking) sea turtle: "hembra" (female), he proclaims with satisfaction after lifting off the shell and digging into the exposed meat. Plastic surgeon Ramiro reads a book, *Orígenes del sexo*, while his oblivious son zones out to unheard music playing through his headphones. Underwriting all the characters is the forest/marine Uruguayan landscape that Érika will proclaim to be "el paraíso" (paradise) and that the viewer experiences as an alien, chilly site. The motivation for the plot comes from Alex's mother, Suli. She feels that time is running out in their isolated world, and, over Kraken's objections, has invited the plastic surgeon and his wife to their home to explore the options for surgery on Alex—something neither Kraken nor Alex wants.

The struggle between the parents allows for the film's long pedagogical asides as Alex's mother talks about wanting her child to be normal and happy; the surgeon offers reassuring guarantees of expertise and success; and Kraken conducts his own research, including seeking out a local intersex person for an intimate conversation. This mechanic—shades of John/Joan—had been castrated as a child, was brought up as a girl, had now officially changed his/her sex to male, and was happily married with an adopted child. He warns Kraken that surgery is the worst thing that the parents could do to a child they love, making the child afraid of his/her own body, which must have something wrong or monstrous with it. (Interestingly enough, neither Kraken nor Suli thinks about introducing Alex to this compassionate, articulate intersex person in their neighborhood, thus keeping Alex's isolation from other intersex people complete.)

Toward the end of the film, after Kraken's discussion with the intersex man and after the rape attempt on Alex, he watches his sleeping child. Alex awakens, and asks what he is doing. "Te cuido," he says, "hasta que puedas elegir . . . lo que quieras" [I'm taking care of you until you can choose what you want], to which Alex responds with the unanswerable question: "¿Y si no hay nada que elegir?" [And what if there is no choice to make?] It is by now clear to both of them that Alex will never be/become a woman, but it is just as clear that this does not mean he will necessarily be a man. Implicitly, in the context of the film's symbolic structure, the positing of an obligatory choice—to be either man or woman—along with the self-mutilation attendant upon this decision, is like asking an amphibian to choose between sea and land, or—even more extreme—aquarium and desert. A sea turtle is not a lizard, after all.

The exteriors in this film tend to be expansive and unencumbered, as befits the desolate landscape of this chilly seaside fishing village. In contrast, the interiors are dark and crowded, like the murky seas of the establishing shot. They are full of people and things that the film viewers (and several of the characters) glimpse only through the obstructed views that turn the interiors into fish tanks, and the characters framed by them into other forms of marine life, supplementing the film's many images of sea turtles, fish, and eels—often in the process of being butchered.[5] We constantly observe the languid movements of the characters through house or car windows, shower curtains, doorways. We catch ourselves peeking through bookshelves and become voyeurs on Álvaro's voyeuristic obsession with watching Alex, including watching Alex's self-examination in a mirror. This insistent framing echoes the strangeness of the first underwater movements in the opening title sequence, while also taming those movements for us.

Alex's room is the richest and most layered space in the film, full of toys, books, artifacts, furniture, bedding. We catch glimpses of it throughout the film, frequently with the visual leitmotif of a lizard crawling around the space, or the camera's lingering on a naked baby doll with a cigarette glued between its legs, as a penis. Most importantly, at the halfway point of the film (minutes 44–45), shortly after their aborted sexual relations, Álvaro explores the room while the other characters are out of the house. Already, eight minutes earlier, the camera has lingered on a shot of Álvaro in the rain, coming back to the house after his frustrated masturbation following their aborted sexual encounter, looking through the window into Alex's room as

Alex gazes at his/her own image in a full-length mirror and then turns from the mirror to the window to catch Álvaro's eyes. The incomplete image of Alex's body (Alex sees the full image; implicitly Álvaro and the film viewers see only the top half) suggests to us the film's and the characters' insistence on the body's materiality and its surface legibility, and the audience's demand to see the whole body in its (in)coherence. In this way, the film prods at the familiar demands of filmic decorum (no full frontal nudity of teenagers) while constantly flirting with the possibility of its violation, creating in us the film viewers desires that we must deny, and will have to be frustrated.

Alex's room becomes the proxy for Alex's body. When Álvaro explores the room, we viewers again become voyeurs, now on Álvaro's physical invasion of Alex's space, first seeing him through a gap in the bookshelves before the camera fully enters the room. We observe him gazing at the lizard, then at Alex's diary/scrapbook of drawings, full of monstrous faces alongside poetic children with long flowers extending from their genitals,[6] and then pan down a shot of the doll with the cigarette glued between her legs. In the background, raised white letters on various surfaces read "RARO" and "ALEX" along with the nearly perfect anagram "EXALA." The series of frames—window, mirror, diary—reminds us over and over again that the self never completely coincides with the image of the self. No matter how persistently framed and visualized, the very nature of the definitional structure—the allegorical frame, we might say—involves selectivity, highlighting, and seeing some things through a masking out of partially occluded references. Thus, we see the doll but not Alex, the upper body in the mirror but not the desired lower body. The imperative to see, which in the film substitutes for the desire to know, does not reveal the body's physical conformation or the self's truth, which, in any case, the deeply vulnerable Alex hides under an armor of irascibility, like a turtle in its shell.

As in Bizzio's story, the first significant conversation between the two adolescents has to do with masturbation, though the film version reduces the dialogue to a much tighter exchange. In "Cinismo," this first significant dialogue between the two adolescents is drawn out over several pages and includes a longer exchange on their masturbatory habits, as well as an additional, prickly exchange of mutual rejection after twelve-year-old Rocío offers to have sex with the fifteen-year-old boy. After Rocío leaves, Álvaro stays behind, meditating about Rocío and the conversation they just had: "Era honesta, sincera, valiente, y había que reconocer que dominaba como pez al agua la economía de palabras; con apenas un puñado de frases había llegado al extremo de invitarlo a coger, además de sacarle que era un pajero" (13) [She was honest, sincere, brave, and you had to recognize that she dominated the economy of words like a fish in the water; with only a handful of sentences, she had arrived at the extreme of inviting him to fuck as well as getting out of him that he often jerked off]. In the film, Alex joins Álvaro on the beach and asks if he's just been jerking off in his room. Álvaro returns the question: "¿Y vos, te hacés la paja también?" [Do you jerk off, too?]. Alex responds with a smile, "Todos los días" [Every day]. Álvaro, clearly bemused by this conversation, says, "Yo nunca había estado en Uruguay" [I've never been in Uruguay before]. Alex indignantly replies, "Estamos hablando de la paja y salís con Uruguay" [We're talking about jerking off and you come out with Uruguay]. Álvaro's response is to ask Alex's age—fifteen, and Alex follows with, "Yo nunca me acosté con nadie. ¿Vos te acostarías?" [I've never slept with anyone. Would you sleep with someone?] Thus, while Puenzo follows the basic outline of the story, and many of the dialogue lines are drawn directly from Bizzio, on the whole, she tends to tighten and abbreviate the spoken exchanges, allowing pregnant pauses and intercut reaction shots to carry much of the film's emotional weight. More clearly than in the short story, in Puenzo's film Álvaro is trying out the hypothesis that Uruguay has different sexual mores than Argentina, that the strangeness of the conversation has something to do with their being in that country.

In Bizzio's story, Rocío convinces Álvaro to allow her to watch him masturbate, but refuses his pleading to let him see her masturbate in return (28), violating an implicit contract among adolescent boys to speak about sexuality in the grunts and moans of a jerk-off circle. Kraken, too, meditates on the stakes involved in seeing and in telling what one has seen: "Había llegado la hora de ser cobarde: jamás le contaría a Suli, ni a nadie, lo que había visto. . . . Después de todo, ¿qué tenía de inquietante que su hija hermafrodita y menor de edad le rompiera el culo al hijo de su invitado?" (Bizzio 21) [The time to be cowardly had arisen. He would never tell Suli, nor anyone else, what he had seen. . . . After all, what was disturbing about his underage hermaphrodite daughter fucking the son of his guest in the ass?]. Kraken's "cowardice" in the story contrasts with what we imagine as his compassionate discretion in the film. Likewise, in Bizzio, the brutal violence of what he would tell, if he did tell—his daughter "breaking the ass" of his friend's son—is perfectly available to the story's reader.

In Puenzo's film, the violence that shades from telling to seeing to breaking is displaced, first in the anticipatory dissection of the turtle to discover its sex, but more bluntly in the scene, two-thirds of the way through the film, when a gang of boys drive their motorboat up onto the beach before attacking Alex, forcing him/her down in the sand and rocks, and lowering his/her pants, with the stated intention of trying out all his/her parts to see if they work. Alex had confided the secret of his/her intersexuality to Vando, Alex's former best friend, and Vando let it slip in conversation to other schoolmates, turning Alex into a freak. It is only Vando's timely intervention, beating the attackers away, that stops the rape. In this violent scene, the slippage from the desire to see (the voyeurism so pervasive throughout the film) is implicated in the prohibition of sight, along with the prohibition of telling. (As Alex explains to his/her father, if there is nothing wrong with him/her, why can't s/he talk to his/her friends about it?). Thus, the desire to see, to hear, to tell, becomes the desire to rape this amphibious, nonhuman being. Desire becomes barbarian, a desire to try out Alex's hole and see how it feels.

Elizabeth Scharang's pressbook to her documentary about Alex Jürgen cites Professor Werner Grünberger of the Frauenklinik der Rudolfstiftung in Vienna on one of the horrific consequences of intersex surgery. Intersex babies who have had vaginas created through surgery are required to submit to "vaginal dilation" throughout their childhood, since the artificial vagina does not grow with the child and would be subject to closing or growing over. This means that at various points, a hard rod is inserted in the vagina to "dilate" it and to maintain a functional hole for later sexual intercourse. As Grünberger notes, "At the age of three, a child begins to recognize its sexuality. If the child has to sleep with a rod inserted, this is truly traumatizing," and many intersex people report that they experience this repeated insertion as a form of rape.

Knowing that Alex Jürgen was an important informant for her—to the degree that she gave her character the same first name—it is tempting to read Puenzo's plot in this context. We see the haunting of Alex Jürgen's life in the fictional story of the South American intersex teenager, and we read the pain and mutilation and trauma that the Austrian experienced in the trauma that the Argentine narrowly avoids. This reading, from freak to human, though fully endorsed in the film, does not completely engage the challenge that Alex poses. If we take Uruguay as the symbolic location of the borderline "mundo raro" where sexuality expresses itself outside the narrow confines of the Argentine imaginary, even there the taxonomic imperative underwrites social exchange. Kraken needs to know if the turtle is male or female. Alex is not allowed to share a bed with a girlfriend on a sleepover at her house. Vando expresses himself best with his fists, as do Kraken himself and Vando's father, when the need arises to clarify their feelings.

At the same time, Álvaro's struggle to find a level of self-acceptance is in some ways more difficult than Alex's. Uruguay upsets all of Álvaro's precarious accommodations between his hidden homosexuality and his father's harsh expectations; it is not just food Álvaro is talking about shortly after his arrival when he comments, "No me gusta probar cosas nuevas." He admires his father more than anyone in the world. And yet, in a rare moment of father-son confidential exchange provoked by the foreign setting and fueled by alcohol, finally, Ramiro openly confesses his lack of interest in his talentless offspring, venturing the additional comment that despite his general disappointment in his son, he was at least relieved when Álvaro took up with Alex, because "tenía miedo de que fueras puto" [I was afraid you were a fag]. In the course of the film, Alex and Uruguay help him learn about himself in an affirming way, counterbalancing Ramiro's blunt judgmentalism. In contrast, as opposed to the tense disappointment between Álvaro and Ramiro, Alex and Kraken walk off together in perfect harmony with each other at the end of the film. After saying farewell to Ramiro's family at the ferry, Alex catches up to his/her parents, reaching over in silence to put his/her father's arm over his/her shoulders as they walk away from the dock—a final framing of the father and child in a far less dysfunctional family than the one returning to Argentina. It is ultimately the two framed images of the family that remain, in juxtaposition: each child running after the father, but in Álvaro's case, always remaining behind, always at a distance, never meeting his father's eyes. Argentina and Uruguay: two unsettled expectations of what is normal, what is right, what is good.

Gayle Salamon cites from "The Ego and the Id" on Sigmund Freud's fascination with the intersex body, reminding us of Freud's temptation to extend the allegory of the hermaphrodite to the brain, and to think of mental development with respect to a bisexual psychical disposition: "The importance of these abnormalities lies in the unexpected fact that they facilitate our understanding of normal development. . . . It was tempting to extend this analysis to the mental sphere" (Freud, qtd. in Salamon 97). In analyzing this passage, Salamon lingers on the issue of a temptation that must be refused, playing with how it radicalizes and undermines the more conventional reading of "normal" sexual dimorphism that precedes it (98–99). The intersex body, then, by our very acknowledgment of its difference, presents a cultural challenge, a temptation that unsettles our understanding, forcing it onto new paths, new temptations: "The body's stubborn insistence on a legible binary is precisely what renders a categorical binary illegible . . . The usefulness of the body image for theorizing gendered embodiment is precisely not that the body image is material, but that it allows for a resignification of materiality itself" (Salamon 97, 117). It is an allegory that haunts our desire to see and to know with, to use

Salamon's terminology, the resignifying inevitability of knowledge's permeable boundaries.

In her article on John/Joan, Butler asks us to do a mental experiment, "to do justice to John," intentionally mixing pronouns in the discussion, by asking us to ask Joan what she saw when looking at himself in the mirror:

> When Joan looked in the mirror and saw something nameless, freakish, something between the norms, was she not at that moment in question as a human, was she not the specter of the freak against which and through which the norm installed itself? What was the problem with Joan, that people were always asking to see her naked . . . ? John seems to understand that the norms are external to him, but what if the norms have become the means by which he sees, the frame for his own seeing, his way of seeing himself? (631)

In her reference to the specter of the freak haunting her reconstruction of John/Joan's encounter with him/herself in the mirror, Butler engages all the central concepts that have informed this discussion of Lucía Puenzo's *XXY*. Like Butler with her thought experiment, Puenzo, too, asks us to follow Alex and Álvaro's gaze, looking at each other, and, through their direct gaze into the camera, back at us, asking us in our turn to look around at the way we frame our own local realities, our own bodies, our own comfortable and uncomfortable spaces. In this refracted image—in a mirror, in the flickering of light on a screen—we find the shadows of our displaced desires.

Notes

1. While there are still few fiction films dealing with intersex persons, the path has been prepared by a range of popular films sensitive to gender dysphoria. Recent U.S. feature films include *Transamerica*, *Boys Don't Cry*, and *To Wong Foo, Thanks for Everything! Julie Newmar*. A sample from the long list of international productions includes *En Soap* (Denmark), *Breakfast on Pluto* (Ireland), *The Crying Game* (UK), *Todo sobre mi madre* (*All About my Mother*, Spain), and *Shabnam Mausi* (India), as well documentaries such as Manoj Raghuvanshi's 2006 film about India's *hijras*, which won a Golden Globe award but, because of its "X" rating, was not circulated. In Latin America, documentaries such as *Butterflies on a Scaffold* (1996) and feature films including *Mi novia el travesti* (*My Fiancée the Transvestite*, 1975), *El lugar sin límites* (*Hell Without Limits*, 1978), *Simón, el gran varón* (*Simon, the Great*

Male, 2002), *Danzón* (1991), and *Madame Satã* (2002) have opened the question of how to create sympathetic and believable trans people in mainstream cinema.

    2. Grammatical gender constraints present problems when talking about intersex people, even as fictional characters. This chapter will doubtless generate some confusion, though we will try to follow the logic of the characters' point of view.

    3. Dreger comments that many of the surgeries done in the United States could be considered genital mutilation, which is prohibited by U.S. federal law, and "it is not at all clear if all or even most of the intersex surgeries done today involve what would legally and ethically constitute informed consent."

    4. This is only one of the film's various utopian qualities, and the reason Alex's character cannot have been submitted to the kinds of genital "reconstructions" typically inflicted on intersex babies—in the name of achieving "normality," such operations often leave the genital area numb, destroying the ability to experience orgasm.

    5. Fittingly enough, Puenzo has announced that her next project will be a screen adaptation of her novel *El niño pez* (Mayer). The novel tells of the doomed love affair between Lala, an Argentine girl, and a Paraguayan indigenous maid. Guayi, the maid (described as not quite human, not quite animal [20]), before coming to Argentina, has given birth to a child who starts to asphyxiate in the air, so the family releases him into the water, where he can breathe (54). Lala later learns that this story is a myth, told to explain why Guayi drowned the baby at birth (162–63).

    6. The scrapbook was created by Inés Efron, who plays Alex in the film. Puenzo comments that she had shown the young actor images by "a German painter who painted small girls with male genitals, and then asked her to invent Alex's diary. She came up with this amazing piece of art, which I decided to include in the film" (Mayer).

Works Cited

Bizzio, Sergio. *Chicos*. Buenos Aires: Interzona, 2004. Print.

Butler, Judith. "Doing Justice to Someone: Sex Reassignment and Allegories of Transexuality." *GLQ A Journal of Lesbian and Gay Studies* 7.4 (2001): 621–36. Print.

"De cerca nadie es normal." Interzona Editora. Web. March 9, 2008.

Dreger, Alice Domurat. "'Ambiguous Sex'—Or Ambivalent Medicine?" *Intersex Society of America*, reprint of *Hastings Center Report* 28.3 (1998): 24–35. Web. Aug. 7, 2008.

Jürgen, Alex. "Pressbook." *Tintenfischalarm*. Web. April 26, 2008.

Mayer, Sophie. "Family Business." *Sight and Sound* 18.6 (June 14, 2008). Web. July 7, 2008.

Puenzo, Lucía. *El niño pez*. Buenos Aires: Beatriz Viterbo, 2004. Print.
Salamon, Gayle. "The Bodily Ego and the Contested Domain of the Material." *differences: A Journal of Feminist Cultural Studies* 15.3 (2004): 95–122. Print.
Sanchez, Diana. "Film Description and Director Biography." *Toronto International Film Festival 2007*. Web. Oct. 4, 2007.
Scharang, Elisabeth. "Facts about Intersexuality." "Pressbook" of *Tintenfischalarm*. Web. April 26, 2008.
Suárez, Pablo. "Palmas para tres." *Agenda de las mujeres*. Web. Sept. 9, 2008.
Tehrani, Bijan. "An Interview with Lucía Puenzo, Director of *XXY*." *Cinema without Borders*. Web. March 7, 2008.
Wilkinson, Amber. Review of *XXY*. *Eye for Film*. Web. March 7, 2008.

Part III

Bisexuality Experiences and Lesbian Identities

10

Excluded Middle?
Bisexuality in *Doña Herlinda y su hijo*

(Jaime Humberto Hermosillo, 1984)

DANIEL BALDERSTON[1]

In late 1994 I gave a paper on the cinema of Jaime Humberto Hermosillo at the Queer Studies Conference at the University of Iowa, and in it used the word *bisexual* to describe the character Rodolfo, the son in *Doña Herlinda y su hijo* (*Doña Herlinda and Her Son*).[2] In one of those comments from the audience for which one is forever grateful, someone (still unknown to me) asked where the bisexuality was in Rodolfo and in the film. I had thought the answer was transparent, because by the end of the film he is married and the father of a son and also still involved in a passionate relationship with the musician Ramón. But several more viewings of the film—and a reading of the contentious but not overly persuasive book by Marjorie Garber, *Vice Versa: Bisexuality and the Eroticism of Everyday Life*—have returned me to the question from the audience, for Hermosillo's 1984 film, like the more recent *Wedding Banquet*, posits the gay male relationship as primary and the heterosexual marriage as a screen created as a response to parental pressure. The late 1970s and early 1980s were a moment of effervescence for the nascent gay liberation movement in Mexico, with the emergence of small but vibrant groups, the Frente Homosexual de Acción Revolucionaria (FHAR) in Mexico City and Grupo Orgullo Homosexual de Liberación (GHOL) in Guadalajara, and the forging of international connections between the Mexican activists and their U.S. counterparts, particularly in San Francisco.[3] Luis Zapata had published *El vampiro de la Colonia Roma* in 1979 (later translated as *Adonis Garcia*), José Joaquín Blanco published his important essay "Ojos que da pánico soñar" in 1981, and the FHAR was publishing *Política sexual: Cuadernos del Frente Homosexual de Acción Revolucionaria*, the first (undated) issue of which circulated three thousand copies. Before 1984 Hermosillo had made at least one implicitly homoerotic film, the 1974 *El cumpleaños del perro* [*The Dog's Birthday*]. It concerns the murder of a young wife by her athlete husband and the protection granted him by a former employer, who eventually murders his own wife when she protests too loudly that her husband has become an accomplice to the first crime. There is nothing overtly sexual about the relation between the two men, and some quite explicitly sexual situations between the young athlete and his new wife. Yet the emotional core of the film is clearly the bond between the athlete and the singularly unattractive older man. As Francisco Sánchez notes in his essay on Hermosillo, at the time the film came out he and other critics were uncertain what to call that bond. He quotes from a review that he himself wrote at the time: "Hay una posibilidad de que los protagonistas de *El cumpleaños del perro* estén señalados por una inclinación homosexual, pero también hay otras muchas posibilidades: relación padre-hijo, sentimiento fraterno, camaradería viril o, simple y sencillamente, afinidad electiva de dos machos mexicanos" (14). [It is possible that the protagonists of *El cumpleaños del perro* are marked by a homosexual inclination, but other possibilities also exist: a father-son relationship, a fraternal feeling, virile camaraderie or, simply, the elective affinity of two Mexican machos], a comment that Sánchez immediately qualifies as "Tonterías, yo sólo le estaba dando vueltas a la simulación, no queriendo aceptar lo que era por demás evidente, que Hermosillo nos había obsequiado la primera película gay de nuestro cine" (14) [Pure foolishness: I was just going round and round in a pretense, not willing to accept what was more than obvious, that Hermosillo had given us the first gay film in our cinema]. But although gay subtexts were present in this and several others of Hermosillo's 1970s films, *Doña Herlinda* looks in retrospect like a response to the "coming-out" narratives of the post-Stonewall period, which impacted strongly in Mexico as elsewhere, a filmic example of which is the 1982 *Making Love*.[4] But these narratives are inflected by Hermosillo with a Mexican twist, here provided by the dominating (and perhaps domineering) presence of an archetypal Mexican mother, Doña Herlinda.

Rodolfo, though he may seem the "macho" of the gay couple, is a weak figure pulled in opposite directions by the two strong individuals in his life, his lover Ramón and his mother Doña Herlinda. Ramón says to him at one point, "Define yourself," but Doña Herlinda has already defined her son as "perfectly ambidextrous." Garber reminds us of the connection in the early Wilhelm Fliess and Sigmund Freud theories of bisexuality between handedness and sexual orientation, so Doña Herlinda is calling on strong cultural models when she asserts—surreptitiously; as always—her son's "native" bisexuality. Her precise statement is that he was born left-handed but that she made him into a perfect ambidexter; his bride's family has already confessed that Olga, the bride-to-be, is left-handed (which would imply lesbianism in the same old theories, an idea hinted at when Olga quickly shifts from skirts to pants).

The sexual politics in the gay couple are set out fairly overtly early in the film. Rodolfo is portrayed with deliberate touches of the filmic image of the famous film actor Jorge Negrete (whom he somewhat resembles),[5] though updated with a beeper in his belt: he wears cowboy boots and white pants, and his appearances in the film, beginning with the opening street scene in which he crosses from the plaza in front of the cathedral of Guadalajara toward the boardinghouse where Ramón lives, are frequently enlivened with the mariachi music about Guadalajara and Jalisco, the very songs sung in so many films by Negrete, considered the very archetype of the macho Mexican male.[6] In the early scene in the boardinghouse, Rodolfo explodes with jealousy at Ramón's friendship with another boarder, Eduardo, who is shown in one scene carving wood and in another knocks on Ramón's door to ask for the return of his hammer. Ramón will have none of Rodolfo's implication that he is attracted to Eduardo: "Es bien buga," he says. Now *buga* (*bugarrón* in the Caribbean) is an equivocal term in Mexican and Caribbean slang; the new *Oxford Spanish Dictionary* defines it as "straight," but a fuller translation would be "straight-acting, but willing to fuck gay men." In working-class Mexico and elsewhere in Latin America (and in working-class New York at least until 1930, as shown by the research of George Chauncey), sexual identity has more to do with roles played than with the sex of the partners; on this point see the eloquent article "Chicano Men; A Cartography of Homosexual Identity and Behavior" by Tomás Almaguer. Ramón is saying that he is interested in being "used as a woman" not by a "straight" man but in a gay relationship; he is defining himself, that is, as an "international," someone whose maps of sexual identity have been redrawn according to modern U.S. and European models.[7] Interestingly, he is apparently of a lower class background than Rodolfo, who resolutely refuses the "international" categories, and whose behavior throughout the film is marked by gender and class privilege.[8] What Almaguer, following Carrier, calls the "bisexual escape hatch"[9] shapes Rodolfo's resistance to the imposed "international" sexual categories, which seem to demand that he "come out" or "define himself" as gay. And yet things are not so simple in the gay couple. Were the "Mexican" or "Latin American" sexual mapping as dominant as Almaguer and others have held, we would expect that Rodolfo would consistently take the "active inserter" role, while Ramón would be cast into the "anal receptive, *pasivo* sexual role."[10] Given the type-casting of Rodolfo as Jorge Negrete and Ramón as a long-haired, pretty, smooth ephebe, it is no surprise that in one early scene in the film Rodolfo is cast as the top, but a later scene unequivocally shows him as the bottom (although in both scenes the men are shown only from the waist up). This looks like "international" behavior, which would demand a remapping and renaming of Rodolfo as gay. But Rodolfo escapes anyway, through the emphatic public devices of marriage and fatherhood.

The straight couple in the film, Rodolfo and Olga, also proves more complicated than first meets the eye. Though there are a few embraces or gestures of Rodolfo's arm around Olga's shoulder, there is relatively little physical passion there. And Olga confirms in a conversation with Ramon that for her too this has been a marriage of convenience, to get away from dictatorial parents (or, as she puts it, to go from the *dictadura* [harsh dictatorship] of her parents to the *dictablanda* [soft dictatorship] of Doña Herlinda). Olga so quickly moves from a rather severe skirt and blazer ensemble to pant suits with ties and even jeans, and is so emphatically interested in pursuing a career, volunteer work with Amnesty International, and her studies (of German of all things, seemingly in response to her father's foreign accent) that she is decisively rejecting the role of the submissive, martyred Mexican wife and mother. She is a "new woman" in an explicitly international mode, while her husband clings to an earlier model of Mexican male identity.

Garber, in one of the few persuasive moments in her book, has argued that bisexual plots always involve triangles, and that the third side of the triangle is often the most interesting. In this case, the relationship that emerges between Olga and Ramón is fascinating. Connected only through Rodolfo, they forge a friendship or complicity that is reminiscent of the women's pictures of the forties, and indeed the gender ambiguities are considerable. Ramón is the more feminine of the two, while Olga in her ties and pant suits plays a very butch number to his femme (though at the end of the film, during the baptism, they are dressed the same, in white jackets, ties, blue slacks, their haircuts similar). The scenes in which the two look radiantly into the cradle are in ironic counterpoint to Rodolfo, the biological father of the baby, who is out in the patio reciting a poem to his mother and her guests. Ramírez Berg, commenting on this relationship, declares: "There's one gentle scene like this after another in the film, and they accumulate to depict a new social order based on the politics of cordial communal interest and mutual respect" (132); his reading no doubt takes Hermosillo too straight, since the director undoes his utopian solutions with cognitive dissonances—here, the gender reversal chat casts Olga as butch and Ramón as femme, in contradiction to so much that is explicit elsewhere in the film. Indeed, it is to Ramón that Olga confesses, "Siempre deseo cosas contradictorias" (I always desire contradictory things), a statement that bears as much on Rodolfo as on herself.

The poem Rodolfo is reciting, meanwhile, is Manuel Acuña's "Nocturno" (a poem he earlier memorized in the sauna with the help of Ramón, who seems to have a better memory for poetry than he does, despite his pretensions as a "declamador"). This poem by the Mexican romantic poet is famous for its association with the poet's suicide in 1873, and the dedication of it to Rosario de la Peña has spawned the persistent theory that Acuña committed suicide after being rejected by Rosario. In this context, though, what is most jarring about the poem is the poet's yearning for a world where he would share his life with his beloved Rosario and also with his beloved and saintly mother (to whom he dedicates a series of other poems). The middle stanzas of the poem (191–92), read by Rodolfo with great emotion at the end of the film, are

> A veces pienso en darte mi eterna despedida,
> borrarte en mis recuerdos y hundirte en mi pasión;
> mas si es en vano todo y el alma no te olvida,
> ¿qué quieres tú que yo haga, pedazo de mi vida,
> qué quieres tú que yo haga con este corazón? . . .
> ¡Qué hermoso hubiera sido vivir bajo aquel techo,
> los dos unidos siempre y amándonos los dos;
> tú siempre enamorada, yo siempre satisfecho,
> los dos una sola alma, los dos un solo pecho,
> y en medio de nosotros, mi madre como un dios!
> [Sometimes I think of saying goodbye to you forever
> erasing you from my memories and sinking you into my passion
> but if it is all in vain and the soul does not forget
> what do you want me to do, piece of my life,
> what do you want me to do with this heart?
> How beautiful it would, have been to live under that roof,

> the two of us united forever and loving one another;
> you always in love, I always satisfied,
> the two of us a single soul, the two a single heart,
> and between us, my mother like a god!]

This melodramatic lyric is worthy of being transformed into a bolero or *canción ranchera* of the kind sung by Lucha Villa earlier in the film, in the scene in which Doña Herlinda lends her handkerchief to the weeping Ramón, so eloquently discussed by José Quiroga in "(Queer) Boleros of a Tropical Night." If the Acuña poem is dedicated implicitly in the film to Ramón (rather than to Rodolfo's wife, Olga), Hermosillo is playing here with multiple ironies. What was impossible in the Mexico of 1873, the coexistence of passionate love with the bourgeois family, and is posed as a utopian dream of a home with both the beloved Rosario and the beloved mother is made real in the film. Rodolfo has it all: a household where he shares life simultaneously with Ramón and with Olga. Ramon is his "compadre" by virtue of being the godfather of the son at the baptism, and is more obviously paternal in his relation to his godson than is the biological father himself. And all of this in a household presided over, administered, by Doña Herlinda herself. When Rodolfo and Olga return from their honeymoon in Hawaii, a period during which Ramón toyed with finding his own way into the gay community but is prevented from doing so by the ever-meddling Doña Herlinda, it is she who proposes the ultimate wedding present for the complicated ménage: architectural drawings showing various new rooms added to the house, including a tower room where Ramón can practice his French horn. The already opulent house must be quite literally expanded into the walled garden to accommodate the new extended family, and all of this at the initiative of the matriarch.

So overpowering, indeed, is Doña Herlinda that one begins to wonder who is in charge of the complex relationships between Ramón, Rodolfo, and Olga. When Ramón dances with a girl at the resort in Chapala so as to annoy Rodolfo (who does indeed become visibly jealous), Doña Herlinda intervenes by saying that *she* is too jealous of Ramón to allow him to dance with other women. When Ramón is tempted to pick up a man during Rodolfo and Olga's honeymoon in Hawaii, Doña Herlinda's presence again interferes. Similarly, Rodolfo seems weak and indecisive when his mother is in action. Ramon's heartfelt cry—"¡Defínete!"—uttered when Rodolfo's engagement to Olga is being defined by others, is the closest we come to a conventional gay liberation narrative in the film. Doña Herlinda, however, proceeds by refusing to define her terms; her only reference to bisexuality, as noted above, comes when she calls Rodolfo "perfectly ambidextrous." It is precisely because of her refusal to define the relationships taking place under her roof that their polymorphous perversity can flourish.[11] Stephen O. Murray calls the arrangements worked out in the film "more wish-fulfillment (a fairy tale?) than representative, even of the upper class," (41) and indeed Joseph Carrier's says of his some seventy-five informants, mostly in Guadalajara (though of a lower-class background than Rodolfo and his mother), that "*none* of my respondents has looked upon homosexual encounters as behavior generally acceptable to his family, nonhomosexual friends, or to society at large" (14).[12]

Doña Herlinda y su hijo transgresses gay cultural expectations as much as it tries to educate straight audiences. The "families we choose"[13] in this film are annoyingly conventional, perhaps, but that seems to be Hermosillo's point: that for an utterly normal and unimaginative gay (or perhaps bisexual) man like Rodolfo, pleasing his mother is the safest way of pleasing himself. Ramón and Olga, the more sympathetic of the younger generation in the film, clearly turn the bizarre situation to their mutual advantage. The fag hag friend of Ramón's at the conservatory is scandalized by the conventional nature of her friend's dreams, but he seems happy with the panoramas that open for him in the new house. And Doña Herlinda can preside over the entire arrangement with poise and self-possession: she knows that she has made it all happen.

In an interview with Hermosillo in *Cineaction* by Florence Jacobowitz, Richard Lippe, and Robin Wood, which took place after the screening in Toronto of the third film in the *tareas* series, Lippe comments:

> You are interested in gay thematics but your films aren't restricted to gay themes. Do you ever find yourself thinking "I should do a gay film" just because you're gay? How do you feel about that or how do you judge your films and your work in relation to your identity as a person? Do you feel a commitment to do a certain amount of work that is gay orientated? (31)[14]

Hermosillo responds: "I never plan my films in that way. It's only most of the time the necessity of telling a story" (Jacobowitz et al. 43). The need to tell a story is inclusive, and does not necessitate the choice of gay material or the avoidance of it. Hermosillo is acutely conscious, though, of the fact that there are limits to what he can do. In the same interview he explains that in the third work in the *tareas* series he showed mother-son incest, but that the producers would not entertain the idea of a father-son incest plot. Perhaps the mother figure in Doña Herlinda is the inscription in Hermosillo's films of censorship and self-censorship. Hermosillo himself has commented on the negative aspects of Doña Herlinda in the interview quoted above (42), but this only serves to open questions posed but not resolved in the film (and elsewhere in his cinema) on the extent to which he is parodying or critiquing Mexican family structures, and on just how radically he is challenging those structures as they impinge on the expression of sexual desire.

In a country where the Monument to the Mexican Mother sits a short block from the downtown intersection of Reforma and Insurgentes in the capital, it is not too far-fetched to hear an echo of the name of the famous Frida Kahlo painting *Madre México y yo* (Mother Mexico and I) in the title of this film. In any case, in the course of the film Doña Herlinda is identified so thoroughly with Mexico—with its cuisine, its art, its sexual mores, its dreams of order and progress—that Olga's comment on the "dictablanda" (soft dictatorship) of Doña Herlinda serves to identify her with the national party, the PRI (Partido Revolucionario Institucional). Like the party, she holds everything together in her anaconda-like deadly grasp. The pop political science terms used by Olga, "dictadura" for her parents' regime and "dictablanda" for Doña Herlinda's, reinforce the identification of Doña Herlinda with the PRI, with its democratic trappings and consensual framework but ultimately dictatorial powers.

Ramírez Berg has called *Doña Herlinda y su hijo* a "Utopia of tolerance."[15] Perhaps, if we remember that most utopias, starting with Thomas More's, have a strong authoritarian streak. Hermosillo himself, in the interview already cited, expresses considerable reservations about the "dictablanda" of Doña Herlinda: "Well, I don't think that Doña Herlinda is a very positive character. She's very sinister, too, because otherwise she wouldn't have asked her son to marry that woman. She helps her son to be happy as a gay man. She's very sinister. She's controlling things the way she wants but she's not giving them freedom" (42). A bit later in the interview he adds: "She's a nice character but some things she does are not fine, but it's beautiful to have those kinds of contradictions in the character" (42). Contradictions: the very word used by Olga to define her objects of desire, and apparently a touchstone of Hermosillo's aesthetics.

In his essay on Hermosillo in the catalog published by the Cineteca National, Francisco Sánchez notes that even in his first films in the 1960s and 1970s Hermosillo was interested in dissonant sexualities and in "freaks," and that the homoerotic elements only gradually became central to his filmography. Indeed, after *Doña Herlinda* Hermosillo has not continued making what one might call "gay" films, though *Clandestino destino* [*Clan-*

destine Destiny, 1987] has one gay male character (out of four) and plays with the possible bisexual nature of the other three characters. In any case, both before and after *Doña Herlinda* Hermosillo has homosexuality present as only one element of a sexual spectrum, and, having said that, the anomalous nature of *Doña Herlinda* itself in the international context of gay filmmaking become more clear, in that in his "gayest" film Hermosillo insistently inscribes homosexuality in the context of the Mexican family structure and seemingly takes for granted the natural bisexuality of one of its main characters.[16] *Doña Herlinda* is not a "coming out" film but a "bringing back in" film, in which the homosexual side of one of the central characters is accommodated within the family structure.

Notes

1. I am grateful to Oscar Chong and Jorge Ruffinelli for help in gathering material on Hermosillo, including videotapes of many of his films, and to José Quiroga and Donna J. Guy for their readings of several versions of this essay. It was previously published in *Sex and Sexuality in Latin America: An Interdisciplinary Reader*, by Daniel Balderston and Donna J. Guy (New York: New York UP, 1997. 190–99).

2. The 1984 film is available from Macondo Video.

3. For a good account of the emergence of gay liberation movements in Mexico, see Ian Lumsden, *Homosexualidad, sociedad y estado en México*, which includes a brief discussion of the work of Luis Zapata and of Hermosillo as emblematic of the period. On the activities of GHOL in Guadalajara (where Hermosillo has been based since the late 1970s,) see Joseph Carrier, *De los otros: Intimacy and Homosexuality among Mexican Men*.

4. On the bisexual plot in *Making Love*, see Marjorie Garber (393–94).

5. In a story in the same volume as the narrative version of *Doña Herlinda y su hijo*, Jorge López Páez writes that his character Emmanuel "resulta una combinación perfecta de Pedro Armendáriz, Jorge Negrete y Pedro Infante y ciertos detalles de Carlos López Moctezuma" [was a perfect combination of Pedro Armendáriz, Jorge Negrete, and Pedro Infante, with certain details of Carlos López Moctezuma] (8).

6. John King refers to the "ebullient machismo of Jorge Negrete" (50), and Charles Ramírez Berg notes "Jorge Negrete's ready smile and unselfconscious demeanor singing songs celebrating *machismo*" (5).

7. See Carrier (193–95).

8. It is hard to say anything very definite about Ramón's class, because when his parents come to visit from the North, it is apparent that they are cultured and bourgeois, though not in the same ostentatious (and urban) way as Doña Herlinda and Rodolfo.

9. See Almaguer (259).
10. See Almaguer (261).
11. In the López Páez story "Doña Herlinda y su hijo," Ramón is the narrator, commenting frequently on the perfect communication that existed between Doña Herlinda and Rodolfo, who seem almost telepathic in their messages in unison.
12. Carrier reiterates the point on page 61.
13. I am thinking of course of the fine book by Kath Weston, *Families We Choose: Lesbians, Gays, Kinship*.
14. In the same issue, see Robin Wood, "Homework Times Three" (28–32).
15. For a virulent attack on Doña Herlinda and on Hermosillo's work in general, see Jorge Ayala Blanco, *La condición del cine mexicano* (356–75). Ayala Blanco observes: "Cruel paradoja: Hermosillo era cada día más festejado y cada día filmaba peor" (366) [A cruel paradox: every day Hermosillo became more famous and yet every day made worse films]. His observations on the amateur acting, poor sound, and cinematography are quite telling, in my opinion.
16. However unlikely the living arrangement in the film, the notion of a more fluid bisexuality in Mexico than in the United States is borne out in the literature, as for instance in Joseph Carrier's "Mexican Male Bisexuality" (especially 83–84).

Works Cited

Acuña, Manuel. *Obras: Poesías, teatro, artículos y cartas*. Ed. José Luis Martínez. México, D. F.: Porrúa, 1949. Print.

Almaguer, Tomás. "Chicano Men; A Cartography of Homosexual Identity and Behavior." *The Lesbian and Gay Studies Reader*. Eds. Henry Abelove, Michele Aina Barale, and David M. Halperin. New York: Routledge, 1993. 255–73. Print.

Ayala Blanco, Jorge. *La condición del cine mexicano*. México, D. F.: Posada, 1986. Print.

Carrier, Joseph. *De los otros: Intimacy and Homosexuality among Mexican Men*, New York: Columbia UP, 1995. Print.

———. "Mexican Male Bisexuality." *Bisexualities: Theory and Research*. Eds. Fred Klein and Timothy J. Wolf. New York: Haworth, 1985). 75–85.

Chauncey, George. *Gay New York: Gender, Urban Culture, and the Making of the Gay Male World, 1890–1940*. New York: Basic Books, 1995. Print.

Garber, Marjorie. *Vice Versa: Bisexuality and the Eroticism of Everyday Life*. New York: Scribner's, 1995. Print.

Hermosillo, Jaime Humberto, dir. *Doña Herlinda y su hijo*. Condor Media, 2006. DVD.

Jacobowitz, Florence, Richard Lippe, and Robin Wood. "An Interview with Jaime Humberto Hermosillo: The Necessity of Telling a Story." *Cineaction* 31 (1993): 155–73. Print.

King, John. *Magical Reels: A History of Cinema in Latin America*. London: Verso, 1990. Print.
López Páez, Jorge. *Doña Herlinda y su hijo y otros hijos*. México, D.F.: Fondo de Cultura Económica, 1993. Print.
Lumsden, Ian. *Homosexualidad, sociedad y estado en México*. Trans. Luis Zapata. México, D. F.; Toronto: Soledicions; Canadian Gay Archives, 1991.
Murray, Stephen O. "Family, Social Insecurity, and the Underdevelopment of Gay Institutions in Latin America." *Latin American Male Homosexualities*. Ed. Stephen O. Murray. Albuquerque, NM: U of New Mexico P, 1995. Print.
Quiroga, José. "(Queer) Boleros of a Tropical Night." *Travesía: Journal of Latin American Cultural Studies* 3.1–3 (1994): 199–213. Print.
Ramírez Berg, Charles. *Cinema of Solitude: A Critical Study of Mexican Film, 1967–1983*. Austin, TX: U of Texas P, 1993. Print.
Sánchez, Francisco. *Hermosillo: Pasión por la libertad*. México, D. F.: Cineteca Nacional, 1989. Print.
Weston, Kath. *Families We Choose: Lesbians, Gays, Kinship*. New York: Columbia UP, 1991. Print.
Wood, Robin. "Homework Times Three." *Cineaction* 31 (1993): 28–32. Print.

11

The Construction of the Bisexual Subject in *No se lo digas a nadie*

(Francisco Lombardi, 1998)

ALFREDO J. SOSA-VELASCO

According to Stephen Hart, Latin American cinema has established itself in the international film industry in the past few decades because it offers a new vision of reality that combines "the grit" associated with the New Latin American cinema of the 1960s and 1970s—typified by such directors as Tomás Gutiérrez Alea, Julio García Espinosa, Jorge Sanjinés, Fernando Solanas, and Patricio Guzmán, recognized for their subaltern vision of the world—with "the slick" of cinematographic masters such as César Charlone and Alejandro González Iñárritu. Hart affirms that such a cinema offers a new version of authorship that combines "a gritty view of life with a slick cinematographic vision" (160). Latin American cinema provides, then, a vision of reality that is not "cute," "political," or conveniently "Third-World" (160). Hart demonstrates this in the work of the Peruvian cinematographic director Francisco Lombardi. For Hart, Lombardi's work offers an interesting field of study regarding the notion of authorship, given the number of films that are adaptations of literary classics. These include *La ciudad y los perros* (*The City and the Dogs*, 1985), based on Mario Vargas Llosa's 1963 novel; *Pantaleón y las visitadoras* (*Captain Pantoja and the Special Services*, 1999), inspired by a 1973 Vargas Llosa novel; *No se lo digas a nadie* (*Don't Tell Anyone*, 1998), based on Jaime Bayly's 1994 novel; and *La tinta roja* (*Red Ink*, 2001), inspired by Alberto Fuguet's 1996 novel. Hart points out that *La ciudad y los perros, Pantaleón y las visitadoras*, and *No se lo digas a nadie* allow us to analyze more precisely the cinematographic vision associated with the author through the process of "filmic subtraction," in which we can measure the originality of Lombardi's version and compare it to the vision of the world expressed in each of the novels (161). For Hart, it is precisely in the instances where Lombardi is most unfaithful to the original that his vision as an author emerges and shines. Lombardi chooses novels that are centered in dialogue, and the filmic version intensifies the strength of the original text. He simplifies the original plot through his use of an astute cast and constructs his films around a series of conflictive moments in which the conflictivity is inserted just when this element does not appear in the original text:

> There is no denying that Lombardi has retained a number of motifs that were present in the original texts, specifically the shocking portrayal of the underbelly of an intrinsically subaltern social reality (animalistic practices in the army, prostitution in the jungle, and sexual promiscuity). In his films Lombardi shows himself to be fascinated by the mechanics of social beliefs, and the ways in which they produce moral dilemmas between individuals. Indeed, he enhances the shock value of this vision—the sense in which these conflicts result in murder, suicide, or torture—by recourse to a set of carefully selected filmic sequences, and it is here where the personal stamp of his vision—its slick grit—lies. (Hart 166–67)

Regarding *No se lo digas a nadie,* Hart affirms that while Bayly's novel is an exploration of gay identity, Lombardi's film "heterosexualizes" the novel to a certain point, gaining dramatic intensity: "It is at points like these that Lombardi's film version demonstrates that it departs radically from Bayly's original novel and, in doing so, formulates its own personal vision of human relationships" (166). *No se lo digas a nadie* presents the life of Joaquín Camino (played by Santiago Magill), a young man from the Peruvian upper class who battles against his own sexual identity. Joaquín's identity is defined by a snobbish society, embodied by his father's (Hernán Romero) machismo and his mother's (Carme Elías) religious zeal, in which, at the end, the idea that in Peru "se puede ser cualquier cosa, menos maricón" [you can be anything except a fag] is reaffirmed. Throughout the film, we see Joaquín as a child, an adolescent, and a university student, trapped in a society that dictates acceptable social behavior, as his parents and his lovers Gonzalo (Christian Meier) and Alfonso (Giovanni Ciccia) explain, and that understands homosexuality as a treatable illness, as Alejandra (Lucía Jiménez) claims in offering to cure Joaquín of his trauma. David W. Foster points out in *Queer Issues in Contemporary Latin America Cinema* (2003):

> [M]uch of the film has to do with examples of the way in which those who have the power to enforce the proscription of being gay—priests, parents, teachers, colleagues, friends, and lovers—read one's body in order to determine if a violation of the deontic meaning of *possible* is to be found. The implication is that if no such violation is discernible, fulfillment of the injunction obtains and society progresses free of the taint of homosexuality (again, whatever it precisely means) and from its threat to the patriarchy. (96)

While Bayly's novel ends with Joaquín living as a homosexual "in exile" in Miami, Lombardi's film "reinserts" him in Lima as bisexual. In the last scenes of the film, the audience sees Joaquín at his law school graduation party. Here, Joaquín bumps into Alfonso, who has married and whose wife is expecting his child, and Gonzalo, who tells Joaquín that whether they get married or not, he has not changed his way of thinking and is still willing to keep having sexual relations with Joaquín. Alejandra arrives at the moment when Joaquín and Gonzalo kiss each other, and tells Joaquín that his relatives and friends are waiting for him to take a picture. The final image of the film (taken as a picture) shows clearly the social construction of Joaquín as a bisexual subject. In this photo, Alejandra is in the middle, with Gonzalo and Joaquín on either side. Just before the picture is taken, Gonzalo touches Joaquín's cheek, and then Joaquín and Gonzalo look directly into each other's eyes, above Alejandra's head, as she looks directly at the camera. This is the moment when the photographer takes the picture and the camera zooms in on the three characters as the film ends, as if the viewer were looking at a black-and-white photo of Joaquín's party. As Pércio de Castro, Jr. (2000) suggests, in Lombardi's filmic adaptation, "el protagonista termina aceptando la idea de que para ser homosexual y poder sobrevivir en la sociedad latinoamericana, tendrá que contraer matrimonio y traicionar a su pareja como a sí mismo, traicionando la naturaleza de su propio ser y vivir una doble vida de apariencias y secretos" (201) [the protagonist ends up accepting the idea that to be gay and be able to survive in Latin American society, he will have to get married and cheat on his spouse as well as himself, betraying the nature of his own self and living a double life of appearances and secrets].

Lombardi's film, then, reinforces the idea that "Latino society/ies regard heteronormativity as the basis of sexuality and that any 'alternative' forms of sexual desire, i.e., homosexuality, are to be eliminated from the realm of such societies" (Subero 201). Through the photograph of the bisexual triangle, the end of Lombardi's film reaches back and redefines the meaning for the entire filmic adaptation, whereas Bayly's novel remains ambiguous by not offering any such closure. Through Joaquín and Alejandra's engagement, *No se lo digas a nadie* supposedly resolves the conflict stated in the film—that of the construction of Joaquín as a bisexual subject—as a textual element adapted from Bayly's novel, seeking the viewer's response. But Lombardi's film does not produce an opposite reading of the protagonist's sexual identity to that in Bayly's novel; rather, the film invites the viewer to read the literary text through a lens affected and controlled by the film.

By heterosexualizing Bayly's novel, suggesting that Joaquín will assume a double life by marrying Alejandra and having affairs with Gonzalo, Lombardi's film not only demonstrates the impossibility of Joaquín's "coming out of the closet" in heteronormative Peruvian society, as some of the film's critics point out. Rather than the homosexual subjectivity constructed in the novel, the film proposes a bisexual subjectivity that criticizes such a society all the more strongly, doubly reaffirming its hypocrisy. This could be the reason why Foster qualifies Lombardi's filmic adaptation as excellent in comparison to Bayly's novel, for which he uses the adjective "mediocre" (94). If Bayly's novel can be read as an exploration of the concept of "coming out of the closet," Lombardi's film can be seen as an answer to the literary text, suggesting that the impossibility of "coming out" brings with it the emergence of a bisexual subject that attacks the discourses on sexuality and gender of normative heterosexuality. For this chapter, "bisexuality" refers to a different subjectivity from the one defined by the "constitutional" model used by film critics such as Robin Wood (1986) and Dennis Bingham (1994), for whom each individual is composed of masculine and feminine aspects. Even more apt is the notion proposed by Maria Pramaggiore (1996), for whom bisexuality is constructed in light of, and in spite of, the cultural practices that define subjects as masculine and feminine, and normalizes heterosexual differences as complementary. For a masculine, feminine, or multiple subject can construct its choice of sexual object as "both/and" instead of "either/or."

The construction of the bisexual subject in *No se lo digas a nadie* subverts the notion of one gender identity as a discursive practice result of such heterosexuality. Judith Butler, in *Gender Trouble: Feminism and the Subversion of Identity* (1990), argues that subversion becomes the way that established categories are destabilized, in which gender parody reveals an identity that is an imitation of an imitation (138) and in which "drag implicitly reveals the imitative structure of gender itself" (175). This subversion (displacement) constitutes, for Butler, an opening for resignifying and recontextualizing, since it is characterized by the process of repetition: "There is no possibility of agency or reality outside of the discursive practices that give those terms the intelligibility that they have. The task is not whether to repeat, but how to repeat or, indeed, to repeat and, through a radical proliferation of gender, to displace the very gender norms that enable the repetition itself" (148). Lombardi's film, then, subverts the construction of homosexual subjectivity that Bayly's novel aims to convey. By constructing Joaquín as a bisexual subject, the filmic adaptation destabilizes any notion of identity as a fixed category. The film also suggests to the viewer that Joaquín's story continually repeats itself. Such a repetition is diegetically shown in the film through the use of Fito Páez's song "El amor después del amor" ["Love after Love"] (1992)—which we hear twice (first, in Joaquín's apartment in Lima when he is with Alejandra, and later, in the Miami club when he runs into her again)—and also through the black-and-white photograph with which the film ends and the credits begin. The song's lyrical voice realizes that after pain he cannot live without love and that "nadie puede ni debe vivir sin amor" [nobody can nor should live without love]. The photo represents what "el amor después del amor" [love after love] is; that is, it leaves us with proof of Joaquín's love for Gonzalo. If this is the proof, then Joaquín's is genuinely homosexual in his intimate life, while ambivalently bisexual in social settings. This would suggest something of an authentic homosexuality in private contexts, versus a purely functional bisexuality in public contexts.

No se lo digas a nadie proposes precisely that, just like the stories of Gonzalo and Alfonso, Joaquín's story will be repeated so that he has to lead a double life. Unlike in Bayly's novel, the film's characters display these double lives through the diverse triangles formed by Joaquín-Gonzalo-Alfonso and their various partners throughout Lombardi's filmic adaptation. Despite the supposed heterosexualization that the film portrays, the bisexual triangle brings to mind how to examine the filmic adaptation against the literary text, and the implications of such an examination. While Bayly's novel ends with Joaquín "exiled" in Miami, the film shows that if he wants to return to Peru, he is left with no other option than to comply publicly with social expectations—becoming a lawyer and getting back together with

Alejandra—in order to maintain sexual relations with Gonzalo, through a supposedly heterosexual life with his future wife, just as Gonzalo pretended when he went out with Rocío (played by Lita Baluarte). Unlike in Bayly's novel, in which, toward the end, Joaquín thinks that he would like to tell his mother about his homosexuality—tell her that she has to understand that he is gay, that it is his nature, and that he cannot stop, and doesn't even want to stop, being himself (357)—the film is totally pessimistic (Foster 109). We also cannot forget that the filmic adaptation, like Bayly's novel, alludes to the author's own bisexuality. Bayly has acknowledged having lived a heterosexual life in Miami while he was a spokesperson for gays, and, later, publicly declaring himself bisexual (Ruz 31). What matters here is, first, how the construction of a bisexual subjectivity functions within the film *No se lo digas a nadie* and, second, what aesthetic (of creation and representations) and social effects (of reception and consumption) such a construction has for the public. As Alexander Doty (1993) notes, "queerness is a mass cultural reception practice that is shared by all sorts of people in varying degrees of consistency and intensity" (xi, 2). And as Pramaggiore adds, even when texts are about "queer" or "queerness," the textual elements can repress or express possibilities for bisexual desire; that is, "nonsingular desires that may be attached from strict sex and/or gender oppositions [. . .] bisexual readings may be available to anyone reading cultural texts, but they are also a specific product of historical and cultural circumstances which authorize these readings" (276). For Foster, Lombardi's film is centered in the parenthetical "anyway":

> [N]o matter what, one is gay anyway; no matter what, one has same-sex partners; no matter what, one adjusts one's accommodations with the heteronormative patriarchy in order to have same-sex partners. And no matter what, the business of society proceeds apace despite the violation to its integrity which—it is at least implied by the intensity of the homophobic screed—threatens its very survival in the form of disrupted procreation and disrupted family life. In other words, Lombardi's film is about the powerful force of hypocrisy that works in appallingly efficient tandem with homophobia to ensure what is *possible* both defies social truth and permits that which is disallowed. (97)

Even though, as Foster points out, the film denounces society's hypocrisy, it seems equally important that Lombardi presents such a denunciation by constructing a bisexual subject. It is precisely through Joaquín's suggested

The Construction of the Bisexual Subject in *No se lo digas a nadie*   191

bisexuality—as well as Gonzalo's and Alfonso's—that Lombardi's film makes the viewer question the genealogies of gender and sexuality.

For the study of *No se lo digas a nadie*, as Clare Hemmings affirms in *Bisexual Spaces: A Geography of Gender and Sexuality* (2002), it is important to rethink the specific formations of bisexuality as "not produced as middle ground at all but as a subset of either heterosexuality or homosexuality, for example, or in close association with other subjects or communities" (2). As Hemmings points out, the bisexual subject becomes the carrier of heterosexist hegemony within the lesbian, gay, or queer community: the bisexual subject incarnates the cultural body or hologram of a psychic model of sexual subjectivity. That model makes the opposite sex the only possible object. From there, according to Hemmings, the bisexual subject cannot be structurally produced from the gender of the chosen sexual object, or from the position of the subject itself, or from the chronology of the subject's sexual identity. In the case of *No se lo digas a nadie*, then, we should ask ourselves how bisexuality is generated—what meaning it acquires in such a context, when its purpose is to underline the limits of the discourses on sexuality and gender. Hemmings identifies three primary forms of a bisexual epistemological approach: first, locating bisexuality as a conventional category beyond those of sexuality and gender; second, making an inner critique of those three categories; and third, underlining the importance of bisexuality in the discursive formation of "other" identities (31).

More than explaining or defining bisexuality in Lombardi's film, we should locate bisexuality in *No se lo digas a nadie* as a tool that underlines the structural problem within sexual identity. If we view bisexuality as an epistemological identity more than as an identity that integrates heterosexual and homosexual orientations, then we can examine that the construction of a bisexual subject in Lombardi's film refers to the reconfiguration of a subject as a double agent: the bisexual subject not only wants to *be* a man and a woman; he also wants to *have* the man and the woman. In *No se lo digas a nadie*, such a reconfiguration is represented in two moments, when Joaquín asks Alejandra to explain to him her sexual acts with her ex-boyfriend Carlos: first, in Joaquín's apartment, when Alejandra comes to see him after a fight with Carlos and tells him that Carlos called her a "puta" [whore] and threatened to tell everyone that she had performed oral sex on him; and, second, at the beach, when Joaquín and Alejandra spend the day together and have sexual relations for the first time. As a result of his conversations with Alejandra, Joaquín tries to get aroused twice so that he can initiate sex with her. The first time ends in failure and pushes Joaquín tell Alejandra that although he really likes her, he also likes guys. The second time is a success. They consummate the relationship on the beach, when Joaquín gets excited after asking her where and how she used to make love with Carlos. This instability between wanting to be and wanting to have—represented by Joaquín in Lombardi's film—is what, for Jonathan Dollimore, makes the position of the bisexual voyeur demand our attention because bisexuals are not confused or undecided but, rather, go beyond the limitations of identification and desire (531). By asking Alejandra for information, Joaquín not only becomes a kind of voyeur of Alejandra and Carlos's sexual acts (the ones she tells him of) but also makes the viewers voyeurs of such acts as well as those of himself and Alejandra. Finally, *No se lo digas a nadie* puts the viewer into the same position as voyeur of the triangle formed by Joaquín-Alejandra-Gonzalo and shows that bisexuality—whether of Joaquín, Gonzalo, or Alfonso—has a discursive impact as much for the bisexual as for the nonbisexual. What functions does bisexuality have in the discourses on sexuality in *No se lo digas a nadie*? When and how is bisexuality invoked in Lombardi's film? When and why does it disappear, and what effects does the disappearance bring to the filmic adaptation? What questions come to the viewers' attention?

In *No se lo digas a nadie,* the construction of a bisexual subjectivity is the option that Joaquín has not only to keep having sexual relations with Gonzalo but also to integrate himself into Peruvian society, as shown at the end of the film. Both Gonzalo and Alfonso explain to Joaquín that under these terms, "se puede ser maricón en el Perú" [you can be a fag in Peru]. The difference between them and the "cholo rosquete" [Indian fag] (played by Aníbal Zamoa), whom Joaquín and his friends insult and beat up in the park, establishes the separation between those who are publicly recognized as gays and those who are not, at the same time that it shows the differences in race and class among the young men of Lima's upper class, to which Joaquín and his friends belong, and those who cross-dress and prostitute themselves for economic reasons like the young man in the park. While Bayly's novel presents the aggression against the "rosquetes travestis" [cross-dressing fags] in two different scenes—first, the attack against Pelusa in Javier Prado and, second, against the man in the Olivar who says he is a woman (227–31)—Lombardi's film unites these two as one, showing only the rumble in the park. If the film denounces the hypocrisy of society's accepted sexual behaviors by suggesting the double life Joaquín will lead, such criticism, on the other hand, also shows the gulf between certain members of society given the race and class to which they belong. Also, it is worth remembering the scene in which, on the way back to the city from the mountains, Joaquín's father hits a "cholo" [Indian] on a bike and tells his son, "No cacé nada, pero maté a un cholo de regreso" [I didn't hunt anything, but I killed an Indian on the way back]. Ultimately, bisexuality appears invoked, when the film ends with the apparent black-and-white photograph so that the viewer thinks about not only what Joaquín has become—a result of circumstances—but also the cultural representation of such a bisexuality.

This analysis benefits from the contributions of Stacey Young (1997) and Jo Eadie (1997), for whom bisexuality is a trope for "something else"—typically confusion, madness, or greed. Its metaphorical presence, or invocation, appears associated with other anxieties—for example, those concerning race, since the "cholos rosquetes" [Indian fags] are distinguished from those who are not. Besides the "cholos rosquetes," we also see another "cholo"—Dioni (played by Elmiran Cossío)—whom Joaquín physically attacks after asking him not to tell his father that he made a pass by suggesting that they touch each other. The "rosquetes" [fags], then, are different from those who would not identify themselves as "rosquetes," such as Gonzalo, who would have married Rocío if Joaquín had not spoken with her, and Alfonso, who is already married and expecting a child. Joaquín, who thinks he will possibly marry Alejandra, in some ways fits into this group, despite the clear awareness he has of his stigmatized sexuality.

However, bisexuality disappears in the moment when it is not expressed publicly, when it is not articulated as a discourse on "coming out" but is instead suggested and is understood by the viewer. The effect of such a disappearance is to play with the viewer's expectations, since Joaquín is constructed as a bisexual subject precisely in the moment when he rejects the possibility of coming out after having understood who he is. Unlike the "rosquetes," whose homosexuality is clearly readable in terms of what Lee Edelman (1994) has called a "homograph"—the opposition between the "unwritable" and the "already written"—since homosexual desire is represented as it is inscribed in the bodies of its participants, Joaquín has signed on to a "cultural repudiation," which ensures his identity within heteronormative society. Joaquín refuses to help the guy in the park when he is beaten, since he doesn't identify with him, and at the end, he lets the viewer foresee that he will marry Alejandra while continuing to have sexual relations with men such as Gonzalo. With this in mind, Foster's comment on the film scene of Joaquín with the prostitute (played by Vanessa Robbiano) is interesting. Foster says that one of the possible reasons for Joaquín's semi-erect penis in the scene is to mark the sexuality of his body in violation of conventions, since "the queer is always portrayed as an effeminate nerd for whom sexual practices involve a repudiation of what is believed (what is enforced to be) the female role in the sexual act" (105). Thus, the representation of Joaquín contradicts the stereotype of the homosexual subject as effeminate and passive.

No se lo digas a nadie shows, then, that there are no finite sexual or social practices that adhere to a bisexual identity. Rather, the nature of a bisexual existence is, as Hemmings affirms, always partial, mostly experienced within the communities that do not recognize bisexuality as viable and are filtered through discourses on identity (38). The construction of Joaquín as a bisexual subject should be understood as "something more" than a heterosexual or homosexual subjectivity. That is, his sexuality refers to "living realities" that do not resonate with accepted experiences of sex, gender, or sexual practices. *No se lo digas a nadie* subverts the discourse of Bayly's novel and the critique that the novel itself makes by heterosexualizing its protagonist, by placing Joaquín in the center of the construction of a bisexual identity that is not reduced to the heterosexual/homosexual dyad or to the binary constructions of gender. As many theorists of bisexual feminist epistemology—for example, Donna Haraway, Elspeth Probyn, Rosi Braidotti, and Judith Butler—are concerned about articulating an understanding of "subject in process," which is formed *through* experiences and not *before* them, *No se lo digas a nadie* shows that the construction of such a subject results from questioning the heterosexist oppositions regarding sexuality and gender.

Lombardi's filmic adaptation presents such questioning by playing with the notion of representation. If his film is an adaptation of Bayly's novel, it represents the novel on various levels. Among the many entries of "representar" [to represent] in the *Diccionario de la Lengua Española,* one about political representation is particularly interesting: "sustituir a alguien o hacer sus veces, desempeñar su función o la de una entidad, empresa, etc." [substitute for someone or do his duties, to carry out his function or that of an entity, enterprise, etc.]. For the editors of *The Bisexual Imaginary: Representation, Identity and Desire* (1997), the term "representation" invokes a political representation as a link between a visual or textual representation of a community and the party, candidate, or spokesperson said to represent that community (3). To represent, visually or textually, a community or a group means to participate in a form of politics. In this fashion, *No se lo digas a nadie* is a representation of Bayly's novel as an adaptation that "makes something present," "declares or refers," and "is an image or symbol of something," as well as a "persona que representa a un ausente, cuerpo o comunidad" [person who represents someone absent, a body, or a community] (*Diccionario de la Real Academia Española*). Viewers of Lombardi's film who are familiar with Bayly's novel will notice the filmic adaptation's changed ending from that of the novel. And they can think about the implications for the novel and the film as cultural products. Lombardi's film has added an invention not present in the novel. The entire sequence of Joaquín's return to Perú and resumption of his relationship with Gonzalo is a deviation from the novel—which the reader of the novel cannot ignore. Although Lombardi's film presents the viewer with "la historia más escandalosa de Lima" [Lima's most scandalous story] (as characterized by the Internet Movie Database [IMDB]), he comforts the viewer with the final scenes, in which it is evident that, as Foster notes, Joaquín ends up "fine—despite his alienation and anguish, accompanied by alcohol, drugs, and prostitution (99).

By proposing the construction of a bisexual subject, *No se lo digas a nadie* provides representation for those who are not represented, although they are present, and for those who form part of a community. Beyond the mere stereotypical representation of a subjectivity, it seems important to keep in mind that any visual representation implies a repertoire of images before which the viewer has certain expectations about what is represented. Thus, the truly important thing is not so much the image's content as how the content acquires meaning. Representation is an arena filled with contradictory messages. In such an arena, the availability of images and the fidelity of what is represented participate in the process of constructing a specific subjectivity. In this theoretical perspective, filmic images serve as a touchstone for identification. Here we have two metaphors associated with the concept of the screen itself: that of the *window* (as developed by the film thinker André Bazin and the realists) and that of the *frame* (as developed by the theorists Sergei Eisenstein, Rudolf Arnheim, and the formalists). Although cinema is at once the window and the frame, it is also a mirror. Jacques Lacan, in his *Écrits* (1989), postulates that the child is constituted as a subject that enters into the imaginary order just when he begins to recognize his reflection in the mirror, when his image appears complete and unified, as an individual separated from the rest of the world, against the experience of being fragmented, disunited, and chaotic. According to Lacan, the "mirror phase" is what constitutes us as human subjects, and that phase has as much to do with identification as with alienation: to become a subject, one needs an image, but that image is always illusory, and being oneself is always precarious in that it is based on a fictional illusion (2). If we constitute ourselves as subjects through an image that is not our own (since the mirror always gives us an inaccurate image of ourselves, more complete and perfect that we really are), then to look at ourselves in the mirror is to realize that we are not what we thought we were after all. The imaginary order is, therefore, a space of possibility and affirmation but also of disorientation and confusion.

Through showing the construction of Joaquín as a bisexual subject, *No se lo digas a nadie* exposes such a process as authentic and artificial at the same time. Just like the novel, Lombardi's film shows Joaquín looking at himself in the mirror after his father tries to teach him how to box. The film points out that heteronormative society's discourse on sexuality and gender does not recognize bisexuality as an identity. The viewer must therefore ask, is Joaquín bisexual because he is left with no other option, or is it his own choice? If it were possible to come out of the closet as gay, would Joaquín still end up engaged to Alejandra to fulfill social expectations? The bisexual subjectivity is configured through an ironic imaginary in that "[t]he bisexual imaginary is both iconic (setting up an image) and ironic (destabilizing that image), without having to choose between the two" (Davidson, Eadie, Hemmings, Kaloski, and Storr 11). *No se lo digas a nadie* provides the viewer with the representation of the bisexual subject while destabilizing it at the same time. From the point of view of the representation of the image, Lombardi shows that the characters Joaquín, Gonzalo, and Alfonso in the film are conventionally masculine: the man who is firmest in terms of his erotic rights, Gonzalo, is the most conventionally "macho" of the three. Foster notes:

> While this hypermasculinity may be legitimate in the effort to reject the effeminate stereotype integral to someone like the elder Camino's version of sexual deviation (as seen in what he views to be his son's effeminacy in handling the boxing gloves), it is purchased with the cost of seeming to naturalize homoerotic love: these men are conventionally masculine figures in appearance, without the threatening, disruptive force of effeminacy. (108)

Lombardi destabilizes the image of the three by showing that Joaquín, Gonzalo, and Alfonso are bisexual, since, as Gustavo Subero (2006) points out, Alfonso's attitude toward homosexuality is similar to Gonzalo's:

> He believes that engaging in man-to-man sex is not a problem as long as the individual lives a pretended heterosexual life. Alfonso does not even regard himself as *entendido* but as someone who is experiencing with his sexuality; his homosexual tendencies are *un vicio pasajero* (a temporary vice). His fear of accepting his

homosexuality is the fear of assuming a sexual dysphoria that contravenes the fixity of sexual roles within macho society. It is the "fear of becoming, feeling, or representing female desire within the phallocentric order." (195–96)

Laura Mulvey, in "Visual Pleasure and Cinema" (1975), has affirmed that traditional cinema invokes and satisfies the scopophilic impulse through the obvious voyeurism of the theatrical situation while, at the same time, appealing to the narcissistic impulse of the ego through the characters on the screen with whom the viewers identify. These impulses are encountered in a standard film in which the female star serves as an object as much for the gaze as for the action of the masculine hero:

> A male movie star's glamorous characteristics are thus not those of the erotic object of the gaze, but those of the more perfect, more complete, more powerful ideal ego conceived in the original moment of recognition in front of the mirror . . . But in psychoanalytic terms, the female figure poses a deeper problem . . . her lack of a penis, implying the threat of castration and hence unpleasure. (34–35)

The viewers identify themselves, then, with the hero, and through him they experience pleasure. For Mulvey, all the resources of cinema function to promote the pleasures associated with the values of the viewers' sexual differences, with the goal of assuring them that these obsessions are natural and that the fictions of cinema would simply mirror the facts of their own lives. By talking about bisexual characters, Pramaggiore proposes analyzing this kind of triangle considering the narrative structure and the viewer's identification:

> The fence is a position from which "same" and "opposite" sex desires of particular characters can be explored rather than viewed as mutually exclusive and is a location from which spectators may be expected to form multiple identifications among variously sexed and gendered characters. Reading from the fence also calls into question the foreclosure of bisexual desire by monosexual, coupled resolutions. (273)

Thus, Pramaggiore seeks to eroticize identification and to explore the fluidity of desire. Marjorie Garber, in *Viceversa: Bisexuality and the Eroticism of Everyday Life* (1995), notes that in an erotic triangle, desire depends on the subject's *position* in that triangle more than on gender or sexual identity. She emphasizes the importance of analyzing "the connections among the 'other' partners that need articulating" (443). Relationships between the members of the erotic triangle are characterized by rivalry, jealousy, and competition. The erotic triangle offers the possibility of identification and desire simultaneously through different positions—regardless of the gender of the characters occupying these positions—the triangulation underlines, according to Pramaggiore, the "both/and" quality of bisexual desire (277). In *No se lo digas a nadie,* Joaquín, Gonzalo, and Alfonso are, for the viewer, the perfect object of temptation, since the three are attractive, available, and can be desired both by men and by women. Alejandra is equally attractive and available and can be desired by the viewers. As for the masculine characters, *No se lo digas a nadie* proposes that the bisexual subject will always be unfaithful. Joaquín and Gonzalo will keep having relations with each other whether they have a female partner or not, whether they are married or not. In this sense, Lombardi's film explores the construction of the bisexual subject through the establishment of its relationships. The identification with the characters and with the story is based on an identification with the process of watching; the viewer becomes a voyeur and, ultimately, observes everything through the camera lens. At the end of the film, the viewers see before them the photo of the final scene. This photo can suggest to the viewer that both Joaquín and Gonzalo are bisexual because they can embody the social dangers of a kind of person that does not fit totally within the expectations of heteronormative society. The film shows that the homosexual subject does not exist in such a society, and the representation of the bisexual suggests under what terms that subject can maintain a relationship, operating within society and dealing with its sexual desire. Joaquín is bisexual because of his passion and appetite for men. The bisexual subject is not reduced to a restrictive space dictated by what is permitted. That is why that subject tries to integrate itself, to fit into society—and yet, in the process it disturbs the social equilibrium.

In *No se lo digas a nadie,* the bisexual subjectivity is explicitly represented, and the Joaquín-Alejandra-Gonzalo triangle, among the others that exist in the film, is crucial to representing it. Bisexuality becomes a metaphor and an agent for the structural instability of heterosexual relationships—more than a mere obstacle that the homosexual or heterosexual characters must overcome. The tension between identification and desire created by the triangle assumes the form of an opposition between identification and desire (heterosexuality), or a mixture of both (homosexuality), and gives resonance and permanence to monosexual formations, rejecting the game of identifications and desires between sex and gender that characterize bisexuality. The construction of the bisexual subject in *No se lo digas a nadie* prevents the viewer from identifying completely with any of the masculine (Joaquín, Gonzalo, Alfonso) or feminine (Alejandra) characters. It is a metaphor for the division between masculine and feminine in the subject that is problematic. It has to do more with *wanting to be* one of the characters (narcissism, according to Mulvey) or *having* one (scopophilia, fetishism, erotic position through the gaze) than with identifying with them. Joaquín, Alejandra, and Gonzalo are potential sexual objects for other characters and viewers. What distinguishes the masculine bisexual characters (Joaquín, Gonzalo, and Alfonso) from the homosexual characters is that they resist any type of codification between identification and desire. Lombardi's film resists a "closed ending" resolution as much for the heterosexual as for the homosexual couple, emphasizing the importance of desire among the characters of the triangle. That is why the construction of the bisexual subject in the film cannot be limited to the viewers who identify themselves as bisexual subjects.

Finally, *No se lo digas a nadie* shows, through the construction of Joaquín as a bisexual subject, the fluidity of identity: Joaquín acts like what he is not, and makes those around him believe it. He pretends to live as a heterosexual with Alejandra so that his family believes it, although the viewer realizes that he is constructed as a bisexual subject who will continue having sexual relations with Gonzalo. The film's phallic rhetoric demonstrates that the representation of sexuality escapes definition by heteronormative society. The film also offers viewers alternatives to the constitution of a heterosexual subjectivity and of couples, since, according to what the photo at the end suggests, Joaquín and Alejandra's relationship is shown through observing Alejandra as an object of desire—Joaquín's apparent attraction—that does not conform to the stereotypical vision of heterosexuality. The representation of the bisexual subject in Lombardi's film permits an exploration of sexuality beyond the discourses on gender and sexuality, in that desire becomes the force that moves the characters. The triangular relationship between Joaquín, Alejandra, and Gonzalo is the movie's political statement to Peruvian society. *No se lo digas a nadie* not only shows a new vision of Latin American cinema, as Hart proposes, but also exemplifies new practices in how viewers observe this new cinema. The movie's "queer" theme seeks to give representation and agency to certain individuals who have no place in society, while at the same time denouncing the overwhelming social discourses that marginalize and oppress them.

Works Cited

Bayly, Jaime. *No se lo digas a nadie*. Barcelona: Seix Barral, 1994. Print.
Bingham, Dennis. *Acting Male: Masculinities in the Film of James Stewart, Jack Nicholson, and Clint Eastwood*. New Brunswick, NJ: Rutgers UP, 1994. Print.
Butler, Judith. *Gender Trouble: Feminism and the Subversion of Identity*. New York: Routledge, 1990. Print.
Castro Jr., Pércio de. "Gritemos a plenos pulmones y contémoselos a todos: revelando secretos en *No se lo digas a nadie* de Jaime Bayly y Francisco Lombardi." *Cine-Lit 2000: Essays on Hispanic Film and Fiction*. Ed. George Cabello-Castellet, Jaume Martí-Olivella, and Guy H. Wood. Portland, OR: Oregon State UP, 2000. Print.
Davidson, Phoebe et al., eds. *The Bisexual Imaginary: Representation, Identity and Desire*. London: Cassell, 1997. Print.
Diccionario de la Real Academia Española. 2009. Web. Sept. 21, 2009.
Dollimore, Jonathan. "Bisexuality, Heterosexuality, and Wishful Theory." *Textual Practice* 10.3 (1996): 523–39. Print.
Doty, Alexander. *Making Things Perfectly Queer: Interpreting Mass Culture*. Minneapolis, MN: U of Minnesota P, 1993. Print.
Eadie, Jo. "'That's Why She Is Bisexual': Contexts for Bisexual Visibility." *The Bisexual Imaginary: Representation, Identity and Desire*. Ed. Phoebe Davidson et al. London: Cassell, 1997. 142–60. Print.
Edelman, Lee. *Homographesis: Essays in Gay Literary and Cultural Theory*. New York: Routledge, 1994. Print.
Foster, David W. *Queer Issues in Contemporary Latin America Cinema*. Austin, TX: U of Texas P, 2003. Print.
Garber, Marjorie. *Viceversa: Bisexuality and the Eroticism of Everyday Life*. New York: Simon and Schuster, 1995. Print.
Hall, Donald, and Maria Pramaggiore, eds. *Representing Bisexualities: Subjects and Cultures of Fluid Desire*. New York: New York UP, 1996. Print.
Hart, Stephen. "'Slick grit': Auteurship versus Mimicry in Three Films by Francisco Lombardi." *New Cinemas: Journal of Contemporary Film* 3.3 (2005): 159–67. Print.
Hemmings, Clare. *Bisexual Spaces: A Geography of Sexuality and Gender*. New York: Routledge, 2002. Print.
Lacan, Jacques. *Écrits: A Selection*. Trans. Annette Lavers. London: Routledge, 1989. Print.
Lombardi, Francisco, dir. *No se lo digas a nadie*. Lolafilms, 1998. DVD.
Mulvey, Laura. "Visual Pleasure in the Narrative Cinema." *Screen* 16.3 (1975): 6–18. Print.
Phelan, Sean, ed. *Playing with Fire: Queer Theory, Queer Politics*. New York: Routledge, 1997.

Ruz, Robert. *Contemporary Peruvian Narrative and Popular Culture: Jaime Bayly, Iván Thays and Jorge Eduardo Benavides*. Woodbridge, UK: Tamesis, 2005. Print.
Subero, Gustavo. "The Different *Caminos* of Latino Homosexuality in Francisco J. Lombardi's *No se lo digas a nadie.*" *Studies in Hispanic Cinemas* 2.3 (2006): 189–204. Print.
Wood, Robin. *Hollywood from Vietnam to Reagan*. New York: Columbia UP, 1986. Print.
Young, Stacey. "Dichotomies and Displacement: Bisexuality in Queer Theory." *Contemporary Peruvian Narrative and Popular Culture: Jaime Bayly, Iván Thays and Jorge Eduardo Benavides*. Ed. Sean Phelan. Woodbridge, UK: Tamesis, 2005. 51–74. Print.

12

Lesbians Made in Mexico: Sexual Diversity and Transnational Fluxes

María de la Cruz Castro Ricalde[1]

The cinematic production of Mexico has followed paths quite similar to those of the country's literature, insofar as the theme of sexual diversity is concerned. In both cases there have been outstanding depictions of male homosexuality, even if their presence is not overwhelming; but that does not necessarily mean that these depictions have had considerable mass readership, or that they appear in canonic publications or anthologies. Some paradigmatic cases would be the novels *El diario de José Toledo* (*Jose Toledo's Diary*, 1964) by Miguel Barbachano Ponce, *El vampiro de la colonia Roma* (*The Vampire of the Roma Neighborhood*, 1979) by Luis Zapata, *Utopía gay* (*Gay Utopia*, 1983) by José Rafael Calva, *Las púberes canéforas* (*The Adolescent Canephoras*, 1983) by José Joaquín Blanco, *Agapi Mu* (*My Love*, 1993) by Luis González de Alba, and, in a way, *Fruta verde* (*Unripe Fruit*, 2007) by Enrique Serna. Curiously, the titles mentioned form a timeline that begins in the sixties and, if listed exhaustively, would show much more prevalence in the eighties and nineties. In turn, to the two most widely known films, *El lugar sin límites* (Arturo Ripstein's *The Place Without Limits*, 1977) and *Doña Herlinda y su hijo* (Jaime Humberto Hermosillo's *Doña Herlinda and Her Son*, 1984) one can easily add the movies of the best-known contemporary producer of films of this variety, Julián Hernández: from his opera prima *Mil nubes de paz cercan el cielo, amor, jamás acabarás de ser amor* (*A Thousand Peace Clouds Encircle the Sky*, 2004), to *El cielo dividido* (*Broken Sky*, 2006) and *Rabioso sol, rabioso cielo* (*Raging Sun, Raging Sky*, 2009). If one were to mention subplots, the list would be even vaster. In other words, even if the gay topic is not continually revisited in Mexican narrative and film, a body of work does exist that allows for the identification of existing depictions of male homosexuality in the last half-century.[2]

Lesbianism, on the other hand, would seem to not form part of the national imaginary of Mexico, given that there are few notable novels; *Amora* (1989) by Rosamaría Roffiel, *Dos mujeres* (*The Two Mujeres*, 1990) by Sara Levi Calderón, *Infinita* (*Infinite*, 1992) by Ethel Krauze, and more recently, *Te seguiré buscando* (*I Will Keep Looking for You*, 2003) by Josefina Estrada, and *Casa de la Magnolia* (*House of the Magnolia*, 2004) by Pedro Ángel Palou. In Mexican cinema lesbians have been invisible, as opposed to the large contingent of effeminate men and transvestites that filled the screens between the seventies and eighties. Nods like *Tres mujeres en la hoguera* (Abel Salazar's *Three Women in the Bonfire*, 1979) have multiplied in the last decade, still without any titles focusing on lesbian identity.

The inclusion of actresses recognizable by their presence on the Mexican small screen—primarily by way of their telenovelas—and lighthearted plots with uncomplicated structures ensured a public that could appreciate these films in movie theaters, television broadcasts, or thanks to their DVD sales. Some of those films, such as *Niñas mal* (*Charm School*, Fernando Sariñana [2007]) and *Hasta el viento tiene miedo* (*Even the Wind is Afraid*, Gustavo Moheno, [2007]) include lesbian characters in secondary roles, in the form of quasi-adolescents; *Así del precipicio* [*Close to the Edge*] (Teresa Suárez, 2006) and *Todo incluido* [*All Inclusive*] (Rodrigo Ortúzar, 2009) present two young women who have recently separated from their male partners, and their encounters with two attractive women reveal to them their homosexuality. Deploying certain stereotypes by showing sex scenes based on frontal nudity (in the case of the first film) or avoiding them (in the case of the second), these characters are ultimately quite innocuous for the heterosexual spectator, and hardly suggestive for audiences with more diverse orientations. Even so, although both films depart from the pathological perspective and the homophobic slant so characteristic of Hollywood cinema of the fifties and sixties, they do not escape the suggestion of compulsive heterosexuality. On the contrary, this is reinforced by these characters, whose orientation does not disturb their families, or their friends, or society in general.

My analysis will focus on one of the aspects of the depiction of lesbians in Mexican cinema of the twentieth century: young, beautiful, upper-middle class, and inhabitants of urban enclaves are the prevalent traits in the characters who suddenly "discover" in their attraction to another woman, their "true" sexual preference. *Así del precipicio* and *Todo incluido* offer scenes of courting and seduction that are evidently organized around a desire that is both male and heterosexual. The present analysis contemplates a transnational configuration, which perhaps makes visible some lesbian exchanges in a Mexican environment; but these exchanges only originate in cosmopolitan settings, are reduced to members of a privileged social class, are posed either as a game or a "need" for experimentation, and are explained by a foreign presence, alien to the idiosyncrasy of Mexico.

Made in Mexico

Así del precipicio and *Todo incluido* portray a modern country, with a lifestyle and atmosphere similar to that of any other major world capital. Both are structured around several stories that function in chorus to portray the dysfunctionality of a society in the first case, and that of a family in the second. In both cases, the young women Hanna (Irene Martz) and Macarena (Ana Serradilla) have just separated from their husbands, and a geographic displacement can perhaps help them clarify their ideas. Hanna moves to the apartment of her friends Lucía (Ana de la Reguera) and Carmen (Gaby Platas), both addicted to cocaine. Macarena settles in with her immediate family to spend a week on vacation at an expensive resort in the Mexican Caribbean. The anecdotes of these characters, however, do not serve as the primary thread in their respective films. Hanna's story in fact, is the plot that is given the least attention of the three presented in *Así del precipicio*, whereas Macarena's does serve the principle idea of *Todo incluido*. Notwithstanding the difference in plots, I would like to point out the multiple coincidences in the way they construct lesbian identity, and in what way this identity fits into society at large.

Suárez's movie prepares the spectator to comprehend Hanna's doubts regarding her sexual orientation. She belongs to the Jewish community and this itself constitutes a mark of "foreignness," or otherness, in a nation that holds Catholicism as a part of its unifying traditions. Upon discovering the infidelities of her wealthy husband—an overprotected "mama's boy"—she abandons their home and, instead of following her first impulse (to sign the divorce papers immediately), she concedes to giving time to consider whether or not to return to Abraham. Surrounded by a luxurious environment, in the exclusive jewelry store where she works, she meets a client who impacts her, Sandra. Sandra instantly shows interest in Hanna, and provides her with her private phone number, which will result in a couple of dates: enough for the young woman to accept the physical attraction she feels for Sandra. In the interim, Hanna dreams about the attractive and married blonde. At the end of the film, the spectator comprehends that the two are now a couple when they show up together to Carmen's funeral.

Promoted by powerful corporations such as Televisa and Fundación Jumex, this movie poses homosexuality, whether male or female, as part of an open and diverse society. Carmen's best friend is a transsexual who assures that the son of the president is gay, and Carmen herself is in love with a handsome, young, gay man. At different moments, at parties and gatherings, men kiss and touch one another; they hook up with ease. Only on one occasion is a same-sex couple jailed by police for "offending the public morality," when they are discovered kissing in public. One hears phrases such as Carmen's, "Cuando una se enamora, se enamora de una persona, no de un sexo" [when one falls in love, one falls in love with a person, not with a sex]. In other words, the possibility of Hanna feeling attracted to another woman becomes plausible, as the transgression that the discovery of her sexual preference could otherwise signify fades, given its normalization within the context of the film.

Hanna and Sandra could be sisters: both are blonde, thin, white, light-eyed, from a moneyed social class, and their union can come to be without having to confront any obstacles. Regarding economics, Sandra keeps half of her husband's fortune. Socially, Hanna's close friends encourage her to explore another type of amorous connection. The conservatism of this Jewish girl, who forms a part of a religiously traditional nucleus, is not a major factor either. At no time is she shown to suffer from any type of moral remorse, or to worry about what people might say. The male partners of these women are much more concerned with appearances, although they are less concerned about their wives being lesbians or unfaithful. For example, in response to Hanna's claims of Abraham's infidelity, he responds in English: "Please don't say that in front of these people," alluding to a gardener who can hear them. The change in language marks the difference in social and cultural status between them and the gardener; but, despite the gardener's lower status in the hierarchy they are still compelled to hide the reason for their separation. Additionally, when Octavio (in the home he and Sandra share) surprises Sandra and Hanna kissing, his reaction is similar to what it would be if he had found her in bed with a man ("Le voy a tirar los dientes a esa lesbiana" [I'm going to knock that lesbian's teeth out]). In reality, Sandra's behavior is no different than Octavio's, as he has had a lover for the last ten years. Apparently, the sex of the person with whom his wife has love affairs is the least concerning, as can be inferred based on his comment on the topic: "No voy a discutir enfrente de desconocidas" [I am not going to argue in front of (female) strangers].

The scenes of seduction copy the stereotypes of heterosexual courting, from a binary and oppositional focus. That is, Sandra is the older woman, with more experience (she has had an affair with at least one other woman) and, predictably, takes the initiative in different sequences. It is she who provides her phone number upon their first meeting, who later suggests that they see one another, who begins the physical approach, and who touches Hanna's breasts and covers her with her own body. The context also allows us to suppose that it is Sandra who will become the provider in the relationship. The passive/active pairing corresponds with the common areas in the use of color, as the young Jewish woman always dresses in white or light hues (pinks and blues), while Sandra dresses either in dark colors or bold prints. In fact, in Hanna's dream this color scheme is extended to Sandra's now-black hair, as she is transformed into a pastry chef who bakes a cake in the shape of an enormous breast.

The kisses and caresses of these women do not problematize heterosexual normativity, both because of the way the lesbian relationship is approached, and above all, because of the strategies of cinematographic discourse employed: the elements of the *mise en scène* (the management of color palette, and the actresses' interpretations), the point of view, and the use of zoom, primarily. This aspect becomes particularly interesting, because—while Hanna personifies sexual innocence—immersed in typical adolescent confusion ("Sandra, no está bien lo que estamos haciendo. Yo estoy pasando por una crisis" [Sandra, what we're doing is not right. I'm having a crisis]), it is her gaze that guides the spectator toward Sandra's elegant figure as she comes up in the elevator, and toward the volume of her breasts, highlighted by the tailored suit she wears.

The close-up of the female body and the subsequent fragmentation of the same invoke both the stereotype of the objectification of desire, and the geography of the heterosexual spectator's imagination. Hanna's dream sequence illustrates this quite clearly: the pink cake that the pastry chef ("Sandra Li") puts into the oven is shaped like an enormous breast with a cherry as the nipple, but Hanna's favorite flavor is carrot, in frank reference to the penis. Sandra dribbles some batter onto Hanna's chest as if it were semen, she rubs Hanna's breasts, and lays her down on the table to then mount her. Before consummating the act, they are surprised by a character evoking "Aunt Jemima" who confronts them with a "What are you doing?"

Hardly surprising, therefore, is the insistence on the caress of the female breast, as well as the frontal nudity in medium shots; as opposed to the heterosexual scenes between Lucía and the bullfighter Matías. These scenes favor more open shots that allow one to take in Lucía's pubis and Matías' buttocks, as well as their copulation in various positions.

And so, the impulses of Hanna's gaze are the telltale signs of her desire for Sandra, and it seems to be a gaze that she cannot control. Her lesbianism, therefore, comes from an instinct; from an attraction that is at no time questioned by any line of reasoning. Just as autonomous as Hanna's gaze is the dream sequence, which is preceded by shots of her grieving, crying over footage of her wedding, while she gobbles up a "Sara Li" brand cake.

The lesbian relationships are validated inasmuch as minimal importance is given to the sexual preference itself. The young Jewish woman experiences, with Sandra, true love and the richness of the act of sex for the first time, while she is simultaneously configured as a virginal character. Time and time again we hear from her lips phrases like "No sé qué hacer, estoy muy confundida" [I don't know what to do, I'm very confused], "no sé qué soy" [I don't know what I am], "¿Qué es el amor?" [What is love?]. Moreover, she reveals to Lucía that she did not like to have sex with Abraham because "era muy tosco" [he was very rough]. She also confesses to her therapist that she could not stand to have him touch her, that they never talked, and he was always working. Her love scenes with Sandra, conversely, favor the placidness of their chitchat, their smiles, and their tender caresses, while the camera allows us—by means of an objective point of view—to admire the harmony of the two women's bodies and imagine the long hours they spend together.

Female Homosexuality:
An Irreparable Evil, Consequence of Modernity?

In synthesis, Teresa Suárez's film does not have an interest in deeply studying the mechanisms of sexual self-identification, the problems that arise upon the choice of an unorthodox object of desire, or the possible differences that may exist between heterosexual and homosexual courting. Instead, the movie proposes that the preference for one sex or another is discovered depending on whether the sexual relations are pleasurable or unsatisfactory. Tradition, family, and social circles are not viewed as possible barriers to assume a given orientation, perhaps because some key factors do not interfere with that affective bond: factors such as economic, social, or cultural differences. Hanna's belonging to the Jewish community is irrelevant to this focus, since religion itself does not appear as part of the text's discourse.

The shaping of Hanna's character as part of a non-Catholic collective, however, responds to another type of interest. On one hand, it contributes toward the portrayal of a diverse and cosmopolitan Mexico, which I mentioned in the beginning of these remarks. The naturalization of the LGBTQ community in the context of the plot can be understood to do the same. Nor is sexual diversity drawn as a threat to society: on the contrary, it is completely innocuous. Of the three friends, only Hanna's romantic bond prospers, and curiously, she is the only one of the three who is not an addict. Desperate to get cocaine, Carmen falls from the heights of a building, having failed to conquer the young gay man with whom she is in love. Lucía witnesses the wedding of the bullfighter who has cheated on her repeatedly and with whom she is obsessed; and as a happy ending she decides to cure herself of all her addictions. In this context, female homosexuality is presented as part of a contemporary world. The lesbian couple is accepted and integrated into the social circle within the film (showbiz, the media, the moneyed social class, and the highest political spheres). Everything rests on the will of one individual's subjectivity: that Hanna conquers her fears and overcomes indecision (both of which could have occurred even if her suitor were a married man, for example).

The ease with which questions are posed regarding sexual preference, the acceptance of the same, and the meeting and success of the suitable couple generates a paradox of interpretation for the movie's spectators. The observations made by Claudia Schaefer on the novel *Dos mujeres* by Sara Levi Calderón are valid for *Así del precipicio*: "In the schema of modernity, then, this text must be negotiated by the critical reader not only as a highly visible sign of Mexican "progress" in the arena of social tolerance, but as a marker of more complex societal relations as well. The "splendors" of modernity can be merely surface phenomena, leaving untouched the core of daily life and its victims" (Schaefer 102).

Teresa Suárez's film premiered amongst discussions about the legalization of *las sociedades de convivencia* (civil unions) in the Federal District of Mexico City, and amongst the repudiation of the same by certain groups, so much so that it was the subject of debate in the Supreme Court of Justice of the Nation in 2010. As can be inferred, the film also fails to reveal anything about the "other" Mexico: the Mexico of homophobic attitudes, with alarming numbers of verbal assaults, physical attacks, and murders of gay community members.

Hanna and Sandra's relationship does not harm anyone: their marriages have stopped working and neither woman is the guilty party. Their dates take place in public places, but do not make anyone around them uncomfortable because, aside from the sustained exchange of looks and word games, they avoid any other physical manifestation of their love. In private spaces, stereotypically assigned to women (the kitchen, the bed, and the bathroom,) is where their love scenes are developed. In this way, the film contends with a limited idea of acceptance: the notion of tolerance only when it does not disrupt the dominant heterosexual normativity (whereas Lucía and Matías kiss each other shamelessly in a bar). In this line of reasoning, Carmen's accidental death, caused by her hurry to recover the kilos of cocaine stashed in the attic of her building, can be understood as a punishment. Lucía's rehabilitation after this traumatic event forms part of the film's moral lesson.

Nevertheless, the naturalization of female homosexuality in *Así del precipicio* faces the risk of being interpreted as one of today's modern evils. The existence of sexual diversity is positioned within a world of indiscriminate drug consumption and trafficking, corruption, and indifference toward any social problems. This naturalization becomes part of the price that society pays for reaching the heights of other large metropolises, and in this sense, the consequence of society's distancing itself from tradition. Raquel, Abraham's cartoonish mother, reproaches Hanna for not having had a child immediately, an expectation that Abraham shares. (Hanna tells her therapist: "Yo sentía que lo único que quería era embarazarme para correr a contárselo a su mamá" [I felt that all he wanted to do was get me pregnant to run and tell his mother about it].) Abraham, who is still her husband, asks her to spend the period of reflection he has requested staying at her parents' house, not at Lucía's apartment since she's "a bad influence." Her attraction to another woman then, could well be the product of the young woman's successive transgressions against the role of women in the past: tolerance of the partner's infidelities, the purely reproductive function of sex, the transfer of the woman from her father's home to her husband's, and the perception of alliances with other female friends as highly risky bonds.

Such violations of the canonic moral order could be attributed to exposure to foreign customs, alien to Latin American morals. Let us remember that Hanna's Jewish origin is emphasized, and that in their first meeting, Sandra's dialogue allows us to infer the frequency of her trips outside of Mexico, and specifically, to Paris. As opposed to what occurs within Mexican literature at the beginning of the twentieth century, in which effeminate men are depicted as "national archetypes" and "a rich vernacular vocabulary to address the topic" is generated (Irwin 20), *Así del precipicio*, rather, tends to conceive of homosexuality as an imported behavior, the result of modernity and the fruit of a longed-for globalization, even if it has diminished the "intrinsic" values of the Latin American nations—not just Mexico.

Furthermore, there are few clues as to where the plot actually takes place. The spectator only sees luxurious commercial centers, high-end restaurants, neighborhoods of grand houses or spacious, impeccable apartments, and wide avenues. Poverty is quickly eliminated, in the figure of the window-cleaner shot by a strung-out Lucía, without any consequence for her; or in the nighttime orgy of cocaine, alcohol, and sex in a miserable place from which she flees, horrified, the next day. In any case, the scenes and the stories would not be at all difficult for the public to identify with those of any other Latin American country, and in this way, Teresa Suárez's movie circulates as yet another object within a culturally globalized world.

All Inclusive in the Mexican Caribbean

The movie by Rodrigo Ortúzar, which premiered on Mexican screens in the summer of 2009, is a paradigm of transnational cinema if we take into account its financing and production: the Chilean company Jazz Films and the enterprise established in Miami, Panamax Films, whose slogan is: "There are 40 million Latinos in the United States. We make movies for them." The companies that distributed the movie were Lions Gate Film in the United States and Universal Picture Corporation of Mexico. This knowledge helps in understanding the decisions about the film's cast and the origins of the same, of the director Ortúzar and the scriptwriters (all of whom are from Chile), as well as the exploitation of certain thematic veins. The origins of the protagonists are Mexican (Jesús Ochoa, Ana Serradilla, Martha Higareda, Jaime Camil) and Chilean (Leonor Varela, Valentina Vargas) and there is even a small part for the Spaniard Mónica Cruz, sister of the famous Penélope. The executive producers were born in the United States, but boast great experience in relation to Latin America. Take, for example, Ben Odell: he lived in Colombia and worked for almost a decade as a writer and producer for that country's television. Such antecedents invite an interpretation of the film's beginning: the dialogue of Ochoa's character ("Soy Gonzalo Fernández. Fui educado para creer en Dios, en la familia, en mi mujer, en mis hijos . . ." [I am Gonzalo Fernández. I was taught to believe in God, in the family, in my wife, in my children . . .]) as an ideological link with a certain type of spectator, by invoking traditional values (religion and family), and marking his possession of his wife and his offspring. Both social heteronormativity, and a couple's biological functions of reproduction are taken as a given. This is why the character's process of accepting Macarena—his oldest daughter—regarding her homosexuality, is characterized by doubt and fear.

The paradox—which fades as the film advances—is that traditional vision of identities (that of the individual subjectivity, and that of its insertion into a culturally delimited area) in the surroundings—simultaneously exotic and cosmopolitan—of Playa del Carmen in the Mexican Caribbean. That is, the luxurious and modern hotel—primary setting of the story—would seem to challenge the discourse of the patriarch Gonzalo who endorses stable and ancestral beliefs. This space is enriched with the large number of nationalities that coexist without conflict, which are expressed in the Chilean accents of Carmen (the mother of the protagonist family) and of Miranda (the young wife of one of the hotel managers—a Spaniard); the Castilian accent of Héctor's girlfriend; the Cuban accent of Usnavy; and the feigned French pronunciation of the "gigolo." This dialectal hybridism describes the coexistence of those who are passing through or those who live in and around that grand all-inclusive resort: Spaniards, Cubans, supposed Frenchmen, and South Americans moving about among large Greek columns and eating to the rhythm of the mariachis. The representation of this number of countries deterritorializes the Mexican nation, and paints it as a place that invites multicultural coexistence—the idea of a country with open doors—always hospitable to others. Upon invitation, they become part of the Mexican community: the Chilean Carmen by her marriage to the Mexican Gonzalo; the Chilean Miranda because her Spanish spouse works in Mexico; and Usnavy, her grandmother, and her Cuban friends who have established themselves in that part of the Yucatán Peninsula.

In Miranda's words, that place is perfect as "un sistema comunitario para divertirse" [a communal system for having fun]. Wearing an identification bracelet is enough to erase social differences: "no hay dinero, nada" [there is no money, nothing]. The illusion is set in motion, as from the first minutes of the story the economic costs of a family vacation in a luxurious hotel—in one of the most expensive zones of the country—disappear. The notion of border is also resignified, in that touristic Babel, within which Europeans and South Americans can apparently mingle freely. The mirage is based on the dividing wall that is raised between those who can, and those who cannot pay their entry into that vacation paradise, and on the metamorphosis of the passport into an indispensable bracelet needed to stay in the place. Otherness, therefore, is only welcomed if it passes through the filter of financial wealth, which redefines the world citizen: s/he who can be so by virtue of his economic and social status. Acceptance of others, determined by a measuring stick for abundance that evens them out and makes them similar, reaches its limits when the variable ceases to be an economic one. This is even clearer in the discourse that prevails in the film regarding sexual diversity.

Gonzalo's initial monologue is the backbone of the film, and is developed alongside the less important stories: that of his wife Carmen (tired of her matrimonial routine), and those of his children Macarena (recently separated from her spouse), Camila (rebel and stoner), and Andrés (the adolescent, anxious for his first sexual adventure, and fan of digital technology). With the exception of the outlier Camila, the big problem of the other family members is tied to their experiences regarding their sexuality. The experiences of each of them on that vacation, marked by the imminent hurricane that will batter the region, will eliminate any type of anxiety and will sanction the accustomed family social structure: Gonzalo will attenuate his fear of death by fraternizing with an extremely young Cuban who will give him back the pleasure and confidence in life; Carmen will feel beautiful and desired again by the handsome young man, who will reject her because in reality, he is not who she is looking for; Macarena will accept her homosexuality, after a terrible crisis; and Andrés will sleep—literally—beside the sensual Spaniard, the girlfriend of his acquaintance Héctor. With the exception of the father, who does partake in intimacy, the rest (Carmen, Macarena, and Andrés) will be rejected by the people they feel attracted to, and, far from feeling frustrated, all three will accept it as a "lesson" that leaves them satisfied and at peace with themselves. It is evident, then, that within that "all inclusive" is a discourse buried within the traditional notions of patriarchy, in which adultery invigorates the man and sexual abstinence is a virtue for the woman and a necessity for the adolescents, who must wait until they are more mature to practice their sexuality.

As opposed to *Así del precipicio*, this movie supports both the polarity of gender, as well as heterosexuality, both structural norms of society, as can be inferred by the words with which Gonzalo opens the film. And if the notion of family gives way to the correlate of the nation, a meaningful paradox is generated, given that the central nuclei (God and family) actively dialogue with a global society characterized by the multitude and regularity of international fluxes that do not necessarily appeal to those values as systemic axes. Therefore, an analysis of the audiovisual strategies with which the notion of lesbianism is constructed becomes intriguing once again, as it emerges from such a conservative context as the one posed here, albeit within a much wider sociogeographic frame.

Unified Perceptions in a Transnational Frame

Historically, global fluxes have produced a variety of familial structures marked by transnational hybridism (Shapiro 122). *Todo incluido* is a testament to this; however, the film's subplots favor a coherent and unified model of the family, which tends to diminish or put aside the possibility that contemporary diasporas could have a disruptive function in relation to national idiosyncrasies. The Chilean origins of both the mother and of Macarena's new friend do not contribute in any way to the fracturing of the beliefs about "God and family" with which Gonzalo was educated. Nor is any allusion made to the reasons why Carmen comes to Mexico and meets her husband. The dictatorship of Augusto Pinochet, and the resulting exile that prompted the arrival of thousands of Chilean immigrants to Mexico in the seventies, are obvious motives; however, Miranda's reason for residing at the splendid resort is less evident.

The sophistication and beauty of the scenery portrayed, and the luxurious hotel it surrounds, harmonize with the bodies that move within both spaces. Svelte and attractive youths are most prominent, and the only shots of an excessively overweight and unattractive woman are included as a humorous counterpoint to the sexual desires of the desperate adolescent Andrés. Hence, the zumba class offered on the beach displays more than a dozen ladies, nearly all of them in bikinis, Miranda and Macarena among them. The latter's lack of rhythm is the pretext for the former to grab her by the hips, and move together rhythmically, in shots that focus on their thin and curvaceous torsos and drift into a medium long shot that highlights the closeness and the semi-nudity of both women. The conversation that later ensues in the pool illustrates very well a series of default assumptions, relating to the sex-gender pairing (Whittle 2005, 122). That is, Miranda assumes that Macarena is either honeymooning or on vacation with her husband. When she denies both options, Miranda asks if she is divorced. In other words, a young and beautiful woman is associated unequivocally with a male counterpart, or in a state of availability to quickly acquire another. In the Chilean's case, she describes her husband, Javier as "un hombre guapo, inteligente, divertido, con dinero y con mente liberal . . . ¿qué más se puede pedir?" [a handsome, intelligent, fun man with money and an open mind . . . What else could one ask for?].

Javier is in charge of the recreation activities at the hotel. His physical traits and character conform to the nature of his work role. Thus, the film begs the question: is it possible to entertain others if one lacks personal charm? Even the cause for Carmen—part of a generation that could not be unaware of the political circumstances in Chile that expelled so many compatriots—to reside in Mexico is silenced. The fact that the Spaniard Javier and the Chilean Miranda reside in a country that is not their own, is not. The labor market has propelled new migratory currents, enshrined within the framework of the law. For these currents, political borders no longer exist, given that—due to global demands—national spaces have all but disappeared symbolically. For this same reason there is no interest in including regional issues, verbal exchanges that denote cultural differences, or the problematization of such differences as points of convergence or divergence.

If the movie is directed toward a transnational and primarily Spanish-speaking spectator, the title, *Todo incluido*, then can be read as that great territory in which the term "Latino" becomes indiscernible. Neither hybridity, nor differentiated subjectivities, nor cultural plurality distinguish it. The physical resemblance between Hanna and Sandra, both blondes with prominent breasts, is repeated in that of Macarena and Miranda: tan, very svelte, with brown hair and eyes. Although Miranda is more confident, both dress almost the same, with clothing designed to emphasize the attractiveness of their bodies: bikinis, two-piece outfits, belts, large earrings, and high-heeled shoes. The camera shots privilege the rubbing together of their bodies in the pool, on the dance floor, in the intimacy of their bedrooms. Overall, the camera highlights Macarena's point of view, anxious to take in her friend's figure, with her gaze stuck on the stereotypical zones of male desire: the buttocks, the hips, and the chest. Subjectivities are interchangeable, therefore, not only where national identities are concerned, but also gender. Being a lesbian implies, in this film, replicating the constructions forged by masculinity, which augments the attractiveness of the movie for an audience that does not find itself questioned by counternarratives that displace or reconfigure familiar stereotypes. For that reason, when Miranda refuses Macarena's kiss, apparently surprised after so much emotional and physical closeness, the spectator can naturally accept her explanation: "[. . .] Mira, si me gustaran las mujeres me gustaría alguien como tú" [. . . Look, if I liked women I would like someone like you]. Similar in social class, age, and appearance, the Latin American women form part of a vast geographic space, lacking historical memory and culturally distinctive features. Bonding with others is not particularly difficult, thanks to this homogenization.

Ad hoc Products for International Audiences

The films analyzed here can be considered an example of what Judith Mayne calls "the paradox of lesbian visibility," namely, an existence and an inexistence of lesbianism. In other words, an "invisible visibility," a simultaneous opening and closing of the possibilities of other types of sexual identities (xvii–xviii). We could call those films "semi Sapphic" because of some aspects of their content, as well as the appearance of female characters who desire other women. Both titles are significant because of the nature of the representations they structure: they confirm that in Mexico, lesbian cinema made for the big screen and for commercial exhibition still legitimates the stereotypes imposed by male desire. The plots and the audiovisual features of both films are imagined for a "modern" Latin American, and specifically, the Mexican audience that accepts plurality and diversity, in the broadest sense of the terms.

The women are independent and recognize their homosexuality. Even so, the importance of the traditional family is continually emphasized, or, in any case, the substitute family, such as a family made up of friends. The values promoted by films of the forties are very similar to those of Latin American films from the twenty-first century: the relevance of the basic social group within which individuals find support and space for identification; the setting in motion of the parabola of prodigal children who have the luxury of living outside the accepted social norms—adultery or drug addiction—but who ultimately recognize their errors; and the social environments that privilege a middle or upper-middle class, that is neither indigenous nor politically active.

The excess of pleasant scenery/spaces in these two movies contrasts with the growing levels of poverty and the existing economic gaps in this region. The two films develop, with very few exceptions, in places marked by opulence, where work takes a back seat and leisure becomes the main aspiration. The dual contrasts within society are enduring, insofar as the erasure of overcrowding, homelessness, or the tasks necessary for day-to-day survival. These place both *Así del precipicio* and *Todo incluido* among the films being produced currently. These films are destined for a Latin

American public, belonging to the middle class, which has normalized "certain" differences regarding accepted morals—only when these differences do not alter or upset them. Consequently, the lesbian couples carry on as if they were simply friends, and their relationships—during courting and sexual exchanges—reiterate the rites and the images associated with those of heterosexuality.

Despite the marked difference in the plots of these two films, the role and the portrayal of the young woman who doesn't know whether or not she is a lesbian are similar. Each character discovers her own desire for another woman without excessive worries or tribulations. For Macarena it is slightly complicated, given that Miranda rejects her. Nevertheless, in both cases friends or family support them, and at no point are the women expelled from these nuclei. Seeing Hanna and Sandra, or Macarena and Miranda, is like seeing a reflection in the mirror: there are not rifts or fissures regarding the depiction of lesbian figures; their portrayal is monolithic given that no diversity is shown between them physically, economically, nor in their age, social class, or culture. Even the stereotype of the tomboy or the "butch" is erased, and replaced with images of the young women who are attractive and desirable for a male viewer.

In this sense, Teresa Suárez and Rodrigo Ortúzar's films stand within a comfortable zone, thanks to their clarity and breadth. There are no liminal spaces or gray areas of any kind. Lesbianism does not signify any type of transgression, perhaps because both Hanna and Macarena appear only outside of lesbian communities, distant from groups or practices that espouse alternative ways of being. Their isolation from these communities can be understood as cases of rare exception, and possible precisely for that reason, inoffensive as a political position.

There are two additional risks that befall both movies: one pertains to the sale of this topic as an example of the economic and cultural progress of Latin American metropolises. The other consists of the recognition of a market of spectators who are virgins to viewing images of other sexual orientations. The inclusion of actors from varying geographic regions— which blends well with the stories being told (characters that are world travelers like Sandra and Miranda, or Carmen's Chilean origin which she chooses to prolong, marking her family members with this sense of belonging as well)—adds additional interest for viewers around the world. However, the incorporation of the lesbian topic would seem to be more related to the diversification of sales strategies for a product, rather than to the genuine desire to tell the story of Sapphic encounters that bear their own complexities.

Notes

1. Both the author and the editors want to express their heartfelt gratitude to Michael Clarkson for the English translation of this essay.
2. Bernard Schulz-Cruz explores more than thirty Mexican films, including several that enjoyed nationwide distribution and have sexual diversity as axes of their stories, such as *Las apariencias engañan* (*Deceitful Appearances*, Jaime Humberto Hermosillo [1977 or 1983]) and *Dulces compañías* (*Sweet Company*, Óscar Blancarte, [1996 or 1994]). The vast majority of the films analyzed, however, were included in the collection because they make homosexuality visible even if only in a marginal way, as is the case in *Danzón* (María Novaro, 1991), *El evangelio de las maravillas* (*The Gospel of Wonders*, Arturo Ripstein [1997]) or *Crónica de un desayuno* (*A Breakfast Chronicle*, Benjamín Cann, [1999]).

Works Cited

Castro Ricalde, Maricruz. "Hijas de buena cuna: 'Historia a cuatro manos' de Aline Pettersson desde un enfoque *queer*." *Caleidoscopio crítico de literatura mexicana contemporánea*. Ed. Adriana Hernández. México, D. F.: Miguel Ángel Porrúa, 2006. 411–25. Print.

Irwin, Robert McKee. "*Los cuarenta y uno*: la novela perdida de Eduardo Castrejón." *Los cuarenta y uno: novela crítico-social*. México, D. F.: Difusión Cultural; UNAM, 2010. 7–34. Print.

Mayne, Judith. *Framed. Lesbians, Feminists, and Media Culture*. Minneapolis, MN: U of Minessota P, 2000. Print.

Muñoz, Mario. *De amores marginales: 16 cuentos mexicanos*. Veracruz, Mex.: Colección Ficción Universidad Veracruzana, 1996. Print.

Schaefer, Claudia. *Danger Zones: Homosexuality, National Identity, and Mexican Culture*. Tucson, AZ: U of Arizona P, 1996. Print.

Shapiro, Michael J. *Cinematic Political Thought: Narrating Race, Nation and Gender*. New York: New York UP, 1999. Print.

Schulz-Cruz, Bernard. *Imágenes gay en el cine mexicano: Tres décadas de joterío 1970–1999*. México, D. F.: Fontamara, 2008. Print.

White, Patricia. *Uninvited: Classical Hollywood Cinema and Lesbian Representability*. Bloomington, IN: Indiana UP, 1999. Print.

Whittle, Stephen, (2005), "Gender Fucking or Fucking Gender?" *Queer Theory (Readers in Cultural Criticism)*. Eds. Iain Morland and Annabelle Willox. Hampshire, UK: Palgrave Macmillan, 2005. Print.

Part IV

Queer Relations with Families, Government, and Nation

13

Clothes Make the Man:
Closet, Cabaret, Cinema in *El lugar sin límites*

(Arturo Ripstein, 1977)

Claudia Schaefer

The Mexican director Arturo Ripstein, a cinematic auteur already identified by audiences with the sordid, shadowy, brooding worlds of his previous melodramatic productions, takes on Hell itself as the *mise-en-scène* of *El lugar sin límites* (*Hell Without Limits*, filmed in 1977, released in Mexico in 1978). The zero degree of "extreme melodrama" (Joßner 2), everything appearing before the camera—clothing, props, set, lighting, actors, color, a predominance of nocturnal scenes—as well as extra-diegetic spillovers into the frame contributes to the creation of an inferno of pain and failure that drags what critic Sergio de la Mora terms the "fragile, complex, and fiercely intelligent idealists" ("Mexican Movies" 2) who populate his films into a maelstrom of ruination. Even those characters who hold day jobs as long-haul truckers, gas-station owners, and landowning caciques cannot resist the temptations in the dark and dreary recesses of brothel bedrooms as they turn into creatures of a night difficult to escape.

El lugar sin límites was released in Mexico a decade after the violent confrontations of 1968 between the government and students, the state and workers, that pitted dreams of modernity against tradition, youth against age, openness against secrecy. The October Olympic Games officially touted as Mexico's entry into international sports competition and economic visibility on the world stage instead flung protest and tension into the spotlight of the media. Black American athletes with raised fists put race on display;

patriarchal ideologies of family and state were questioned as legacies of a dying past. The government of President Gustavo Díaz Ordaz pulled out all stops to keep the nation's image both at home and abroad under control. This, of course, meant the use of violence and not negotiation. The law of the father in all its glory was under attack by new generations eager to be part of a different world.

Adding to the anxiety over losing power over social and political issues as well as over public images was a turn to the cinema as a site for skirmishes if not outright battles. It was in this medium that "virility as a metonym for Mexicanness" (de la Mora, *Cinemachismo* xiii) had prevailed, and then where it began to be strongly questioned. From the massacre in the plaza of Tlatelolco in 1968 to the 1971 paramilitary crushing of student demonstrations in Mexico City, there was a constantly volatile and irreconcilable backdrop against which Ripstein shot his films. By 1977, Díaz Ordaz's handpicked successor, Luis Echeverría, was about to leave office and anxiety about the elections infused Ripstein's film. Later, the Mexican Miracle carried on by President José López Portillo would create inflation, invite extraordinary amounts of foreign investment in future oil drilling, and turn Mexico City into a metropolitan nightmare.

Eric Zolov examines a general turn to popular culture in the wake of Tlatelolco, especially to the counterculture of rock music (*La Onda*) but also to film and other media, as "an important vehicle for channeling the rage and cynicism felt toward a political system that denied democratic expression and toward a family structure that seemed to emulate it" (132). Left with few directions to turn in dissent, the "cumulative crisis of patriarchal values" (1) was confronted with psychedelics, music, and a continued attitude of rejection toward authority. The "irrevocably frayed" national family lay in tatters (Zolov 1) and wanton spending was not going to weave it back together.

El lugar sin límites is by no means a flash in the pan, but fits perfectly into this cultural and political framework and into a series of productions influenced by politics, literary texts, and the director's enraged sense of social stagnation. From first to last, Ripstein's films of the period start with social anxiety—concerning political dissidence, religion, family values, sexuality and gender, freedom or containment—and closed communities as anachronistic legacies of the past. The characters are forced to negotiate with men in control, men in community, and structures such as the police, the family, the church, the state, brothels, bars, and jails—spaces "cerradamente, obligadamente masculinas" (Paranaguá 126) in which masculinity itself assumes different and conflicting forms. He begins this period of

1972 through 1978 with *Castillo de la pureza* (*Castle of Purity*, 1972), a film that deals with a shuttered world—a home where a father keeps his children imprisoned and isolated from the outside world—and ends with the punishment and incarceration of the patriarch but only after the family is irreparably torn apart. In 1973, Ripstein's *El Santo Oficio* (*The Holy Office*) turns to the suffocating, secret world of Mexican history's *conversos* or Jews who had officially converted to Christianity but kept their Jewish religious rituals alive behind closed doors. Those dark and shadowy corners are then expanded outdoors to the moribund small towns and inside the seedy brothel of *El lugar sin límites* whose chromatic register is decidedly sordid and static, evoking a timeless and immobile infernal space.

In 1976, Ripstein was commissioned to film a documentary on the Lecumberri federal prison, which had held the detainees of the 1968 demonstrations and had recently been shut down. Titled *Lecumberri, el Palacio Negro* (*Lecumberri*), referring to the detention center's popular name, the film documented the last days of that grim structure built on the model of Jeremy Bentham's panopticon system of surveillance. In 1978, Ripstein made the film *Cadena perpetua* (*In for Life*), a tense mix of money, power, and male aggression ending once again with a prison sentence—this time for life in the Federal Penal Colony of Las Islas Marías. Built in 1905 by Porfirio Díaz as a model of escape-proof detention for those too dangerous to be housed in Lecumberri, this colony represents a paradox: it is an all-male community shut off from the mainland with few means of escape and the open sky as witness to a closed, claustrophobic, dead-end future. The *mise-en-scènes* of the 1970s films compact and condense images into allegories of the state and its officially celebrated attributes while they recode the recognizability or what Marjorie Garber calls the "legibility" (39) of the characters and their performances.

As the "currency of the moment" (Quiroga 41), cinema is a privileged site of communication, and a tool that Ripstein uses to provide the audience with ways of reading change: insight as opposed to blindness, demystification as opposed to mythologizing, and mobility as opposed to stasis. As each successive Mexican federal government has built monuments to state-sponsored modernity (the Olympic venues that survived beyond the games, for example), Ripstein has emptied traditional structures of meaning and turned them into cenotaphs, empty façades erected to the memory of people whose remains do not even lie within them. In this context, the muted sepias, grays, and jaundiced yellow tones of the brothel in *El lugar sin límites* produce an effect on that enclosed space that makes it look like a museum. A public institution that houses and preserves the cultural heritage of a nation or group, the brothel indeed condenses the history of patriarchy and economics into the aging bodies of its inhabitants and makes them available to all. In addition, the cacique don Alejo closes his election campaign and celebrates his victory inside the same walls. Not just the desires of the flesh age here, those of politics and power do as well. Point-of-view (POV) shots position the spectator alongside the characters within the brothel, but at a distance from the landowner. In this way, those shots are challenging and limiting the cacique's vision of reality.

The spectator of *El lugar sin límites* gets frustrated by the static camera shots—what Spanish filmmaker Pedro Almodóvar calls "*carne trémula*." Those shots capture the tics of the live flesh of the actor Roberto Cobo as a link between his previous character Calambres (Leg Cramps, Electric Shocks, Charley Horse), and the performance drag queen La Manuela. Desire is displaced from the traditionally available bodies of women (prostitutes) as queens of the *fichera* genre (De la Mora, "Facing Machismo" 84) to bodies of more ambiguous gender (La Manuela) much as street dress shifts in Mexico City to create what becomes a confusion of genders. As Zolov concludes, satirical essays and cartoons in conservative magazines "evoked a common fear among conservatives that the bedrock values which had kept men masculine and women feminine were at risk" (134). Clothing on and off the human body is made visible and legible as it condenses the warp and woof of the fragments of "the national fabric" (Quiroga 13). The power of the cinema—as both myth and weapon—is equated with the power of cross-dressing to cross boundaries, the power of performance (the song and dance of the cabaret) to provoke, and the power of culture to produce a new image of heroism, replacing fallen revolutionary idols.

The central story is fairly simple despite the plethora of additional details: a young man, Pancho (Gonzalo Vega) sexually attracted to an older queen, La Manuela (Roberto Cobo), is driven to deny his feelings by outdated forces of masculine authority that demand that he maintain his macho image and not become a threat to national values as a "*maricón*." Despite Pancho's redefining masculinity with words but not deeds—"un hombre debe ser capaz de todo, ¿no cree?"—he ends up killing the object of his desire with pitiless violence and reproducing the same scenario the state had in its repression of youth in 1968. This time, however, a young man does the dirty work himself, internalizing the fear and hatred, and the state comes out clean since its role in the end is to punish the killer.

Ripstein's hellish vision is built of a set of descending concentric circles of the asphyxiating Mexican nation, the dying town of El Olivo, the brothel owned jointly by La Manuela and La Japonesita (Ana Martín), a transvestite queen and her daughter by prostitute La Japonesa Grande (Lucha Villa). The final scene, at the inmost circle, ends with a shot of an unpaved street and the lifeless body of La Manuela, lying in a rut after being brutally pummeled and kicked by Pancho and his brother-in-law Octavio (Julián Pastor). Hell may be confined technically to the visible limits of the frame, but if the human mind is the last infernal redoubt, no spatial limits can contain it. The cinema delves into that psychological mechanism.

La Manuela's valise—a closed mind, a door locked to keep danger (Pancho) at bay—containing the remnants of her lost dreams, in the shape of red and black Spanish *manola* dresses that accompany her everywhere, along with a sealed trunk filled with secret, melancholic souvenirs, add up to a limitless hell each time either of them is breached. La Manuela's colorful, over-the-top presence is a haunting visitation by the repressed within masculine-centered Mexican society. That repression, embodied in the men she encounters, calls up what Shoshana Felman refers to as "The feminine . . . [which] is not outside the masculine, its reassuring canny opposite, but [which] is inside the masculine, its uncanny difference from itself" (Solomon-Godeau 99). The range of masculinities and femininities cut from this cloth of multiple selves encompasses much more than it excludes. It seems no coincidence that De la Mora uses the expression that La Manuela "plays with fire" (105) when she twice emerges from hiding, first from her bedroom and then from the chicken coop where she has run to avoid contact with Pancho, aware that her reappearance will provoke a remembrance of things best kept hidden. The smoldering ember of desire has brought the trucker Pancho back after a long haul on the road, to pick up where he left off with La Manuela rather than returning home to his wife in nearby San Juan de Dios. And when that spark finally ignites during the second of her two musical performances; there is no way to stop the spread of the flames that consume her.

Before the two establishing shots that unlock the gates of this Mexican hell (the place names reflect those of José Donoso's eponymous novel, but the road signs indicate small towns in Mexico), *El lugar sin límites* opens with a voice-over. White letters on a dark background are read by the director himself, this element of visual style creating a link between the audience and the film narrative to come, as in the soliloquies of Christopher Marlowe's play *The Tragicall History of the Life and Death of Doctor Faustus* (1604) that are its source. The dramatic soliloquy that opens the play reveals the character's inner doubts about offering his soul to the devil in exchange for power and knowledge, while his closing words are a meditation on the fate he chose for himself and the material failure of his quest. In Marlowe's very Anglo-Saxon version of the story filled with necromancy and magic, angels and devils, the knowledge found in books by wise men such as Aristotle is not enough for the good doctor who chafes at convention and seeks the forbidden. As the prototype of a modern scientist not content with secondhand information, Dr. Faustus longs for access to new details about the natural world, which divine sources keep from human beings and which only the devil will provide. Mephistopheles, Lucifer's representative on earth, informs Faustus that hell actually has no boundary and is a state of mind, not a physical location. The doctor's pride leads not to a fall in the physical sense, then, but to an itinerant fear that accompanies him—like La Manuela's "fire"—from within, forever. In an allegory of both the dangers and the promises of integrating the traditional and the modern—and, on the side, a fascination with the forbidden—Faust's final confrontation with the devil tellingly occurs offstage, unseen. Unlike Faust's end, La Manuela's occurs before our very eyes. We see her chased by a brand-new red truck we have seen since the film's opening shots. Driven by Pancho who is goaded to hunt her down rather than admit his feelings for her, the demonic vehicle whines its way across the frame, around even the tightest corner, to set up the final attack. The spectator is forced to stare at the crushed and bloodied La Manuela, lying unburied like Polynices outside the protecting walls of the city of Thebes, abandoned by all who could save her (the cacique don Alejo [Fernando Soler] witnesses the dénouement but decides not to intervene). Faust's friends discover his empty clothes on stage and him gone—whether to salvation or to damnation is left uncertain. In a tight close-up shot, we see the torn frills of the dress still worn by La Manuela, her body draped in the garments that both cover and uncover her. Nothing of her end is left to the imagination. What might become of the criminals is insinuated by the dialogue and is a sign of a transition from the personal authority of an old system to the public discipline of a new one. The ultimate (closed) space for machismo is the hellish confines of prison.

El lugar sin límites opens with two emblematic shots that situate the narrative in place and time and present the spectator with a critical triangle of characters. Suggesting the diegesis of the entire film, these shots both open and close the narrative of what happens among the three. After the voice-over reference to hell's omnipresence and inescapability, extradiegetic music forms a bridge to the first establishing shot. Lyrics sung by Lucha Villa announce, "cuán falso fue tu amor" [How false was your love] and refer to "sentimientos fingidos" [pretended sentiments] and to the disillusionment of finding that this was not the angel of her dreams. Her strong performance of these emotionally charged words recycles the bolero that Pancho listens to as his own confession—the lasting remains of the sexual tension between La Manuela and Pancho. José Quiroga indicates that "boleros play with a border where masculinities and femininities are to be seen in ways that do not necessarily correspond to the ways gender acts out in the public sphere" (155), making these lyrics startlingly prophetic of the closing sequence. Pancho's repression of his own sexual desire for the *loca* Manuela in order to calm the horrified anxieties of his brother-in-law Octavio requires "falsity" and "pretense" to the extreme, at least when witnesses are around. Even if La Manuela is indeed the angel he cannot help dreaming about, Pancho is not about to break the code of "manliness" on his own. But he is caught on the horns of a dilemma. Pancho's hypermasculine muscled arms, and his public show of physical strength by picking up barrels and women and holding them over his head, in this context look more and more like compensatory acts, for he is also caught crying in private. Maybe youth is not ready to take on the guise—the garments—of adulthood and come to terms with choices of its own rather than fall back on the heritage of empty family values.

If La Manuela is a performance queen, lip-synching lyrics and mimicking dance moves, then Pancho is a performer with little faith in what he does. His character is filled with visible moments of hesitation, as seen by the diegetic audience of other men, by the real audience, and by Octavio who is the only one who pushes him over the edge. He ends up being a failure as a husband, as a lover, and as a breadwinner, who will never earn enough to buy his wife the house of her dreams. We see in Pancho none of the pride displayed by young men testing the limits of parental authority (don Alejo and Octavio are the surrogates for that), but instead an emulation of outdated virility. As part of the fleet of trucks that link Mexico's urban and rural spaces before the 1970s, Pancho has been on the road, has seen new people and places; he has no reason to be stuck in the lyrics of old songs and old values, or in old patterns of infidelity. His tragic flaw is that he does not "return the gaze of the father . . . [and thereby] rewrite the gestures of authority that have held the [national] system in place" (Zolov 35). Contrary to what an audience might anticipate, the older Manuela is not the anachronism; Pancho is. His development was arrested in childhood by don Alejo and his wife Doña Blanca (Blanca Torres) who had him play with their sickly daughter to keep her company. Doña Blanca, now in a twilight zone of what onscreen looks like the puzzlement of someone sinking into Alzheimer's disease, is treated like a child by her husband. She, in turn, sees Pancho only as a young boy. He can never grow up in the eyes of the forces imbued with power in the town, even when those forces are vestigial.

The soundtrack of the lyrics begins when the written words of the seventeenth-century dramatist are on the screen, but they bridge into the interior of a shiny red truck making its way slowly and unevenly across the jarring and scarred dusty surface of the road leading into the almost-totally abandoned small town of El Olivo. A faded sign leaves Pancho at a crossroads: should he go toward El Olivo (icon of the past, where La Manuela is) or toward San Juan de Dios (harbinger of promising things to come, where his wife and family are)? The music emanating from the luminous dashboard of the vehicle, foregrounded by the strong arms of the driver holding tight to the steering wheel, a look of expectation on his face, precipitates a memory tied to an anticipated rest-and-recreation stop in El Olivo. On his last visit, Pancho had violently attacked La Manuela, ripping her red dress during a dance performance. That dress, kept by Manuela, functions as what José Quiroga calls "coital reminiscences" (146): lipstick traces, trembling, and other vestiges of sexual encounter that linger after the fact. While we have no evidence that such an encounter was consummated—there are indications of intent but nothing more—the embrace between Pancho and La Manuela was close to one.

The camera leaves the interior of the truck's cab, and the next take is a medium-long shot of a dusty street, chipped and peeling paint on walls, and a lone old woman shuffling along the narrow sidewalk—absence and loss personified. This image, with its lack of dynamism, also frames the previous rush of apprehension of a return to the scene of the crime, with the subsequent angst over the victim's greatest fears coming true. In *El lugar sin límites,* the material "reminiscence" of a sexual encounter between the two men is a red dress. Earlier, Manuela wears red pants, too, but that dress encapsulates the look of femininity, the color of desire, the (gendered) skill needed to keep images intact and in their place, and the state of the "national fabric."

La Manuela's red clothing is tied diegetically to La Manuela herself as well as to her performance of a paso doble entitled "El Relicario," which ends with a similar fetishizing of a piece of cloth. Within the architectures of masculinity—here the brothel, as a unifying space for all desire, whether political, sexual, or discursive—an almost autonomous power is given to the clothing worn or alluded to by La Manuela. The lyrics of "El Relicario," sung by Sara Montiel and later parodied both by her (on Spanish television when already much older) and then by La Manuela (for the entertainment pleasure of the customers), parallel the fate of La Manuela's red dress and, by displacement, of herself. La Manuela's first performance in the film occurs in the middle of a long flashback to the moment of conception of La Japonesita, and the financial temptation that precipitates it. La Japonesa Grande, madame and businesswoman with a fondness for difficult men and with a fascination for "different" modes of masculinity, which she concludes she can "enderezar," or set on the straight and narrow, is an outsider, like La Manuela. Both come from so far north as to be "foreigners" and, therefore, share both gender and origins. La Japonesa Grande bets don Alejo she can get La Manuela to have sex with her as a man does—as La Japonesa Grande did with the love of her life, who has left her. The song, linked with Spain and, therefore, significant to La Manuela, who learned it from a Guadalajara guitar player she also has loved and lost, has a love-struck bullfighter lay down his cape so that the dark (outsider, gypsy) woman he falls in love with will step on it and leave him that patch of satin as a souvenir to inspire him for the next day's bull fight. The *relicario* is associated with the tiny box or chest used to keep bits and pieces of the bodies of saints or their clothing for veneration, but here there are no saints. Obviously, having power to make the viewer perceive them in singular and exceptional ways, relics and their containers work as metonymies, substituting for the absent but without calling up a specific image. The bullfighter's muse leaves her imprint on the cloth.

 The attention of the viewer does not shift to the guitar player (absent) or the bullfighter (also absent) but stays on vision itself, "immobilized" (Kibbey 33). The tragic outcome of the paso doble narrative, foreshadowed by the beloved's premonition of death, is the matador's death in the ring. As he falls, fatally gored, he pulls out the tiny piece of his cape, whose bright red color is visible to all, but which is imbued with a more impassioned meaning only by the two of them. La Manuela, turned off by the brutish behavior of the men at the party celebrating don Alejo's political triumph, almost doesn't perform. These lyrics are sacred to her in the way the scrap of the cape was a relic for the bullfighter; La Manuela learned them from a musician "con dedos de brujo" [with a sorcerer's fingers] who took her to a flamenco dancer for private lessons. She is convinced by the cacique, who promises protection and admiration, but that is not exactly what follows in the next scene. Alcohol and violent embraces fill the packed diegetic space with frenetic dancing with both male and female partners, ending with the heat of the moment cooled off in a ritual cleansing in the nearby river.

 Half immersed in the water, La Manuela is revealed as a physically well-endowed man, who turns away from the camera so that only her buttocks are visible over the torn dress and wet garter belt and stockings. Just as La Japonesa told La Manuela when she and the other women arrived at the brothel from San Juan de Dios years before, Manuela is Manuela only when her flat, bony buttocks or her red Spanish dress stand in for her. "No te reconocía sin el vestido" [I didn't recognize you without the dress], she tells the dancer; that is, clothes make the man. If La Japonesa Grande is named thus because she needs to squint to see, we *see* La Manuela only when she appears as a *loca*, an insider in the cabaret who is simultaneously an outsider represented by another figure of foreignness: the Spanish flamenco dancer. This leitmotif will be carried on in the dance of death orchestrated to "El beso," another composition related to Spain. With La Manuela's evocation of that musical version of a legend, the curtain comes down and the outsider is erased (killed).

After establishing the rural environment, the camera places us in a semi-darkened interior where La Manuela and her daughter, La Japonesita, lightly covered by dingy, red-striped sheets, sleep back-to-back at dawn after a night's entertainment of local clients. The street sounds of gears grinding and music playing filter into the bedroom and wake La Manuela. She sits up, startled, and reaches for the sheets to cover herself. Pancho's voice is not heard, nor is he visible to her—instead, the air horn substitutes, announcing the return of the repressed. With widened eyes, La Manuela asks a question out loud but infers the duality of her feelings in both tone and grammar: "¿Crees que venga?" [Do you think he'll come?] While she asks breathlessly and in detail about the doors and windows that have to be kept locked to keep this force of nature from penetrating their space, she does so with a subjunctive: maybe, maybe not; he loves me, he loves me not. And she articulates this with more than a tinge of expectation. Enough time has gone by that La Manuela both fears and has her "illusions" about Pancho's return.

Spectators are placed outside again as Pancho pulls into the gas station of his brother-in-law Octavio. Octavio, unable to lift some heavy barrels, asks Pancho if he still has the strength to move them out of the way. Between challenges to his physical prowess, laments about being left behind in "pinche Olivo" [shitty Olivo] and imprecations of "A la mierda con este pueblo" [to hell with this town], Octavio makes it clear that to get out of poverty, they should move with everyone else to San Juan de Dios. Blindly following the dream of economic success, Octavio may seem sympathetic, but the flashback that will follow a few scenes later reveals that El Olivo itself was populated by similar ideals, as La Manuela, La Japonesa Grande, the "güilas" [prostitutes], and a whole town moved from San Juan to enjoy the benefits flowing from recently elected *diputado* [member of the House of Representatives] don Alejo. The cacique's power was displaced onto the new values of "democratic" elections, and the population followed the money and the promises. But the pendulum is swinging back to San Juan de Dios, and the cacique is old.

Old values, old structures, and unpaid debts are not for "la gente decente." The exaggeratedly tight jeans and shirt of the truck driver can perhaps signal his social and economic backwardness and provincial status. Extreme close-ups of Pancho's body, both above and below the waist—as if to make him appear bigger than he is—cinematically contour the dialogue of two men also at a personal crossroads: those extreme close-ups emphasize apprehension and posturing. They discuss a lingering fear of power, as if to reassure themselves that no real "man" should be afraid of an aged landowner. Curse follows curse as this tiny community of two reassures itself that it can survive threats from outside (no electricity, old landowners, and a potential move). Octavio recognizes that to get ahead, he needs to go with the flow, but this is a decision he has been forced to make. Stay behind, and you end up like Pancho: with a shiny vehicle and a collection of women along the highways, but with no money, no house, and no future. Octavio has convinced his sister Emma (Marta Aura) that owning a home is the sign of progress and of a strong provider. But Pancho sticks to his childish stance, affirming, "No le tengo miedo a nadie." This will be contradicted shortly by a scolding from the patriarch don Alejo, with the patriarch in full view while Pancho is always partially seen, framed by doors and entryways but never taking a full stride into any space. Don Alejo reduces Pancho to tears of impotence. His bravado will be challenged in subsequent shots both with the cacique, to whom he owes the truck, and with La Japonesita, who realizes her power to control masculinity, both physically (she grabs his crotch) and politically (like the Partido Revolucionario Institucional [Institutional Revolutionary Party], she promises transparency but doesn't deliver). The feminine has been the object of the gaze in society as well as in the media, but here the reversal is startling and radical. A shift of power occurs when La Japonesita and Pancho meet inside the enclosed space of an alfalfa storage bin. She caresses him while demanding that he leave her and La Manuela alone. She is a direct threat to the traditional segregation of gender roles; he is not. Like traditional (male) politics, she entices him with an act of pleasure while, at the same time through her erotic gestures, telling him a different story.

Inside Octavio's small store, the two men hatch a plot, based on the purportedly successful breadwinner's guidance: Octavio urges Pancho to bring his finances out of public view and into the family by paying off don Alejo with money Octavio has at hand. The power of the lender over the indebted then turns inward, bringing all the anxiety back into the home, where it will fester as it has inside the brothel. Octavio moves outside to tend to business; Pancho lies back on a cot and falls deeply asleep. The fear of falling asleep at the wheel, or in the face of great social change, closes the scene. Octavio shows annoyance, but Pancho is unfazed.

The camera cuts to La Manuela, whose own fear focuses on the torn outfit from her last encounter with Pancho. In the sordid brothel filled with faded dolls, flower garlands, and memories, a torn dress is not out of place. A year has gone by since Pancho did "something" that ended up ripping an iconic dance costume to shreds and turning it into a rag ("una hilacha"). Like the fabric of the nation since 1968, La Manuela's dress is torn open for the world to see, and she muses about how she will sew it up, since the darning should be invisible and she has no red thread. La Manuela gets out of bed, ties a thin robe about her, and sits down at a dressing table mirror to apply lipstick. Her preparations to be publicly presentable are accompanied by recollections and self-affirmations: "Me gustaba [Pancho]." "Lo provocó, ¿no?" "No le bailo a ese bruto, sólo para caballeros" [I liked him. He provoked it, right? I won't dance for that brute, only with gentlemen]. She sounds unsure: he is to blame, right? As if with a stamp of the foot, but with an unconvincing tone, she vows not to dance for him again, since he is no gentleman. That will be impossible, but it takes most of the film to reach a turning point. She puts on an orange shirt and red pants—not just the dress but everything La Manuela wears is encoded as passionate—and walks, bouncing and determined, into the patio, starting her quest for red thread. Why does she not just avoid Pancho? That would turn them into one-dimensional beings and not the "fragile, complex, and idealist" (De la Mora) characters exposed by Ripstein in their dreams and vulnerabilities. Neither the younger women in the brothel, such as Lucy (Carmen Salinas), nor the older ones, such as Clotilde (Hortensia Santoveña), has what she needs, but in the kitchen of Ludovinia, or La "Ludo" (Emma Roldán), La Manuela finds a treasure trove of sewing materials that doña Blanca had given to the old woman long ago. Her eyesight failing, Ludo cements the bond between the two by affirming that thread (*el hilo*) is not lent but given as a gift, as it was to her. A pact is sealed over the right color, as if a perfect color match would almost hide the suture, in parallel to the way La Manuela hides under the "failed realness" (De la Mora, *Cinemachismo* 113) of her costume and makeup. The act of stitching—La Manuela uses the less common verb "zurcir" rather than the very Mexican "remendar"—unites her with aging femininity whose future is in doubt. Ludo remarks with some tenderness, "a vieja como yo tú no vas a llegar nunca" [you'll never get to be an old woman like me]. Melodrama's master narrative has to be woven together—*zurcida*—to bring the fragments together for a tenuous present. The *hilo* (*de la historia*) is, literally and metaphorically, passed along from Blanca to Ludo to Manuela. But then what? Cinematic narrative is left without storytellers, just as don Alejo is left without descendants and finds no pressing need to sign his will.

Manuela puts on the red dress and, in a series of crosscut shots between inside and outside, Pancho and La Manuela, she faces her fears and desires head-on. Supposedly in San Juan and not at home, Manuela hides among the chickens when Pancho makes his reappearance. "Si no lo ve, no va a pasar nada," La Manuela says of the sexually provocative garment. We peer at La Manuela behind the fronds of the courtyard, where she can't take her eyes off La Japonesita, Clotilde, and Lucy, who play the jukebox and dance with Octavio and Pancho. Octavio doesn't let Pancho out of his sight. When he finally does, that act of trust will bring down the house. The camera never moves closer to La Manuela than a medium distance, but is focused on the buttocks of La Japonesita—perhaps a metonym for La Manuela's own anatomy—and Pancho's bear hug. In retaliation for her acts in the alfalfa storage bin, Pancho's macho brazenness defies La Japonesita: he will bring La Manuela out or he will make her cry. La Manuela dips back behind the tree and emerges from nature (a Garden of Eden), dressed to kill, to become "el plato fuerte" [the main dish] of the night. As La Manuela sets up the performance of "La leyenda del beso" ["The Legend of the Kiss"] the shot widens to encompass the entire club for the first time. She assumes the role of storyteller, as well as protagonist, of this myth founded on a hostile encounter between two cultures and on the carryover of revenge into the next generation.

The music, a Spanish *zarzuela,* or light opera, bridges two genres—the gypsy tragedy of *La tempranica,* and a comedy of the hunt, *La montería*—to reach a bloody conclusion. La Manuela's performance centers on the well-known *intermedio* of the zarzuela. During that precise musical movement, the fatal attraction between a Spanish gentleman and the gypsy beauty Amapola plays out. The gentleman and the gypsy cannot unite, just as rich and poor cannot meet. Donoso/Ripsteins's work mirrors the zarzuela: La Manuela and Pancho cannot be on the same stage, without dire consequences. No matter what oaths the count swears, the bloods cannot mix. La Manuela tells the story and then performs the role of the woman whose kiss is supposed to revive a dead man. In and out of character, La Manuela defies Pancho to let her kiss him and wake him from his slumber, for he is merely asleep and not dead. The displacement of the kiss, from his eyes to his knee, then to his buttocks, breaks the peace, bringing Pancho from the chair to his feet. "La mujer divina," La Manuela enchants the object of her desire face-to-face and a hairsbreadth away. The camera focuses on the mirror images of desire awakened in both characters; their kiss, finally, is mutual. Reappearing, Octavio is both horrified into silence (except for a primal scream "¡Pancho!") and confirmed in his fears about Pancho. Evidence comes from his own sight. The ensuing chase scene of a woman fleeing two men who want to make her disappear before anyone comes forward as a witness could come straight out of any tabloid where *locas* and other social outsiders are always framed in communities imbued with violence.

If hell is a place without limits, and Pancho is tempting the devil, Ripstein's inferno does not end with the closing credits. The reticent cacique who hides from the brutal attack but looks on, fascinated, from behind the huge tree outside his patio warns his ranch hand that justice will be done, but elsewhere. "Son muy machos en la cárcel" [they are real manly men in prison] he assures himself—more macho even than Pancho. Male fantasy will be displaced from the brothel to the prison as the patriarch's voice closes the film, narrates from the fadeout darkness, and guarantees a continuation of this story. In the last frames of *El lugar sin límites,* there is no one. Octavio and Pancho have fled, Alejo and his servant go inside and close the door, La Manuela is dead, and La Japonesita and Lucy go to sleep and hope the errant La Manuela will come back the next day, after the party is over. This is her pattern. Silence reigns, but hell will continue in new places and new guises. Like the bar, the brothel, the town, the nation, and hell, the prison is another microcosmic allegorical space in which meaning is multiplied and abstracted from the concrete, and in which subjects (characters) must negotiate their identities. As John Ochoa says in his study of the trope of "failure" in Mexico, such a "transitional, possibly destructive, moment . . . precipitates new knowledge" (5) and is ultimately related to a "fall" with unexpected and far-reaching consequences. Through allegory, *El lugar sin límites* unwraps the origins of certain national failures to give access to the human bodies behind them, but the director refuses to cover them up again. As Ochoa concludes (and Ripstein appears to desire), there is "insight gained through failure" (192) facilitated by the privileged position of the spectator and the cinematic eye.

Works Cited

Donoso, José. *El lugar sin límites*. Caracas: Biblioteca Ayacucho, 1970. Print.
Garber, Marjorie. *Vested Interests: Cross-Dressing and Cultural Anxiety*. New York: Routledge, 1992. Print.

Joßner, Ulrich. "Arturo Ripstein: Extreme Melodrama." Web. Dec. 6, 2011.
Kibbey, Ann. *Theory of the Image: Capitalism, Contemporary Film, and Women.* Bloomington, IN: Indiana UP, 2005. Print.
Ochoa, John A. *The Uses of Failure in Mexican Literature and Identity.* Austin, TX: U of Texas P, 2004. Print.
la Mora, Sergio de la. *Cinemachismo: Masculinities and Sexuality in Mexican Film.* Austin, TX: U of Texas P, 2006. Print.
———. "Fascinating Machismo: Toward an Unmasking of Heterosexual Masculinity in Arturo Ripstein's *El lugar sin límites*." *Journal of Film and Video* 44.3–4 (1992–1993): 83–104. Print.
———. "Mexican Movies for the New Millennium." Web. Dec. 6, 2011.
Paranagúa, Paulo Antonio. *Arturo Ripstein: La espiral de la identidad.* Serie Signo e Imagen/Cineastas Latinoamericanos. Madrid: Cátedra; Filmoteca Española, 1997. Print.
Quiroga, José. *Tropics of Desire: Interventions from Queer Latino America.* New York: New York UP, 2000. Print.
Ripstein, Arturo, dir. *El lugar sin límites.* Conacite Dos, 1977. Film.
Solomon-Godeau, Abigail. *Male Trouble: A Crisis in Representation.* London: Thames; Hudson, 1999. Print.
Zolov, Eric. *Refried Elvis: The Rise of the Mexican Counterculture.* Berkeley, CA: U of California P, 1999. Print.

14

Families, Landowners, Servants, and Siblings in *La ciénaga*

(Lucrecia Martel, 2001)

David Oubiña[1]

The elements that make up *La ciénaga* (*The Swamp*, 2001) are quite simple: a hot summer, an estate in the remote regions of Salta province, and two families. Mecha, who owns the estate, suffers a small accident, and her friend Tali comes to visit. Over the next few days, the two women's families cross paths and are reunited, children come and go, and a bit of life penetrates the deteriorating farmhouse. José, Mecha's oldest son, journeys from Buenos Aires to visit his mother, the boys go hunting in the hills, and the girls take naps and chat by a swimming pool of filthy water. Meanwhile, the women plan an outing to Bolivia to buy school supplies—a trip that never takes place. Elsewhere, someone claims to have sighted the Virgin Mary, and toward the end there is a tragic death. Not much else happens in this world as observed attentively by Momi, the youngest of Mecha's daughters.

On one hand, the horizon of possibilities in *La ciénaga* is limited by the decrepit regional economies where the story unfolds. It is a suffocating world with no good way out and from which nothing new can arise. The characters form part of a web of relations that acts as a closed system in which traits are passed immutably from one generation to another. There are no transitions, because to show a transition is to capture the moment in which a situation transforms. Here, situations are indefinitely suspended states. The problem of *La ciénaga* is how to allow for progress without advancing; that is, how to increase the dramatic tension without accelerating the narrative pulse? Lucrecia Martel's film advances like a log on a slow-moving river. It is methodical but elusive. A large group of characters are involved in small conflicts that, rather than articulating themselves as axes of a defined story, sketch muted tales that are barely insinuated and reach only a low narrative intensity.

Swampy Scenes and Ambiguous Boundaries

Trapped in a story that does not advance and is continually bogged down, the characters form groups that manage to oppose each other as often as they blend. There are few frames with fewer than two or three people, and practically no scenes (except, perhaps, Luciano's death) that follow one person alone. The images are hyper-populated, but that is not the only issue. The film makes no effort to distinguish its characters: at first sight, it is difficult to identify them and establish the links between them. Nevertheless, that confusion is not due to any sparse elaboration of their personal qualities—although they intermingle, each conserves his or her singularity. In this way, the prevailing style of overcrowded images in the film is no mere accumulation but, rather, a conglomeration of minutely drawn figures. If, on one hand, individual personalities do not impede the bending of traditional molds, on the other hand, promiscuity never prevents confrontations. In any case, Lucrecia Martel works with this light but abrupt disparity between similarity and difference. The characters belong to different classes, different generations, and different families. Although this may not prevent them from permanently mixing, it does not suppose that there is anything to share, either. Their relationships oscillate between small differences, blown out of proportion to emphasize distance, and a tight-knit closeness that, by accentuating itself, shows nothing so much as incompatibility.

In a significant way, just as Martel does not allow for a protagonist character or a central line of narration, neither does she choose a choral structure for telling different, parallel stories. She is less interested in advancing different fronts to construct a sequence than in passing from one situation to another in a drifting or flowing fashion. The tale is constructed not by exposing several stories but by linking them horizontally, and it progresses in a diffuse manner without knowing which direction it is heading. It is based on an associative and recursive model. There is no development, no continuity, and no alternation. The effect is of promiscuity and contamination. The characters are limited to retracing their orbits, passing again and again through the same places; but as these orbits share a common space, they sometimes intersect and lead to exchanges that can materialize as approximation or as rejection—or, sometimes, as both at once. The film is developed through this system of encircling (Mecha and Tali's families, landowners and servants, children and parents), oriented along an apparently whimsical path full of curves and reversals. It is not so much a polyphony as it is a monotonous and often discordant sound. This is literally the case with the dialogues: instead of occurring in an alternating fashion, they overlap and pile on top of one another. The same idea applies to the composition of the frames, in which there are always many people and the main action is never clearly distinguishable. Thus, the problem is not only in how things are oriented in space (what should be seen) but also in the story (what should be understood).

A choral structure always clearly proclaims its narrative goal: that we see what there is to see when it needs to be seen. The narration changes from one line to another to find the important element of each moment. *La ciénaga*, in contrast, clings to an acceptance of indecision, indeterminacy, and uncertainty. The camera never seems to select the situation or to locate itself in a privileged position. Of course, this style of narration does not follow documentary protocol. Instead, the idea is not to film what is possible, when it is possible, and from where it is possible, but rather to have a careful shot selection that leaves out potentially strong dramatic moments to create the effect of an eccentric viewpoint that never knows where to look and is always on the brink of not being able to see *anything*. According to Martel in Emilio Bernini's "Tres cineastas argentinos":

> That was the main idea of the movie: not to show beginnings of scenes, but instead to stumble upon situations that had already begun. If one sees both the inception and conclusion of a situation, much of the drama is lost. And in a film without a strong dramatic base, my challenge was to maintain—but not increase—the initial intensity level. Or in any case, if the drama were to be escalated, it would be due to the accumulation of small things and not because there were any great expectations. (136)

That "accumulation of small things" comes from the little separation between those who seem similar, or from the points of contact between those who should keep themselves separate. Mecha and Tali are two different representations of women. One runs her own house and disregards her husband, a bumbling deadbeat stripped of all rights and conjugal obligations.

The other, conversely, is completely submissive to her husband, who, in apparent bonhomie, always imposes his authority in an unequivocal manner.[2] In Mecha's family, the women are certainly more diligent: Vero, Momi, and Isabel are the ones who look after Mecha when she is injured. The men are useless (like Gregorio), slackers (like José), or slightly wild (like Joaquín). Gregorio barely objects when Mecha expels him from the bedroom and sends him to sleep in the small room in the back of the house. Rafael is the opposite: a selfless husband and an overprotective father. But if he is able to resolve all problems in the household, it is at the cost of suppressing any opportunities for others to make decisions. Only he knows where the papers for the car are and what documentation is necessary for leaving the country; it is he who buys the school supplies so that Tali does not journey to Bolivia; and, when his wife says that the children are better off at Mecha's house because they can cool off there, it is he who goes to buy a swimming pool for the patio of their own house. Whereas a question posed to Gregorio falls on empty ears, Rafael's answers stifle any further questioning. It is impossible to have dialogue with one, because what he says is insubstantial. However, it is equally impossible to talk to the other, because he never listens.

In the beginning, Tali's family is presented as diametrically opposed to Mecha's. While one seems swamped with domestic and family obligations, the other lounges around a pool with a group of friends. When Mecha has the accident, almost nobody pays attention, and it seems a miracle that she finally makes it to the hospital. Tali, in contrast, dotes over Luciano and keeps her concerned husband informed of his son's health. But this contrast gradually diminishes, even though the families do not abandon their different traits. It becomes apparent that these are two sides of the same coin: two complementary aspects of a common patriarchal tradition. Tali and Mecha need to escape to Bolivia because both, for different reasons, feel suffocated. And if, ultimately, the trip never materializes, it is because neither woman manages to free herself from what binds her in place: Mecha because she cannot get out of bed, and Tali because she cannot face up to her husband. There is very little mobility. Each woman is a prisoner of her role, and both are ultimately paralyzed, as always.

The characteristics of the two families, which tie them together as much as differentiate them, work on other levels as well: outwardly, in the links the family maintains with others (the servants, those belonging to a lower class: the "Indians"), and inwardly, in the ways that the family members are linked among themselves (above all, the relationships between the siblings). In both cases, certain lines of prohibition established by common law are at risk of being transgressed. Given that all social order must be based on prohibition (which defines inclusions as well as exclusions), the concept of transgression as necessary and essential violence takes on a central role. For Georges Bataille in *Literature and Evil*, transgression is not liberation (49). It does not deny or annul prohibition; it does not suppose mere disorder. In this sense, transgression is not located outside the system of prohibition; rather, it integrates or completes prohibition. Prohibition is not an antisocial force or exogenous agent, but a dynamic element of strong cohesion.

Every transgression supposes a theater, a visible space in relation to others. According to Bataille in his book *Erotism: Death and Sensuality*, transgression is never animalistic violence (38–39). Abandonment to this passion is not a loss or dissociation with one's self (as it is understood in the Augustinian tradition). Instead, it contains a cognitive dimension or seeks to create a certain meaning. Abandonment has more to do with productivity than with negativity or submission. It is not a mere replacement of the law of prohibition with the law of disorder, but rather the articulation of a complex and hidden system of logic connecting both laws. Bataille is interested in the inevitable interdependence of the two. He does not postulate transgression as an alternative mode to the law, because in reality, transgression does more: all law is derived from the so-called law of disorder.[3] In Martel's work, that very relationship is the point from which forces opposed to the law and transgression begin to function. Familial order imposes itself over certain prohibitions and taboos, but instead of eliminating them, it establishes them as areas of resistance. They remain latent and threatening, in a double relationship of attraction and rejection.

Boggy Symbiosis: Affection and Contempt; Attraction and Repulsion

The relationships between Mecha's family members and their employees are as much symbiotic as they are refractory. The movie neither tries to show that these people are similar nor that they are different; instead, it is concerned with what happens when these distinct (and distant) classes coexist in the same space. Their relationship is built as much out of friction as out of closeness, and each action in this space has meaning as the reaction to another. Curiously, class relations are grounded in a racial essentialism that should minimize any confusion: the servants are "the Indians," and that nomenclature establishes an uncrossable boundary. Still, the separation between the two castes does not prevent communication, although, of course, it plays out according to a hierarchy. Communication occurs not in spite of the differences but by exploiting them; not because the differences are forgotten but because they are present.

José feels entitled to flirt with Isabel. Not that she is particularly appealing to him, but he believes he can seduce her because he is the son of the landowner. He is merely exercising his power. If he later gets injured, it is because he has gone too far into unwelcoming territory: a public Carnaval dance in which he is the person out of place. Vero uses her power similarly when she asks El Perro to try on the shirt she is considering buying for José. This minor situation, which might seem perfectly innocent, quickly ends up violent and humiliating. El Perro is invited to undress in front of his girlfriend (or, rather, Isabel is forced to witness how the landowner's daughters take advantage of her boyfriend), only for Vero to smell the sweat he leaves on the shirt, and toss it aside in disgust.

Joaquín is the one who most explicitly shows class prejudice, but at the same time, he is the one who best blends in with the other group. On the way back from the dam, he disgustedly throws away the fish they have caught: "They're nothing but mud. These damn Indians will eat anything." Nevertheless, since he does not notice that Isabel picks up the fish and takes them home, he later praises the delectable dish she has made with those very catfish. In another scene, he complains about those Indians living one on top of the other, together in one house: the mother, father, grandfather, cat, and dog. Curiously, that seems a near perfect description of his own family. He later curses the Indians who spend all day caressing the animals and who "have probably already fucked the dog because they like smooth skin," while he himself strokes that very dog. In his fantasies, Joaquín projects an image of savages onto others, which allows him to establish differences and distance himself. In reality, that projection is a way to conjure up a primitivism that he comes dangerously close to: not only does he spend time inspecting the hindquarters of the dogs, but he also eats with his hands ("You're like a beast," Momi tells him), and it is in the woods, among the animals, where he seems to enjoy himself most.

But the point where the ties of attraction and repulsion (of submission and domination) undeniably weaken is in the relationship between Momi and Isabel. Because Momi never forgets their unequal positions, she cannot help but fall in love. Momi is vulnerable because she loves. She is the only person in the film who loves, and she suffers because her love is not reciprocated. Momi naps in the servants' room and watches television in her room with Isabel. When José calls on the phone, Momi commands:

"Mom says that you have to answer"; but later, when her brother tells Isabel she cannot be there, and kicks her out, Momi tries to keep her and cover up the offense. Mecha says that Isabel steals towels and that she is going to fire her, but it is later revealed that Momi has taken a bracelet of Isabel's. Isabel gives her clothing to wear, and Momi ridicules her—sweetly although with a certain paternalism—because a servant does not know how to choose garments ("They don't match: stripes and flowers don't match"). But later, when Isabel is getting ready to go to the dance, Momi becomes jealous and tries to keep her home. Finally, because the servant has other responsibilities and pays her no attention, Momi insults her with purely classist spite: "dirty Indian." Affection and contempt are contiguous. And if they implicate each other, it is because one can morph into its opposite at any moment.

Effectively, the different instances of intimacy or mimicry among residents of the house and servants constantly signify both rejection and difference, simultaneously. Conversely, within the relationships between family members lies an ambivalent tension determined by desire that never quite defines itself as attraction or as friction. Better put, there is attraction and friction at the same time. It is like a magnetic field in which the two forces are inseparable rather than counteractive. The forces of attraction and repulsion among residents and servants ultimately drive them apart. They are not cohesive; they work like a centrifugal force, responding to one another in contradiction and alternation (sometimes one making itself felt, and sometimes the other). Between the siblings, however, those two opposing forces converge: they are integrative, simultaneous, and tend to concentrate and fuse into a conflictive identity closed over itself.

There is only one scene in which the family is seen eating together around the table, and it turns out to be an awkward, abnormal, strange situation. Every other time, the natural place of gathering or receiving visits is around Mecha's bed. *La ciénaga* can even be considered a film about beds. Everybody gets between each other's sheets: Momi in the servant's bed and in Vero's bed; Vero in José's bed; José and Joaquín in Mecha's bed. Within this morbid promiscuity, the innocence of childish games is confused with barely repressed aggression and sexuality. The collisions between bodies are always violent, but it is impossible to determine how much is hostility and how much is attraction.

A similar phenomenon happens in *La niña santa* (*The Holy Girl*, 2004), another film by Lucrecia Martel: Amalia and Josefina kiss in a deck chair at the hotel (in the final scene, her friend even says, "I'm always going to take care of you because you have no siblings; I'm your sister"); Josefina and her cousin lie down in the grandmother's bed; Amalia sleeps in a bed with her mother, and Uncle Freddy joins them. In an interview with Juan Aguzzi, Martel remarks:

> The family is a particular group of people among whom, for reasons that seem unnatural to me, sex is banned for all except the parents. Nevertheless, desire is present wherever there is a group of people, whether or not they have blood relations; desire is in fluctuation, with no need for the concrete act of sex, but it circulates, and to avoid it is a very middle class attitude. . . . When a person lives with those attitudes is when these desires are seen most easily, which are totally anarchical and always throbbing and alive. For me the sensuality or sexuality of the movie was important for counteracting that element of despair. (27)

Thus, in *La ciénaga*, desire as a vital impulse is absent between the parents and, instead, flows in all other directions. In the midst of this great confusion of characters, in which it is never quite clear who is related to whom, hints of incest arise among the promiscuity and come almost unexpectedly to serve as signs of intense vitality.

José lives in Buenos Aires with his father's old lover; but after arriving in Salta he sleeps in the bed of his mother, who, in turn, has expelled his father from the bedroom. Meanwhile, Vero is jealous of Mercedes and tries to get in bed with José; he rejects her, but after the fight at the Carnaval dance, she and her cousin undress him while he is unconscious. When Mercedes decides not to travel, José seems to feel liberated: although he announces the news to Vero as a provocation, to annoy and anger her, he is also evidently seeking her complicity. He steals a pair of her panties, puts them on his head, and runs away; she follows him and catches him, and they struggle; both fall to the ground and end up fighting and pawing each other as they roll around in the mud. The corollary is no less significant. Vero is showering when José comes into the bathroom: barely separated from his sister by the shower curtain, he first urinates in the toilet and then sticks his muddy foot under the shower water as his sister covers herself, more amused than appalled. The whole situation unfolds as a game between brother and sister, but what is unsettling is that it becomes difficult to distinguish when it is merely mischief and at what point the doors are opened to a sexuality that has been there all along, lurking beneath the surface. Desire is unpredictable and uncontainable. That is why it challenges the limits imposed by a familial order consisting of atavistic repetition: it opens a gap within a monolithic structure that otherwise seems to swallow everything and leave nothing out.[4]

Mired: Passengers on a Sinking Ship

But to what extent do these transgressions of domestic law (from within, from without) truly materialize? If it is true that desire counteracts that hopeless horizon awaiting the characters, does it direct them to another place? What lies in the future for Vero or José? And what might be expected for Momi, who suffers from an impossible love? For just as there exists in each character a sense of asphyxiation, there is also an impulse to complacently settle oneself within already familiar situations. The family house is called La Mandrágora (The Mandrake), and Lucrecia Martel explains that she was interested in the name because it describes a plant used in ancient times for its anesthetic power and aphrodisiac properties. "I wanted the film to oscillate between two polar extremes: numbness and sensuality. That is, perhaps, the deepest drama of the film" (75).[5]

Both potentials exist in the picture, but the final shot casts serious doubt over the realization of any change. Seated at the poolside, back to back, Vero and Momi reproduce the same visual image as their parents at the beginning of the film. In this circular structure, realities seem doomed to repeat themselves: all indications suggest that the girls will continue the cycle and replicate the familial order; so Mecha, just like her mother, will fail to get out of bed in the end, and José will end up just like his father. These reiterations are as meaningful as the disagreements that accentuate people's distance and abandonment. Vero calls José seeking consolation over Luciano's death, but the line is busy because he has left the phone off the hook, undecided on whether or not to call Tali. Momi, for her part, has gone to ask the Virgin Mary for Isabel's return, but she has found nothing but disappointment: "I saw nothing," she says. A silent telephone and an empty water tank. A better horizon does not seem to await either of the girls. Neither desire nor love has made them any different.

La ciénaga presents a state of things in which any change appears alien to the horizon of possibilities available to the characters. The key is to ask oneself why none of the characters reacts, why none of them warns each other that they are on a sinking ship. The vision of the filmmaker is descriptive and analytic: it observes from the perspective of her characters, but with a clarity they could not attain. Therein lie the power and beauty of film.

Notes

1. Professor David Oubiña and the book's editors express their heartfelt thanks to our colleague Alexander Sugar for the English translation of this essay, written originally in Spanish.
2. Mercedes, the third friend, is as different from Mecha as from Tali. She is an independent woman without a husband, a matter which both Mecha and Tali judge according to their own perspectives: Tali sympathizes because she never found a partner while Mecha notes ironically, and resentfully, that she is one of the few women who never sleeps alone.
3. See, for example, Bataille's *Erotism: Death and Sexuality* (38–39); also his *Literature and Evil* (49). Perhaps the admiration that Martel has for Osvaldo Lamborghini's works comes through in her films thanks to the concept of transgression as described by Bataille.
4. In a different way, the dangerous situations and appearance of Virgin Mary also question the foreseeable order of repetition. They pose a threat to an established limit. But while desire predicates a vital momentum and involves the active participation of the characters, the dangers lying in wait and the heavenly apparition promising miraculous solutions belong to the fatal or supernatural order. (Thus, both tend to instill a passive attitude in the characters.)
5. In *La niña santa*, there is also an oscillation between two polar extremes, but here it is a difference between passion in the religious and erotic senses. How can we distinguish between the devil's temptation and the divine call? The encounter between Amalia and Dr. Jano is marked from the start by that contradiction: after a meeting with a group of Christians, she stops to listen to a musician playing a tune on a theremin while the doctor stands behind her and rubs up against her. On one side is the music in its most ethereally intangible state (the theremin is an instrument that is played without being "touched"), and, on the other side, desire in its crudest embodiment.

Works Cited

Aguzzi, Juan. "El deseo es algo que fluye; evitarlo es una actitud muy clase (Entrevista con Lucrecia Martel)." *El Eclipse* 4 (2001): 26–28. Print.

Bataille, Georges. *Literature and Evil*. Trans. Alastair Hamilton. London: Marion Boyars, 2001. Print.

———. *Erotism: Death and Sensuality*. Trans. Mary Dalwood. San Francisco, CA: City Lights, 1986. Print.

Bernini, Emilio, et al. "Tres cineastas argentinos (Conversación con Lucrecia Martel, Lisandro Alonso y Ariel Rotter)." *Kilómetro 111* 2 (2001): 125–50. Print.

Lalanne, Jean-Marc. "Le film s'enracine dans des peurs d'enfant (Rencontre avec Lucrecia Martel)." *Cahiers du cinéma* 564 (2002): 75–76. Print.

Martel, Lucrecia, dir. *La ciénaga*. Wanda Visión, 2001. DVD.

15

Mapping Guilt, Betrayal, and Redemption: *En la ciudad sin límites*

(Antonio Hernández, 2002)

CHRIS PERRIAM

This Spanish-Argentine-French production has had a fairly modest theatrical exposure (173,910 box office admissions in the enlarged EU); however, its high-profile cast and its novel combination of queer historical fiction with an engagement with what has come to be called la memoria histórica in the context of Spain give it a dual, if niche, appeal. Festival exposure at Berlin International Film Festival and the Regus London Film Festival in 2002 were followed by the Providence Latin-American Film Festival in 2004, with the not inconsiderable cultural machinery of the Instituto Cervantes including it in their regular program of screenings, for example, in Cairo in 2004, Warsaw in 2005, Dublin and Lisbon in 2009, and in the III Festival Hispano Brasileño de Cine in Rio de Janeiro in 2006. Low-key festival reappearances are still occurring (for example, the 2008 IX Festival de Cine Europeo en Bolivia). Sogepaq/Twentieth Century Fox's DVD release for Europe dignifies the title with Special Edition treatment, including a director's cut and full scholarly filmographies for the cast. The non-spoiling synopsis offered by Film Index International reads as follows:

> Víctor [Leonardo Sbaraglia] has come to Paris to see his father who is seriously ill. However, he finds the old man behaving strangely and trying to run away from the hospital. Finally

gaining his father's trust, Víctor smuggles him out of hospital but his father's memory lapses and other members of the family put a stop to further trips. Víctor is about to give up, when he discovers his father's madness cloaks a terrible secret.

The secret is not fully terrible in itself, though, since its revelation represents in part an affirmative piece of gay personal and left-wing political history: Víctor's father, Max (Fernando Fernán Gómez), had an intense affair as a young man, sharing a modest Parisian left-bank apartment with a radical, out, gay, communist exile, Rancel—now Joaquín—(Alfredo Alcón), who had taken part in resistance assignments within Franco's Spain. However, two factors undermine the positive impact: one is that Max is now convinced of his madness (if it is such), in that he betrayed Rancel and failed to warn him against boarding a train which led to his capture; the other is that Víctor's mother, Marie (Geraldine Chaplin) has all along been fired by jealous rage against Rancel, whom she supplanted, and the memory and mention of whom she has long been able to suppress. The secret is made more surprising to Víctor perhaps because his father is, to him, a wealthy, established head of a substantial family business and stands at the center of a classic wealthy middle-class, emphatically heterosexual family, riddled by betrayals and petty frustrations, and ripe for melodramatic exploitation by the film, following a venerable, mainstream cinematic tradition. The manifest unhappiness of most of the women in the family, the dim, cruel complacency and emotional naivety of one brother, Luis (Roberto Álvarez) and the financially self-interested machinations of the other, Alberto (Álex Casanovas) and a leitmotif of betrayal all become amplified through the trope of the city with no limits, to become indirect signifiers of a larger dysfunctionality.

Betrayal, loss, and being lost heighten the storyline's thematic associations with representations on screen of the Spanish past. Although it stands at an obvious temporal distance from such well-known films as Carlos Saura's *La caza* (*The Hunt*, 1965) and *Cría cuervos* (*Cria!*, 1976) or Víctor Erice's *El espíritu de la colmena* (*The Spirit of the Beehive*, 1973), some of the traces of those films and their motifs persist. Geraldine Chaplin's presence in *Cría cuervos*—as a ghost of past betrayals—and Fernando Fernán Gómez's in *El espíritu de la colmena*—as a man reconstructing yet denying the past—consolidate the impression of persistence. All three films, as so many others of the era, use family bonds and conflicts to signal social, national, and political ones (Hopewell, Kinder 165–72, Saenz "The Absence of Place"). Although Álvaro del Amo feels able to go so far as to bluntly (or journalistically) describe "En la ciudad sin límites" as "a melodrama about the unhealed wounds of the Civil War" (12), the mapping is not that clearly delineated. Instead, several lines of connection back into the film's historical past fill out a general outline of association. Jonathan Holland ("The City of No Limits") and Miguel Ángel Huerta Floriano ("En la ciudad sin límites") pick up on Max's fixation on a button as his link to his lost memories and lost love as a reminiscence of *Citizen Kane* (Orson Welles, 1941) and the Rosebud motif (Max's semi-plutocratic status does so too). As we will be seeing later, the iconic figures of Fernando Fernán Gómez and Geraldine Chaplin bond the film obliquely with the cinema of the Spanish Transition to Democracy. Two useful brief blog-style comments by Rubén Corral ("En la ciudad sin límites") and Rodríguez Chico ("En la ciudad sin límites") draw more pertinent attention to the remote similarities in part of the storyline with Alain Resnais's *La Guerre est finie* (*The War is Over*, 1966), with a script by Jorge Semprún, himself an exiled (and eventually ex-) communist resistance fighter writing in France. Its central plot motif of cross-border resistance to Franco, and its preoccupation with, as the script's second section is entitled, "Les vérités du mensonge" and to "[ce] monde clos [. . .] mouvant, trouble, et rempli de pièges" (Semprún 43, 49) ("The Truths Within the Lie"; "[this] enclosed, blurred and shifting world, full of traps") would certainly appear to underpin some of the connections made in *En la ciudad sin límites* between personal drama and political involvement, between psychological and physical entrapment. A final connection to Spanish history comes through two members of the film's team, Geraldine Chaplin (to whom I shall return shortly) and co-scriptwriter Enrique Brasó, who had both worked on *In memoriam* (directed by Brasó [1977]).

The film was based on Adolfo Bioy Casares's tale "En memoria de Paulina" (in the collection *La trama celeste* [1948]), a subtle ghost story which balances the remembering of its title with the jilted narrator's declaration "Eludí obstinadamente su recuerdo" (87), exploring the protean quality of his dreams and memories of the, as it turns out, murdered woman. In its secondary but significant plots concerning "la situación del país" (by way of the liberal magazine for which both Luis and his rival Julio work) and sexual dilemma (Paulina is torn between the two men; but one is emotionally dysfunctional and the other violently jealous in the machista mold), it linked its haunting qualities to concerns with national and personal identity in a way which was strongly characteristic of its period. The film was a commercial failure, but formally elegant (Torres 76–78) in its treatments of loss, regret, temporality, and uncanniness, and it anticipates much of the atmosphere and the disposition of preoccupations of *En la ciudad sin límites*. Chaplin's playing of Paulina, thwarted in her desire for the writer Luis by his inability to commit erotically and emotionally, at first emphasizes tender vulnerability set against stifling bourgeois interiors, and subsequently her chilly irritation at Luis (reprising Chaplin's skilled representations of anger and distress in Saura's *Cría cuervos*, out one year earlier). In her affair with Luis's professional and romantic rival Julio, Paulina, in Chaplin's interpretation, is ambiguously yielding, almost wanton, but also distant (and still attached to Luis). *En la ciudad sin límites* does not use either the melodramatic jealousy killing which is the narrative core of *In memoriam* or the return to Luis of the dead Paulina (in an eerie scene in which reprised domestic habits give way to the sudden hemorrhaging of her hand as she reaches out to touch him).

However, something of Luis's obsessive voice-over remembrance of Paulina does reappear in Max's fractured monologues in *En la ciudad sin límites*. There are echoes too, in Max's written declaration to Rancel, of Luis's melancholy realization early on in the establishing narrative present of In memoriam, in voice-over interior monologue, that "siempre te quise Paulina [. . .] no he podido olvidarte," intensified by the core temporal ellipsis (of Luis's sojourn in Cambridge, England) and by reiterations of motifs of transience. Where Luis the writer had thought he had to respond to his "voces interiores" alerting him to the conflict between the artistic ideal and reality "[huyendo] de la vida y del amor [para] conformarse con los sueños," the dying businessman Max finds that his own evasion of love and dissidence has played it part in constructing a false dream. Marie has also played her part in this, enclosing Max in a metaphorical space of lies.

Star Memories

A traditional motif of both Baroque drama and mainstream film fantasy, the interchangeability of dreams and reality which informs this film had been exploited to dramatize extreme alienation five years previously in Spain, in a different context, in *Abre los ojos* (*Open Your Eyes*, dir. Alejandro Amenábar, 1997; see Perriam, and Smith 115–30). The motif's equally traditional, spatial counterpart—the labyrinth—will be discussed later in the essay. While in itself the motif might be pure embellishment, it becomes more embedded in the structuring of the film through the actors' own histories and the different stages in their careers. Fernando Fernán Gómez's status as an icon of Spanish cinema—as well as his career in playing and directing quietly dissident, off-beat, and anti-establishment figures (Brasó 14, 144–48, 213–18;

Freixas)—makes his performance stand as a memorial in itself, recapitulating a film-cultural history of the transition while also sustaining, as Fernando Méndez-Leite points out ("En la ciudad sin límites"), the moral weight of the film narrative. Geraldine Chaplin, with her links back into the early days of cinema through her father, her strong professional and sentimental association with Carlos Saura and her status as muse and myth of Spanish cinema of the 1970s, adds another line into the past. Brasó's own interest in Saura, with a book on the period of high dissident cine metafórico (metaphorical cinema), is certainly not betrayed by the film's concern with oblique political references within a clearly indicative frame of intense family drama. As I have already suggested, in discussing *In memoriam*, her chilly, haughty performance recalls the repressive microcosm of *Cría cuervos*; and her role there, in part as a ghost (the mother of the young protagonist Ana), connects with our film's own concern—Max's—with speaking with the dead. Just as her character Marie haunts the family, and is haunted by what she sees as the unacceptable past, so too does Chaplin's playing of her haunt the film. Marie's demeanor is invariably produced through straight-backed, tight-lipped, and gesturally restrained formality mixed with looks of constant reproach (Marie's prime mechanism of control over the family) which tip over into enraged obstinacy once the secret threatens to be out. When Víctor confronts her with the news of his conversations with Rancel/Joaquín and demands to see the letter for him that Max has entrusted to a nurse, Chaplin and Sbaraglia, helped by the hospital *mise-en-scène* play the scene in such a way as to emphasize separateness and the impossibility of reconciliation. Chaplin—glimpsed through a huge sheet of space-separating glass at first, and suddenly made to disappear in a blur leftwards out of frame at the end of the chilly, intense exchange—stands immobile in front of a pair of reflective aluminum lift doors like a ghost who has appeared, and will disappear, through a closed door. The letter she hatefully flings down onto the corridor floor between them is like a life-changing token or message from the other side.

As one blogger in Fotogramas aptly pointed out, the film was the third time that Chaplin and Fernán Gómez had worked together, along with Saura's *Ana y los lobos* (*Anna and the Wolves*, 1972) and *Mamá cumple 100 años* (*Mama Turns 100*, 1979)—each with their own poignant contributions to historical memory—in their shared professional pasts. Their presence here, with those echoes of previous narratives and images of hidden histories, revelations appearing, and collective grief focused down onto domestic and individual emotional life, highlights the motif of dream and reality, veiling and unveiling.

Leonardo Sbaraglia—two generations younger than Fernán Gómez, and with his early career in Argentina not in Spain—brings to the film a forward-looking feel. His role here coincides with the start of an energetic career in mainly Spanish and European-funded films as epitomized by Vicente Aranda's *Carmen* (2003), being filmed that same year. As *Variety*'s reporter noticed, scenes between Sbaraglia, with his "nice combination of the intense and the laid back" and Fernán Gómez's more extrovert interpretation of despair and dementia, looks like "a workshop on how acting has changed down the years." Sbaraglia himself, unsurprisingly, pays tribute to the experience of working with the older actor in an interview in Buenos Aires ("Nunca nadie"). In the same interview he goes on immediately to make the connection, for his Argentine audience, to the general ethical tenor of the story and the specific historical context:

> "Lo conmovedor de esta película es que mi personaje está tratando de recuperar la memoria de los que luchan. Porque tangencialmente intenta recuperar algo que está muy ligado a la historia española y al movimiento antifranquista, que es la trama política que tiene la película muy detrás" [What is moving about this film is that my character is trying to recover the memory of the fighters. Because tangentially, he tries to recover something that is very tied into Spanish history and to the anti-Franco movement, which is the political trauma deeply behind the film].

In what is indeed a highly moving scene in the film the family drama of reconciliation and recognition, and the intensity of Hernández's staging of the semi-autobiographically inspired encounter (Caparrós Lera 149) of disoriented, dying father and belatedly lucid, bereft son, "la memoria de los que luchan" [the memory of the fighters] richly interposes itself. Víctor's tears spread a vicarious haze to the viewer's visualization of the scene, and the slow tracking back of the camera in synchronization with the slow movements of Max's aided struggle to sit up and gulp air into his lungs, are a partial example of the inheritance what Giles Deleuze famously identified as the cinema of the time-image. It draws attention to "the disturbances of memory and the failures of recognition" (55), the "present/pastness" of the film image. As is well known, the crystal-image as proposed by Deleuze shapes time as a constant two-way mirror that splits the present into two heterogeneous directions, "one of which is launched towards the future while the other falls into the past. Time consists of this split, and it is . . . time, that we see in the crystal" (81). The father/son image of certain scenes of *En la ciudad sin límites* is also, in this sense, the crystallized image of past as lived, past as possible (virtual), past projected (in the letter and in the naming of Rancel) into the future, future perfect (the inevitability of loss), and future perfected. Marie and what she represents (again, a past falsely upheld against a future) is challenged; the family's course of history is altered; Víctor is cast adrift but free; and the letter, again, has envisaged how "mis hijos nos ven abrazados, desnudos, pero ya no son mis hijos" [my children see us embracing, naked, but they are no longer my children]— those "hijos" are generalized out into, and interpellated as, the collective new family who witness this drama in but also beyond the space and time of the film. Although Deleuze had in mind a far more experimental and radical, modern mode of cinematic representation than does Hernández, the film manages to stage several crystallizations of this type.

Memoria histórica; Queer History

The blurring of past and present which emanates from Max's disturbed misrecognition of both times (he never did fail Rancel; he is not, in any literal sense, a captive), along with the narrative's concern with denial and reconciliation, places the film in the significant context of Spanish cultural work on historical memory in relation to the Civil War of 1936–1939 and its aftermaths. The crucial moment which haunts Max is one that only makes sense in relation to a specific machinery of political repression designed to hunt down and eliminate the *maqui* or resistance, even though the film seems to be "about" that aspect of history only tangentially. Like the ghosts and ghostly voices which cultural commentators have identified as emerging from cultural and political discourses since 1978 (Resina, ed.; Resina and Winter, eds.), Max's reconstruction of the Rancel he never sees but wishes to conjure up is a hauntological narrative. In the same vein, Rancel's silent appearance at the graveside in the films' last moments and his gothically envisaged emergence from the dark riverside street on the night of his meeting with Víctor, as well as Geraldine Chaplin's embodiment of Marie—so reminiscent of her playing of the ghost of Ana's mother in *Cría cuervos*—all respond to the need identified by, for example, Jo Labanyi (2005) to draw attention to "la historia de la sujetividad" [the history of subjectivity] which constitutes memory ("El cine como lugar de memoria" 168), and to engage with ghosts, as "the victims of history who return to demand reparation" ("History and Hauntology" 66).

The critics writing on historical memory in Spain find themselves returning often to the idea of Places of Memory, as posited by Pierre Nora. In parallel, too, they speak of the agency of amnesia, just as in Spanish (and Argentine) history there have been different "pacts" about forgetting/ignoring the past (Buchenhorst; Vilarós 1–21, 54–9). Max's own contradictory and half-productive amnesia/delusion constructs no real place, but the phantom, blurred border between Spain and France in the past, the *City Without Limits* of the unreal present, and Rancel/Joaquín's own novel of the same name. Again, the Resnais/Semprún film serves as an echo chamber. As in *En la ciudad sin límites*, anxiety (on the part of Carlos/Diego) about warning a comrade (Juan) not to board a train (at Perpignan, headed for Madrid and a potential trap) is enhanced by the motif of being lost and confused: "On dirait que tu tâtonnes, Diego," warns Marie toward the end of Act/Section 3, "que tu es dans le brouillard, que tu ne sais plus où tu vas" (Semprún 150) [you are moving around in a fog and don't know where you are any more]. This fog blurs the boundaries between emotional and political life, eroding both. The voice-over of the narrator alerts Carlos/Diego to the fact, too, that he and his fellow activists are "perdus dans un grand rêve . . . essayant de reconstruire votre pays, de le faire ressembler à vos souvenirs," a fraternity "rongée, pourtant, par l'irréel" (108) [lost in some vast dream . . . trying to reconstruct your home country and make it look like your memories of it].

In both films, the areas of blurring and confusion constitute a metaphorical space for the working through of the grief and pain of separation incurred in political violence. In the case of *En la ciudad sin límites* they respond as well to the alienation and marginalization incurred through homophobic action. Rancel holds the key, as Max often says, to getting out of the city; Víctor's reconstruction of a past through his visit to the Paris apartment, his guiding of Max through the (to Max unrecognizable) streets to get there, and the writing and recovery of the letter to Max all represent a coming out, and for Marie an outing of the truth. Marie and the family act, as Noelia Saenz points out "as a repressive force" their "constant surveillance [. . .] and [that of] the medical staff creates an environment that simulates and perhaps conjures up his past feelings of persecution—his memories of smuggling illicit Communist propaganda between the Spanish exile community in Paris and Madrid" ("The Absence of Place").

Although this film's settings—an expensive Parisian hotel; a private hospital; bourgeois Madrid; the banks of the Seine—create a comfortable mainstream look around the more interesting and unsettling core of sexual dissidence (as had those of Gerardo Vera's *Segunda piel* [*Second Skin*, 1999] with its similar plot based around an explosive erotic secret) that link between personal drama and political involvement is readily strengthened through the character of Rancel/Joaquín. He is represented as something of a forerunner of the radical queer politics of the 1980s in as much as his life has combined uncompromising visibility (interpreted jealously and homophobia as an arrogant flamboyance by Marie) with a rigorous political commitment. He is furthermore coded as the inheritor of a Parisian left-wing political philosophy in two strong ways. *Mise-en-scène* in the café scene where he and Víctor meet—near the site of a former radical bookshop—align him visually with the atmosphere of the archetypal left-bank literary and political scene of the mid-twentieth century, while his cane and demeanor have something of the classic photograph by Alfonso of the Spanish intellectual and poet Antonio Machado (another spirit in exile), "En el café de las Salesas, diciembre de 1933."

As we are seeing, these ghosts are queer ghosts; it is the politics of heteronormativity and the arena of intimate memory which are where the film's interest in conflict lies, rather than in the more usual terrain of the politics of national identity—revindication and conflicting interpretations of the meanings of democracy, transition, commemoration, inheritance, and memory itself. Some of the import of this is borne, again, by the connotations and connections of one of the actors. Despite strong plot connections in Hernández's film with Argentina—Víctor's current country of work and residence—Sbaraglia's strictly Argentine resonances are played down, as is his accent, although that of Víctor's girlfriend Eileen (Leticia Brédice) is not. However, the film that arguably launched his trans-Atlantic career, Marcelo Piñeyro's version (2000) of Ricardo Piglia's novel *Plata quemada* (1997), in which Brédice also played, had associated him strongly with a dramatic scenario which Gabriel Giorgi appropriately describes as "el lugar de los que dicen 'no' al Estado [. . .] a la sujección al estado, a la subordinación al trabajo y—muy sistemáticamente [en la trayectoria de Piglia]—a la normalización sexual" [the place of those who say 'no' to the State . . . to the subjection of the state, to the subordination to work and—very systematically in Piglia's trajectory—to sexual normalization] (68). His body and that of his co-star Eduardo Noriega are highly eroticized in the film, and, as in the novel, represent resistant bodies conformed by "[una] sexualidad alegórica" [an allegorical sexuality] and a series of connections between delinquency, homosexuality, and political and moral non-conformity (Giorgi 68, 48, 68–71; see also Alfeo Álvarez 146). Víctor's sexuality as played by Sbaraglia in *En la ciudad sin límites* stays strictly within the usual limits of heterosexual masculinity's difficulties with commitment on the one hand (helplessly playing off Eileen against Carmen [Ana Fernández], his European ex) and of the conventional and salary-protected rebelliousness of the younger brother refusing to toe the family line. None of the transgressive energy of *Plata quemada* (*Burnt Money*, 2000) comes through. However, there is an interesting transfer of functions: when Víctor tracks down Rancel and the latter agrees to meet him, the tenor of the conversation is, precisely, that of resistance, transgression, and the—to Rancel—radicalizing power of love for a man. Sbaraglia sits there drawn into a new space where it is vital to say no. Rancel's specific revelation—that it was Marie who betrayed him—ineluctably involves Víctor in a love story, in a history of two nations and several factions, and in the struggle for resistance to the normalizing regime that Marie has been so desperate to bolster. It harnesses his undirected rebelliousness, making him take responsibility for the queer coming out of his family history.

Place and Cinematic Space

Part of Max's obsession is with the need to "desandar ese camino" in order to escape forward, as it were, into the past as it should have unfolded. The simple metaphor of retracing binds place and history, real and virtual journeys, destinies and cities. The plot, of course, involves not one city but three, differently represented. San Juan (Víctor and Eileen's Argentine home city) does not appear at all, but has a kind of ancillary role: as a reinforcement of the basic idea of there being no real escape (Víctor might appear to be able to choose to go back there, but the European drama holds him in thrall); and as a low-intensity signal—or, in Saenz's interpretation a "mythic space" ("The Absence of Place")—alerting some viewers at least to the trace of a suggestion that the Spanish and the Argentine historical memories with regard to their different eras of repression echo and inform one another. Madrid is represented visually in its sunlit, bourgeois aspect, with street scenes reminiscent of Almodóvar's glamorous take on the city in his mid-1980s to 1990s phase—the Madrid of the leafy and handsomely developed ribbon up through Retiro, Salamanca, and Chamartín south. When Víctor visits Rancel/Joaquín's second-home apartment his brief conversations at the door with his long-term companion (played by filmmaker Antonio Hernández himself), the approach and the communal areas of the block recall the soberly sumptuous arrangements which so contributed to the straightening out and bourgeois domestication of Javier Bardem's gay character in *Segunda piel* (as noted above). The only (though not inconsiderable) trace, of the Madrid of the war and the dictatorship is the very persistence of these monuments to well-off, comfortable living, built in part out of values certainly not shared in the past by the radical Rancel and more in line with Marie's (and, it has to be said, Max's) worldview. Paris, for its part, not only represents a vital connection with the left-wing past and the brief, intense romance between Max and Rancel, as suggested above, but also a domestication and normalization of the experiences and meanings of that time. This occurs though the operation of conventional visualizations of the Paris of many a heterosexual romantic film—the Paris Eye and the Eiffel Tower as backdrops to a tearful reunion between Víctor and Carmen (Ana Fernández); the Seine, its bridges, the Quai Bourbon;[1] rooftops, food, and wine; an unfeasibly luxurious hotel—and through the narrative connection between the city and Marie; between, that is, its central layout and the structures of power of the bourgeoisie (a connection anyway already there, of course).

However, overriding these very full associations is the problematic though telling clarity with which no space at all is allotted to the intimacy between Max and Rancel; this is only partly due to the narrative imperative of silencing and confusion which arises out of the subjective construction by Max of Paris "paranoiac space," with an attendant "blurring of boundaries between fiction and nonfiction and past time and present space" (Saenz "The Absence of Place").[2] The set of the Paris flat which might have been decorated at least a little like a love nest (Rancel/Joaquín coyly describes their time there as "bonito, muy importante" [nice, very important]) is sparse and sober. Max (excusably at the level of plot) has no clear visual memory of Rancel and has to rely on a single photograph, hidden in the copy of Rancel's autobiographical novel, in its turn hidden from Marie. Rancel has also deliberately buried his own memories of the time; so there are no flashbacks to the physical relationship, only stills in a photo album being leafed through by Rancel/Joaquín's companion in Madrid: text dominates. The letter Max writes for Rancel is the only, and in itself the emphatically non-cinematic, mode of access to the past: "a veces sueño que seguimos allí y que el tiempo es nuestro, y que tu boca recorre mi cuerpo desnudo. Y entonces mis hijos nos ven abrazados, desnudos; pero ya no son mis hijos, son los hijos de ella. No los conozco. No conozco a nadie. ¿Recuerdas?" [sometimes I dream that we are still there and time is ours and that your mouth travels my naked body. And then my children see us embrace, naked; but they are no longer my children, they are her children. I don't know them. Remember?].

The reading, in Fernán Gómez's voice-over, of the full text of the letter is staged with high dramatic intent: panning shots of graves and mourners in the dappled light, and a gentle crane shot back out and up into the trees for Rancel/Joaquín's arrival at the cemetery, against a backdrop of the over-used and repetitive melancholy theme music by Víctor Reyes. The scene soon settles to a theatrical arrangement of confrontation—Marie on one side of the grave and Rancel/Joaquín (and, initially, Víctor) on the other.

In a different narrative key, but a similar tone, toward the end of *La Guerre est finie* (*The War is Over*, 1966) Carlos/Diego imagines himself attending the funeral of a dead comrade, Ramón: "c'est l'ombre de Ramon qui est entrée dans ta vie," the narrator tells him, "L'ombre de la mort qui était sur toi, depuis le premier jour de ta vie" (Semprún 170) [the shadow of Ramon has made it place in your life . . . the shadow of death which has always been over you, since the day you were born]. In a traditional artistic trope, this shadow also permits the highlighting of images of continuation, of the efforts and kindliness of the dead being relived and carried forward. So too in the case of the dead Max, and the living Rancel and Víctor. But only to a certain extent, since the sexual politics of the moment are highly ambivalent. The erasure through mere textualized memorialization of the physical reality of homosexual desire, and the proximity of the dead, once homosexual body, means that—for all the affecting paraphernalia of the scene—queer history is perilously close to being a dead letter, a token. Heterosexuality, though, is represented enthusiastically, though not uncritically, at the level of sexual activity. Sex in the hotel between Luis and Beatriz (Mónica Estarreado)—with Pilar (Adriana Ozores) just down the corridor—leads to a farcical scene of jealousy and fecklessness. Víctor and Carmen make love in her Madrid apartment's richly colored linen in a series of attractive dissolves with slatted, amber light filtering in. His eyes are bright, and her hair is spread out on the pillow: a chiaroscuro of warm sensuousness in exactly the kind of scene which Pedro Almodóvar years ago had already gloriously and parodically claimed for man-on-man sex (between Eusebio Poncela and Antonio Banderas) in *La ley del deseo* (*Law of Desire*, 1987), but, apparently, to no avail. Víctor and Eileen have high-class bathroom foreplay on the day of her arrival from Argentina, permitting some unreconstructed objectification by the camera of Leticia Brédice with her bare breasts above the level of the expensive bath foam all in a joyful celebration of the erotic clichés of heterosexual romance as hegemonically depicted in cinema. But for Max and Rancel, as the letter says, it is too late; there is no image of two bodies; and there is no easy place, no scene, for their story to come back together.

In the postscript to his study of *Confession of the Letter Closet: Epistolary Fiction and Queer Desire in Modern Spain* (as the study's subtitle puts it), Patrick Paul Garlinger notes how:

the genre's formal and historical constraints enable queer desire by allowing for the intimate expression between correspondents who might not otherwise share such thoughts, but they also constrict that expression: queer mail, associated with confession and confidentiality, struggles to articulate a concept of homosexual desire not stained by stigma, shame, and guilt. (186)

Something of that stain clings to Max's unanswerable letter; but Rancel's dignified resistance to Marie goes some way toward dispelling it. As a staging of a confession the film produces and enables a discourse which can "expose the social homophobia and psychic ambivalences around sexuality and identity that were foundational in the emergence of homosexuality as a category and with which gays and lesbians still struggle" (Garlinger xv). Its expression of historicized queer desire escapes the constriction Garlinger describes; the metaphorical limitlessness of the title of the film ceases to be a cause of oppression and confusion and begins to be liberation.

Notes

1. Although, more generally, it is true that "the identity of the city is maintained by the prominent use of the French language, rather than its famous landmarks" (Saenz).

2. Saenz is also arguing that the space as constructed by the film is indicative of displacements caused by transnational flows of power and production.

Works Cited

Alfeo Álvarez. "El enigma de la culpa: La homosexualidad y el cine español 1962–2000." *International Journal of Iberian Studies* 13.3 (2000): 136–47. Print.

Bioy Casares, Adolfo. *La trama celeste*. Ed. Pedro Luis Barcia. Madrid: Castalia, 1990. Print.

Brasó, Enrique. *Conversaciones con Fernando Fernán Gómez*. Madrid: Espasa-Calpe, 2002. Print.

———. *Carlos Saura*. Madrid: Taller de Ediciones J. Betancor, 1974. Print.

Buchenhorst, Ralph. "Los desaparecidos de Argentina: Localizadores múltiples de un discurso de la memoria." *Iberoamericana* 9.35 (2009): 65–84. Print.

Caparrós Lera, José María. *El cine del nuevo siglo: 2001–2003*. Madrid: RIALP, 2004. Print.

Corral, Rubén. "En la ciudad sin límites." *LaButaca.Net* (n. date) Web. Aug. 3, 2009.

Del Amo, Álvaro. "Journal: Madrid." *Film Comment* 38.6 (2002): 12–13. Print.

Deleuze, Gilles. *Cinema 2: The Time-Image*. Trans. Hugh Tomlinson and Robert Galeta. London: Athlone, 1989. Print.
Freixas, Ramón. "Entre la convención y la sumisión." *Fernando Fernán Gómez: El hombre que quiso ser Jackie Cooper*. Ed. Jesús Ángulo and Francisco Llinás. San Sebastián: Patronato Municipal de Cultura, 1993. 59–76. Print.
Garlinger, Patrick Paul. *Confessions of the Letter Closet: Epistolary Fiction and Queer Desire in Modern Spain*. Minneapolis, MN: U of Minnesota P, 2005. Print.
Giorgi, Gabriel. *Sueños de exterminio: Homosexualidad y representación en la literatura argentina contemporánea*. Buenos Aires: Beatriz Viterbo, 2004. Print.
Hernández, Antonio, dir. *En la ciudad sin límites*. Madrid; Buenos Aires: Icónica, S. A.; Patagonik Film Group. 2002. DVD.
Holland, Jonathan. "The City of No Limits (En la ciudad sin límites)." *Variety* May 27–June (2002): 22. Print.
Hopewell, John. *Out of the Past: Spanish Cinema after Franco*. London: British Film Institute, 1986. Print.
Huerta Floriano, Miguel Ángel. "En la ciudad sin límites." *Cine para leer*. Jan.–June 2002. Ed. Equipo Reseña. Web. Aug. 2, 2009.
Kinder, Marsha. *Blood Cinema: The Reconstruction of National Identity in Spain*. Berkeley; Los Angeles; London: U of California P, 1993. Print.
Labanyi, Jo. "History and hauntology; or, what does one do with the ghosts of the past? Reflections on Spanish film and fiction of the post-Franco period." *Disremembering the Dictatorship: The Politics of Memory in the Spanish Transition to Democracy*. Ed. Joan Ramon Resina. Amsterdam; Atlanta, GA: Rodopi, 2000. 65–82. Print.
———. "El cine como lugar de la memoria en películas, novelas y autobiografías de los años setenta hasta el presente." *Casa encantada: Lugares de memoria en la España constitucional (1978–2004)*. Ed. Joan Ramon Resina and Ulrich Winter. Madrid; Frankfurt am Main. Vervuert/Iberoamericana, 2005. 157–71. Print.
Méndez-Leite, Fernando. "En la ciudad sin límites." *Fotogramas* (n.d.). Web. Aug. 2, 2009.
"'Nunca nadie criticó mi acento o mi actuación.' Se estrena el primer film de los cinco que Leo Sbaraglia hizo en España." *La Nación Online*. June 25, 2003. Web. Aug. 3, 2009.
Perriam, Chris. 2004. "Alejandro Amenábar's *Abre los ojos/Open Your Eyes* (1997)." *Spanish Popular Cinema*. Ed. Antonio Lázaro Reboll and Andy Willis. Manchester, UK: Manchester UP, 209–21. Print.
Resina, Joan Ramon. "Short of Memory: The Reclamation of the Past since the Spanish Transition to Democracy." *Disrembering the Dictatorship: The Politics of Memory in the Spanish Transition to Democracy*. Ed. Joan Ramon Resina. Amsterdam; Atlanta, GA: Rodopi, 2000. 83–154. Print.
Rodríguez Chico, Julio. 2009. "En la ciudad sin límites." *LaButaca.Net* (n. date). Web. Aug. 3, 2009.

Saenz, Noelia. "The Absence of Place in a Borderless City: Exploring the Psychic and Transnational Spaces of *En la ciudad sin límites*." *Spectator: The University of Southern California Journal of Film and Television* 29.1 (2009): 47–53. Web. Dec. 12, 2009.

Sbaraglia, Leonardo. "Nunca nadie criticó mi acento o mi actuación." *La Nación Online*. June 25, 2003. Web. Aug. 7, 2009.

Semprún Jorge. *La Guerre est finie: Scénario du film d'Alain Resnais*. Paris: Gallimard, 1966. Print.

Smith, Paul Julian. *Spanish Visual Culture: Television, Cinema, Internet*. Manchester, UK: Manchester UP, 2006. Print.

Torres, Augusto M. *Directores españoles malditos*. Madrid: Huerga; Fierro Editores, 2004. Print.

Vilarós, Teresa. *El mono del desencanto: Una crítica cultural de la transición española (1973–1993)*. Madrid; México, D. F.: Siglo XXI, 1998. Print.

16

Ronda nocturna: A Homage to Buenos Aires

(Edgardo Cozarinsky, 2005)[1]

DIETER INGENSCHAY

According to the gay branch of the Berlin Film Festival and its "Teddy Award"—the world's most important event of this kind—Latin American movies apparently are on the upswing. It is also a blatant fact that the Berlin Film Festival website promotes *queer* cinema worldwide according to demanding criteria of cinematographic quality and thematic novelty. Over the last years—and always because of their innovations in queer themes and their formal challenges—important contributions have come from South America. In 2005, for instance, at the Teddy Award for the best feature film was awarded to *Un año sin amor* (*A Year Without Love*, 2005), Anahi Berneri's adaptation of Pablo Pérez's novel (which is discussed in this volume as well), In 2007 and 2009, respectively, *La León* by Santiago Otheguy and Lucía Puenzo's *XXY* earned a special mention too. *Rabioso sol, rabioso cielo* (*Raging Sun, Raging Sky*, 2009), directed by Mexican filmmaker Julián Hernández, won a Teddy Award for the best feature film. *Ronda nocturna* (*Night Watch*, 2005), Edgardo Cozarinksy's movie, did not win the "Teddy," because its director chose not to compete for such an award.[2] Nevertheless, this Franco-Argentine production succeeded in getting considerable viewers' response and critiques in leading scholarly journals both in Europe and the Americas.

In Argentina, the writer and director of *Ronda nocturna*, Edgardo Cozarinsky (Buenos Aires, 1939), is almost a legendary individual, known for his books and films. From a "highbrow" and educated perspective, both literary works and film creations focus on specific characters of Argentine popular culture—such as tango or everyday life in Buenos Aires. Yet, many of his works have been conceived in Paris, where Cozarinsky went into exile in the 1970s at the beginning of the last dictatorship. After being a victim of government censorship, he stayed for about thirty years. He has appropriated French cultural history (see Sebreli 2001; Weiss 2003) and nowadays divides his time between Paris and Buenos Aires. As a creator, Cozarinsky successfully combines literature and cinema, fiction and essay, documentary and fantasy. To put it the words of Juan José Sebreli, "la unidad de esta triada—cine, ficción, ensayo—está ligada por temas que son constantes, invariables" [the unity of this triad—film, fiction, essay—is intimately connected through constant, invariable themes] (213).

Among Cozarinsky's books it is worth mentioning the following titles: a series of stories, essays, and memories entitled *Vudú urbano* (*Urban Voodoo*, 1985), *Borges/in/and/on Film* (1992), *La novia de Odessa* (*The Bride from Odessa*, 2001)—a volume of short stories as well—a collection of essays and chronicles, *El pase del testigo* (*The Witness Switch*, 2001), the novel *El rufián moldavo* (*The Moldavan Ruffian*, 2004), more stories entitled *Museo del chisme* (*Gossip Museum*, 2005), *Tres fronteras* (*Three Borders*, 2006), *Palacios plebeyos* (*Plebian Palaces*, 2007), the novel *Maniobras nocturnas* (*Nocturnal Maneuvers*, 2007), and *Milongas* (2007)—essays on the history of tango. Between 2009 and 2010, Cozarynksi published *Burundanga* (2009), *Lejos de donde* (*Far from Wherever*, 2009), *Galaxia Kafka* (*Kafka Galaxy*, 2010), *Blues* (2010), and *Biografías y testimonios* (*Biographies and Testimonials*, 2010).

Regarding his productive cinematography—spreading over more than forty years—Cozarinsky's most important films are *Puntos suspensivos o Esperando a los bárbaros*, (*Ellipsis or Waiting for the Barbarians*, 1971), *Les apprentis sorciers* (*The Sorcerer's Apprentice*, 1976), *La Guerre d'un seul homme* (*One Man's War*,1981), *Jean Cocteau: Autoportrait d'un inconnu* (*Autobiography of an Unknown*, 1983), *Haute Mer* (*High Tide*, 1984), *Pour Mémoire: Les Klarsfeld, une famille dans l'Histoire* (*For the Record: The Klarsfeld Family in History*, 1985), *Sarah* (1988), *Guerreros y cautivas* (*Warriors and Captives*, 1989), *Boulevards du crépuscule: Sur Falconetti, Le Vigan et quelques autres en Argentine* (*Sunset Boulevard*, 1992), *Scarlatti à Séville* (*Scarlatti in Seville*, 1994), *Citizen Langlois* (1994), *La barraca: Lorca sur les chemins de l'Espagne* (*Lorca on the Road in Spain*, 1995), *Le Violon de Rothschild* (*The Rothschild*

Violin, 1996), *Fantômes de Tanger* (*Tangier Ghosts*,1997), *Le Cinéma des cahiers* (*Cinema Notebooks*, 2000), *Tango Deseo* (*Tango-Desire*, 2002), *Dans le Rouge du Couchant* (*Red Sunset*, 2003), and, of course, his movie discussed in this chapter: *Ronda nocturna* (*Night Watch*, 2005).

Buenos Aires: Its Places and Its People

Shooting for *Ronda nocturna* first began in Argentina in May 2005.[3] Though it differs significantly from his proceeding films, *Ronda nocturna* unites several of Cozarinsky's favorite subjects, such as the metropolitan (sub)culture of Buenos Aires, ordinary life after the crisis of 2001, tango music, and gay life. The movie's protagonist is Víctor (Gonzalo Heredia), a nineteen-year-old hustler and drug dealer. The film can be easily summarized as a chronicle of Víctor on his way through one night in Buenos Aires. In this sense, *Ronda nocturna*, from the title itself, can be understood as a movie about the constant and restless movement of a character; that is, the film is something like a nocturnal "street movie" that unfolds in the great metropolis. The choice of a hustler instead of a female prostitute seems clear: the hustler moves around the city more easily than any of his female counterparts. Usually positioned on the junction of Avenida Pueyrredón and Santa Fe in the most openly gay district of the Capital, Víctor wanders out to many different neighborhoods: San Telmo, Catalinas Norte, Avenida 9 de Julio with the famous obelisk, Plaza Balvanera, Palermo, past huge and trendy skyscrapers, modest suburban houses, bars of all kinds, an elegant gym, a shabby hotel, parks and sidewalks, and a train station. Still, Víctor returns regularly to a meaningful urban point, that is, a characteristic flower stand where a female florist (Susana Varela) offers him a free red carnation. Here an unusual protagonistic role is given to the extreme close-up of incense smoke, as well as tender, complicit gestures and sincere smiles. These elements construct a place for Víctor, a kind of existential and physical paradise where perhaps the serenity of repose and wordless friendship might still be possible.

The spectator thus is confronted with a large scope of people typical of the metropolis: "ordinary" people mixed up with less "common" individuals, partly exotic figures, as well as with the socially marginalized "cartoneros" (recyclers), and even children. We witness Víctor's colleagues, clients, and friends; diplomatic agents; poor families living in the street; his former boyfriend Mario (Rafael Ferro); and an uncanny young woman—Víctor's female ex-lover (Mariana "Moro" Anghileri). All these character are located on clearly delimited scenarios of the city, a particular city—Buenos Aires, which becomes a type of huge set where the lives of individuals without any apparent connection converge. One might say that *Ronda nocturna* is constructed in correspondence with the expressionistic genre of *Stationendramen*—Station Drama. These *Stationendramen* hark back to medieval theater representations of Christ's *via crucis*. As such, these works were structured around the suffering, crucifixion, and resurrection of Jesus Christ.[4] From the narrative's structural perspective, *Ronda nocturna* might be considered a station drama; from the diegetic perspective of its content, *Ronda nocturna* is on the whole an homage to Buenos Aires: the city, the people—particularly the young men—and more broadly, its lively night culture.

After an impressive start by the means of an extremely high-angle shot and several long-angle shots of the location,[5] spectators are situated right away in Buenos Aires's urban night life: this is Víctor's "headquarters" on Avenida Santa Fe—specifically at the corner of that renowned street and Avenida Pueyrredón. From this unique place filled with resonances mainly for the Buenos Aires gay audience, he is picked up by a private black Mercedes, driven by El Comisario, an elegant police officer (Gregory Dayton). The *comisario* "protects" Víctor in exchange for sexual services. The *comisario* leaves his "protégé" at a popular restaurant/bar whereupon he goes to the men's room to hand over an envelope containing cocaine to a youngster. In the same bar he soon meets his friend Carlitos. Outside this place, we see both friends in a quiet suburban setting—in the script Cozarinsky offers, again and again, clear instructions that refer to real street names and certain neighborhoods of Buenos Aires. A car takes them to a modern office building where they enter a fashionable gay gym in which Víctor rapidly finds a client. Such a scene confirms how well connected Víctor is: instead of waiting on the street as other anonymous male prostitutes do—also portrayed in the movie—the protagonist transversally circulates diverse social and economic strata, and seems to feel comfortable doing so. In the gym, Víctor is shown with that client—a middle-aged man—in a private room. Nevertheless, there is no depiction of explicit sex. Víctor returns to the streets and takes a taxi that drives him through nightly avenues of the city center. During this sequence, a series of shots of a highly unrealistic atmosphere occurs—with tango music in the background. The cab stops next to a couple kissing at a traffic light, where the girl pushes her friend onto the roadway where a truck kills him (at least this is what both Víctor and the audience are supposed to believe). Such a fleeing and uncanny "murder" drags Víctor's *Stationendramen* into an even deeper unrealistic atmosphere, in contrast to the hyper-realism of a *mise-en-scène* at the beginning of the film. Following that, Víctor enters the realm of international politics: in a luxurious apartment located in a modern building there is an ambassador of an unnamed state. He is giving a party and entertains his guests with a number of hustlers. Víctor returns to Santa Fe, to the flower stand and a gay bar located there,[6] accompanied by the tango music of Osvaldo Pugliese's "Negracha." This song, along with "Al atardecer" by the band Los Piojos, are two musical leitmotivs of the movie, providing interpretative clues to Víctor's night wanderings.

His friend Mario, a taxi-driver, comes along in his car. Víctor steps in and they drive to the so-called Red Zone (Zona Roja, near Oro and Godoy Cruz streets) where transvestites prostitute themselves and their friends fool around with them. In a Chinese restaurant, they speak about a common friend who died of AIDS, and finally decide to set off to a cheap hotel to have sex. Once again, Víctor passes by "his" flower stand, plays soccer with children in a playground, and finally joins a group of recycling people—the "*cartoneros*." The "Negracha" song is reprised, and, with the popular Plaza Primero de Mayo (near Avenida Rivadavia) in the background, he shares a cup of mate with these men, until they all jump onto a small truck to collect recyclable goods.

Sequences with or without dialogue, close-ups of Víctor's face, medium or long shots as he continues with relationships that seem very habitual, all create a powerful empathy toward the protagonist. He seems like a night watchman, by which Cozarinsky is able to disarm the facile critiques of spectators who condemn hustlers with moralizing views. The genuine, natural capacity for interaction with the most diverse individuals demonstrates admirable signs of humanity, his honesty and generosity, and more precisely, his magnanimity. Thus, Víctor incarnates what for many is a marvelous cultural oxymoron: an individual who at the same time is a hustler and a model of human social virtues.

The camera follows behind the truck through the dark city streets. Víctor then comes to a bar where the calendar shows that it is the night of November 2, All Saints Day. According to an Argentine tradition, "Día de los Fieles Difuntos" (Day of the Faithful Dead), is when the dead come back to meet the living they love. Such a date is essential to understanding the combination of realist and supernatural elements proposed by the film; a date in the Gregorian calendar, precise and historically documented, annually repeated, seems the propitious time for visits from presences whose historical time is no more. Cecilia, a young woman (Moro Anghileri) enters the bar, comes up to Víctor, tells him that he is not dreaming, that it *is* her . . . She affectionately takes his hands and speaks about past times.

Outside they walk like a couple in love, and in the middle of the trolley-car tracks, Víctor and Cecilia kiss. At the same time Cecilia starts shouting at him and shows him the hook with which she provoked the abortion of their fetus: the uncanny seems to embrace Víctor; like in a crazy circle, the camera turns around the couple through circular dolly shots—until a train approaches. Víctor succeeds in jumping off the track, and once the train has passed, there is no trace of Cecilia left and she must have been a phantom of the Day of the Faithful Dead. While the red sky of the sunrise appears along the horizon, our protagonist meets two elderly ladies waiting for bus no. 47 that will take them to Chacarita, one the two most famous cemeteries of Buenos Aires. The ladies share with Víctor the final goal of their trip to the cemetery: they will be joining their dead friends and lovers. In the final setting, we see Víctor walking along a wall full of graffiti, dribbling a ball with some school boys; the movie ends with the sound of tango music.

This movie, and Cozarinsky himself, have become subjects of an Argentine documentary directed by Carmen Guarini, called *Meykinof* (2005)—a phonetic pun on the English expression "making of" and with the German word "Kino" (cinema) embedded in it. Accompany by the main actor Gonzalo Heredia, Guarini observes and records Cozarinky's "making of" *Ronda nocturna* and his way of working as a filmmaker. She recreates the ambience of the shooting and constructs Cozarinsky's personality both from his own work and from the interaction Cozarinksy entertains with, for example, the cameraman Javier Miquelez.[7]

The Aesthetics of the "Indirect Cinema"

Even before his movie *Dans le rouge du couchant* (2003), both the night (as the time of action) and the city (as its setting) fascinated Cozarinsky. In this sense, *Ronda nocturna* seems to unite Cozarinsky's preferred themes, for both the night and city converge here into a special kind of film aesthetics. Such an aesthetics, described by Jonathan Rosenbaum as the aesthetics of the "indirect cinema" (1995),[8] makes abundant use of nocturnal shots—contrasting with the last sequence of the movie recorded at daylight—interplays of artificial light and natural darkness, and cityscapes built out of noise, smooth sounds, and silence.

The film title as well as its English translation, *Night Watch*, could be echoing Rembrandt's famous and homonymous painting entitled *Nightwatch* (1642). Rembrandt's masterpiece has become a prototypical paradigm of the dialectics of light and darkness in art history. Similar to the painting, where a possible self-portrait of the Dutch painter himself is perceiving the whole scene from its back center-up, *Ronda nocturna* can be also understood as a Cozarinsky's self-portrait: the Argentine filmmaker perceives his city and intimately becomes part of that perception. In some sequences, the film title may also be referring to those half empty bars American painter Edward Hopper (1882–1967) perpetuated in his *Nighthawks* (1942). To this list of artistic creations, it would be possible to add more and more inter-iconic, cinematic references. Although it is already taken for granted that the art of film always plays on the contrasting subtleties of darkness and brightness, it should also be remembered that an aesthetics of the night fundamentally belongs to film as an artistic medium. In fact, Cozarinsky himself speaks about the aesthetics of "nocturnity," which he attributes not only to romantic poetry, but also to special persons of high sensibility:

> Hay gente que vive de día y otra de noche, que es muy distinta. La noche es el negativo del mundo del día, no hablo de la noche banal, de los boliches, sino la de los que hacen su vida de noche. Hay una nocturnidad, como en la poesía y la literatura romántica, con sus himnos a la noche, cuando la sensibilidad percibe cosas que no descubre durante el día, que está contradictoriamente adormecida. Hay una cierta normalidad nocturna que incluso exime de culpa a sus protagonistas. (Minghetti "Cozarinsky")

> [There are people who live by day and others by night, which is very different. Night is the negative of the daytime world. I am not speaking of banal nighttime, that is, that one of the bars, but rather of whose life is threaded together through the night. There is a nocturnity, as in poetry and romantic literature, having its own hymns to the night—when human sensibility perceives things that it cannot discover during the day, On the contrary, during the daytime, human sensibility remains dormant. There is somehow a certain nocturnal normality that exempts its protagonists from feeling guilty.]

Ever since Cozarinsky wrote *Vudú urbano* (*Urban Voodoo*) twenty-five years ago, the subject of the city continues to fascinate him. In *Ronda nocturna*, the city makes its presence felt before the first images: already during the opening credits, one hears urban traffic noise. The movie captures the city, again and again, by the means of shots of city lights. Moreover, these shots sometimes imitate the human eye, for example, when the director strategically sets the camera inside moving cars and shoots the city lights reflected in the rearview mirror.

Other Argentine gay/lesbian films have chosen Buenos Aires as a background, i.e., Diego Lerman's *Tan de repente* (*Suddenly*, 2002), which Cozarinksy mentions as one of his meaningful references. Cozarinsky describes *Tan de repente* as "breathing the same air as the New Argentine Cinema."[9] This statement may sound curious because of his thirty-year-long Parisian exile. We can assume, however, that Cozarinsky's procedures in order to artistically possess his own is based on a perspective I want to call "peripheral view." A peripheral view should be summarized as being a technique that offers an unexpected or "fresh" perception of some city's distinctive features. This is reached through the eyes of a foreigner, or by the point of view of a person coming back to the city after a long absence—such an absence from the city would give the individual "foreign" perspectives. It may be symptomatic, therefore, that Cozarinsky prefers to think, above all, of that Buenos Aires depicted in *Chun gwong cha sit* (*Happy Together*, 1997), by Wong Kar-wai—a non-Argentine, non-Latin American, and non-European director: "Cuando hace cinco años vi *Happy together*, de Wong Kar-wai, me dije,¡caramba!, aquí hay una Buenos Aires que no vi en ninguna película argentina, que ningún cineasta argentino me mostró. No es una Buenos Aires falsa, sino una que reconozco en la pantalla. Creo que tiene que ver con el acostumbramiento." [When I saw *Happy Together* by Wong Kar-wai, five years ago, I told myself, wow! Here there is a Buenos Aires that I haven't seen in any Argentine film, which no Argentine filmmaker has showed me so far. It is not a false Buenos Aires, but rather a Buenos Aires I am able to relate to on the screen. I think this has to do with getting habituated to it.]

Cozarinsky declares that he enjoys the "lyricism" of Wong Kar-wai's film (in particular its city shots), because this sort of movie discovers "the other side of reality that interests me." In fact, *Ronda nocturna* uses a broad register of atmospheric, lyrical, and unrealistic depictions of Buenos—both from a technical point of view (the "swimming" lights of cars and the city itself seen through windows or mirrors, as if the spectator were located within an aquarium) and from parts of the plot. Concerning the plot, there is a strong counterpoint between the fantastic story about Cecilia, the *faithful dead lover*, on one hand, and, on the other, the hyper-realistic trip (in the genre of a documentary of newsreel) with the poor through the nighttime street. This counterpoint successfully illustrates the kind of aesthetic indirect cinema would promote. Rosenbaum states that "indirect cinema" oscillates between individual alienation and human sympathy and, as a final result, indirect cinema directors practice artistic ways of obliquely appropriating the metropolis. In this respect, *Ronda nocturna*'s music plays an essential role by contributing to that goal. In short: the gentle tones of the soundtrack dominate even the passages when in-crescendo melodies and lyrics trigger a sort of aesthetics of sadness, melancholy, and perhaps nostalgia. Nevertheless, the film's general mood never turns into desperation.

Sociohistorical Implications

Decades of exile have left such significant footmarks in Cozarinsky's creation that Jason Weiss addresses in his chapter on the Argentine film, "The Translated Self." In the context of cultural studies, that title seems to anticipate the recent concept of *remigration*. Rosenbaum considers *Guerreros y cautivas* (*Warriors and Captives*, 1989) and *Boulevard du crépuscule* (*Sunset Boulevard*, 1992) as "Cozarinsky's two Argentine 'homecoming' films" (42). Following his line of analysis, I interpret *Ronda nocturna* as a film proving that the director has finally arrived home and feels at ease in Buenos Aires. Moreover, the film would also argue that Cozarinsky is solidly united with a nation still shaken by the consequences of the crisis of 2001 (which not only affected the "lower" classes, but also a wide range of middle-class people). When *Ronda nocturna* was screened in Argentine theaters in 2005, the events of 2001 were over, but their harsh, nationwide consequences were still vigorously disturbing.[10] Emblematic figures of the new precarious situation were the so-called *cartoneros*, people moving around Buenos Aires by night to collect recyclable goods—above all, paper. The *cartoneros* have become subjects of a great many literary works (César Aira's *La villa*) and film productions—I only mention the famous documentary *El tren blanco* by Nauel García et al. (*The White Train*, 2003).

In sequence 35 (0:55:44–0:58:03), Víctor joins the *cartoneros*, and a script fragment clearly reveals other facets of Víctor's cheerful return to his childlike innocence, namely, the reciprocal and almost-wordless acceptance (an emblematic gesture) between Víctor and the *cartoneros* in the Southern Cone of sharing yerba mate (a mate-leaf infusion). The script reads:

> PLAZA. EXTERIOR. NOCHE. VÍCTOR avanza por el borde de una plaza jugando con el láser que compró en la primera secuencia. De pronto, una pelota rueda hasta sus pies. La patea y descubre un grupo de chicos que juegan en la plaza, alrededor de familias de cartoneros que toman mate alrededor de sus carritos. VÍCTOR juega con ellos, un chico más que ríe y se divierte, sin

rastro de los episodios a los que poco antes ha sobrevivido. Otro grupo de cartoneros llega y se une a los anteriores. VÍCTOR comparte el mate con ellos. Una bocina fuerte interrumpe este momento de convivialidad. Niños y adultos se encaminan hacia un camión que ha estacionado al borde de la plaza, empujando los carritos con la cosecha de la noche. (50)

[PLAZA. OUTDOORS. NIGHT. VICTOR walks along the edge of the plaza playing with the laser that he bought in the first sequence. Suddenly, a ball rolls up to his feet. He kicks it and sees a group of kids playing in the plaza, near *cartonero* families drinking mate near their carts. VICTOR plays with the kids, one more kid laughing and having fun, without any trace of the episodes he's survived. Another group of *cartoneros* joins the first one. VICTOR shares their mate. A loud car horn interrupts this moment of conviviality. Children and adults walk toward a truck parked at the edge of the plaza, while pushing their carts that are full of the night's harvest.]

That sequence features the popular Plaza Primero de Mayo (near Rivadavia) in the background. While the hustler is together with *cartonero* families, the audience hears again the sound of the popular tango "Negracha," friendly laughter, social whispers, and Víctor's sincere words of gratitude: "Le agradezco mucho. [El mate está] muy rico" [I thank you very much. The mate tastes really good]. The *cartoneros* (elders, adults, and kids) treat Víctor as if they had known him for a really long time. The soundtrack of this sequence, as a sound-off, seems to be used to express the mood both of Víctor and his marginalized fellows of the night: All of them are enjoying their communitarian existence. Before they all jump onto the truck and the protagonist helps with loading it with heavy carts, Víctor's voice-over even characterizes the relation he entertains with the *cartoneros*: "los amigos"—he warmly says (0:57:26). In the next sequence, the editing allows Cozarinky to present diverse points of view through the dark city streets: second-person shots (a sort of low-angle shot from a *cartonero* kid's POV, who could have been left behind, a second low-angle shot maybe from another *cartonero* who is at Víctor's feet), subjective shots (a pan-shot from Víctor's POV on city lights, tree tops, and a skyscraper all blurred by fog), and an apparent anonymous high-angle shot when the truck is turning left. Thanks to all of these diverse shots, the audience is convinced to conclude that the city is alive, the night is always in movement, and there are nocturnal individuals whose enthralling lives deserve to be told by cinema.

In one of the interviews with Claudio D. Minghetti, Cozarinsky was asked about the "strange way of including" the *cartoneros*'s night world. To answer the question, the director responded with the argument of an aesthetic necessity:

> Cuando uno va caminando por una calle no va mirando lo que tiene alrededor en general: va hacia un lugar. Cuando ponés la cámara, la cámara corta, encuadra dentro de la panorámica que permite al ojo humano, y no podés dejar de ver lo que cayó dentro, y te muestra cartoneros y bolsas de basura en todas esquinas. . . . Es casi imposible no ver cartoneros y basura en las calles.
>
> [Walking down the street, usually one doesn't look around; you just go straight to a specific place. When you make the camera rolling, the human eye only sees what the camera cuts off or captures within its frames in the panorama, and you cannot avoid seeing what has fallen into the camera frame. So, the camera shows you *cartoneros* and garbage bags at every corner. . . . It's almost impossible not to see *cartoneros* and garbage throughout the streets.]

During our conversations, Edgardo Cozarinsky asserted that he considers the moments Víctor spends with the *cartoneros* as the most intimate and harmonious ones of the whole story. The *cartoneros* are not professional actors, but rather *real* people of the post-crisis, precarious situation. And the director told me the anecdote that one of the women, after she learned that Cozarinsky was making a movie, went to the hairdresser the next day to look "nice" for her role. Finally, he had to pay her to *not* go to the hairdresser or use professional makeup.

Despite the stylizations within the *nightwatch* parabola of a hustler—which culminates in the unreal, "indirect" meeting with his female ex-lover on the Night of the Faithful Dead—social reality is another central aspect of the film's aesthetic agenda. During the time subsequent to the crisis, solidarity was a common, new, and widespread feeling which Edgardo Cozarinksy captures when he turns these precarious characters into the main character's "family." This central aspect seems to me one of the truly thought-provoking statements of *Ronda nocturna*.

Even if Claudio D. Minghetti knows Cozarinsky's works very well, unfortunately I cannot agree with him when the critic compares Cozarinsky's aesthetics to that of Jean Genet:

Como Jean Genet, Cozarinsky intenta una representación mitológica de los bajos fondos sociales. Como el marinero Querelle, el Víctor del autor de *Boulevares del crepúsculo*, muestra una sonrisa que puede iluminar la oscuridad. Víctor es un chico dueño de una contradictoria pureza, que con inocencia y sin culpa baila sobre el imperfecto tablero de la ciudad, como lo haría una bola de billar por un paño, viejo y cortado. (Minghetti "Buenos")

[Like Jean Genet, Cozarinksy attempts a mythological representation of the social underground. As the sailor Querelle, the character of Víctor in Cozarinsky's *Sunset Boulevard* shows a smile that can illuminate darkness. Víctor is a kid with a kind of contradictory purity. Both with innocence and without guilt, Víctor dances on the imperfect stage of the city, in the same way a billiard ball would dance on an old, torn pool table cloth.]

Cozarinky's taxi boy in *Ronda nocturna* does in fact belong to the *bajos fondos* (social underground), and a small part of the movie also points at mythological elements. But the taxi boy and Carlitos are everyday hustlers; they lack the mystic halo of Genet's protagonists, and their discussions are much more down-to-earth than the pompous pathos readers find in Genet's gay aesthetics.

Ronda nocturna in the Context of Gay Cinema

The works of Richard Dyer (1977) and Robert Lang (2002), among others, open the debate on whether or not, and in what way, it is accurate to use the metaphor or metonym of the gay or queer character to interpret a work of art in general or any film in particular. This discussion cannot be addressed here—rather I want to point out two possible aspects under which a gay cinema may be defined as such: identity and aesthetics. Let us consider *Ronda nocturna* in this context.

David W. Foster (2004) and Joe del Rio (2005) have traced the question of gay identity in the context of the homophobic and hetero-normative Latin American cinema. Foster stresses that the films analyzed in his book respond, above all, to Latin American paradigms.[11] From this theoretical perspective, *Ronda nocturna* directly responds to a Latin American and particularly an Argentine paradigm: *Ronda nocturna* stands out as a document of the openly gay atmosphere and gay infrastructure of Buenos Aires, one of the most culturally vivid urban centers of Latin America. By focusing on the particularities of Buenos Aires, the city, its people, its culture, and its gay life, this film preempts the cliché of Argentina as a (pseudo)-European country.

There are two main features that characterize Cozarinsky's film as a Latin American gay production: (1) the impact of transvestites which we find in well-known "gay" novels and films, such as *El lugar sin límites* (*Hell Without Limits*) by José Donoso and Arturo Ripstein, and *No se lo digas a nadie* (*Don't Tell Anyone* by Jaime Bayly and Francisco J. Lombardi); and (2) the presence of male prostitution, which has been thought through by Argentine intellectual Néstor Perlongher in his book *La prostitución masculina* (1993), and which is the central subject in hustler novels, such as *Adonis García, el vampiro de la colonia Roma* (Adonis García: A Picaresque Novel, 1979) by the Mexican Luis Zapata, and *Taxi Boys* (2004) by the Argentine Claudio Zeiger. In cinema, one immediately thinks of the following titles: the film version of Barbet Schroeder's *La Virgen de los Sicarios* (*Our Lady of the Assassins*, 2000), based on Fernando Vallejo's homonymous novel; *Sin destino* (*No Future*, 2002) by Mexican filmmaker Leopoldo Laborde; and the recent feature-length *Chamaco* (*The Kid*, 2010) by Cuban Carlos Cremata Malberti.

In *Ronda nocturna*, male cross-dressing is revisited. Mario and Víctor, for instance, decide to make a call on the transvestite prostitutes that work in the Buenos Aires neighborhood Oro, on Godoy Cruz Street. The cross-dressers perform a particular kind of corporality that exaggerates the common places of heterosexual desire through their vamp outfits and silicon breasts. Cozarinsky's camera shows the world of the cross-dressers with sympathy and humor. Such sympathy and humor, completely averse to moral judgments, are particularly present in the shots of a sex worker who looks like a middle-class/middle-aged housewife, called "La Thatcher" (Marcelo Iglesias).

In *Screening the Sexes: Homosexuality in the Movies*, Parker Tyler has shown that the exemplary hustler can be found in the movies of Andy Warhol and his cultural school. In relation to Warhlol's trend in pop culture, we can think of *My Hustler* by Warhol himself, and *Flesh and Trash* by Paul Morrissey, a film featuring Joe Dallessandro, in fact a sexual icon of the 1970s. Even if the handsome actor Gonzalo Heredia ("Víctor") were able to establish his presence in Argentine television after *Ronda Nocturna*, he certainly lacks the charisma of Dallessandro. Tyler comments that, together with the threat of erectile dysfunction, drugs are considered to be Dallessandro's main problem, explicitly in some scenes of *Flesh* (see Tyler 56 *et sequitur*). Thirty years later, in *Ronda nocturna*, drugs still appear, but the central anxiety is no longer focused on erectile dysfunction, but on the HIV/AIDS pandemic. Such global anxiety has been portrayed in numerous Latin American documentaries on male prostitution, including the daring Cuban film *El pulóver* by Michel Hutter (2004), and through a fictionalized biography also studied in this collective volume: Anahi Berneri's *Un año sin amor* (*A Year Without Love*, 2005).

Ronda nocturna expresses concerns about HIV/AIDS: (1) When Víctor and his friend Carlitos discuss in a pizza restaurant about the advantages of having a powerful "protector" against street dangers; (2) when El Comisario, Víctor's protector, exhorts him to use condoms;[12] (3) when, after having performed anal sex in El Comisario's car, the latter opens the car door and his hand lets a condom drop on the soil (0:10:08–0:10:13)[13]; and (4) later on, in a Japanese restaurant, when Víctor and Mario speak about a friend who "died of that' [murió de eso] as a result of practicing unsafe sex. While he was treated in the Muñoz Hospital, one of the Buenos Aires' big clinics, that common friend told to his friends that he had decided to move to the United States.[14]

Buenos Aires and Its Young Gay Men

Whereas Cozarinsky's aesthetics can be characterized by his fondness of Buenos Aires and its night life, it is also necessary not to forget adding the way in which Cozarinky's film represents masculinity. First of all, such a representation takes place under the perspective of gay desire. The set of shots portraying male bodies in the gym, with tattoos on their strong muscles, is a good proof of this thesis. There is another memorable sequence: that one of the hotel where Mario and Víctor go to have sex. The sequence encapsulates some climatic moments of both happiness and uncanniness (*Unheimlichkeit*) that Víctor experiences throughout the film.[15]

The hotel room they go to is partly shabby, partly showy, with a big jacuzzi in which the boys take a bath, with a lot of foam. The melody-off for this sequence imposes its nostalgia over the two protagonists. This piano piece is "Milonga del adiós" ["The Farewell Milonga"], by Carlos Franzetti. After the bath, there is a series of important shots (0:49:02–0:50:35): a really high-angle shot—almost a bird's eye shot—of great tenderness, which abruptly changes into a medium shot of the couple, and then, at last, into a close-up. During this series of shots, the camera presents the two young men and their naked bodies on the mattress, without any explicit (oral or anal) sex, but off-screen space indicates genital touching accompanied by explicit in-frame masturbation noises. Both Víctor and Mario will orgasm at the same time and, also reciprocally, they will caress and will enjoy each other. The script reads: "PLANO MEDIO. Los amigos en la exaltación del orgasmo y pasando a la serenidad siguiente. VÍCTOR sonríe, como aliviado. MARIO lo observa" (47) [MEDIUM SHOT. Both friends in the ecstasy of orgasm and moving to serenity. VICTOR smiles, as if relieved. MARIO observes him]. Another close-up shot shows Víctor's good-looking face while he is happily sleeping on the pillow. Then, a conflicting montage destroys Victor's peaceful moments and security: all of a sudden Mario, seen from behind grasping with another pillow, tries to suffocate Víctor, and magically disappears after a short struggle.

What is Mario's motive for such a behavior? Perhaps drugs or maybe a sudden sadistic stroke of aggressiveness could be blamed for it. Even if the film later answers this question by means of a supernatural legend, those aggressive shots in the hotel sequence serve Cozarinsky's clear purpose: the subject of explicit violence between lovers enters this rather quiet movie. And yet, *Ronda nocturna* does not offer any solutions to social problems such as this. With his own set of aesthetic concepts, those moments of physical violence and others that will take place later in the film, do not distract Cozarinsky from his main objective, that is, to create a piece of cinematic art devoted to his homage Buenos Aires's nightlife as well as the gay young men who live there.

Notes

1. An abridged version in Spanish of this essay was published with the title "Un homenaje a Buenos Aires: *Ronda nocturna* de Edgardo Cozarinsky (Argentina, 2005)." *Borges-Buenos Aires: Configuraciones de la ciudad del siglo XIX al XXI*. Ed. Roland Spiller. Madrid; Frankfurt: Iberoamericana; Vervuert, 2014. 137–48.

2. In several conversations with the filmmaker in Berlin and Buenos Aires between 2009 and 2011, Edgardo Cozarinksy told me that his film creations were not intended for a "ghetto" audience.

3. The screenplay of *Ronda nocturna* is also available. See the complete reference in the list of works cited.

4. In the European context, for example, the trilogy *Until Damascus* (1898, 1904) by the Swedish writer August Strindberg, and *Luces de Bohemia* (1924) by the Spanish playwright Ramón del Valle-Inclán, revisit medieval passion plays. Cozarinsky's *Ronda nocturna* echoes these *Stationendramen* and *viae crucis* of medieval Christianity.

5. This first shot of the film, beginning with a bird's-angle shot—and a long pan from above to below—imposes the city on the spectator with great violence: a tall city building, the afternoon sky, cables in the air, ambient sound, and a street light that anticipates shadows complete the frame and establish the urban premise of *Ronda nocturna*.

6. This bar and restaurant has the name of *Café Oviedo Recoleta* in the film. As a cultural kernel of "la movida gay" de Buenos Aires, the corner of *Café Oviedo Recoleta* is a fascinating microcosm of the whole city. There hustlers wait for their clients or socialize with each other, closeted upper-middle-class men drive by in their cars looking for easy hook-ups, children and adult "cartoneros" work or take a break, taxi drivers slow down their cabs, and street vendors of bric-à-bric items and a florist earn a living. Today that bar-restaurant has another name: *Bar Restaurante El Olmo*, on Avenida Santa Fe 2502 and Avenida Pueyrredón 1396.

7. Claudio D. Minghetti, a journalist who has written a number of articles on Cozarinsky's works, stresses the documentary nature of *Ronda nocturna*: "El resultado deviene interesante, en especial para quienes ya vieron el film de Cozarinsky. Atractivo porque logra rescatar el clima que se generó durante el rodaje, incluso en las escenas—por su contenido—de mayor riesgo, por ejemplo las registradas dentro de un albergue transitorio (según los productores, sin suspender la actividad habitual de aquél) y la relación establecida entre el cineasta y el director de fotografía, Javier Miquelez, uno y otro obsesionados por lograr con su cámara, cuando se trata de calles iluminadas con luces de neón, un registro parecido al del ojo humano" (*Reflexiones*).

8. Indirect cinema "is quite literally founded on a theoretical impossible space—a realm of intervals, on in-betweenness, paradoxically defined by its own conscious marginality and lack of definition. Its only certainty, one might say, is a complete absence of certainty" (Rosenbaum 38).

9. Besides Diego Lerman's film, other films belonging to this cinema trend in Argentina include *La quimera de los héroes* (*The Chimera of Heroes*, 2003) by Daniel Rosenfeld—made with Cozarinsky's support; *Cabeza de palo* (Wooden Head, 2002) by Ernesto Baca; *Caja negra* (Black Box, 2002) by Luis Ortega; and *El nadador inmóvil* (*The Motionless Swimmer*, 2000) by Fernán Rudnik,

10. For critical articles on the 2001 crisis in Argentina, see *Argentiniens (Post) Krise: Symbole und Mythen*, edited by Dieter Ingenschay and Torben Lohmüller, a Special Issue of *kultuRRevolution: Zeitschrift for angewandte Diskurstheorie* 51.1 (2006).

11. "These are Latin American cultural productions, and I wish them to be understood primarily as such. If they also contribute to transnational debates about same-sex desire, patriarchal heteronormativity, homosociality, and homophobia, it is a consequence of the growing internationality of Latin American filmmaking in terms of the ambitions of directors and production companies" (xviii).

12. El Comisario to Víctor: " 'Te cuidás, ¿no? Quiero decir . . . ¿Usás forros? Lo digo por vos.' Por toda respuesta, Víctor saca un puñado de pequeños envases metálicos y se los muestra. VÍCTOR (sonriente): '¿De qué color querés?' " [You

take care of yourself, right? You use condoms? I say it for your sake. In response, Victor takes out a handful of foil-wrapped packages and shows them to him. Victor, smiling, asks: What color do you want?] (*Guión* 16).

13. Undoubtedly, all spectators for the film are aware of Víctor's good nature. Two gestures of his can serve to confirm it: Víctor gives El Comisario one of the condoms he always carries in his pockets, and then, Victor caresses El Comisario's head. Immediately he has an orgasm. In contrast, "the protector" is not a protector: El Comisario not only provides Víctor no sexual protection, but also is not concerned at all whether Víctor is enjoying sexual intercourse or not. In Cozarinsky's words: "El muchacho decide acelerar las cosas y empieza a agitarse con ritmo regular. Sobre su nuca la cabeza del COMISARIO parece sufrir una serie de espasmos. VÍCTOR sonríe aliviado y esboza una caricia en la cabeza del hombre" [The young man decides to accelerate things and begins to stroke himself rhythmically. He appears to have a series of spasms against the Commissioner's neck. Victor smiles, relieved, and sketches a caress on the man's head] (*Guión* 16).

14. The big country to the North appears as a place that may be idealized by some people in Argentina. In *Ronda nocturna*, however, the American way of (gay) life does not seem to represent the preferred alternative to Buenos Aires. For example, Víctor does not enter a McDonald's restaurant, an icon of American culture. First, that restaurant is only a background for three medium shots of Víctor (0:35:49–0:35:53; 0:36:00–0:36:03; 0:36:06–0:36:07) and for two long shots of Víctor as well (0:35:53–0:35:57; 0:36:07–0:36:09). Second, McDonald's is metonymically connected with Víctor's boredom. Finally, Mario, driving a traditional, Argentine, black cab, comes by to rescue his former lover Víctor from moments of a pointless existence.

15. Here, of course, it is necessary to recall Sigmund Freud's essay on "The Uncanny" (*Das Unheimliche*) in order to really grasp what Víctor could have thought of his fantastic night experiences.

Works Cited

Cozarinsky, Edgardo, dir. *Ronda nocturna*. Buenos Aires; Paris: Cine Ojo; Les Films d'Ici, 2005. DVD.

———. *Ronda Nocturna (Guión)*. Buenos Aires: Paidós, 2005. Print.

Dyer, Richard. *Gays and Film*, London: British Film Institute, 1997. Print.

Foster, David W. *Queer Issues in Contemporary Latin American Cinema*. Austin, TX: Texas UP, 2004. Print.

Freud, Sigmund. "Das Unheimliche." *Project Gutenberg*. Web. June 26, 2012.

Ingenschay, Dieter. Entrevista Personal con Edgardo Cozarinsky. July 25, 2010.

Ingenschay, Dieter, and Torben Lohmüller, eds. *Argentiniens (Post)Krise: Symbole und Mythen*. Special Issue of *kultuRRevolution: Zeitschrift for angewandte Diskurstheorie* 51.1 (2006). Print.

Kar-wai, Wong, dir. *Chun gwong cha sit* (aka *Happy Together*). Hong Kong: Block 2 Pictures et al. 1997. DVD.

Lang, Robert. *Masculine Interests: Homoerotics in Hollywood Film*: New York: Columbia UP, 2002. Print.

———. "Buenos Aires y su noche triste." *La Nación*. Web. June 20, 2009.

———. "Cozarinsky y Ronda nocturna: Interview with Edgardo Cozarinsky. Web. June 19, 2009.

Minghetti, Claudio D. "Reflexiones a propósito de Edgardo Cozarinsky." *La Nación*. Web. Dec. 1, 2005.

Río, Joe del. "Identidad gay en el cine latinoamericano reciente." *Temas* 41–42 (2005): 61–70. Print.

Rosenbaumm, Jonathan. "Ambiguous Evidence: Cozarinsky's 'Cinéma indirecte.'" *Filmcomment* (1995). New York: Film Society of Lincoln Center. Web. April 15, 2012.

Sebreli, Juan José. "Cozarinsky: Sobre exilios y ruinas." *Cuadernos Hispanoamericanos* 613–14 (2001): 213–16. Print.

Toibero, Emilio. *Abecedario Cozarinsky*. Web. June 21, 2009).

Tyler, Parker. *Screening the Sexes: Homosexuality in the Movies*. New York: Da Capo, 1993. Print.

Weiss, Jason. "The Translated Self: Edgardo Cozarinsky." *The Lights of Home: A Century of Latin American Writers in Paris*. New York: Taylor & Francis, 2003. 183–90. Print.

Contributors

Daniel Balderston is Professor of Hispanic Languages and Literatures at the University of Pittsburgh, as well as director of the Borges Center and editor of *Variaciones Borges*. An expert on Borges, Southern Cone literature, Brazilian literature, and Latin American gender and sexuality studies, Balderston's recent publications include: *Approaches to Teaching Puig's Kiss of the Spider Woman*; *El deseo, enorme cicatriz luminosa: Ensayos sobre homosexualidades latinoamericanas*; and *Borges, realidades y simulacros*.

Debra A. Castillo is Stephen H. Weiss Presidential Fellow, Emerson Hinchliff Professor of Hispanic Studies, and Professor of Comparative Literature at Cornell University. She is 2014–15 president of the international Latin American Studies Association. She specializes in contemporary narrative from the Spanish-speaking world (including the United States), gender studies, and cultural theory. Among her most recent books are *Cartographies of Affect: Across Borders in South Asia and the Americas* (Worldview 2011, with Kavita Panjabi), *Hybrid Storyspaces* (Hispanic Issues online, 2012, with Christine Henseler) and *Mexican Public Intellectuals* (Palgrave 2013, with Stuart Day).

María de la Cruz Castro Ricalde is a Professor at the Instituto Tecnológico de Monterrey, 19 Toluca Campus, Toluca. Since 2003 she directs the Cátedra de Humanidades de la Asociación Mexicana de Análisis Cinematográfico y miembro del Sistema Nacional de Investigadores, nivel 2. Her fields of research cover gender studies and audio-visual discourse. Professor Castro Ricalde coordinates the series entitled *Desbordar el canon: Escritoras mexicanas del siglo XX*. This scholarly series twice received the Consejo Nacional para la Cultura y las Artes Award (México, 2006/2009). Since 1998, she has been an active member of Diana Morán Workshop of Theory and Literary Criticism. Professor Castro Ricalde also founded the Mexican Association of Film Studies (Asociación Mexicana de Análisis Cinematográfico). Recent coedited books include: *Un vacío siempre lleno* (Instituto Tecnológico de

Monterrey; FONCA, 2006) with Aline Pettersson and Josefina Vicens, and *Después del silencio* with Laura López Morales and Guadalupe Dueñas (Instituto Tecnológico de Monterrey et al., 2010)

David William Foster is Regents' Professor of Spanish and Women and Gender Studies at Arizona State University. Foster is President of the Latin American Jewish Studies Association. His research interests focus on urban culture in Latin America, with emphasis on issues of gender construction and sexual identity, as well as Jewish culture. He has written extensively on Argentine narrative and theater, and he has held Fulbright teaching appointments in Argentina, Brazil, and Uruguay. He has also served as an Inter-American Development Bank Professor in Chile. His most recent publications include *Nuestro Ambiente: Chicano/Latino Homoerotic Writing* (Bilingual Press, 2006) and *Argentine Urban Photography* (McFarland Publishers, 2007). In 2006, Foster conducted a seminar on *Brazilian Urban Fiction* as part of the National Endowment for the Humanities (NEH) Summer Seminars for College and University Teachers, and in 2007 he also conducted an NEH seminar, in Argentina, on Jewish Buenos Aires.

Dieter Ingenschay, since 1995, is Full Professor at the Department of Romance Literatures at Humboldt-Universität Berlin (Germany). He is also a member of the "Georg-Simmel-Institut" for Metropolitan Studies and of the "Zentrum für Interdisziplinäre Geschlechterstudien" (Center for Interdisciplinary Gender Studies) at the same university. His main fields of research and teaching are contemporary literatures and cultures from Spain and Latin America, with special attention to postcolonial, post-dictatorial, queer/gay and metropolitan subjects. He is General Coordinator of ProSpanien, a program of the Spanish Ministry of Culture to promote research in Germany on Spanish topics. Recent titles include *After-Images of the City*, coedited with Joan Ramon Resina (2003), and *Desde aceras opuestas: Literatura/cultura gay y lesbiana en Latinoamérica* (2006). In 2008, the volume *El andar tierras, deseos y memorias. Homenaje a Dieter Ingenschay* was published by Iberoamericana (Madrid/Frankfurt).

Cecelia Burke Lawless is a Senior Lecturer in Romance Studies at Cornell University. She has taught at Hamilton College as well as Hobart and William Smith Colleges and the Université de Montréal. While on a Fulbright in Venezuela, Professor Lawless pursued research on documentary film. She has published several articles on architectural manifestations in

Latin American film, as well as *Making Home in Havana* (Rutgers University Press, 2002), a cultural studies investigation of the concept of home through photography and testimonials.

Andrés Lema-Hincapié is an Associate Professor of Ibero-American Literatures and Cultures in the Department of Modern Languages at the University of Colorado Denver, where he teaches and does research on the connections between Hispanic literature and Western philosophy, and especially on modern metaphysics in the work of Jorge Luis Borges. His most recent book *Borges, . . . ¿filósofo?* [*Borges, . . . a Philosopher?*] was published in 2012 by the Instituto Caro y Cuervo (Bogotá, Colombia). With Professor Joan Ramon Resina, Lema-Hincapié coedited *Burning Darkness: A Half Century of Spanish Cinema* (Albany, NY: SUNY, 2008), a collection of essays on fifteen of the most influential Spanish films of the past sixty years. Andrés Lema-Hincapié is the cofounder/codirector of the *Gabriel García Márquez Proyect* at the University of Colorado Denver.

Óscar Osorio is Professor at Universidad del Valle (Cali-Colombia). His recent publications include: *Hechicerías* (2008), *El cronista y el espejo* (2008), *Una porfía forzosa* (2012), *La Virgen de los Sicarios y la novela del sicario en Colombia* (2013), and *El narcotráfico en la novela colombiana* (2014). He has received the XXXII Cáceres Award of Short Novel for his *El cronista y el espejo* (España, 2007); the Gutiérrez Mañé Award for the Best Doctoral Dissertation (New York, 2013); and the Jorge Isaacs Award of Vallecaucanos Essayists (Cali-Colombia, 2013).

David Oubiña is an Adjunct Investigator of CONICET and lecturer at the UBA, University of Cinema, and New York University. He has been a visiting professor at the University of Bergen and visiting scholar at the University of London. He is part of the board of directors for *The Frogs* (the arts, essay writing and translation), and of the editorial board of *Cahiers du cinéma* (Spain). He has been a scholarship recipient of the Guggenheim Foundation, the Fulbright Commission, the British Council, the Fundación Antorchas, and the National Fund for the Arts (Argentina). He has served as a script consultant on a number of feature films and as an adviser for the Fundación Antorchas and the TyPA Foundation. He is coauthor of the scripts for *Música nocturna, Asesinato y muerte* y *Notas de tango*, by Rafael Filippelli. His most recent books include: *Estudio crítico sobre* La ciénaga *de Lucrecia Martel* (2007), *Una juguetería filosófica: Cine, cronofotografía y arte* *digital* (2009) and *El silencio y sus bordes: Discursos extremos en la literatura y el cine argentinos* (in press).

Chris Perriam is Professor of Hispanic Studies at the University of Manchester. His research interests are in contemporary Spanish Cinema, Latin American and Spanish poetry, and queer popular writing in Spain. Chris Perriam's publications include: *Carmen on Film: A Cultural History* (Bloomington, IN: Indiana UP, 2007), coedited with Phil Powrie, Bruce Babington, and Ann Davies; and *From Banderas to Bardem: Stars and Masculinities in Recent Spanish Cinema* (Oxford University Press 2003). With Susan Frenk, Vanessa Knights, and Michael Thompson, Chris Perriam coauthored *A New History of Spanish Writing: 1939 to the present day* (Oxford University Press, 2000).

Esteve Riambau is a Full Professor in the Department of Audiovisual Communications at the Autonomous University of Barcelona. Professor Riambau has taught and delivered invited lectures at many academic institutions, such as Université de Paris III, Roma, Stanford, and the Escuela Internacional de Cine y Televisión de San Antonio de los Baños in Cuba. He is also coauthor of the documentary *La passió possible: L'Escola de Barcelona* (Barcelona Television, 2000). *La doble vida del faquir* (2005) and *Màscares* (2009), two feature-length films cowritten and codirected with Elisabet Cabeza, premiered in Spain at the renown San Sebastián Film Festival. Both films have been honored in various international film festivals. His most recent publications are: *Ricardo Muñoz Suay: Una vida en sombras* (2007), *El poder de les formes: Francesc Galmés i l'art del protocol* (2011) and *Hollywood en la era digital* (2011). Currently, Professor Riambau is the director of the Film Archives of Catalonia and the vice-president of the FIAF (Fédération Internationale des Archives Filmiques).

Claudia Schaefer is Professor of Spanish and Comparative Literature, Rush Rhees Professor, and Chair of the Department of Modern Languages and Cultures at the University of Rochester. She is the author of *Bored to Distraction: End-of-the-Century Cinema of Excess in Mexico and Spain* (2003), *Danger Zones: Homosexuality, National Identity, and Mexican Culture* (1996), *Textured Lives: Women, Art, and Representation in Modern Mexico* (1992), and *Juan Goytisolo: Del 'realismo crítico' a la utopía* (1984), as well as the most recent publication *Frida Kahlo: A Biography* (2008). Two of her books have been chosen by the American Association of University Presses as Books for Understanding the World. Other distinctions include a Mellon

Grant and the 2007 Goergen Award for Distinguished Achievement and Artistry in Teaching.

Paul Julian Smith is a specialist in the cinema, television, and visual culture of Spain and Latin America. He has been the Professor of Spanish in the Faculty of Modern and Medieval Languages of the University of Cambridge since 1991 and Visiting Professor in ten universities (including Stanford, University of California–Berkeley, New York University's King Juan Carlos Chair, Johns Hopkins, Universidad del País Vasco, and Lund, Sweden). He is the author of fourteen books (with translations into Spanish and Chinese). In July 2008 he was elected a Fellow of the British Academy, where, in November 2008, he gave a lecture on Transnational Cinemas in Latin America: the cases of Mexico, Argentina, and Brazil. He is one of four founding editors of the *Journal of Spanish Cultural Studies* and was the editor of the book series Oxford Hispanic Studies, published by Oxford University Press. His most recent books are: *Spanish Screen Fiction: Between Cinema and Television* (Liverpool; Chicago: Liverpool UP; Chicago UP, 2009), *Spanish Visual Culture: Cinema, Television, Internet* (Manchester: Manchester UP, 2006), and *Television in Spain: Franco to Almodóvar* (London: Boydell and Brewer; Tamesis, 2006).

Alfredo J. Sosa-Velasco was an Assistant Professor of Spanish in the Department of Romance Languages and Literatures in Southern Connecticut State University. Dr. Sosa-Velasco specializes in nineteenth-, twentieth- and twenty-first-century Modern Peninsular Spanish Literature. His interests are ample, ranging from the relationship between literature and medicine to aesthetics, history, and memory. He has recently published a book on the role of Spanish physician writers as intellectuals (*Sanadores de la nación: Médicos escritores en España, 1855–1955*), and he is currently working in another one based on the representation of the Spanish civil war in narrative and film (*Remembering, Forgetting, and Memory in Spain: Representations of the Spanish Civil War in Novel and Film, 1936–2006*).

Robert Tobin, after 18 years at Whitman College, accepted the Henry J. Leir Chair in Foreign Languages and Cultures at Clark University in Worcester, Massachusetts, where he teaches courses in comparative literature and film studies. His book, *Doctor's Orders: Goethe and Enlightenment Thought* (Bucknell UP, 2001), looks at the relationship between literature and medicine, especially in Goethe's seminal *Bildungsroman*, *Wilhelm Meister*. Tobin's *Warm Brothers: Queer Theory and the Age of Goethe* (University of Pennsylvania Press, 2000) has been widely acknowledged to be a significant contribution to gay and lesbian studies in the fields of eighteenth-century literature and German literature. His work has been supported by the Deutscher Akademischer Austauschdienst (DAAD), the Fulbright Commission, and the Rockefeller Foundation.

Cristina Venegas is an Associate Professor of Film and Media Studies at the University of California–Santa Barbara. Her research focus is on international media with an emphasis on Latin America, Spanish-language film, television in the United States, and digital technologies. Her book, *Digital Dilemmas: The State, the Individual and Digital Media in Cuba* (Rutgers 2010), explores how conflicts over media access play out in their both liberating and repressive potential. She has curated numerous film programs on Latin American and Indigenous film in the US, and is cofounder and Artistic Director of the Latino CineMedia International Film Festival in Santa Barbara.

Index of Terms

Abre los ojos (Amenábar), 250
Addams Family, The (TV Series), 105
Adiós a Cuba (Cervantes), 45
Adiós, Roberto (Dawi), 12, 29n18
Adonis García, el vampiro de la colonia Roma (Zapata), 173, 203, 275
Advocate, The (magazine), 82, 90
Afinidades (Perugorría and Cruz), 49
Agapi Mu (González de Alba), 203
Alicia en el pueblo de Maravillas (Díaz Torres), 35
Amora (Roffiel), 204
Amores perros (González Iñárritu), 147
Ana y los lobos (Saura), 251
And the Band Played On (Spottiswoode), 79
Angels in America (Kushner), 79
Año sin amor: Diario del SIDA, Un (Pérez), 71–73, 84, 87–89, 91
Año sin amor, Un (Berneri), 6, 12, 71–80, 81–84, 87–93, 263, 276
Apariencias engañan, Las (Hermosillo), 218n2
Apprentis sorciers, Les (Cozarinsky), 264
Ardiente oscuridad (Skármenta), 94n8
Argentiniens (Post) Krise: Symbole und Mythen (Ingenschay and Lohmüller), 278n10
Así del precipicio (Suárez), 9, 204–05, 209–11, 213, 216

Barraca: Lorca sur les chemins de l'Espagne, La (Cozarinsky), 264
Basket Case (Henenlotter), 109n3

Batalla en el cielo (Reygadas), 144, 147, 152n5
Beso de la mujer araña, El (Puig), 12, 77
Besos en la frente (Galettini), 12
Bestia desnuda, La (Vieyra), 101
Biografías y testimonios (Cozarinsky), 264
Bisexual Imaginary: Representation, Identity and Desire (Davidson), 194
Bisexual Spaces: A Geography of Gender and Sexuality (Hemmings), 191
Biutiful (González Iñárritu), 143
Blood and Sand (Mamoulian), 2
Blood of the Virgins (Vieyra), 101
Blues (Cozarinsky), 264
Blow Job (Warhol), 148
Bonnie and Clyde (Penn), 56
Borges-Buenos Aires: Configuraciones de la ciudad del siglo XIX al XXI (Roland Spiller), 277n1
Borges/in/and/on Film (Cozarinsky), 264
Boulevards du crépuscule: Sur Falconetti (Cozarinsky), 264, 271, 274
Bound (Davis), 56
Boys Don't Cry (Peirce), 158, 168n1
Brain Damage (Henenlotter), 109n3
Breakfast on Pluto (Jordan), 168n1
Breve cielo (Kohon), 29n12
Burundanga (Cozarinsky), 264
Butterfly Kiss (Winterbottom), 56

Caballos salvajes (Piñeyro), 59
Cabeza de palo (Baca), 278n9

Cabinet of Dr. Caligari, The (Wiene), 103
Cadena perpetua (Ripstein), 223
Caja negra (Ortega), 278n9
Callejón de los milagros, El (Fons), 147
Camila (Bemberg), 13, 15n3, 29n16
Cargo de conciencia, (Vieyra), 101
Carmen (Aranda), 252
Cartas del parque (Gutiérrez Alea), 34
Cartero de Neruda, El (Skármenta), 94n8
Casa de la Magnolia (Palou), 204
Castillo de la pureza (Ripstein), 223
Caza, La (Saura), 248
Celluloid Closet: Homosexuality in the Movies, The (Russo), 14
Cenizas del paraíso (Piñeyro), 59
Chamaco (Cremata), 275
Chicos (Bizzio), 156
Cielo dividido, El (J. Hernández), 144, 147, 149, 203
Ciénaga, La (Martel), 10, 12, 237–45
Cinderella (Soliño), 114
Cineaction (magazine), 179
Cinemachismo (de la Mora), 222, 232
Cinéma des cahiers, Le (Cozarinsky), 265
Citizen Kane (Welles), 249
Citizen Langlois (Cozarinsky), 264
Ciudad letrada, La (Rama), 123n5
Ciudad y los perros, La (Lombardi), 185–86
Cinema of Latin America, The (Elena and Díaz), 14
Clandestino destino (Hermosillo), 180
Comandos azules en acción (Vieyra), 101
Companion to Latin American Film, A (Hart) 14
Condición del cine mexicano, La (Ayala Blanco), 182n15
Confesión a Laura (Osorio), 12
Confession of the Letter Closet: Epistolary Fiction and Queer Desire in Modern Spain (Garlinger), 258
Contemporary Argentine Cinema (Foster), 29n18
Contemporary Latin American Cinema: Breaking into the Global Market (Shaw), 14
Correccional de mujeres (Vieyra), 101
Creature from the Black Lagoon (Arnold), 105
Cría cuervos (Saura), 248, 250–51, 253
Crónica de un desayuno (Cann), 218n2
Crying Game, The (Jordan), 168n1
Culture of Queers, The (Dyer), 14
Cumpleaños del perro, El (Hermosillo), 174
Curious Dr. Humpp, The (Vieyra), 6, 12, 99, 101–04, 107–08
Custodio, El (Moreno), 25

Dans le Rouge du Couchant (Cozarinsky), 265, 268
Danzón (Novaro), 168n1, 218n2
Dark Side of the Moon, The (telenovela), 48
De eso no se habla (Bemberg), 19, 28n2
De los otros: Intimacy and Homosexuality among Mexican Men (Carrier), 181n3
Deadly Organ, The (Vieyra), 100
Death in Venice (Mann), 13, 15n5
Detrás de la mentira (Vieyra), 100
Diario de José Toledo (Barbachano Ponce), 203
Diccionario de la Lengua Española, 194
Diccionario de la Real Academia Española, 194
Doña Bárbara (Fuentes and Delgado), 2–3
Doña Herlinda y su hijo (Hermosillo), 8, 50n7, 173, 179–81, 181n5, 182n11, 203
Donovan's Brain (Feist), 105
Dos mujeres (Levi Calderón), 204, 209

Dr. Zoide contra la bestia desnuda, El (Vieyra), 101
Dracula (Browning), 108
Dulces compañías (Blancarte), 218n2

Early Frost, An (Erman), 79
Écrits (Lacan), 195
En la ciudad sin límites (A. Hernández), 10, 11, 247, 249–52, 254–55
Erotism: Death and Sensuality (Bataille), 241, 246n3
Espíritu de la colmena, El (Erice), 248
Eva Perón (Desanzo), 76
Evangelio de las Maravillas, El (Ripstein), 218n2
Extraña invasión (Vieyra), 100

Families We Choose: Lesbians, Gays, Kinship (Weston), 182n13
Fantômes de Tanger (Cozarinsky), 265
Faust (Murnau), 104
Fifty Years of Queer Cinema: Five Hundred of the Best GLBTQ Films Ever Made (Porter and Prince), 14
Flesh (Morrisey), 276
Flesh and Trash (Morrisey), 275
Fly, The (Neumann), 103
Foolish Wives (von Stroheim), 108
Four Horsemen of the Apocalypse, The (Ingram), 2
Frankenhooker (Henenlotter), 109n3
Frankenstein (Shelley), 102
Fresa y chocolate (Gutiérrez Alea and Tabío), 6, 31–50, 50n8
Fruta verde (Serna), 203
Fugacidad del cine mexicano, La (Ayala Blanco), 145

Galaxia Kafka (Cozarinsky), 264
Gender Trouble: Feminism and the Subversion of Identity (Butler), 189
Girl and the Skeleton, The (Henenlotter), 109n3
Gitano (Vieyra), 101

Gran Aventura, La (Vieyra), 101
Guerra contra la sociedad (Pécaut), 129
Guerre d'un seul homme, La (Cozarinsky), 264
Guerre est finie, La (Resnais), 249, 258
Guerreros y cautivas (Cozarinsky), 264, 271
Grandes películas del cine gay (Villalba), 14
Gun Crazy (Lewis), 56

Happy Together [Chun gwong cha sit] (Wong), 77–78, 270
Hasta el viento tiene miedo (Moheno), 9, 204
Haute Mer (Cozarinsky), 264
Historia oficial, La (Luis Puenzo), 27, 73
Hojas de cine (book series), 50n3
Homosexualidad, sociedad y estado en México (Lumsden), 181n3
Horripilante bestia humana, La (Cardona), 107
Hours, The (Cunningham), 79
Hubo un tiempo en que las noches dieron paso... (J. Hernández), 145
Human Condition, The (Arendt), 59

Illiad (Homer), 68n7
Indiana Jones and the Temple of Doom (Spielberg), 106
Infinita (Krauze), 204
In memoriam (Brasó), 249–51
Irrompibles, Los (Vieyra), 101
Island of Lost Souls (Wells), 103
Ismael (Piñeyro), 59

Japón (Reygadas), 144, 152n5
Jar ar nyfiken—en film i gult (Sjöman), 107
Jean Cocteau: Autoportrait d'un inconnu (Cozarinsky), 264
Juguete rabioso, El (Artl), 66
Justine (Durrell), 53

Kamchatka (Piñeyro), 59
Kiss of the Spider Woman (Babenco), 12, 50n7, 75, 77, 83, 93
Kiss or Kill (Bennett), 56

Laberinto de Pasiones (Almodóvar), 46
Lavender Screen: The Gay and Lesbian Films, The (Hadleigh), 14
Laws (Plato), 60
Lecumberri, el palacio negro (Ripstein), 223
Lejos de donde (Cozarinsky), 264
Lengua de las mariposas, La (Cuerda), 15n2
León, La (Otheguy), 263
Lesbianas de Buenos Aires (S. García), 13
Ley del deseo, La (Almodóvar), 258
Literature and Evil (Bataille), 241, 246n3
Living End, The (Araki), 79
Lobo, el bosque y el hombre nuevo, El (Paz), 31
Luces de Bohemia (Valle-Inclán), 277n4
Lucía (Solás), 40
Lugar sin límites, El (Ripstein), 3, 9, 12, 168n1, 203, 221–34, 275
Luz silenciosa (Reygadas), 144

Madagascar (Pérez), 34
Madame Satã (Aïnouz), 168n1
Magical Reels: A History of Cinema in Latin America, (King) 14
Making Love (Hiller), 174, 181n4
Mala educación, La (Almodóvar), 150
Mad Love (Freund), 105
Mamá cumple 100 años (Saura), 251
Maniobras nocturnas (Cozarinsky), 264
Marido argentino promedio, El (Shua), 28n8
Mariposas en el andamio (Bernaza and Gilpin), 12, 168n1
Mask of Fu Manchu, The (Brabin), 106
Mauvaise Conduite (Almendros and Jiménez), 39
Mecánicas celestes (Torres), 7, 111–22

Memorias del subdesarrollo (Gutiérrez Alea), 34, 38, 45
Método, El (Piñeyro), 59
Mexican Screen Fiction: Between Cinema and Television (Smith), 152n1
Meykinof (Guarini), 268
Mi novia el travesti (Cahen Salaberry), 168n1
Mil nubes de paz cercan el cielo (J. Hernández), 7, 8, 12, 143–53, 203
Milongas (Cozarinsky), 264
Modisto de señoras (Jiménez Pons), 152n3
Momentos (Bemberg), 28n3
Montería, La (zarzuela), 233
Mother and Child (R. García), 143
Muerte de un burócrata (Gutiérrez Alea), 34
Museo del chisme (Cozarinsky), 264
My Hustler (Warhol), 275
My Teenage Fallout Queen (Henenlotter), 109n3
Mystère de la chambre jaune, Le (Leroux), 102

Nadador inmóvil, El (Rudnik), 278n9
New Latin American Cinema: Theory, Practices, and Transcontinental Articulations (Martin), 50n3
New Queer Cinema (Aaron), 14
New York Times (newspaper), 80, 89–90, 123n3
Night of the Bloody Apes (Cardona), 107
Niña santa, La (Martel), 243, 246n5
Niñas mal (Sariñana), 9, 204
Niño pez, El (Lucía Puenzo), 157, 169n5
No se lo digas a nadie (Bayly), 8, 185–99, 275
No se lo digas a nadie (Lombardi), 8, 185–99, 275
Nosferatu (Murnau), 104
Novia de Odessa, La (Cozarinsky), 264
Nueve minutos (Lucía Puenzo), 157

Ocean's Eleven (Soderbergh), 56
Octopusalarm [*Tintenfischalarm*] (Scharang), 156–57
Orgy at Lil's Place (Intrator), 107
Oso rojo, Un (Caetano), 25
Otra historia de amor (Ortiz), 12, 29n18
Out at the Movies: A History of Gay Cinema (Davis), 14
Oxford Spanish Dictionary, 175

Palacios plebeyos (Cozarinsky), 264
Pantaleón y las visitadoras (Lombardi), 185–86
Parfum de la dame en noir, Le (Leroux), 102
Parting Glances (Sherwood), 79, 82
Pase del testigo, El (Cozarinsky), 264
Pelea cubana contra los demonios, Una (Gutiérrez Alea), 34
Philadelphia (Demme), 79, 82
Pietà, La (Michelangelo), 58, 63
Placer sangriento (Vieyra), 100
Plata quemada (Piglia), 54–63, 255
Plata quemada (Piñeyro), 6, 12, 53–69, 255–56
Poesia in forma di rosa (Pasolini), 152n4
Poetics (Aristotle), 60, 68n8
Política sexual: Cuadernos del Frente Homosexual de Acción Revolucionaria (magazine), 174
Postman, The [*Il postino*] (Radford), 83–84, 94n8
Pour Mémoire: Les Klarsfeld, une famille dans l'Histoire (Cozarinsky), 264
Prostitución masculina, La (Perlongher), 275
Psychopathia Sexualis (Krafft-Ebing), 90
Púberes canéforas, Las (Blanco), 203
Púlover, El (Hutter), 276
Pulp Fiction (Tarantino), 56
Puntos suspensivos o Esperando a los bárbaros (Cozarinsky), 264

Quatermass Experiment, The (Guest), 103
Queer Issues in Contemporary Latin American Cinema (Foster), 14, 28n2, 187
Quiero llenarme de ti (Vieyra), 101
Quimera de los héroes, La (Rosenfeld), 278n9

Rabioso sol, rabioso cielo (J. Hernández), 144, 203, 263
Rasputin and the Princess (Henenlotter), 109n3
Rear Window: Tales from Havana (Channel Four), 47
Red Horror (Vieyra), 101
Reel Views (Berardinelli), 123n2
Reina del Sur, La (TV series), 3
Reservoir Dogs (Tarantino), 56
Rocco and His Brothers (Visconti), 43
Ronda nocturna (Cozarinsky), 11–12, 263–79
Rosario Tijeras (Maillé), 3
Rudo y Cursi (Cuarón), 143
Rufián moldavo, El (Cozarinsky), 264
Rules of Art, The (Bourdieu), 145

San Francisco Chronicle (newspaper), 123n3
Sangre de vírgenes (Vieyra), 101, 108
Santo Oficio, El (Ripstein), 223
Satan in High Heels (Intrator), 107
Scarlatti à Séville (Cozarinsky), 264
Screening the Sexes: Homosexuality in the Movies (Tayler), 275
Secreto de sus ojos, El (Campanella), 15n2
Segunda Piel (Vera), 254, 256
Señora de Nadie (Bemberg), 5, 12, 15n3, 19–30
Sex and Sexuality in Latin America: An Interdisciplinary Reader (Balderston), 181n1
Sexperts, The (Intrator), 107
Shabnam Mausi (Bharadwaj), 168n1

Sheik, The (Melford), 2
Sight and Sounds (magazine), 89
Silence = Death (Praunheim), 79
Simplemente una rosa (Vieyra), 101
Simón, el gran varón (Barreda), 12, 168n1
Sin destino (Laborde), 12, 275
Soap, En [A Soap] (Christensen), 168n1
Sobrevivientes, Los (Gutiérrez Alea), 34
Stanford Encyclopedia of Philosophy, 152n8
Stay Tuned for Terror (Vieyra), 100
Sucedió en el internado (Vieyra), 101

Tan de repente (Lerman), 270
Tango deseo (Cozarinsky), 265
Tango feroz, la leyenda de Tanguito (Piñeyro), 59
Taxi Boys (Zeiger), 275
Te seguiré buscando (Estrada), 204
Tempranica, La (zarzuela), 233
Testimonials (Cozarinsky), 264
Testosterone (Moreton), 77–78
Thelma and Louise (Scott), 79
Them! (Douglas), 103
Thing that Couldn't Die, The (Cowan), 105
Tinta roja, La (Lombardi), 185
Titón: de la Habana a Guantanamera (Ibarra), 39
Todo incluido (Ortúzar), 9, 204–05, 214–16
Todo sobre mi madre (Almodóvar), 15n2, 168n1
To Wong Foo, Thanks for Everything! Julie Newmar (Beeban Kidron), 168n1
Tragicall History of the Life and Death of Doctor Faustus (Marlowe), 225
Trama celeste, La (Bioy Casares), 249
Tres fronteras (Cozarinsky), 264
Tres mujeres en la hoguera (Salazar), 204
Transamerica (Tucker), 157, 168n1
Tren blanco, El (N. García), 271
Tropics of Desire (Quiroga), 33

Última cena, La (Gutiérrez Alea), 34

Ultimate Guide to Lesbian and Gay Film and Video, The (Olson), 14
Último cuplé, El (Orduña), 150
Until Damascus (Strindberg), 277n4
Utopía gay (Calva), 203

Variety (magazine), 82, 90, 252
Venganza del sexo, La (Vieyra), 6, 12, 99–109
Venus in Furs [Venus im Pelz] (Sacher-Masoch), 90–91
Vice Versa: Bisexuality and the Eroticism of Everyday Life (Garber), 173, 197
Vida continúa, La (Vieyra), 101
Vigan et quelques autres en Argentine, Le (Cozarinsky), 264
Villa Cariño está que arde (Vieyra), 101
Villa, La (Aira), 271
Violent Life [Una vita violenta] (Pasolini), 146
Violon de Rothschild, Le (Cozarinsky), 264
Virgen de los Sicarios, La (Schroeder), 7, 125–41, 275
Virgen de los Sicarios, La (Vallejo), 7, 125–41, 275
Virus Knows No Morals, A [Ein Virus kennt keine Moral] (Praunheim), 79
Viudas de los jueves, Las (Piñeyro), 59
Vuelven los García (I. Rodríguez), 2
Vudú urbano (Cozarinsky), 264, 269

Wedding Banquet (Lee), 173
White Peacock, The (Lawrence), 67

XXY (Lucía Puenzo), 8, 12, 29n12, 155–69, 263

Yo gané al prode . . . ¿y Ud . . . ? (Vieyra), 101
Yo, la peor de todas (Bemberg), 15n3, 19
Yo soy la felicidad de este mundo (J. Hernández), 144

Zero Patience (Greyson), 79

Index of Names

Aaron, Michele, 14
Acuña, Manuel, 177–78
Aeschylus, 56
Aguzzi, Juan, 244
Aira, César, 271
Alcón, Alfredo, 248
Almaguer, Tomás, 175–76, 182n9, 182n10
Almendros, Néstor, 39
Almodóvar, Pedro, 4, 15n2, 46, 121, 150, 224, 256, 258
Alterio, Héctor, 13
Álvarez, Roberto, 248
Álvarez, Santiago, 37
Alzate, Gastón, 138
Amenábar, Alejandro, 250
Anaya, John Didier, xi
Angelino, Joel, 42
Anghileri, Mariana "Moro," 265, 267
Antigone, 60
Araki, Gregg, 79
Aranda, Vicente, 252
Arias, Imanol, 29n16
Aristotle, 60, 68, 226
Arizmendi, Diego, 146–47, 151
Armendáriz, Pedro, 181n5
Arnheim, Rudolf, 195
Arnold, Jack, 105
Arroyo, Fernando, 149
Artl, Roberto, 66
Aura, Marta, 231
Ayala Blanco, Jorge, 145–46, 151, 182n15

Baca, Ernesto, 278n9

Bakhtin, Mikhail, 42
Baluarte, Lita, 190
Banderas, Antonio, 258
Barbachano Ponce, Miguel, 203
Bárbara, *Santa*, 43
Barbero, Aldo, 101
Bardem, Javier, 256
Barnard, Timothy, 45
Barreda, Miguel, 12
Bataille, Georges, 241, 246n3
Bauleo, Ricardo, 101
Bayly, Jaime, 8, 9, 185–90, 192, 194–95, 275
Bazin, André, 195
Beltrán, Susan, 101
Bemberg, María Luisa, 4–6, 13, 15n3, 19–20, 23–24, 26–29
Berardinelli, James, 123n3
Berdoulay, Vincent, 117
Bernaza, Felipe Luis, 12
Berneri, Anahí, 6, 71–72, 76, 78, 82, 84, 89, 91–92, 263, 276
Bernini, Emilio, 239
Bingham, Dennis, 188
Bioy Casares, Adolfo, 249
Bizzio, Sergio, 156, 158–61, 164–65
Blancarte, Óscar, 218n2
Blanco, José Joaquín, 174, 182n15, 203
Blasco Ibáñez, Vicente, 2
Bó, Armando, 100
Bond, James, 101
Bosch, Rosa, 143
Bouloukos, Beth, xi
Bourdieu, Pierre, 145

Brabin, Charles, 106
Braga, Sonia, 12, 77
Braidotti, Rosi, 194
Brando, Luisina, 19, 29n16
Brasó, Enrique, 249, 250, 251
Brédice, Leticia, 255, 258
Bresson, Robert, 145
Browning, Tod, 108
Bruno, Guiliana, 116, 118–20
Buscemi, Steve, 82
Butler, Judith, 29n12, 155–57, 168, 189, 194

Caballero, Rufo, 49
Caetano, Adrián, 25–26
Caillois, Roger, 104
Callas, Maria, 41, 45, 118, 120
Calva, José Rafael, 203
Camil, Jaime, 211
Camino, Joaquín, 186, 196
Campanella, Juan José, 4, 15n2
Cann, Benjamín, 218n2
Carr, Michael J., 67n1
Cardona, René, 107
Carpentier, Alejo, 45
Carrier, Joseph, 175, 179, 181n3, 181n7, 182n12, 182n16
Carvajal, Edwin, 125, 131, 140n2, 140n3, 141n5
Casanovas, Álex, 248
Castellanos, Alma Rosa, 123n2
Castro, Fidel, 12, 35
Castro, Mariela, 48
Castro, Raúl, 48
Catalá, Delfina, 36
Cervantes, Ignacio, 45
Chaplin, Geraldine, 248–51, 253
Charlone, César, 185
Chauncey, George, 175
Chávez, Julio, 25, 29n16
Chijona, Gerardo, 48
Chong, Oscar, 181n1
Ciccia, Giovanni, 187
Clarkson, Michael, xi, 140n1, 218n1

Cobo, Roberto, 3, 10, 12, 224
Conte, Richard, 100
Cossío, Elmiran, 193
Couter, Javier van de, 74
Cowan, Will, 105
Cozarinsky, Edgardo, 11, 73–77, 263–71, 277n1, 277n4, 278n7, 278n9, 279n13
Cremata Malberti, Carlos, 275
Cruz, Mónica, 211
Cruz, Penélope, 211
Cruz, Vladimir, 35, 49
Cuarón, Alfonso, 143, 152n2
Cuerda, José Luis, 15n2
Cunningham, Michael, 79

Dallessandro, Joe, 275
Dargis, Manohla, 147
Darín, Ricardo, 12, 15n2
Darwin, Charles, 103
Davidson, Phoebe, 196
Davis, Steven Paul, 14
Dawi, Enrique, 12, 29n18
Dayton, Gregory, 266
de Castro, Pércio, Jr., 187
de la Cruz, Sor Juana, 15n3, 19
de la Mora, Sergio, 221–22, 224–25, 232
de la Peña, Rosario, 177
de la Reguera, Ana, 205
del Amo, Álvaro, 248
del Rio, Joe, 274
del Toro, Guillermo, 143, 152n2
Delany, Samuel, 122
Deleuze, Giles, 90, 193, 252–53
Díaz, Porfirio, 223
Díaz López, Marina, 14
Díaz Ordaz, Gustavo, 222
Díaz Torres, Daniel, 35
Dollimore, Jonathan, 192
Dombasle, Arielle, 121
Doyle, Sir Arthur Conan, 102
Donoso, José, 3, 9, 225, 233, 275
Doty, Alexander, 190

Douglas, Gordon, 103
Dreger, Alice Domurat, 155–56, 169n3
Durrell, Lawrence, 53
Dyer, Richard, 14, 274

Eadie, Jo, 193, 196
Echarri, Pablo, 6, 54
Echevarría, Carlos, 83
Echeverría, Luis, 222
Edelman, Lee, 193
Efron, Inés, 169n6
Eisenstein, Sergei, 195
Elena, Alberto, 14
Elías, Carme, 186
Enkidu, 68n6
Epps, Brad, 46
Erice, Víctor, 248
Estarreado, Mónica, 258
Escobar, Pablo, 137
Estrada, Josefina, 204
Euripides, 56
Évora, José Antonio, 40

Fassbinder, Reiner Werner, 144
Faust (Faustus), 6, 100, 103, 226
Feist, Felix E., 105
Félix, María, 3
Felman, Shoshana, 225
Fernán Gómez, Fernando, 12, 15n2, 248–52, 257
Fernández, Ana, 255, 257
Fernández, Emilio "El Indio," 147
Fernández L'Hoeste, Héctor, 141n7
Ferro, Rafael, 265
Fiesco, Roberto, 147
Figueras, Marcelo, 54–55, 61, 63, 66
Fleming, Ian, 101
Fliess, Wilhelm, 175
Flowers, John, 109n2
Fons, Jorge, 147
Fontana, Clara, 29n16
Foster, David William, 14, 28n2, 29n18, 46, 55, 187–88, 190, 193, 195–96, 274

Franco, Francisco, 46, 249
Franzetti, Carlos, 276
Fresedo, Emilio, 67
Fresedo, Osvaldo, 67
Freud, Sigmund, 113–14, 167, 175, 279n15
Frizler, Paul, 109n2
Fuguet, Alberto, 185

Galettini, Carlos, 12
Garber, Marjorie, 173, 175–76, 181n4, 197, 223
García, Nauel, 271
García, Santiago, 13
García, Sara, 2
García Espinosa, Julio, 185
García Joya, Mario ("Mayito"), 43, 50n5
García Márquez, Gabriel, 34
Garlinger, Patrick Paul, 258–59
Gattorno, Francisco, 36
Gaviria, César, 137
Gelormini, Nicolás, 84, 94n9
Genet, Jean, 147, 273–74
Gilgamesh, 68n6
Gilpin, Margaret, 12
Ginsberg, Allen, 86, 92, 94n10
Giroud, Pavel, 48
Goethe, Johann Wolfgang von, 103–04
González de Alba, Luis, 203
González Iñárritu, Alejandro, 143, 145–46, 152n2, 185
González Vargas, Carla, 146
Grimm, Jacob, 112, 116
Grosz, Elizabeth, 113, 114, 116
Grünberger, Werner, 166
Guarini, Carmen, 268
Guest, Val, 103
Guevara, Che, 33, 42
Gutiérrez Alea, Tomás, 4, 5, 31–32, 34, 36, 38–40, 44–45, 47, 49, 50n5, 185
Guy, Donna J., 181n1
Guzmán, Patricio, 185

Hadleigh, Boze, 14
Halperin, David, 68n6
Hanks, Tom, 82
Haraway, Donna, 194
Hart, Stephen M., 14, 185, 186, 199
Hegel, Georg Wilhelm Friedrich, 113
Hemmings, Clare, 191, 194, 196
Henenlotter, Frank, 99, 105, 109n3
Heredia, Gonzalo, 11, 265, 268, 275
Hernández, Antonio, 10, 247, 252–53, 255–56
Hermosillo, Jaime Humberto, 8, 50n7, 144, 173–74, 177–82, 203, 218n2
Hernández, Julián, 7, 8, 12, 143–52, 203, 263
Higared, Martha, 211
Holden, Stephen, 123n3, 147
Holland, Jonathan, 249
Homer, 59
Hopewell, Kinder, 248
Hoppe, Miguel Ángel, 149
Hopper, Edward, 269
Huerta Floriano, Ángel, 249
Hurt, William, 12, 77
Hutter, Michael, 276

Ibarra, Mirta, 35–36, 38–40
Iglesias, Marcelo, 275
Infante, Pedro, 2, 181n5
Ingenschay, Dieter, 278n10
Intrator, Jerald, 107
Irving, Washington, 105
Irwin, Robert McKee, 211

Jacobowitz, Florence, 179
Jácome Liévano, Margarita Rosa, 125
Janus, 65
Jaramillo, Germán, 135
Jarman, Derek, 145
Jasan, Muhabid, 160
Jesus, 63, 266
Jiménez Leal, Orlando, 39
Jiménez, Lucía, 187
Jiménez Pons, Eduardo, 152n3

Joan of Arc, 115
Johnson, G. Allen, 147
Julia, Raul, 12, 77
Jürgen, Alex, 156–57, 161, 166

Kahlo, Frida, 180
Khan, Omar, 56, 109n4
Kibbey, Ann, 229
Kinder, Marsha, 46, 248
King, John, 14, 29n19, 181n6
Kohon, David José, 29n12
Krauze, Ethel, 204
Kristeva, Julia, 63
Kushner, Tony, 79

Laborde, Leopoldo, 12, 275
Lacan, Jacques, 195
Lamborghini, Osvaldo, 246n3
Lang, Robert, 274
Lawrence, D. H., 67
Lecuona, Ernesto, 45
Leduc, Paul, 144
Lema, John Byron, xi
Lenne, Gérard, 102–03, 106
Lerman, Diego, 270, 278n9
Leroux, Gaston, 102
Leutrat, Jean-Louis, 104
Levi Calderón, Sara, 204, 209
Lewton, Val, 99
Limbacher, James L., 109n2
Lippe, Richard, 179
Lohmüller, Torben, 278n10
Lombardi, Francisco J., 8–9, 185–92, 194–96, 198–99, 275
Lombardo, Bárbara, 74
López, Alejandro, 140n2
López Moctezuma, Carlos, 181n5
López Páez, Jorge, 181n5, 182n11
López Portillo, José, 10, 222
Lumsden, Ian, 181n3

Machado, Antonio, 255
Madonna, 76, 93
Magill, Santiago, 186

Mann, Thomas, 13, 15n5
Marlowe, Christopher, 225
Martel, Lucrecia, 4, 10, 237–39, 241, 243–45, 246n3
Martín, Ana, 224
Martz, Irene, 205
Mastroianni, Marcello, 19
Mayer, Sophie, 169n5, 169n6
Mayne, Judith, 216
Medak-Seguín, Bécquer, xi, 109n1
Medici, Italo, 115
Meier, Christian, 187
Menem, Carlos, 73–75
Merkin, Ricardo, 74
Meyer, Russ, 99
Michael Archangel, Saint, 138
Michelangelo, 58, 63
Mihanovich, Mónica, 100
Ming Liang, Tsai, 144
Minghetti, Claudio D., 273, 278n7
Minujín, Juan, 71–72, 82
Miquelez, Javier, 268, 278n7
Moheno, Gustavo, 9, 204
Montiel, Sara, 149–50, 228
More, Thomas, 180
Moreno, Rodrigo, 25
Moreton, David, 77
Morrissey, Paul, 275
Mulvey, Laura, 197, 199
Murnau, W. Friedrich, 104
Murray, Stephen O., 179

Nixon, Nicholas, 82
Negrete, Jorge, 175–76, 181n5, 181n6
Neruda, Pablo, 6, 83–86, 92, 94n8
Neumann, Kurt, 103
Noriega, Eduardo, 6, 12, 53, 56, 65, 255
Novaro, María, 218n2
Núñez, Omar, 74

Ochoa, Jesús, 211
Ochoa, John, 234
Odell, Ben, 211

Oedipus, 60
Olivella, Martí, 113
Oliver, Felipe, 135
Olson, Jenni, 14
Orduña, Juan de, 150
Ortega, Luis, 278n9
Ortiz de Zárate, Américo, 12, 29n18
Ortuño, Juan Carlos, 148–49
Ortúzar, Rodrigo, 9, 204, 211, 217
Osorio Gómez, Jaime, 12
Osorio, José, 131, 138, 140n3
Ospina, Claudia, 134–35
Otheguy, Santiago, 263
Ozores, Adriana, 258

Padrón, Frank, 41, 48
Páez, Fito, 189
Palou, Pedro Ángel, 204
Pasolini, Pier Paolo, 144–47, 152n4
Pastor, Julián, 225
Patrocles, 68n7
Paz, Senel, 31, 49
Pécaut, Daniel, 128–29
Pecoraro, Susú, 22, 29n16
Pérez, Fernando, 34
Pérez, Pablo, 71–72, 84, 86, 92, 94, 263
Perlongher, Néstor, 158, 275
Perón, Eva ("Evita"), 75–77, 93
Perugorría, Jorge, 12, 32, 49
Philip II of Macedonia, 57
Piglia, Ricardo, 55, 60, 62–63, 255
Pinochet, Augusto, 214
Piñeyro, Marcelo, xi, 4, 6, 53–67, 67n1, 67n3, 68n4, 255
Platas, Gaby, 205
Plato, 60, 113
Plutarch, 57
Poe, Edgar Allan, 102
Poncela, Eusebio, 258
Porter, Darwin, 14
Prado, Javier, 192
Pramaggiore, Maria, 188, 190, 197–98
Praunheim, Rosa von, 79

Index of Names

Prat, Gloria, 101
Pratt, Douglas, 109n2
Probyn, Elspeth, 194
Puenzo, Lucía, 8, 29n12, 155–61, 165–69, 263
Puenzo, Luis, 4, 27, 73, 156
Puig, Manuel, 9, 12, 77
Pugliese, Osvaldo, 267

Quintrala, La, 3
Quiroga, José, 33, 35, 178, 181n1, 223–24, 227–28

Raghuvanshi, Manoj, 168n1
Rama, Ángel, 118, 123n5
Ramírez Berg, Charles, 177, 180, 181n6
Ranni, Rodolfo, 20
Ray, Jean, 102
Reimer, David, 155–58
Resnais, Alain, 249, 254, 258
Reygadas, Carlos, 144, 147, 152n5
Ripstein, Arturo, 3–4, 9–10, 144–45, 203, 218n2, 221–24, 232–34, 275
Robbiano, Vanessa, 193
Rodó, José Enrique, 152n7
Roffiel, Rosamaría, 204
Roldán, Emma, 232
Romero, Hernán, 186
Romilly, Jacqueline de, 56–58
Rose, Gillian, 117, 123n6
Rosenbaum, Jonathan, 268, 270, 271, 278n8
Rosenfeld, Daniel, 278n9
Rossini, Gioachino, 112, 118
Rudnik, Fernán, 278n9
Ruffinelli, Jorge, 181
Russo, Vito, 14
Ruz, Robert, 190

Sacher-Masoch, Leopold von, 90–91
Sade, Marquis de, 90
Saenz, Noelia, 248, 254, 256–57, 259n2
Salamon, Gayle, 167–68

Salazar, Abel, 204
Salinas, Carmen, 232
Samper Pizano, Ernesto, 137
Sánchez, Diana, 155, 157
Sánchez, Francisco, 174, 180
Sanjinés, Jorge, 185
Santoveña, Hortensia, 232
Sariñana, Fernando, 9, 204
Sarli, Isabel, 100
Saura, Carlos, 248, 250, 251
Sbaraglia, Leonardo, 6, 12, 53, 56, 65, 247, 251–52, 255–56
Schaefer, Claudia, 209, 221
Scharang, Elizabeth, 166
Schroeder, Barbet, 7, 125, 129, 275
Schubert, Franz, 117
Schulz-Cruz, Bernard, 218n2
Sebreli, Juan José, 264
Semprún, Jorge, 249, 254, 258
Serna, Assumpta, 19
Serna, Enrique, 203
Serradilla, Ana, 205, 211
Shapiro, Michael J., 214
Shaw, Deborah, 3, 14
Shelley, Mary, 102, 103
Siodmak, Curt, 105
Sjöman, Vilgot, 107
Skármenta, Antonio, 94n8
Smith, Paul Julian, 32, 76, 78, 82, 84, 89, 91, 152n1 250
Solanas, Fernando, 185
Solás, Humberto, 40
Solaya, Marilyn, 40
Soler, Fernando, 226
Solomon-Godeau, Abigail, 225
Soloviov, Vladimir, 102
Sophocles, 56
Spielberg, Steven, 106
Spinoza, Baruch, 113
Stack, Peter, 123n3
Stevenson, Robert Louis, 103
Stoker, Bram, 101
Strasberg, Ann, 100
Strindberg, August, 277n4
Stroheim, Erich von, 108

Suárez, Pablo, 157
Suárez, Teresa, 9, 204–05, 208–09, 211, 217
Subero, Gustavo, 14, 188, 196
Sugar, Alexander, xi, 67n1, 246n1

Tabío, Juan Carlos, 5, 31, 34, 36, 39, 44, 49
Thiriard, Paul-Louis, 38
Todorov, Tzvetan, 102, 109
Torres, Fina, 7, 111, 117
Tyler, Parker, 275–76

Valentino, Rudolph, 2
Valle-Inclán, Ramón, 277n4
Vallejo, Fernando, 7, 125–26, 129, 135, 140n1, 275
Varela, Leonor, 211
Varela, Susana, 265
Vargas Llosa, Mario, 185
Vargas, Valentina, 211
Vásquez, José Antonio, 131
Vázquez, Luis Bernardo Jaime, 152n6
Vera, Gerardo, 254
Vega, Gonzalo, 224
Videla, Jorge Rafael, 101
Villa, Lucha, 178, 225–26
Villalba, Susana M., 14
Vieyra, Emilio, 6, 7, 99–109
Virgen de la Caridad del Cobre, 43
Virgen del Pilar, 58, 63, 64

Virgin Mary, 63, 136, 237, 245, 246n4
Visconti, Luchino, 43
Vitier, José María, 37

Walde Uribe, Erna von der, 140n3
Walsh, María Elena, 29n14
Warhol, Andy, 148, 152n9, 275
Weiss, Jason, 264, 271
Welles, Orson, 62, 249
Wells, H. G., 103
Weston, Kath, 182n13
Whittle, Stephen, 214
Wiene, Robert, 103
Wilde, Oscar, 104
Wilkinson, Amber, 159
Wong, Kar Wai, 77–78, 144, 270
Wood, Ed, 99
Wood, Jason, 144
Wood, Robin, 179, 182n14, 188
Wynne, Marsea, xi, 140n1

Yi-Fu, Tuan, 117
Young, R. G., 109n2
Young, Stacey, 193

Zamoa, Aníbal, 192
Zapata, Luis, 173, 181n3, 203, 275
Zeiger, Claudio, 275
Zolov, Eric, 222, 224, 227
Zorrilla, China, 21
Zorrilla, Raúl, 99

Index of Concepts

activism, homosexual, 75, 77, 173; HIV/AIDS 79, 81
adaptation (of literature to film), 103–05, 169, 263; in Lombardi's filmography, 8, 185–90, 192, 194–95; of *La Virgen de los Sicarios*, 7, 125–26, 131, 139, 140n2
aesthetics, 5, 11–13, 38, 40, 57, 79, 158, 180, 190, 269, 273–74, 276–77; aesthetic-ethical intent in *La Virgen de los Sicarios*, 126, 130, 132, 135, 139, 140n2; art film aesthetics, 8, 144–47, 150–51; indirect cinema aesthetics, 268, 270; gay aesthetics, 274
agency, 189, 199, 253; queer agency, 5–8
alienation, 148, 195, 250, 254, 270
allegory, 32, 155–57, 161–62, 164, 167, 223, 226, 234, 255
androgyny, 114, 121
animation, 116, 120
Ariel Awards, 146, 152n7
art cinema, 7, 39, 46, 143–44, 151, 269, 270, 274, 277
audience, 6, 8, 13–14, 24, 29n15, 31, 33–36, 40, 42–43, 46, 49, 55, 72, 75–76, 92, 100, 121, 144, 150, 156, 158, 164, 204, 215–16, 221, 223, 225, 227, 252, 266, 277; audience appeal, 49; gay, 76, 82, 266; global/transnational, 8, 32, 35–36, 46, 72, 82, 147, 151, 216; straight, 179; as voyeur, 106

auteurism, 5, 7, 143–47, 151–52

Bildungsroman, 65
bisexual triangle, 176, 188–89, 192, 197–99
bisexuality, 5, 8–9, 65, 121, 167, 181n4; in *Doña Herlinda y su hijo*, 8, 173, 175–76, 178–79, 181; in *No se lo digas a nadie*, 8–9, 187–99
body, 24, 42, 63–65, 82–83, 89, 106, 116, 152n5, 156, 158, 164, 167, 187, 207, 214–15, 224, 226, 229, 231, 234, 243, 255, 258, 277; and the city, 119; and desire, 193, 224; heterosexual, 63; intersex, 157–59, 162, 167; feminine/female, 2, 207; masculine/male, 63, 82 144, 276; lesbian, 113, 208; transsexual, 156
Bollywood, 1, 2
bondage, 90, 91; *see* sadomasochism
butch, 3, 163, 176, 177, 217
camp, 26, 29n15, 76, 93, 145, 150
cartoons, 77, 224; in *Mecánicas celestes*, 121
catholicism, 43, 63, 68, 117, 205

censorship, in Argentina, 24, 264; in Cuba, 34–36, 38–39, 47; in *Doña Herlinda y su hijo*, 179–80; of *Plata quemada*, 55; of *Señora de Nadie*, 29n11; of sex films, 108
César, Prix, 152n7
cinéma d'auteur, *see* auteurism

cinematography, 263–64; in Hermosillo's films, 182n15; in Hernández's films, 146–47, 150; in Lombardi's films, 185–86; in *Plata quemada*, 55; in Piñeyro's films, 58–60; in Reygadas's films, 144; in *La Virgen de los Sicarios*, 140n2

cinephilia, 7, 151

city, cityscapes, 119, 248, 256–57; in *Fresa y chocolate*, 32, 41, 44–45; in *Ronda nocturna*, 11, 266, 268–70, 272, 274–75, 278n5, 278n6

class, classism, 238, 241–44

close-up (shot), in *Un año sin amor*, 81, 83, 86, 89; in *Así del precipicio*, 207; in *El lugar sin límites*, 226, 231; in *Ronda nocturna*, 265, 267, 276, 277

clothes, 114, 121, 215, 221, 223–24, 228–30

colonization, 1, 43, 117, 133

comedy (genre), 34, 38, 116, 122, 158, 233

coming out, in *Doña Herlinda y su hijo*, 174, 176, 181; in *En la ciudad sin límites*, 254, 256; in *No se lo digas a nadie*, 9, 188, 193, 196

community, 46, 65, 78–80, 84, 112, 117, 133, 136, 191, 194–95, 205, 209, 212, 222–23, 234; leather/BDSM, 74, 88, 90, 93; LGBTQ, 146, 178, 209

confessional, 49, 71, 84, 86, 93

cross-dressing, 192, 224, 275

desire, 6, 8; in *Así del precipicio* and *Todo incluido* 204–05, 207–08, 213–17; in *Un año sin amor* 74, 81–82, 84, 86, 90–92; in *La ciénaga*, 243–45, 246n4; in *En la ciudad sin límites*, 250, 258–59; in *Doña Herlinda y su hijo*, 177, 180; in *Fresa y chocolate*, 27, 32–33, 41–42; in *El lugar sin límites*, 224–25, 227–28, 233–34; in *Mecánicas Celestes*, 113–16, 118, 120; in *No se lo digas a nadie*, 188, 190, 192–94, 197–99; in *Plata quemada*, 53–55, 58–60, 63, 66–67, 67n2; in *Ronda nocturna*, 275–76, 278n11; in *La venganza del sexo*, 109; in *XXY*, 158–59, 164, 166–68

detective story, 100, 102

dialogue, in *El cielo dividido*, 149; in *La ciénaga*, 239–40; in Lombardi's films, 186; in Pyñero's films, 57, 60, 62; in *Ronda nocturna*, 267; in *La Virgen de los Sicarios*, 125; in *XXY*, 164–65

dichotomy, 115, 129

dictatorship, 20–21, 27–28, 28n5 29n15, 73, 75, 85, 101, 108, 176, 180, 214, 256, 264

discourse, 22, 32, 38, 41, 42, 44, 47, 71, 92–93, 133, 144, 194, 199, 209, 213, 259; cinematographic, 207; gender/sexuality, 9, 10, 42, 47, 86, 188, 191–94, 196, 199; HIV/AIDS, 83; medical, 81, 83, 93; national, 33; patriarchal/homophobic, 6, 28, 212; poetic, 86; political, 34, 42, 253; queer, 25, 71, 75

Disney, 114, 120, 121

distribution, film, 6–7, 11, 13, 46, 75, 99–100, 107–08, 143–46, 152, 211, 218n2

diversity, sexual and gender, 3, 9, 12, 48, 55, 203, 209–10, 213, 216–17, 218n2

divorce, in Hollywood film, 23; law in Argentina, 28n6, 75; in *Señora de Nadie*, 21

documentary, 89, 271; in *Un año sin amor*, 72, 91; in Cozarinsky's films, 264, 268, 270; Cuban documentary,

12, 38–39, 47; in Ripstein's films, 223; in *XXY*, 156–57, 166
drag, drag queen, 77, 93, 151, 189, 224–25, 227
dysphoria, gender/sexual, 4, 156, 168n1, 197

editing, 32, 144, 150, 153, 272
effeminacy, in *Un año sin amor*, 88; in Argentina, 64–66; in *Kiss of the Spider Woman*, 77; of the "latin lover" stereotype 2; in Mexico, 204, 210; in *No se lo digas a nadie*, 193–94, 196
erotic cinema, 109
eroticism, 5–7, 53, 67, 82, 100, 113
exile, 83, 119, 214; Cozarinsky's exile, 264, 270, 271; in *Fresa y chocolate*, 45; gay "exile," 84, 187, 189
exploitation, 150–51, 248

fairy tale, 7, 111–12, 114–16, 122, 179
family, in *Un año sin amor*, 88; in *Así del precipicio* and *Todo incluido*, 208, 211–14, 216–17; in *La ciénaga*, 10, 237, 240–45; in *En la ciudad sin límites*, 10–11, 248, 251–56; in *Doña Herlinda y su hijo*, 178–81; in *El lugar sin límites*, 222–23, 227; in *Ronda nocturna*, 273; in *XXY*, 167
fantasy, fantastic (genre), 6, 7, 11, 99, 100–06, 108–09, 109n3, 114, 250, 264
father, fatherhood, 158–60, 162, 166–67, 173–74, 176, 179, 251–52
feminism, 19, 26, 28n7, 119, 194
femme fatale, 2
fetish, fetishization, 82, 90, 138, 199, 228
fichera, 9, 224
film noir, 56
fragment, 115–16, 195, 207, 224, 233

frame, framing, in *La ciénaga*, 238–39; in *Fresa y chocolate*, 42; in J. Hernández's films, 152n9; in *El lugar sin límites*, 221, 225–26, 228, 234; in *Plata quemada*, 58, 64, 66, 68n7, 68n9; in *Ronda nocturna*, 277, 278n5; frame theory, 195; in *La Virgen de los Sicarios*, 135, 139; in *XXY*, 163–64, 167–68
Freudian theory, 65, 113, 167, 175, 197
funding, 101, 143, 147

gangster film, 56, 67n3
gay bashing, queer bashing, 25, 151
gaynster, 53, 67n3
gaze, *Así del precipicio*, 207–08; feminist gaze, 28n7; in *Fresa y chocolate*, 32–33, 41–42, 49; Lesbian, Machorra, 2, 13; masculinist gaze, 197, 215, 231; in *XXY*, 158, 164, 168
genitals, genitalia, 138, 158–60, 164, 169n3, 169n4, 169n6, 277
geography, 117–19, 123n4, 123n6, 214
gesture, 6, 44, 58, 64–65, 176, 231
globalization, 211
global cinema, 71, 77–78, 122n1, 143, 145
Golden Age of Mexican cinema, 2, 147
Goya Awards, 29n12, 46, 156

hegemony, 191, 258
hero, heroine, 3, 13, 42–43, 56, 59–60, 68n4, 116, 197
heteronormativity, 1, 8, 27, 188, 190, 193, 196, 198–99, 212, 255, 278n11
heterosexual, heterosexuality, 2, 9–10, 33, 36, 39–40, 46, 65, 188–91, 198–99, 213, 217, 258

HIV/AIDS, in *Un año sin amor* 6, 71–72, 80–83, 86–87, 92–93, 94n7; in global cinema, 78–80; in *Ronda nocturna* 276
Hollywood, 2, 3, 23, 121, 157–58, 204
home, 118–20, 123n6
homoeroticism, 27, 144, 147, 174, 180, 196
homophobia, 28n5, 64, 76, 144, 152n3, 160, 204, 209, 190, 274; in *Fresa y chocolate*, 6, 31–35, 37–39, 41, 44
homosociality, 278n11
horror (genre), 102, 106
humor, 106, 132, 135, 214, 275
hustler, 11, 265, 267, 272–75, 278n6
hybrid, hybridism, hybridity, 44–45, 67n3, 113, 116, 147, 212, 214–15

identity, national, 10, 46, 141n7, 249, 255
identity, sexual and gender, 4, 5, 8, 33, 34; in *Así del precipicio* and *Todo incluido*, 205; in *Doña Herlinda y su hijo*, 8, 175–76; in *Fresa y chocolate*, 42; in *En la ciudad sin límites*, 259; in *Mecánicas celestes*, 115–18; in *No se lo digas a nadie*, 186, 188–89, 191, 193–94, 196, 198–99; in *Señora de Nadie*, 20, 22; in *XXY*, 156–59; in *Ronda nocturna*, 274
identity politics, 147, 152n8
ideology, 19, 27, 32, 36, 38, 42–45, 49, 106, 126, 140, 211, 222
immigration, 118, 120, 122; illegal, 112–14, 119, 122
incest, 109, 179, 244
indirect cinema, 268, 270, 278n8
industry, film, 3, 143–44, 152, 185
intersex, intersexuality, 8, 155–68, 169n2
irony, in *El cielo dividido*, 148, 151; in *Doña Herlinda y su hijo*, 176, 178; in *No se lo digas a nadie*, 196; in *Señora de Nadie*, 23, 24; in *La Virgen de los Sicarios*, 139; in *XXY*, 159

leather, 71–74, 87–93, *see* sadomasochism
leitmotif, 63, 119, 163, 230, 248
lesbian, lesbianism, 3, 5–6, 9, 13, 15, 19, 113, 175, 203, 204; in *Así del precipicio* and *Todo incluido*, 9, 205–09, 214–17
LGBTQ, 1, 3–5, 14, 14n1, 209
liberation movements, 75, 173, 181n3
lighting, 66, 89
location (film), 8, 40, 44, 55, 125, 147, 150, 151, 166, 266

macho, machismo, 1–3, 6; 29n17, 181n6; in *Doña Herlinda y su hijo*, 174–75; in *El lugar sin límites*, 224, 226, 234; in *No se lo digas a nadie*, 186, 196–97; in *Señora de Nadie*, 20, 22–23, 26
machorra, 2–3
mapping, 11, 176, 247, 249
marginality, marginalization, 11, 27, 33, 46, 65, 76, 117, 122, 149, 152n8, 199, 254, 265, 272, 278n8
maricón, 14n1, 25, 76, 186, 192, 224
marriage, 5, 7, 13, 28n2, 28n6, 68n6, 75, 212; in *Así del precipicio*, 206, 209–10; in *Doña Herlinda y su hijo*, 173, 176; in *Mecánicas celestes*, 7, 111–12, 114–16; in *Señora de Nadie*, 19–24, 27; in *No se lo digas a nadie*, 187, 193, 198
marriage, same-sex/gay, 4, 5, 28n6, 75
masculinity, 1, 2, 13, 25–26, 33, 42, 77, 87, 215, 255, 276; in *El lugar sin límites*, 10, 222, 224–25, 227–29, 231; in *No se lo digas a nadie*, 196–99; in *Plata quemada*, 64, 65; in *Señora de Nadie*, 22, 25–26; in *La Virgen de los Sicarios*, 138–39

masturbation, in *El cielo dividido*, 149; in *XXY*, 160, 163–65
matriarch (archetype), 8
medicine, 71, 80–81, 83, 86–87, 92–93, 94n7
melancholy, melancholia, 39, 45, 94n4
melodrama, 38, 78, 82, 93, 101, 178; in *En la ciudad sin límites*, 11, 248–50; in *Fresa y chocolate*, 32–35, 40–43, 48; in *El lugar sin límites*, 9–10, 233; in Ripstein's films, 221, 223
memoir, 71, 84, 87, 88
memory, 216, 250–53, 255–57
metaphor, 9–10, 29n17, 32, 44, 61, 65, 68n5, 72, 139, 157, 193, 195, 198–99, 251, 254, 256, 259, 274
metonym, metonymy, 65, 222, 229
micronarrative, 21–23
minimalism (technique), 148
mise-en-scène, 9, 34, 40, 68n4, 221, 223, 251, 255, 266
misogyny, 134–36
monster, in Vieyras's films, 103–05, 107; in *XXY*, 160, 162, 164
montage, 86, 89, 121, 277
morals, morality, moralism, 61, 206, 210, 217
mother, motherhood, lesbian motherhood, 15n3; in *Mecánicas celestes*, 112; Mexican mother, 8, 174, 176–80; in *Señora de Nadie*, 21–23, 25
mujer abnegada, 2
music, in *La ciudad sin límites*, 258; in *Doña Herlinda y su hijo*, 175; in *Fresa y chocolate*, 37, 40–43; in *El lugar sin límites* 233; in *Mecánicas celestes*, 112–13, 116–17, 122; in *Plata quemada*, 63; in *Ronda nocturna*, 265–68; in *La Virgen de los Sicarios*, 130, 136
mutilation, 8, 156, 158, 163, 166, 169n3

myth, mythology, 129, 169n5; *Un año sin amor*, 93; in Cozarinsky's work, 274; in *Mecánicas celestes*, 112; in *Plata quemada*, 53–54; in Vieyra's work, 6, 100–01, 103, 106

narrative, in *Un año sin amor*, 72, 75, 83, 91; in *Doña Herlinda y su hijo*, 174, 178; in *En la ciudad sin límites*, 250–51, 257; in *Fresa y chocolate*, 2, 37, 42–43, 47; in J. Hernández's films, 144–45, 147, 151; in *El lugar sin límites*, 225–26, 233; in *Mecánicas celestes*, 111, 116; in *No se lo digas a nadie*, 197; in *Plata quemada*, 55–56, 58–60, 62–64; in *Ronda nocturna*, 266; in *Señora de Nadie*, 21, 26; in *La Virgen de los Sicarios*, 127–28, 130; in *XXY*, 156–58, 161
nation, 11, 33, 212–13, 224, 232, 234, 271; national audience, 8, 46; national cinema, 7; national gay rights, 4, 75, 209; national identity, 9, 205
nature, 54, 102–04, 117, 230, 233
neoliberalism, 73, 77
neorealism, 32–33, 44
normalization, 155, 206, 217, 255–57
nostalgia, 32, 45, 120, 126, 129, 139, 271, 276
nudity, frontal nudity, 145, 150, 152n5, 204, 208; semi-nudity, 214; soft-porn nudity, 107

opera, in *Mecánicas celestes*, 112, 113, 115, 116, 118, 121, 122
orgasm, 67, 102, 160, 169n4, 277, 279n13

pastiche, 7, 116
patriarch, in *El lugar sin límites*, 223, 231, 234; in *Todo incluido*, 212
patriarchy, in *El lugar sin límites*, 224; in *No se lo digas a nadie*, 187, 190;

patriarchy *(continued)*
  in *Señora de Nadie*, 6, 21, 23, 27, 28n2; in *Todo incluido*, 213
performance, 145, 158, 223–28, 233, 251
performativity, 8, 41, 120, 123, 159
perspective, in Cozarinsky's work, 270
perversion, perversity, in *La venganza del sexo*, 6; in *Doña Herlinda y su hijo*, 179
pharmakon, 83
photograph, photography, 187–89, 193, 198–99
poem, poetry, 6, 71, 83, 85–86, 92–93, 94n10, 145, 176–78, 269
point-of-view (POV), in *Así del precipicio*, 207–08; in Cozarinsky's films, 270, 272; in J. Hernández's films, 150; in Lombardi's films, 196; in *El lugar sin límites*, 224; in *Mecánicas celestes* 117; in *Todo incluido*, 215; in *La Virgen de los Sicarios*, 138
porn, pornography, 6, 13, 107
promiscuity, in Martel's films, 10, 238, 243–44; in *Un año sin amor*, 84
promotion, film, 143, 206, 263
pronouns, gendered, 168
psychoanalysis, 28n9, 92, 112, 197

queer couples, 27

race, racism, in *La ciénaga* 241–43; in Cuba 37–38; in *No se lo digas a nadie* 192–93; in *La Virgen de los Sicarios* (Vallejo) 133–35
reader, 7, 64, 86–87, 127, 131–32, 136
realism, 44, 149; social realism, 151
resistance, 43, 93, 116, 175, 241, 248–49, 253, 256
repression, in Argentina 73, 77, 256; in Cuba 6, 32–36, 41, 47–49; in *El lugar sin límites* 224–25, 227; in *Plata quemada* 65–66, 73; in *XXY*, 160

sadomasochism, SM, S/M, S&M, BDSM, 6, 71–72, 87, 89–92, 93n1
screen, 106–07, 121, 173, 195
screenplay, 7, 9, 54–55, 125–26, 129–32, 135–40, 140n2, 277
self, 34, 114, 164, 241
sex (category), 8, 156, 159, 162, 175, 190–91, 194, 197, 199, 206, 214
sex (act), 2; in *Un año sin amor*, 80, 85–87, 93; in *Así del precipicio*, 208, 210–11; in *La ciénaga*, 244; in *En la ciudad sin límites*, 258; in *Fresa y chocolate*, 32, 36, 48–49; in *El lugar sin límites*, 229; in *Mil nubes de paz* 148; in *No se lo digas a nadie*, 191, 194, 196; in *Ronda nocturna*, 11, 266–67, 276–77; in *Señora de Nadie*, 24, 26; in *La venganza del sexo*, 101–02, 106–09; in *La Virgen de los Sicarios*, 130, 138–39; in *XXY*, 164
sexploitation film, 6, 99, 107–08
shot (composition), in *Un año sin amor*, 81, 82, 86, 88–89; in *Así del precipicio*, 208; in *El cielo dividido*, 148; in *La ciénaga*, 239; in *El lugar sin límites*, 224–26, 228, 233; in *Mecánicas celestes*, 116–17; in *Plata quemada*, 65–66; in *Ronda nocturna*, 266–70, 272, 275–77, 278n5, 279n14; in *Todo incluido*, 214–15; in *La Virgen de los Sicarios*, 139
sound, in Cozarinsky's work, 268, 278n5
soundtrack, in *El cielo dividido*, 149–51; in *Fresa y chocolate* 45; in *El lugar sin límites*, 226, 228; in *Plata quemada*, 55, 66–67; in *Ronda nocturna*, 271–72
space, in *Así del precipicio*, 210; in *La ciénaga*, 239, 241; in *Fresa y chocolate*, 32, 34, 40, 42–45; in *En la ciudad sin límites*, 11, 250, 256–57, 259n2; in *El lugar sin límites*, 10, 222–26, 224, 228–31, 234; in *Mecánicas celestes*, 7, 111–14, 116–22, 123n4; in *La Virgen de los Sicarios*,

7; in *Plata quemada* 68n4; in *Señora de Nadie*, 25–26; in *Todo incluido* 212–14, 216–17; in *XXY*, 162–64
Special Period (Cuba), 34–35, 44, 50n2
spectator, spectatorship, 7–8, 10, 20, 32, 116, 197, 204–07, 209, 215, 217, 224, 226, 230, 234, 265–67, 270, 278n5, 279n13
stereotype, 1, 2, 14n1, 25, 160, 194, 196, 204, 207, 215–17
straight, in *Doña Herlinda y su hijo* 175–76, 179; in *Fresa y chocolate*, 37; in *XXY*, 159
station drama [*Stationendramen*], 266
subject, subjectivity, 5–6; in *Así del precipicio*, 209, in *Fresa y chocolate*, 31, 41; in *En la ciudad sin límites*, 253; in *No se lo digas a nadie*, 8–9, 185, 187–96, 198–99; in *Todo incluido*, 212, 215
submission, 71, 90, 93, 241–42
surgery, 104, 155, 157, 162, 166
symbol, symbolism, in *Un año sin amor*, 72, 82; in *La ciudad sin límites*, 11; in *No se lo digas a nadie*, 194; in *Plata quemada*, 63, 65–66; in *La Virgen de los Sicarios*, 126, 138–39; in *XXY*, 160–61, 163, 166

taboo, 34, 38, 44, 47, 241
Teddy Awards, 46, 75, 146, 263
terror, terrorism, terrorist, 59, 73, 77
terror (film), 13, 99
theater, 68n4, 197, 241, 258, 266
therapy, 23, 25–26, 28n9, 80
thriller, 6–7, 100–02
time, temporality, 32, 127, 129, 138, 257
time-image, 10, 252
tolerance, 32, 36, 39, 48, 75, 76, 82, 108, 180, 209–10
tomboy, 217
tragedy, 53, 55–59
transgresion, 24, 28n2, 41, 179, 210, 217, 241, 245, 246n3, 255–56

transnational (cinema), 7, 11, 278n11; in *Así del principio* and *Todo incluido* 205, 211, 214–15; in *La ciudad sin límites* 259n2; in *Fresa y chocolate* 46–47; in J. Hernández's films 144, 147, 150–51; transnational flux 9, 203, 213
transsexual, transsexuality, 155–57
transvestite, transvestism, 12, 100–01, 204, 224, 267, 275
triangle, 176, 189, 192, 197–99, 226

uncanny, 10, 249, 266, 268, 276, 279n15
utopia, 68n9, 169n4, 177–78, 180

vampire, vampirism, 6, 100–01, 104
video clip, 121
viewer, viewership, 8, 11, 36, 54–55, 57, 61, 82, 129, 131–32, 135, 137–38, 148, 157, 159, 161, 162–64, 187–89, 191–99, 217, 229, 252, 256
violence, in *La ciénaga* 241–43; in *En la ciudad sin límites*, 249, 254; in *El lugar sin límites*, 222, 224, 228–29, 234; in *Ronda nocturna*, 277, 278n5; in *Señora de Nadie*, 25; in *La Virgen de los Sicarios*, 7, 126, 128–34, 138–40, in *XXY*, 165–66
virgin, virginity, 114–15, 217
voyeur, voyeurism, 6, 24, 41, 61, 105–06, 159, 163–64, 166, 192, 197–98

wandering, 100, 105, 265, 267
weapon, 3, 101, 126, 133, 136, 138–39, 224
Weltschmerz, 149
wife, 19–20, 24, 26, 28n10, 106, 160, 162, 174, 176, 178, 190, 206, 211–13, 225, 227–28, 240, 275

zoom, 10, 26, 44, 63, 112, 117, 136, 187, 207

www.ingramcontent.com/pod-product-compliance
Ingram Content Group UK Ltd.
Pitfield, Milton Keynes, MK11 3LW, UK
UKHW041924140426
5217IPUK00014B/309